Drama and Theatre Studies

NEW REVISED AND EXPANDED EDITION

for use with all Drama & Theatre Studies A & AS specifications

STANLEY THORNES

Sally Mackey ▲ Simon Cooper

First edition published in 1995 and reprinted six times
New Revised and Expanded Edition published in 2000 by:
Stanley Thornes (Publishers) Ltd
Delta Place
27 Bath Road
CHELTENHAM GL53 7TH
United Kingdom

03 04 05 06 / 10 9 8 7 6 5

A catalogue record for this book is available from the British Library

ISBN 0-7487-5168-8

For David

In memory of Dorothy Cooper

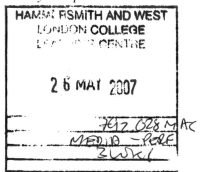
Cover photo shows the Forkbeard Fantasy

Typeset by Tech-Set Ltd, Gateshead, Tyne & Wear
Illustrated by Richard Barton and Mark Dunn
Picture research by Amanda Davidge and Christina Morgan
Printed in Great Britain by Scotprint

Contents

PART 3   KEY THEATRE PRACTITIONERS

Acknowledgements

The authors and publishers wish to thank the following for permission to use copyright material:

Faber and Faber Ltd for an extract from Brian Friel, *Translations*, 1981; Samuel French Ltd on behalf of the author for extracts from David Campton, *The Cagebirds*, 1976; Nick Hern Books for an extract from Peter Flannery, *Singer*, 1989; Michael Imison Playrights Ltd on behalf of The Trustees of the Terence Rattigan Trust for an extract from Terence Rattigan, *Separate Tables*, Hamish Hamilton, 1955. © 1954 The Trustees of the Terence Rattigan Trust; International Creative Management, Inc on behalf of Maurice Valency for an extract from Friedrich Duerrenmatt, *The Visit*, adapted by Maurice Valency. © 1956, 1984 by Maurice Valency, as an unpublished work entitled 'The Old Lady's Visit', adapted from 'Der Besuch Der Alten Dame' by Friedrich Duerrenmatt. © 1958, 1986 by Maurice Valency; Reed Consumer Books for an extract from Caryl Churchill, *Vinegar Tom*, Methuen London, 1982; Tessa Sayle Agency on behalf of the authors for Theatre Workshop, *O What a Lovely War*, Methuen Drama, 1965. © 1965 Joan Littlewood Productions Ltd;

Sarah Ainslee/Photostage (p.390); Catherine Ashmore (p.157 bottom); (pp.274, 278) taken from *Artaud and After* by Ronald Hayman (Oxford University Press, 1977); The British Library (p.198); Chichester Festival Theatre (p.7 bottom); Nobby Clark/Forkbeard Fantasy (cover), Nobby Clark/Theatre de Complicite (p.164 top), Nobby Clark/Royal National Theatre (p.7 top); Dee Conway Library (p.355); Donald Cooper/Photostage (pp.157 top, 164 bottom, 363, 382); (p.236) design for *A Doll's House*, courtesy of Huntley Carter/taken from the *Twentieth Century Stage Decoration* by Fuerst and Hume (Dover, 1967); Gordon Craig Estate (p.200); Hulton Deutsch Collection (pp.191, 264); Philip Jackson/The Minack Theatre (p.4); Mander & Mitchenson Theatre Collection (p.297); Martin Charles (p.11); Mary Evans Picture Library (pp.225, 266); (pp.234, 238, 248) Taken from *Moscow 1900–1930* by Serge Fauchereau (Rizzoli, 1988); Morris Newcombe, South Coast Photographic Workshop (pp.373, 376, 379); Odin Teatret/Nordisk Teaterlaboratorium (p.283); Ohatani Women's College, Osaka, Japan (pp.204–206); John Roan Photography, Northampton (p.5); Roger-Viollet (p.256); The Royal Court Theatre (p171); Stadtische Galerie im Lenbachaus (p.292); Adrian Gatie/The Stephen Joseph Theatre, Scarborough (p.8); (p.313) Ulrike Stoll/taken from *Caspar Neher* by J Willett (Methuen, 1986); total theatre designs, two solemn tragedians (pp.268, 272) taken from, Walter Gropius & Arthur Wensinger (Eds.), *The Theatre of the Bahaus*, by permission of the University Press of New England, 1961; (pp.331, 339, 343, 344, 345, 347, 349) Taken from *Towards a Poor Theatre* by Jerzy Grotowski © Methuen Publishing Ltd, 1969; The Victoria and Albert Museum (pp.209, 211).

Every effort has been made to trace all the copyright holders but if any have been inadvertently overlooked the publishers will be pleased to make the necessary arrangement at the first opportunity.

There are various people we would like to thank for their assistance, support and advice in helping create the first edition of the book.

Peter Murby encouraged our original idea and Caroline Arthur was a most helpful and good humoured editor. Many people have been knowing or unknowing recipients of the trialling of much of this material. We would like to acknowledge retrospectively our gratitude to: the pupils from The Bourne Community College, Thomas Bennett Community College (both in West Sussex), Roade Comprehensive School, Northants and, particularly, drama education students at The Central School of Speech and Drama; teachers in London and Northamptonshire, amongst others, who have taken part in courses where first drafts of this material have been used and who have offered useful comments; Clare Jeffery, Sarah Ream, Jonathan Goodwin and Tim Armitage for their help and constructive comments in the writing of Part 3.

Authors' note on the second edition

The need for a new edition of *Theatre Studies* became clear as the Dearing report in the UK focused on a change in the post-16 system. With advice from Stanley Thornes, we decided to undertake a new edition rather than a completely new text primarily because there was still much in the original edition that would be useful in the new (e.g. reviewing productions, practitioners, analysing texts).

The response to the first edition that we have had from teachers and students took us by surprise. When we first started on the book (with encouragement from people such as Andy Kempe at Reading University), we did not expect it to be so welcome and so successful. Thank you to all of you who have taken the time to say something to us or who have written. It has been deeply appreciated. We have taken your advice for the new edition!

What are the changes? The new Part 1 combines the old 1 and 2 into a simpler framework. Some of the old material is still present, often with new examples, bearing in mind new texts. There is entirely new material as well. This new part is versatile enough to cover the study of full texts, our prime consideration, and unseen extracts (currently in two of the three post-16 specifications). We have taken into account the particular needs of each of the specifications – you should find familiar terminology used in the specifications' contents.

Part 2 remains the same as the old Part 3. All the specifications ask students to review live theatre now so this chapter has additional use. There is a new review, of *The Weir*, which brings the part more up to date. We felt that there was much material in the old reviews that would still be useful, however.

Part 3 is the old Part 4 with the addition of new sections on Grotowski and Brook. Although only one of the specifications requires the study of particular practitioners, the other two use them. Recent material from EdExcel suggested the section on Brecht as key reading for a unit on Brecht's Epic Theatre, for example. The original four practitioners stay the same with additional summaries to help students gain an overview of their work. We have not included question and suggested answer frameworks in the two new sections on Grotowski and Brook as these kinds of activities have been superseded by material from the boards.

We have not included as many questions and answers in this edition. Again, we note that the boards are a great deal more organised in producing sample questions and answers now. On the whole, these are a closer match than the ones we write. We have maintained the 'questions and frameworks' in Part 1, however, because these offer a solid, incremental way of learning and because the boards are not quite so helpful in this area of the examinations.

A/S and A2 specifications and this book

There are three new A and A/S specifications in 'Drama and Theatre Studies' – EdExcel, AQA and WJEC. In this section we attempt to map the new specifications on to the book. We have not attempted to support devised and performance work; there are other texts that do this (e.g. the partner book to this, *Practical Theatre: A Post-16 Approach*). Therefore, some modules or units from the specifications are not directly referred to below. We have written the mapping from this book in bold, in brackets.

EDEXCEL DRAMA AND THEATRE STUDIES

GENERAL
The EdExcel specification has a list of 'Terms and concepts' with which students have to become familiar. Most of these are described in the Performance Spaces section on pp.3–11, the language terms on pp.78–81, the stage terms list on pp.11–14, the Glossary on pp.409–11 or within certain sections of the book e.g. 'Ubermarionette' can be found in the Craig section.

UNIT 1: (A/S and A2) EXPLORATION OF DRAMA AND THEATRE
The unit asks candidates to explore texts, developing ideas for workshops. Elements to be understood include 'plot (and subplot)', 'use of language', 'characterisation', 'interpretation of meaning'. (**Use 'Presenting theatre' and 'Textual analysis' in Part 1.** These have a number of sections that will fully support the terms and concepts students have to understand.)

UNIT 2: (A/S and A2) TEXT IN PERFORMANCE I
This is a practical unit, performing or designing a text, but the sections on '**Approaching the text as an actor, director, designer**' in '**Presenting theatre**', **Part 1** will be useful.

UNIT 3: (A/S and A2) TEXT IN CONTEXT I
Section A is linked with Unit 2. Students have to write about the text produced in Unit 2, evaluating their work but also placing the text in its cultural and historical context. (**Use 'Support research' in Part 1 for this. Use sections from Part 3 where relevant.**)

Section B asks students to comment on live productions seen, with reference to the playwright's intentions and the social, cultural and historical background of the text. (**Use Part 2 mainly, for a comprehensive** coverage of reviewing live productions. Also, use 'Support research' in Part 1 for research frameworks into the social, cultural and historical background.)

UNIT 5: (A2) TEXT IN PERFORMANCE II Like Unit 2, this is primarily a practical unit. However, students have to explore a text from the point of view of a director, designer or performer. (**Use 'Approaching the text as an actor, director, designer' in 'Presenting theatre', Part 1. Use sections from Part 3, where relevant.**)

UNIT 6: (A2) TEXT IN CONTEXT II Section A asks students to take on the role of director with a view to directing one of two plays. The student must understand the context. (**Use most of Part 1.**)

Section B asks students to study a text from between 1575 and 1720 with a view to its performance history and to see a live performance. (**Use 'Support research' in Part 1, Part 2** (for the contemporary performance), **possibly relevant sections from Part 3.** Also, look at the bibliographies on pp.135–8, particularly on past staging. See the Index for particular references to individual texts. For example, there are references to Gay's *The Beggar's Opera* on pp.18, 56, 89, 122 and 402.)

AQA DRAMA AND THEATRE STUDIES

MODULE 2 (A/S and A2) APPROACHES TO TEXT – WRITTEN The module says 'candidates are expected to gain a practical awareness of theatre as a process, of the relationship between the text and its performance potential, and of the work of the actor, director or designer'. (**Use 'Presenting theatre' in Part 1.**) In addition, it lists a number of aspects that need to be considered such as 'character motivation and interaction', 'creation of mood and atmosphere' and others. (**Use 'Textual analysis' in Part 1.**) Candidates are also asked to 'take account of the original social and cultural context of each play as well as its genre and style'. (**Use 'Support Research' in Part 1** – paying particular attention to the frameworks offered as guidance for further research if your period is not in this text.)

See the Index for particular references to individual texts. For example, there are references to Shakespeare's *A Midsummer Night's Dream* on pp.4, 13, 33, 56, 58, 77, 89, 94, 366, 372 and 381–3.

MODULE 3 (A/S and A2) THEATRE IN PRACTICE – WRITTEN Section A asks students to understand the work of Stanislavski, Craig or Artaud and their significance on contemporary theatre. (**Use the relevant section in Part 3.**) Section B asks students to discuss live productions. (**Part 2 covers this.** The review notes are particularly useful as a model for other productions seen.)

MODULE 4 (A2) PLAY IN PRODUCTION – PRACTICAL Whilst this is a practical module, support information for the form of theatre chosen can be picked out from the book by careful use of the Index. For example, the form described as 'Ibsen's naturalism' can be supported by looking for all the references under naturalism and Ibsen and reading the section of Stanislavski in Part 3.

MODULE 5 (A2) TEXT INTO PERFORMANCE – WRITTEN

Further texts have to be studied in this section with a specific directorial overview. The 'original social and theatrical context' needs to be addressed again. (**Use all parts of Part 1** – these should have been covered for Module 2 and can be revisited.)

MODULE 6 (A2) THEORY INTO PRACTICE – WRITTEN

Section A asks students to apply knowledge of a practitioner (Brecht, Brook or Grotowski) to live productions or their own practical work. (**Use the relevant section in Part 3 and combine with 'Presenting texts' in Part 1 and/or Part 2.**)

Section B requires students to interpret an unseen extract/s for potential performance. (**'Presenting theatre' and 'Textual analysis' in Part 1 address this comprehensively**. This part is written to combine knowledge needed for studying set texts and interpreting unseen extracts.)

WJEC DRAMA AND THEATRE STUDIES

GENERAL

WJEC expect a knowledge of theatre practitioners for all aspects of its specification. 'Knowledge of the theory and practice of the following theatre practitioners is considered essential for a full understanding of modern theatre practice'. They name Stanislavski, Craig, Brecht, Meyerhold, Artaud, Grotowski, Boal, Brook. (**See Part 3 for most of these.**)

UNIT 1: (A/S and A2) PERFORMANCE WORKSHOP

This is a practical unit where candidates offer acting or technical production skills in the presentation of an extract (and a devised piece) on a set text. (**'Approaching the text as an actor/ director/ designer' in 'Presenting Theatre', Part 1 will be useful, as would 'Support Research', Part 1 for researching the text.** Use the Index for particular references to individual texts.)

UNIT 2: (A/S and A2) DIRECTORIAL ANALYSIS and UNIT 3: (A/S and A2) TEXT ANALYSIS

Unit 2 requires students to prepare an unseen extract/s for production. Unit 3 asks for an analysis of scenes from two set texts, again with a view to performance. (**'Presenting Theatre' and 'Textual Analysis' in Part 1 address these comprehensively.** These sections of Part 1 combine knowledge needed for studying set texts and interpreting unseen extracts.)

UNIT 4: (A2) PERFORMANCE ANALYSIS

Section (a): Theme Project Report. Candidates are expected to bring a broad range of theatrical knowledge to a 3,000-word analytical and evaluative report that supports Unit 5. (**Depending on the topic chosen for Unit 5, see the Index reference according to the relevant genre, style, topic, influences.**)

UNIT 5: (A2) PRACTICAL PERFORMANCE FROM A SET THEME

This is primarily a practical unit presenting two text extracts and one devised piece. (**Some reference to Parts 1 and 3 may well be useful in preparing the text extracts selected.**)

UNIT 6: (A2) TEXT IN CONTEXT

Candidates sit an examination analysing aspects of two set texts. (**Part 1 covers this comprehensively.**)

General introduction

Drama is a combination of text, production and reception

Drama is a *performed* art. To engage with any dramatic work, you should always consider **text, production** and **reception** as interwoven. The **text** is written by the playwright or company, the **production** is the text as it is realised by a company in a performance and the **reception** describes the reaction of the audience. Analysing the text on the page is simply not enough.

The earliest forms of drama arose from a ritual base where very few of the performers could read or write; a written text was not necessary since the components were handed down through an oral tradition. Drama would have been a shared experience where performer and audience would have been barely distinguishable. The remnants of such drama can still be seen in Britain, albeit in a commercialised setting where there will be a force of spectators. The Padstow Hobby Horse can still be seen dancing the streets of Padstow, Cornwall, on Mayday, intent on providing a spectacle. Although it has long since lost its original purpose as a symbol of forthcoming fertility, an echo of such a rite can be sensed. Some rituals are of more recent origin. The rolling tar barrels of Ottery St Mary in Devon (or Lewes in East Sussex) on 5 November provide spectators with a sense of communal ritual. These rituals are a form of 'performance art' where the 'text' is often wordless and the audience participation is part of the whole ritual. This is in contrast to early *plays* which had a story, spoken text and a clearer definition between performers and audience.

Drama as performance art without a script is not confined to traditional rituals. Whilst we have scripted records of early mystery and morality plays, no such forms were used with the medieval jongleurs and only scenarios were used in the great *Commedia dell'Arte* performances of the Italian Middle Ages. We tend to allocate too much importance to the written text, even for plays of Shakespeare's time.

> These plays [Shakespeare's] were made and mediated in the interaction of certain complex material conditions, of which the author was only one. When we deconstruct the Shakespeare myth what we discover is not a universal individual genius creating literary texts that remain a permanently valuable repository of human experience and wisdom; but a collaborative cultural process in which plays were made by writers, theatrical entrepreneurs, architects and craftsmen, actors and audience; a process in which the plays were constructed first as performance, and subsequently given the formal permanence of print.
>
> [Holderness, G. (ed.) *The Shakespeare Myth*, Manchester University Press, 1988. p.13]

Holderness suggests that Shakespeare's plays were a combination of text, production and reception, not merely treasured pieces of manuscript. Theatre was created and formed through a collaboration of playwright, performers and offstage members of the company and through the audience reaction. For example, the heckling of the audience and the response from actors would be as much a part of the performance as the original script and the 'text' would alter accordingly. Any study of theatre must hold this as a prerequisite: theatre is a performance art focused upon audience reception.

Drama is about humanity and conflict

It is possible to identify another constant that helps describe the nature of drama. Drama addresses humanity; it tells us about ourselves. More than that, it concerns humanity and conflict. (The word protagonist is derived from the Greek *agonistes* which actually means actor or *combatant*.) If the human race lived in a world of moral, social and political harmony, there would be little for dramatists to draw upon. Very few plays exist without an element of conflict, because the world in which human beings exist is not a Shangri-La of harmony and deep contentment.

There are three broad areas of conflict: with the self, with the environment and with another person. It is difficult to think of a dramatic text that does not contain one of these three areas of conflict within its subject matter.

Whilst conflict is generally present, a dramatist is likely also to have far more specific themes or issues within her or his text. Caryl Churchill's *Mad Forest* (1990) examines the hypocrisy of ordinary lives during the overthrow of Ceauşescu in Romania; *Everyman* (anonymous), a medieval morality play, tells us that only our good deeds on earth will help us in the next world. Whilst the specific issues in these two examples are vastly different, both are broadly dealing with conflict. Churchill asks us to understand the individual Romanian family struggling with pragmatism and ideals in a strife-ridden society and under two corrupt dictatorships. In *Everyman*, we share Everyman's struggle to find aspects of himself that will serve him well in death. Both plays are underpinned by this notion of conflict.

Drama has to be accessible to our belief system, part of our common sense

For the reception of drama to be part of the creative equation, drama has to make sense to us, the audience; it has to be understandable within our cultural system, part of our 'common sense'. The drama may well be from an entirely different culture, but there must be something that fits into our own structure of beliefs, values and experiences in order to make sense of the piece to us.

Whilst you may find the most abstract 20th-century Western European expressionistic drama hard to understand, it does come within your belief system and, once the code is cracked, the meaning behind the piece is accessible to you. Similarly, however strange a fantasy land is used for the setting of a piece of children's television, the moral codes used in the fantasy world will be understood by its audience. However, take as a comparison a ritualistic drama of early 19th-century Bali, where the three widows of a recently dead king jumped to their deaths over a cliff; this was then the norm. A Danish anthropologist, Helms, witnessed the rich, colourful and dramatic spectacle surrounding this event. His report shows that he greatly admired the aesthetic beauty of the occasion but completely failed to understand the drama. His belief system could not accept or comprehend the event itself, just as we would have the same difficulty if we saw that spectacle today. It is outside our cultural sense. An audience is likely to respond more fully the more they recognise a performance as part of their own *broad* cultural system.

If drama is basically a performance art concerned with the conflicts of the human race within an accessible cultural context, what is its purpose? The earliest ritualistic drama took place as a form of religious worship, praise or supplication. Predominantly pre-Christian, such rituals were often directed at natural forces represented by gods or the equivalent. As drama acquired more formal settings, where the actor became an identified part of the drama and separate from the audience, the religious focus was still implicit but the expression of *human* conflict began to take precedence.

Drama seeks to entertain and enlighten an audience

Since the earliest forms of audience-focused drama, theatre has sought to **entertain** and **enlighten**; 'to instruct by pleasing' is an old adage concerning the purpose of art. However, the relative weight given to entertainment or enlightenment has varied considerably through history according to the demands and desires of the audience and the dramatist.

For example, in Britain the appalling lives of the Victorian working classes in overcrowded cities led to an overwhelming need for escapism, with a clear-cut system of moral absolutes and instantly recognisable stereotyped characters presented on stage. The resulting melodramas were one of the most obvious examples of a dramatic genre to develop from market forces. Here, the market clamoured for a high percentage of entertainment and the results were weighted towards the 'pleasing' of an audience.

In contrast, Brecht is an example of a playwright who wished to enlighten (to teach, even) his audience, asking them to take action as a result of watching his plays. His strength is that he did this in such a way that it married 'pleasure' with 'instruction'. The decadent society of pre-Second World War Germany and the rise of Fascism contributed to his desire to educate audiences through his own particular brand of didactic, political work. Some plays are overt examples of this: *Fear and Misery in the Third Reich* (1938) and the more subtle *The Resistible Rise of Arturo Ui* (1941) are worth noting as excellent examples of plays that seek to enlighten their audiences. Both teach the audience about the evil of Hitler and the Third Reich.

Drama can inform the aesthetic senses

Whilst considering entertainment and enlightenment as the principal purposes of drama, it is worth noting that some drama would emphasise the development of the aesthetic senses of an audience. (This can loosely be included within the brackets of both entertainment and enlightenment, of course.) Frequently culturally determined, the audience's aesthetic appreciation is sometimes of prime importance. The Japanese Noh theatre is such a style of drama; the art and skill of its gliding performers are the focus of the drama and the audience would be expected to applaud and appreciate the aesthetic beauty of the work. Developing this sense would be a chief purpose for such drama.

PART 1

EXPLORING TEXTS

1.0 *Introduction*

Part 1, *Exploring Texts*, offers a number of important frameworks for addressing texts from a theoretical *and* practical perspective. As the introduction to Section 1.1, 'Presenting theatre', suggests, playtexts should always be considered with the realisation or production of the text in mind. If you are studying playtexts for an examination, all specifications ask students for a combined theoretical and practical perspective. For any theatre practitioner, there will be moments of analytical study *and* moments of practical experimentation. Part 1 moves between the two and should be considered as a whole, therefore. (We do not attempt to consider *devised* work here; for the purposes of Part 1, it is assumed that we are engaged with the understanding and realisation of *published* playtexts.)

The information in Part 1 is useful for full playtexts or extracts.

With an emphasis on playtext realisation, the first section, '**Presenting theatre**', identifies key practical areas that students of theatre need to consider when responding to playtexts. Performance venues, stage terms and approaching the text as an actor, director and designer are discussed.

In the second section, '**Textual analysis**', we suggest methods of studying playtexts so that the student actor, director or designer is supported in the analysis of texts.

'**Support research**', the last section, engages with the further research that theatre students have to undertake when working on a playtext. This looks at the social, historical and cultural background of texts, the theatrical history and plays of a similar genre, time or theme.

1.1 *Presenting theatre*

1.1.0 INTRODUCTION

When realising or writing about the production of playtexts, you will be expected to have some understanding of theatrical staging and approaches to text from an actor's, director's and designer's perspective. This will take you clearly into the areas of **production** and **reception**. Here we are directly engaged with the expected and/or desired response of the audience. To achieve this desired reception, the text has to be staged and interpreted.

This section helps you think of the text as a living art form that should be approached practically. Even if you are only *writing* about the practical realisation of the playtext, you should initially consider it 'on its feet' and not as a piece of literature on the page. With this in mind, the section starts with **Performance spaces** in an attempt to make you immediately think about staging texts in appropriate venues. Then we suggest a number of **Stage terms** that are a natural part of any theatre practitioner's vocabulary. Finally we look at **Approaching texts as an actor, director and designer**.

1.1.1 PERFORMANCE SPACES

Performance spaces are not just stages

There are many different types of performance area, from Punch and Judy kiosks to circus arenas. It is too easy to think merely in terms of different types of *stage*. Whilst stages are more conventional for theatre performances, other spaces can be most effective. Quite recently, Hull University made excellent use of a Punch and Judy-type kiosk for a real-head-with-puppet-body adaptation of Jarry's *Ubu Roi* at the Edinburgh Fringe Festival.

It is worth considering other performance spaces

Whilst certain texts (and unseen extracts) may not immediately appear to lend themselves to highly unusual performance spaces, it is worth considering a number of alternatives. You must be aware of the range of possibilities and the *effect* of such venues. You are free to think laterally, as long as there is a reason for your unusual choice and it is feasible. If the notion of setting a 20th-century adaptation of *Beowulf* in a quarry can be fully *justified*, then you should not be completely put off. (This has actually been done – at the 1987 National Student Drama Festival, Bretton Hall grounds.)

This section looks more closely at the more *usual* stages and types of production within them. The exceptions are endless, but it is always worth remembering the wide range of possibilities.

Amphitheatres

These were originally Greek, were adapted slightly by the Romans and are still occasionally reproduced. They were built on a huge scale; Epidavros, in Greece, seats around 20,000 people (it is still used). The acoustics were (and are) exceptionally good, although the traditional Greek masks contained a mouthpiece that, some researchers believe, acted like a small megaphone to assist the sound.

Greek influence is important

It is worth looking further at Greek theatres as they were the first known specifically designated theatre spaces and as such influenced all later designs. (Most drama and theatre arts books have a section on Greek theatre.)

Figure 1.1 The Minack Theatre at Porthcurno Cornwall: an example of a British theatre that uses the Greek amphitheatre as its basic idea.

Amphitheatres are suitable for large-scale productions

In terms of discussing the staging of plays, there are several points to be considered concerning amphitheatre stages. Amphitheatres are appropriate for large-scale productions. There is an awesome grandeur about such theatres which could match the chosen production. This need not necessarily be a modern production of a Greek play; other pieces may well suit such an environment, although some would be extremely difficult to justify. Chekhov's *The Three Sisters* doesn't leap to mind as a primary choice for a summer festival at the Theatre of Dionysus (Athens). However, Shakespeare's *A Midsummer Night's Dream* could well be a contender. The style of the play is the important consideration. Chekhov's play has an intimate quality and is naturalistic, and this would be difficult to marry with a huge amphitheatre. Shakespeare's play, on the other hand, is full of ceremony and movement.

Proscenium arch theatre

Proscenium arch theatres are still the most recognised form of theatre space. The name derives from the Greek word *skene*. This was the building for actors changing at the back of the acting area in a Greek amphitheatre; it suggested an early version of permanent sc(k)enery. Thus, pro(before)-scenium would be a space in front of the back scenery. The word 'proscenium' is now taken to be the front opening of the stage and its surround.

Proscenium arch theatres are still popular

The *arch* is the frame surrounding the front of the stage, solid and usually immovable. The impression is that the audience is watching the production through a picture frame, an archway (see Fig. 1.2). Many local and West End theatres are proscenium arch theatres; the basic design was popular from the late 17th century to the early 20th century. Not surprisingly, there are many still in existence. Whilst the public regard proscenium arch theatres as the norm, they can be most restricting for companies performing within them. In addition, the audience often feels removed or cut off from the action on stage because of the arch.

Proscenium arch theatres are generally equipped with a range of possibilities for scenery. Drapes or side flats can be used to blank off the wings. In many, it is possible to drop in scenery from above the stage (or 'fly' it in), to have a revolve in the middle of the stage, to have trap doors or stages that drop and so on.

There are classic proscenium arch productions

There are certain types of play that are most suited to 'pros. arch' theatres, plays where the company is deliberately aiming for a 'fourth wall' effect. This is when the audience is expected to see the production as if through an invisible fourth wall, with the scenery forming the other walls. Naturalistic dramas are often deemed appropriate for proscenium arch theatres.

Yet there have been large-scale productions in proscenium arch theatres. Melodramas, complete with waterfalls or Gothic castles, played in the Victorian proscenium arch theatres. The stages were vast in those times and audiences witnessed huge spectacles. The Covent Garden Theatre Museum, London, has a model of a Victorian theatre with a ship sinking on stage; extravagant scenery was expected and theatre technology became quite advanced.

Figure 1.2   The Royal Theatre, Northampton, with a highly decorated safety curtain

Of course, proscenium arch companies produce much effective drama that is not in the traditional 'pros. arch' manner. What you need to consider, however, is which performance area is *most suitable*. Just as *The Three Sisters* would not be terribly suited to an amphitheatre, the *Chester Mystery Cycle* (originally performed on wagons with the audience promenading) does not come to mind as a key choice for a proscenium arch interpretation. Ibsen's *Hedda Gabler* might be most appropriate for proscenium arch staging, however.

It is important that you *justify* your choice of proscenium arch theatre if you are discussing staging. Whilst it is the most traditional form of theatre now, it has enormous limitations for communicating with the audience. When you are visualising the staging of a text, make sure you have good reasons for performing it in a proscenium arch theatre.

End on (open) stage

The end on (open) stage, like the proscenium arch theatre, has the audience facing the stage; the stage is at one end of the building (i.e. 'end on'). It is not encumbered with a formal proscenium arch – it is 'open' – and is therefore more flexible than the 'pros. arch' theatres. The seating is generally raked up. (See Fig. 1.3)

Modern theatres and school theatres are often end on (open) or a hazy mix between this and proscenium arch. They suit many kinds of production without being very exciting venues conceptually. They are perfectly functional, allowing for a reasonable feeling of audience involvement (depending on size, of course) and yet taking full sets and lighting rigs.

End on (open) stages are suitable for many different types of play

These are popular theatres and can take a wide variety of productions. You would be safe in suggesting such a stage for many texts, as long as you gave an explanation of what effect you hoped to achieve by using such a stage.

Open stages are those which almost merge with the audience; there is no barrier, such as a proscenium arch. Most of the following examples of stages are open.

Thrust/apron stage

'The Theatre' was the first theatre ever built in this country (in 1576 by James Burbage). This took many of the features of an inn yard (the previous typical performance venue), with a raised platform (or stage) thrusting out into the audience, who surrounded it on three sides. You have doubtless seen the reconstructed Shakespeare's Globe Theatre in London. This is the essence of a thrust theatre today. Occasionally, stages will be essentially end on, or proscenium, but with an *apron* put on the front, so that the audience is both watching the main stage and surrounding the apron on three sides. This has a similar effect to a thrust stage. (See Fig. 1.4)

Like theatre in-the-round, thrust allows for excellent actor–audience contact. The audience is drawn into the action. Obviously, tall scenery is limited to the section of stage behind the thrust: otherwise, the audience's view is blocked.

If you decide to stage a playtext on a thrust stage, you presumably want quite close contact with the audience. Is this a play where several of the

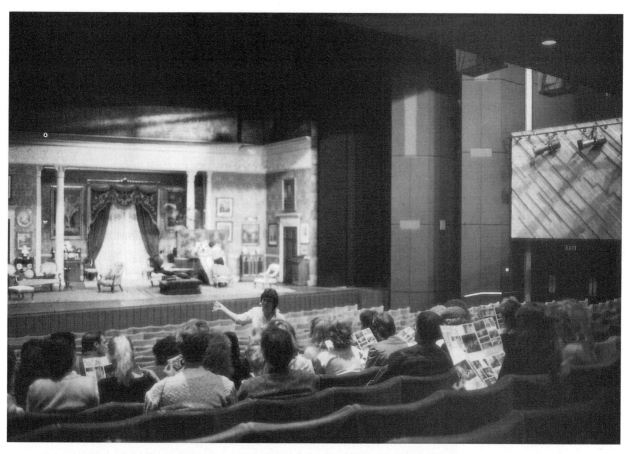

Figure 1.3   The Lyttleton Theatre, Royal National Theatre, London.

Figure 1.4   Chichester Festival Theatre before recent refurbishment.

characters speak directly *to* the audience, perhaps? This would be an excellent reason for selecting a thrust venue.

Theatre in-the-round/arenas

In this form of theatre the audience is not necessarily seated in a circle; it could be seated in a square, for example. However, it does surround the acting space. This form of theatre is ideal for close, intimate work which requires little scenery.

You would be forgiven for thinking that theatre in-the-round can be limiting, as there seem to be many drawbacks. For example, it can be difficult to light, actors can easily be blocked by others and there is little scope for scenery. However, a remarkable variety of productions takes place, most successfully, at the Stephen Joseph Theatre in Scarborough, for example. Of course, some plays lend themselves to theatre in-the-round perfectly; Claire Luckham's *Trafford Tanzi* is one example. This is literally and symbolically set in a wrestling ring.

You would be advised not to dismiss theatre in-the-round for staging texts, but again you must think carefully about justifying your choice. If you see a theatre in-the-round production, try and assess how well the production suited that style of performance.

Abnormally large theatre in-the-round venues are called arenas (for example circus arenas).

Figure 1.5   The Stephen Joseph Theatre, Scarborough.

Corridor/traverse

Corridor (or traverse) theatre is pleasantly self-explanatory. The acting space is directly between two parallel groups of audience. It is doubtful whether there are any permanent corridor theatres, but they are occasionally constructed for productions on the Fringe, for example.

Figure 1.6   A corridor/traverse theatre.

Again, you need to think about *why* one would stage a piece in a traverse format and what this method of staging brings to the text. For example, you may wish to constantly remind the audience that they are in a theatre, as in a Brecht production. A traverse stage would be an interesting choice as audience members can see across the performance space to another block of the audience.

Promenade

Promenade performances take place without any formal stage area, with the actors and audience occupying roughly the same space. The actual performance of a scene is indicated by an actor speaking loudly and/or that particular area being lit. In addition, there will sometimes be small areas of raised staging or rostra placed strategically around the area, which are occasionally used by the actors. The performance will move around all over the space; if members of the audience are standing in an acting space that is about to be used, the actors will 'move' them.

Promenade performances can make most effective theatre. The proximity of the actors and the constant movement around the space combine to create an unusual and exciting event.

Perhaps promenade works best when there is a *particular* point in performing in that style. Modern adaptations of the medieval Mystery Cycles (e.g. York and Chester) have been successfully performed in promenade. This works well as it represents a modern version of what happened in medieval times, when an audience moved from station to station (platforms on carts) to see various different parts of the bible stories.

A modern classic, *Road* by Jim Cartwright, is usually performed in promenade; it was written for this purpose. We are given glimpses of the lives of people who live in one road. The audience is encouraged to 'visit' different houses or areas in the road. This is a wonderful piece of modern theatre.

In 1974, the fringe theatre company Joint Stock put on a promenade production called *The Speakers* by Heathcote Williams. This was centred around the lives of people who gave impromptu speeches on tea chests at Speakers' Corner in Hyde Park. When you entered the hall, there was a tea stand in the centre with one of the actors in role serving tea. It was clear that you were at Speakers' Corner, particularly when the first speech started. The audience moved around the area, reflecting the movement of listeners at Hyde Park Corner. Again, there was an appropriate point in setting this as promenade theatre and again it was most successful.

Figure 1.7   A promenade performance of *The Mysteries* (the Nativity).

Courtyard

The key distinguishing feature of courtyard theatre is the additional layer (or layers) of seating/standing. Usually basically thrust, it more closely follows the Elizabethan tavern yards and early theatres.

Again, this is a flexible theatre. In terms of responding to staging playtexts, there would be little to choose between this and thrust.

Figure 1.8   The Swan Auditorium, The Royal Shakespeare Theatre, Stratford upon Avon.

ACTIVITY   Using a playtext you know, discuss possible performance venues, as suggested above, highlighting the merits and problems of each type. Ensure that the *meaning* of the play is taken into consideration fully, and whether the various venues can help reflect that meaning.

1.1.2 STAGE TERMS

You will need to become familiar with the following list of stage terms. You will know some already, but it is worth reminding yourself of them; they are an important part of your knowledge of the theatre in general. You will find they are of use as well when you are writing about productions you have seen and production work that you are undertaking.

Some of these terms are annotated to suggest *how* you might use them. (For an extended list of stage terms, see Frances Reid's *The Staging Handbook*, A. & C. Black, 1990.)

Auditorium
The area for the audience, generally filled with seats. The term becomes hazardous when talking about promenade productions or street theatre, of course.

There is little point in simply mentioning the auditorium as an assumed fixture. Sentences such as 'I would have the Captain and his troops entering from the auditorium to create an impact' would not be sufficient. The auditorium needs to be defined first. An auditorium which surrounds a theatre in-the-round stage with four gangways and blocks of sixty audience members may well provide good entrance possibilities for the Captain and his troops; it would still be necessary to describe what *sort* of impact is desired, however. A four-tiered auditorium in a typical 19th-century West End theatre, where three of the tiers wouldn't even see the entrance, provides more of a problem.

Backcloth

The cloth, most familiarly made from canvas, which covers the back of the stage. Frequently painted with some form of scenery – not necessarily naturalistic of course. Backcloths are rather old-fashioned now on the high-tech modern stage, except in pantomimes and less well-equipped venues.

Blacks

Drapes, traditionally black, which curtain off the sides (and sometimes back) of the stage area or performance space.

Centre stage (CS)

The stage is divided up into areas, as shown in the diagram. These are *always* seen from the viewpoint of the actor standing on stage and facing the audience.

These terms are an important form of performance shorthand. It is far easier for you to explain your suggestions for character moves using this shorthand. For example: 'By moving Giovanni from centre stage (CS) to down stage left (DSL), he is demonstrating a distaste for Annabella. If he moved back up to CS later, this would match his tone of conciliation.' If you had written 'to the part of the stage nearest the audience on the audience's right', you can see how clumsy your writing would become.

Whilst CS would still make sense, remember that DS, US, DSL, SL, etc. would become meaningless in a theatre in-the-round venue.

Cyclorama

The back 'wall' (frequently made of stretched cloth) of the stage, which is sometimes slightly concave so that it can receive projected images effectively. It is often used to represent a large expanse, such as sky.

Figure 1.9   The stage area

Downstage (DS)

(See *Centre stage*.) The front of the stage or performance space, nearest the audience. As the actor stands in the middle of the performance space, to get to a downstage right position (DSR), she would move *down* the stage towards the audience, bearing to her *right*.

Flies

The area above the stage, which should be at least the height of the stage area again. Scenery is 'flown' up there on a series of pulleys, usually operated electronically in modern theatres.

It is likely that you would only make a passing reference to 'flies' or 'flying' if describing a set change. (This is true of many of these terms.)

Front of house (FOH)

This refers to any job in the theatre that involves dealing with the audience, from box-office sales to ushering. It also refers to all aspects of staging that are outside the stage area, for example in the auditorium.

FX

Sound effects.

Gels

See p.66.

Ground plan

The diagram of the stage and set and/or LX (lighting) plan, seen from a bird's-eye perspective. (See p.62)

House lights

The lights in the auditorium, which traditionally dim and go out as the action on stage begins.

Occasionally a production will keep the house lights up for the opening or, indeed, the whole show. There is likely to be a particular reason for this. If you are analysing a production where this has happened, you might write something like:

> 'At the beginning of *A Midsummer Night's Dream*, the cast were in the audience and they encouraged us to talk and comment on the action in the auditorium. The house lights remained up, which added to the feeling that we, the audience, were integral to the action. It seemed that this company wished to emulate the atmosphere in Elizabethan theatres as far as possible.'

LX

Lighting.

Rake

This refers to a tilt in the floor of the stage, usually from US to DS. This could be simply to improve the view from the auditorium, particularly if much of the auditorium is below the level of the stage. Alternatively, a rake of some description might be designed deliberately as part of the set to highlight an aspect of the meaning of the play.

A possible use of the term might be:

'I would want the set to reflect the gradual decay and disintegration of the society that the dramatist portrays here. In addition to representing walls and tenement buildings on flats which are askew, I would want the floor to be on a rake which is also askew, tilting slightly from SR to SL as well as from US to DS.'

Stage left (SL)
The left-hand side of the acting space as the actor faces the audience. (See p.12)

Stage right (SR)
The right-hand side of the stage as the actor faces the audience. (See p.12)

Strike
To dismantle the set completely. The term also refers to the removal of a certain object or piece of scenery.

Tabs
Any curtains on stage. This term was originally 'tableaux curtains', the proscenium arch curtains that opened by being gathered from the middle to the side and then up. These proscenium arch curtains are now frequently referred to as 'house tabs'.

Trap
A trapdoor in the stage, conventionally used for unusual entrances and exits.

Upstage (US)
The back of the stage, away from the audience. (See p.12)

Wings
The areas at the side of the stage not seen by the audience.

ACTIVITIES

1. Go to a traditional performance space: a theatre, a studio, or a hall with a stage. Run through the list of terms identifying and locating as many as possible.

2. Read the following extracts from the opening stage directions for Peter Weiss's *Marat/Sade* and a version of Euripides' *The Trojan Women*. Roughly sketch out your visual interpretation of the set for ONE of these. Either label it or explain the drawing in words, contriving to use as many terms from the list above as appropriate. This is simply an exercise to use terminology. You may want to include additional items and terms, particularly if you are familiar with the play.

The stage shows the bath hall of the asylum. To right and left bathtubs and showers. Against the back wall a many-tiered platform with benches and massage tables. In the middle area of the stage benches are placed for the actors, sisters and male nurses. The walls are covered with white tiles to a height of about ten feet. There are window openings high up in the side walls. There is a metal framework in front of the platform and around the baths at the sides.

[Weiss, Peter, *Marat/Sade*, Marion Boyers, 1965.]

The scene represents a battlefield, a few days after the battle. At the back are the walls of Troy, partially ruined. In front of them, to right and left, are some huts, containing those of the Captive Women who have been specially set apart for the chief Greek leaders. At one side some dead bodies of armed men are visible. In front a tall woman with white hair is lying on the ground asleep. It is the dusk of early dawn, before sunrise. The figure of the god Poseidon is dimly seen before the walls.

[Euripides, *The Trojan Women*, trans. Murray, 1905]

1.1.3 APPROACHING TEXTS FOR PRODUCTION

This section does not provide a 'handbook' of skills for actors, directors or designers. There are other textbooks that provide detailed hands-on training techniques for these professions (see the bibliography at the end of Part 1). What it does do is provide some clear guidelines for *approaching* a text as an actor, director or designer. In other words, what do we need to do, what do we need to think about and what stages do we need to go through when studying a playtext with a view to realising it in performance? In addition, it offers ways of *writing* about these approaches. Whilst many students engage successfully with practical drama work, writing about practice can be problematic. Clearly, as we have said in the introduction to Part 1, this section cannot be read in isolation. For example, it is impossible to develop a character study as an actor without detailed textual analysis; this is covered in the second section of Part 1, 'Textual analysis'. Similarly, it would be foolish to consider directing a text without undertaking substantial background research of the kind suggested in Section 1.3, 'Support research'.

There are common areas of thought and study that must be undertaken by any practitioner involved in realising a text. All must seek the meaning of the text. This section starts with 'finding the meaning' therefore. After this, the section splits into particular concerns for actors, directors and designers. Again, however, *all* these subsections would be useful for theatre students.

FINDING THE MEANING

All practitioners should seek the meaning or purpose of a playtext. This can be a complex task. Themes and issues are not identified simplistically. Malcolm Kelsall makes the point:

The clumsy critic digs out a slogan. Consider Irena's ''I'll go on working and working!'' from Chekhov's *The Three Sisters*. Taken as Chekhov's 'message' it turns the dramatist into a proto-Marxist critic of a decadent, lazy, land-owning society – or consider Edgar's ''The Gods are just'' from *King Lear* which might be used to recruit Shakespeare as a Christian optimist. But it is like extracting the role of a trombone from a symphonic score and saying *that* is what the symphony is about. Instead, we must learn to hear the entire orchestra, and not just at one moment, but through the total experience as it is shaped in time.

[Kelsall, M. *Studying Drama: An Introduction*, Edward Arnold, 1985. p.62]

Identifying the meaning of a text is more complex than picking out individual 'soundbytes', then.

You cannot identify a theme without detailed analysis of all elements of a text

You need to hear what the characters say and see what they do; you need to assess the structure of the play and see how the mood changes; you need to see where it is set; you need to form some conclusions about the style of the play (which is also only possible after all these first levels of analysis are completed). When you have done all this, you will be able to discuss the themes and issues present in the play. This detailed text analysis is covered in Section 1.2.

However, there are many sources that can help you to begin to identify themes and issues and the author's intentions even before you thoroughly analyse the text. Consulting these is a perfectly legitimate thing to do, although your own analysis will give you a much wealthier understanding of the central preoccupations in the play.

Sometimes the author tells you what he or she is writing about

Some authors make it particularly easy for you. An author will often give an introduction or comment upon her or his play. In his Preface to *Miss Julie*, for example, Strindberg explicitly tells us about the issues he is addressing. George Bernard Shaw uses his play prefaces in a similar way. This is a useful and perfectly valid way into the play. It has the same purpose as a good programme in the theatre; it can *introduce* you to the play. Here are a couple of examples which help you identify the author's intentions.

To this end I chose, or let myself be caught up by, a theme which may be said to lie outside current party conflicts. For the problem of social ascent and decline, of higher and lower, better or worse, man or woman, is, has been and will be of permanent interest.

[Strindberg, A., *Preface to Miss Julie* (1888), trans. Michael Meyer, Methuen, 1964. p.92]

[I] rapidly left aside the interesting theory that witchcraft existed in the minds of its persecutors, that 'witches' were a scapegoat in times of stress like Jews and blacks. I discovered for the first time the extent of Christian teaching against women and saw the connections between medieval attitudes to witches and continuing attitudes to women in general. . . . I wanted to write a play about witches with no witches in it; a play not about evil, hysteria and possession by the devil but about poverty, humiliation and prejudice, and how the women accused of witchcraft saw themselves.

[Churchill, C., Notes after *Vinegar Tom*, in *Plays by Women, Volume 1*, Methuen, 1982. p.39]

Research scholars may relay the author's intentions in a play

If the author does not tell you what he or she is writing about in a preface, afterword or introduction, it is possible that he or she might have discussed the play as it was being written. This discussion, verbal or written, may have been recorded and critical texts about the play or author will refer to it. Undertaking some critical research yourself would therefore be most useful. You may not need to go far for this research; some editions of playtexts include comprehensive notes and essays about the text and author.

For example, in the Penguin 1961 edition of Lorca's play *Yerma*, Lorca's brother, Francisco Garcia Lorca, writes the introduction. This gives us a close insight into Lorca's intentions when he wrote *Yerma*.

> Of the trilogy contained in this book [the others are *Blood Wedding* and *The House of Bernarda Alba*], *Yerma* is the play which has the smallest number of elements directly inspired by reality. Federico turned to a theme present in all his lyric and dramatic work – that of a frustrated instinct for motherhood; this theme he embodied in the character that is the most symbolic in all his theatre, perhaps the most dramatic and, I was about to say, the most poetic.
>
> The drama centres about the violence with which the main character lives her personal conflict. It has been argued – a little childishly, to my notion – that Yerma's dramatic obsession is not entirely justified psychologically, since it could have a solution. And, in effect, it could have one, and there would be no drama, by making Yerma cease to be Yerma – that is to say, by making her cease to feel her maternal instinct tragically. Or, with the easy solution . . . of changing men. It would not be worth the effort to falsify Yerma's character by making her violate her sense of duty – another defining trait of her character – so that afterward she might continue being Yerma as before. This solution is raised in the play and rejected.

From this we see that Lorca is using the figure of Yerma to represent the tragedy of a woman who is trapped in her need to bear a child; this is his central theme.

Editors usually give clear guidance about the text

Often, introductions are written by scholars of a play rather than the author or, as in Lorca's case above, a member of the family. An academic authority will have thoroughly researched the play and will often encapsulate the heart of the piece. Here, Edward Braun, formerly professor of Drama at Bristol University, writes about Nikolai Gogol's *The Government Inspector* (written in 1835):

> Whereas Gogol had conceived *Marriage* [his previous play] as pure farce, his intention with *The Government Inspector* was altogether more ambitious. Condemning the cheap sensations of the melodrama and the irrelevant trivialities of the vaudeville, he sought with his comedy to bring out the significance of everyday happenings. Much as he admired the satirical force and technical brilliance of Molière and Beaumarchais, he rejected their decorum, their refined dialogue, their traditional characters. Modern drama, he asserted, must reflect the problems of modern society, and comedy must help us to acknowledge our vices and shortcomings by exposing them to ridicule. With a typically naïve disregard for the furore his observations on society were sure to cause, he had faith in the purifying and elevating power of laughter.
>
> It was Pushkin who suggested to Gogol the theme of mistaken identity for his play, having been mistaken himself for an itinerant government snooper in

Nizhny Novgorod. But in any case it was a common enough anecdote, and Gogol is believed to have based the character of Khlyestakov on a Petersburg publisher, who was a notorious pathological liar and had once posed successfully as an inspector in Bessarabia.

... It may be argued that such situations as the confrontation between Anna Andreyevna and Khlyestakov, after she has discovered him kissing her daughter, and the traditional letter denouement reveal Gogol's debt to French classical models, but mostly we are in the realm of an altogether new and more robust theatre far more closely related to life itself.

[Braun, E. Introduction to Gogol's *The Government Inspector*, Methuen, 1982]

From this we see that Gogol was intent on moving away from the classical theatrical style in the 1830s; this different style helped serve his theme of ridiculing the hypocrisies and minutiae of daily Russian existence.

Editions with a number of plays from the same genre or period can be helpful for wider research

Editions with a number of other plays of the period can be particularly useful as the introductions can give an overview of the whole period which is helpful for background research into the period and genre. John Hampden wrote the introduction for a 1970 edition of *John Gay's The Beggar's Opera and Other 18th-Century Plays*. He gives a useful description of the 18th-century obsession with 'sentimental drama', scathingly suggesting that 'the period suffered on the whole a steady vitiation of taste, until drama was divorced altogether from literature and life'. He goes on to point out the striking contrast that is Gay's play, *The Beggar's Opera*.

To pass ... to *The Beggar's Opera* (1728) is to enter a new world, a Cloud-Cuckoo Land where everything is vigorous, vivacious, entertaining, and morality has no place.... [I]ts enduring qualities may be left to speak for themselves, but topical elements strengthened its first appeal. Everyone recognised in Lockit and Peachum Sir Robert Walpole, then Prime Minister, and Lord Townshend, who had recently quarrelled. Many other characters were identified with less certainty. The satirical element will be more obvious to us if we remember that political life was then extremely corrupt and the highwayman was a common object of the countryside. The pictures of the prison and the spy system, though satirical, are but little exaggerated.... Even Boswell ... owns the fascination of the play: 'There is in it so much of real London life, so much brilliant wit, and such a variety of airs, which from early association of ideas engage, soothe, and enliven the mind, that no performance which the theatre exhibits delights me more.'

[J. Hampden, *Introduction to John Gay's* The Beggar's Opera *and Other 18th-Century Plays*, Dent & Sons, 1970]

Look for copies of playtexts with notes

Some playtexts have extended commentaries and notes that are extremely useful for clarifying meaning. Most obviously, editions of Shakespeare are 'student-friendly'. Another good example is the Methuen Student Edition of Wertenbaker's *Our Country's Good*. Over half the book contains commentary and notes which clarify many different points about the text.

Use good theatre dictionaries
to help pinpoint themes
In addition to playtext introductions, it is always worth referring to a good theatre dictionary for comments upon a play. Editors of theatre dictionaries often pinpoint issues in a play astutely and efficiently. The following are from Griffiths, T. and Woddis, C. *Theatre Guide*, Bloomsbury, 1991:

On Arden's *Sergeant Musgrave's Dance*:

A male-oriented play, where women are seen either as whores (sexual and dangerous) or mothers (asexual and comforting), it seems hard in retrospect to see it as anything other than a passionately pacifist, anti-imperialist play. (p.13)

On Weiss and *Marat/Sade*:

Marat/Sade, which brought him [Weiss] an international reputation through the historic Artaud-influenced 1964 RSC production by Peter Brook (a *tour de théâtre* difficult to match) is exactly what the full title describes. . . . [T]he play does include a variety of arguments about revolutionary violence and an ironic picture of the revolution tamed by the new Empire but very likely to re-emerge. (p.372)

On Osborne's *Look Back in Anger*:

It came to express the disillusion with post-war England that was felt by many, and contains a central statement of frustration from its anti-hero Jimmy Porter, which became a cry for a whole generation: 'there aren't any good brave causes left'. Jimmy Porter became the epitome of the Angry Young Man in his harangue of contemporary values. (p.231)

Theatre programmes are also
useful
Another source for identifying meaning and themes in a play is a decent theatre programme of a production of the text. The programme notes by Lee Hall, who adapted Brecht's *Mr Puntila and his Man Matti* for The Right Size company (Almeida Theatre, autumn, 1998), give a useful insight into Brecht during his early war years. (This play immediately preceded *The Resistible Rise of Arturo Ui*.)

It is difficult not to imagine that Brecht was in someway writing about himself. The picture of an autocrat, split between a determined and deterministic vision of how things must be run, and the Bacchanalian visionary, driven by lust and sentimental overflowings of fraternity, could easily be that of the contradictory playwright. There seems to be too much good in Puntila for Brecht simply to be preparing a little Marxist parable. Puntila's schizophrenic vacillations between monstrous sobriety and Utopian dissipation strike me as a possible essay in self criticism.

. . . While the play is a call to intellectual resolve, it also punctures the sentimentality of communitarian cant. Puntila's final exhortations of the Brotherhood of Man are so close to National Socialist jingoism that we can't leave the theatre with a simple untroubled message.

Despite all this help in identifying themes and issues, your real source for reaching an understanding of the play will be the text. Some authors have refused to say what their work is about in any case, preferring the audience response to be original. Samuel Beckett was famous for such silence. Harold Pinter is another who refutes any intention of meaning as such: 'I have usually begun a play in quite a simple manner; found a couple of characters in a particular context, thrown them together and listened to what they said, keeping my nose to the ground.'

To identify themes and issues in the play yourself, you must analyse the text in detail. To do this you will need to concentrate on the structure, the language and the characterisation.

Identify moments of climax as these often encapsulate the key issues in a play

These are all addressed in Section 1.2, 'Textual analysis'. However, there are two other useful 'short cuts' which may help you identify the essence of the play. Firstly, it is worth trying to identify moments of climax in the play. It is at this point that the major ideas in a playtext can be found. All drama is about conflict (see Introduction) and it is at moments of conflict, most clearly in evidence when the play reaches a point of climax, that key themes are often foregrounded.

The following extract can be used as an example. The Hesseltines, Queenie, Albert and family, have been told they will be relocated by the council from a northern city to the nearby countryside. They are looking forward to this event. Douglas Dobson, from the council, has just arrived to notify them about moving. He tells them that far from being moved to a house with a garden, they are going into a high-rise flat. The play was written in 1963.

QUEENIE: *(formally)* You see, we've been under the impression that we're not going in a flat. We've been given to understand that we're going into a house.

DOUGLAS: *(officially)* Well, whoever told you that had no authority to do so. We've none of us had any authority to tell anybody where they were going to live. Not till you received the official notification.

(ALBERT walks menacingly across and takes the document from QUEENIE. He glances at it.)

ALBERT: *(tearing the paper in two and dropping it on the floor)* You don't get me in a flat.

(ALBERT walks calmly back to his previous position and stands with his back to DOUGLAS. DOUGLAS takes this rebellion with his hysterical amusement.)

DOUGLAS: What the – you're all in flats, man! It's the modern age! It's the modern age! The whole street's in flats! *(Demonstrating with his hands.)* We're going to up-end this whole terrace. It's your whole mode of life. Instead of living next door to each other, you'll be living above and below each other. There's no more horizontal housing. Those days are gone, my friend!

ALBERT: *(dogmatically)* You don't get me in a flat.

QUEENIE: There's hundreds of houses up there. Rows and rows of them. We were told quite specifically we were going in a house.

DOUGLAS: They'll tell you anything down there. There's a woman across the street, she can't get about – she's been labouring under the delusion she's getting a bungalow. They've put her on the twelfth storey! There's another fellow rambling on about what he's going to do and what he isn't going to do in his garden. I says, ''Garden, garden, where did you get that tale from?'' I says, ''You've got your communal area.'' He says, ''Can I dig it up?'' I says, ''Dig it up, they'll dig you up if you do!'' It's all done for you! You're in flats now!

Waterhouse, Keith and Hall, Willis, *All Things Bright and Beautiful*, Samuel French, 1963

By recognising this as a moment of climax and, therefore, paying particular attention to it, one of the key themes of the play can be seen clearly. The authors are criticising the government's policy at the end of the 1950s of relocating people from poor housing areas into high-rise flats, away from the centre of the cities. Douglas is used as a cipher for the authors' disapproval of this short-sighted government policy.

The following extract can be used as another example. *Vinegar Tom* by Caryl Churchill is set in 17th-century Britain. (The dots in square brackets represent cuts in the text for the purposes of this exercise.)

MARGERY: Jack, Jack, come quick – Jack.

JACK: What's the matter now?

MARGERY: The calves. Have you seen the calves?

JACK: What's the woman on about?

MARGERY: The calves are shaking and they've a terrible stench, so you can't go near them and their bellies are swollen up. (*JACK goes off.*) There's no good running. There's nothing you can do for them. They'll die like the red cow. You don't love me. Damn this stinking life to hell. Calves stinking and shaking there. [. . . . .]

JACK: Other people sin and aren't punished so much as we are.

MARGERY: We must pray to God.

JACK: We do pray to God and he sends afflictions. [. . . . .]

MARGERY: Unless it's not God.

JACK: How can I bear it?

MARGERY: If it's not God.

JACK: What?

MARGERY: If it's not God sends the trouble.

JACK: The devil?

MARGERY: One of his servants. If we're bewitched, Jack, that explains all.

JACK: If we're bewitched . . . [. . . . .]

MARGERY: The devil can't bear to see us so good.

JACK: You know who it is?

MARGERY: Who?

JACK: The witch. Who it is.

MARGERY: Who?

JACK: You know who.

MARGERY: She cursed the butter to hell. [. . . . .]

JACK: What we do then? Burn something?

MARGERY: Burn an animal alive, don't we? Or bury it alive. That takes witchcraft off the rest.

JACK: Burn the black calf then shall we? We'll get some straw and wood and put it in the yard and the calf on top and set it on fire.

MARGERY: Will it walk?

JACK: Or I'll carry it.

MARGERY: It stinks terrible.

JACK: Stink of witchcraft it is. Burn it up.

MARGERY: We must pray to God to keep us safe from the devil. Praying's strong against witches. [. . . . .]

Something to Burn [usually sung by Margery and Jack]

What can we do, there's nothing to do,
about sickness and hunger and dying.
What can we do, there's nothing to do,
nothing but cursing and crying.
    Find something to burn.
    Let it go up in smoke.
    Burn your troubles away.

Sometimes it's witches, or what will you choose?
Sometimes it's lunatics, shut them away.
It's blacks and it's women and often it's Jews.
We'd all be quite happy if they'd go away.
    Find something to burn.
    Let it go up in smoke.
    Burn your troubles away.

[Churchill, Caryl, *Vinegar Tom*, (1976), in *Plays by Women, Volume One*, Methuen, 1982. pp.25–26]

ACTIVITY   Is there any kind of message in this passage? If so, what do you think it might be and how would you justify it by reference to the text?

You will find it useful to look at the song, *Something to Burn*, particularly closely. This gives us clear hints about Churchill's message which can then be related to the whole play.

Stage directions at the beginnings of acts can be helpful   In addition to identifying moments of climax, it is worth looking at the stage directions given at the beginning of individual acts (where these are given, of course). Clues about the theme/s of the play may be found.

For example, if you look at the first and last of the stage directions in Duerrenmatt's *The Visit*, you will notice a clear difference. The beginning of Act 1 reads:

> *The scene represents, in the simplest manner, a little town somewhere in Central Europe. The time is the present. The town is shabby and ruined as if the plague had passed there. . . . Left of the station is a little house in grey stucco, formerly whitewashed. It has a tileroof, badly in need of repair. Some shreds of travel posters still adhere to the windowless walls. . . . two* MEN *are lounging cheerlessly, shabbily dressed, with cracked shoes.*

The final scene of the play has these stage directions:

> *The gradual transformation of the shabby town into a thing of elegance and beauty is now accomplished. The Railway Station glitters with neon lights and is surrounded with garlands, bright posters, and flags. What is seen of the town indicates the culmination of the change from squalor*

to a blinding and somewhat technical perfection. The TOWNSFOLK, *men and women, now in brand new clothes, form themselves into a group in front of the station.*

[Duerrenmatt, F., *The Visit* (1956), adapted by Maurice Valency, Samuel French, 1958.]

It is clear that something significant has happened to the town during the play to improve its fortunes. Whilst this does not give us the theme of the play, of course, it does hint at it. It raises the questions of what has happened and how this has happened. On reading the play, it becomes clear that to achieve this new wealth and sparkle the townspeople have sacrificed their morals. Here, we have Duerrenmatt's central theme – the immorality and hypocrisy of the world at the time he was writing and the disenchantment he felt at such fragile virtues.

Thus, whilst the settings have not specifically told us the theme of the play, they have led us to ask the right questions, which have in turn led us to the theme. Obviously, this might not be the case in every play; however, it is another point to be taken into account when analysing the text for themes and issues.

ACTIVITY Look at the stage directions of one of the following:

The beginning of Act 1 of Chekhov's *The Three Sisters*;
The beginning of Act 1 and Act 4 of Ibsen's *Hedda Gabler*;
The beginning of Act 1 of Lorca's *Yerma*;
The beginning of Act 1 of O'Casey's *The Shadow of a Gunman*;
The beginning of Act 1 of Weiss's *Marat/Sade*.

Even if you do not yet know the play, what *impressions* do these stage directions give you about the play? If you have already read the text, how do these support the main theme/s of the play? You could write as much as two pages on this.

ACTIVITY Take another text you have read which does not have detailed stage directions at the beginning of the play e.g. John Gay's *The Beggar's Opera*; Euripides' *The Trojan Women*; Edward Bond's *Restoration*; Jonson's *Volpone*; Becket's *Waiting for Godot*. Having established the themes of the play in your own mind, devise a set of stage directions for the beginning of the play that would give a clear indication of your vision for the play. This would include reference to set, of course, but it should also give a sense of atmosphere reflecting the key themes that you wish to emphasise. (You may find the earlier sections on 'performance venues' and 'stage terms' useful.)

Consider the playwright's broader ideology, if known

Finally, it is important to remember that the meaning of an individual text can be found in the author's broader ideology. For example, Brecht's plays contain a Marxist perspective on human existence. All his plays are intended to suggest codes for living, using Marxism as the basic tenet. Whilst there may be more specific issues in each text (e.g. the parody of Hitler's fascism in *Arturo Ui*), these are framed within the 'meta-discourse' of Marxism. Similarly, it would be possible to suggest that most of Caryl Churchill's plays broadly engage with feminist issues: the frustrated role of women in society across many periods and their oppression by male hierarchies.

ACTIVITY   Below is an example of a 'theme guide' (on Jonson's *Volpone*) based on reading the play, seeing it (at The Royal Shakespeare Theatre, Stratford, September, 1999), reading the programme for that production and undertaking some critical research. Here, we have summarised the themes of the text drawing attention, if appropriate, to how these are evidenced in the plot. Take a text that you have read and produce a similar brief theme guide.

Ben Jonson's *Volpone* (or *The Fox*). English, comedy. 1605/6.

Themes
–   Hypocrisy and vice of English Jacobean society but set in Venice. (Italy was popular in Elizabethan and Jacobean England. Also, perhaps the setting gives a sense of distance, encouraging the allegorical nature of the text.)
–   Human avarice and the power of money. People will sacrifice all morality for money. The avarice is heightened by Jonson's use of carrion birds for the preying characters: Voltore, the vulture; Corbaccio, the crow; Corvino, the raven.
–   Sexual jealousy and erotic desire. The young wife and older husband has been a familiar theme for comedy since Roman times.
–   Gulling: taking people in, often to extreme lengths, for the guller's pleasure alone.
–   Betrayal – private and public. This is seen at obvious times such as Mosca betraying Volpone towards the end of the play and in the sub-plots, e.g. Sir Politic betraying Venice to the Turks.

The following sections suggest methods of approaching a playtext from different perspectives: actor, director and designer. Whilst these are practical roles, most drama examinations expect students to *write* about this approach. With this in mind, we have adopted 'writing about the approach' as the thrust of the following sections. There are clear overlaps between the sections. For example, the on and off text rehearsal methods outlined under the 'Director' section will be useful for the 'Actor' as well.

APPROACHING THE TEXT AS AN ACTOR

As an actor, you will be primarily concerned with one particular character or characters. However, if you are studying a playtext for a written examination instead of, or in addition to, preparing a performance, you should be able to discuss *any* of the characters in the text from an actor's perspective. You will need to consider the indications of characterisation given in the whole text or in an extract. From this, you can establish a character's motivation and interaction with others.

Character should not be considered in isolation

Characterisation cannot be considered without reference to other aspects of text analysis. For example, a dramatist does not write a play just to create some interesting (or otherwise) characters on stage. The characters and the *meaning* or *theme* are interwoven; the characters speak the *language* of the text (see Section 2.1 for a discussion of language). Characterisation clearly does not stand in isolation.

Each historical theatre period has its own forms of characterisation, which should be researched for particular set texts. The end of the 19th and the 20th centuries are worth highlighting here as one of the most important periods of theatre history for character development, however. They are also a popular period for drama examinations.

FORMS OF CHARACTER-ISATION IN THE LATE 19TH AND 20TH CENTURIES

Late 19th and 20th-century theatre has concentrated on realistic characters

Much of 20th-century theatre has been part of a move towards dramatic texts with complex, multi-faceted characters who resemble complex, multi-faceted human beings. Whilst drama highlights and compresses that complexity, many writers root their characters in real life. (Look at any soap opera for an example of the highlighting and compression of characterisation.) This has mainly happened since the development of naturalism early in the 20th century. Strindberg's *Miss Julie* (1888) is an early example of a play containing this complex and psychological characterisation. In his preface to the play, we can see what Strindberg was intending:

> My souls (or characters) are agglomerations of past and present cultures, scraps from books and newspapers, fragments of humanity, torn shreds of once-fine clothing that has become rags, in just the way that a human soul is patched together. [.....] Here I have somewhat broken with tradition by not making my characters catechists who sit asking stupid questions in order to evoke some witty retort. I have avoided the symmetrical, mathematically-constructed dialogue of the type favoured in France, and have allowed their minds to work irregularly, as people's do in real life, when, in conversation, no subject is fully exhausted, but one mind discovers in another a cog with which it has a chance to engage. Consequently, the dialogue, too, wanders, providing itself in the opening scenes with matter which is later taken up, worked upon, repeated, expanded and added to, like the theme in a musical composition. [.....] I have done this because I believe that what most interests people today is the psychological process. Our prying minds are not content merely with seeing something happen – they must know why it happens.
>
> [Strindberg, August, *The Preface to Miss Julie* (1888), translated by Michael Meyer, Methuen, 1964. pp.95, 98, 99]

This wish to address the psychological make-up of a person in drama has continued and developed throughout this century. It is what the audience has come to expect when watching television, films and theatre. Sometimes the *form* varies, of course. For example, in Brian Friel's *Philadelphia! Here I Come* (1965), the protagonist has his 'thoughts' or *alter ego* on stage with him. The audience gains an insight into his mind because we hear his inner thoughts, spoken by another actor. The dramatist is still giving us a detailed, complex, under-standable character, however. This form of characterisation is based on the popularity of psychoanalysis in the 19th and 20th centuries. By contrast, writers in previous periods tended to create more stereotypical or allegorical characters. This was particularly so in the period immediately preceding the 20th century, where melodrama was renowned for its overt stereotypes.

There are many exceptions to realistic characters of course

Whilst much of 20th-century theatre focuses on characters who bear a close resemblance to real life, there are exceptions. The playwright might want to address the bizarre and irrational aspect of human existence. In one example, we see two down-at-heel, intelligent but dislocated tramps waiting by the side of a road for a figure who never appears. To attempt a character study of these two unlikely beings based on 'normal' human psychology would be pointless. They are surreal symbols of the irrational and absurd nature of humanity. (See *Waiting for Godot* by Samuel Beckett.) There have been many instances where 20th-century playwrights have chosen characters to be representative or symbolic rather than realistic.

Alternatively, a dramatist might choose to present just one facet of a personality on stage to highlight that side of human nature. David Campton's short play *The Cagebirds* has a number of 'birds' on stage, such as 'The Long-Tongued Gossip' or 'The Mirror-Eye'd Gazer', who together add up to a depressing and oppressive picture of the human race. Analysing each of these bird-characters as whole individuals would defeat Campton's message.

Another example of unusual characterisation occurs in Ntozake Shange's *for colored girls who have considered suicide when the rainbow is enuf*. These characters are 'Lady in orange', 'Lady in yellow' – all the colours of the rainbow. Each person represents a whole group of women yet has a story of her own to tell.

Other dramatists might gently ridicule their audience by presenting 'heightened' characters. They are familiar and we recognise them, but they are somewhat larger than real life, thus emphasising certain characteristics. Some of Alan Ayckbourn's work is a perfect example of this; his characterisation is particularly centred on the British white middle classes. Another excellent example is the popular *Abigail's Party* by Mike Leigh (developed from an improvisation base). The central character, Beverly, is a parody of a bored, selfish, flirtatious, insensitive, materialistic woman with bad taste. She succeeds in making the audience wince. To analyse Beverly could take you only into the realm of parody and no further.

METHODS FOR CHARACTER STUDY

The character written on the page of any dramatic text is not complete. The **text** is only one third of the equation. When you are analysing and commenting upon plays, this must always be remembered. The **production** and **reception** form the other two thirds. You will be completing the characterisation by discussing how the character will be realised on stage. This should include reference to the audience reponse you hope to elicit. The character is thus lifted off the page and given life.

The text forms the base but the additional elements of production and reception complete a characterisation

How a dramatist gives indications of characterisation

The author will give clear indications of character upon which you can build. These will be communicated through various means:

- the character's own words
- the character's own actions

- other characters' words

- other characters' actions

- stage directions

- the subtext behind any of the characters' words.

How would the character be played?

Even as you first engage with the above list, you will be forming a judgement of the character. As you form the judgement, you should also be thinking about how to interpret that character on stage; in other words, you will begin to include thoughts about **production** and **reception**. For example, you decide that your character is sensitive to others because she says, 'You look apprehensive. Come and sit down and join us, you'll soon see that we're normal.' At the same time you should be working out a method of playing those lines so that the sensitive side of her nature can be most clearly communicated to the audience. For example:

'She stands up and moves to Talitha, taking her arm and gently guiding Talitha back to the group. She speaks in a cheerful, lighthearted tone to relieve any embarrassment Talitha might feel. The audience feels comfortable and reassured by her words and actions.'

The character's own words

The words of the character under analysis are the key method of coming to decisions about his or her character. It is useful to quickly decide on *key examples* from the text that clearly demonstrate characteristics of the role under analysis. An examination question might ask you to look at just one character or perhaps two or more. If the latter, then you must be selective about your choice of examples to allow time for two or more characters to be analysed. You are advised to underline or note suitable speeches as you read the play or extract.

Key examples from the character's words are important

Do not try to be exhaustive. You cannot assess every line said by each character.

The character's own actions

These are most likely to be found within the stage directions. The dramatist will often indicate what a character *does*; this can be a key clue in the communication of character and should be brought into a character analysis. Here is an example from Peter Shaffer's *Equus*:

DYSART: I'm sorry.
         (ALAN *slams about what is now the office again, replacing the benches in their usual position.*)
ALAN: All right, it's my turn now. You tell me! Answer me! . . . Do *you* have dates?
DYSART: I told you. I'm married.
         (ALAN *approaches him, very hostile.*)
ALAN: I know. Her name's Margaret. . . .

[Shaffer, Peter, *Equus*, Penguin, 1976. p.251]

Shaffer is helping us understand Alan's character at this point in the play through his actions. He 'slams about' and 'approaches him [Dysart], very hostile'. Clearly he is a person capable of aggressive anger.

If movement is not stated in the stage directions, it may be implied in the speeches themselves. If there are no obvious suggestions of movement, as is often the case, there is more opportunity for you as an actor (or director) to pick up an implied movement; this was the case with the example concerning Talitha. (See p.27)

Other characters' words

There will not be many examples of this in a short extract. However, the words of other characters may demonstrate a particular view of your character which shifts your thinking. They can provide a balance, a contrast or a confirmation of the impression given by the character's own words and actions.

The following is an example from Alan Ayckbourn's *Confusions*. The character we are analysing is Lucy. Rosemary has gone round to the house of her neighbour, Lucy, to give her a telephone number. Lucy has been acting strangely; the audience and Rosemary sense that her behaviour is abnormal. Rosemary's husband, Terry, arrives and this brief extract is from a hasty conversation between Rosemary and Terry, out of Lucy's hearing.

ROSEMARY:	*(sotto voce)* Come in a minute.
TERRY:	I'm watching the telly.
ROSEMARY:	Just for a minute.
TERRY:	I wondered where you'd got to. I mean, all you had to do was give her the number...
ROSEMARY:	I want you to meet her. See what you think. I don't think she's well.
TERRY:	How do you mean?
ROSEMARY:	She just seems...
TERRY:	Is she ill?
ROSEMARY:	I don't know...
TERRY:	Well, either she's ill or she isn't.
ROSEMARY:	Ssh.

[Ayckbourn, Alan, *Confusions*, Samuel French, 1977. p.5]

If you were analysing the character of Lucy, the person to whom Rosemary is referring, the above would be a perfect example of how other characters' words assist a character study. The obvious *key examples* are the lines 'I don't think she's well' and 'She just seems ...'. Rosemary is indicating to us that Lucy is behaving oddly.

Other characters' actions

The actions of other characters can also give information about the character you are studying. In the same scene, slightly earlier, there is a stage direction that reads:

Rosemary sits nervously. She rises after a second, looks guiltily towards the kitchen and sits again. . . .

[Ibid. p.4]

In context, it is apparent that Rosemary is finding the encounter with Lucy to be unnerving and feels ill at ease with her. The account of her actions given here supports this.

If you were writing about Lucy, you could use Rosemary's words and actions to build a picture of Lucy. For example:

'Lucy's behaviour is unusual and we feel it is abnormal. She does not follow the normal codes of behaviour. Ayckbourn has already set Rosemary up as a 'norm' and we note that she is uncomfortable with Lucy. We, the audience, identify with Rosemary's reactions, so when Rosemary "sits nervously" and says, "I don't think she's well", we share those feelings and thoughts about Lucy.'

Stage directions

Stage directions, particularly descriptions of how the character is speaking, are frequently neglected as a source of characterisation; you may find yourself ignoring the words in brackets. However, these can be an invaluable source of identifying the dramatist's intentions and one of her or his key methods of communicating meaning. For example:

QUEENIE: *(refusing to listen)* Oh, I know you think different. You don't see them like we do. . . .

[Waterhouse and Hall, *All Things Bright and Beautiful*, French, 1963. p.31]

The words in brackets give us a good indication of an aspect of Queenie's character: she is impatient at times and won't always listen to other people. All this adds to a character study.

The subtext behind any of the characters' words

As well as being asked about the author's presentation of a character, you are also likely to be asked about means of communicating that character to an audience. Whilst it is possible to achieve this straight from the text on the page, you will find that you are actually also reading the *subtext* to help you with your interpretation. This is something to recognise and develop.

Reading the subtext gives you the opportunity to discuss a more rounded character than the one that appears on the surface. Just as it is highly unlikely that *your* whole character would be apparent from the things you actually say and do, the same would be true of a character in a playtext. It is *reading the subtext* which will give some insight into a fuller character.

The following extract should help as an example of what we mean. Lorca's *The House of Bernarda Alba* (1935) is a drama about an all-female

Spanish family. Like his play *Yerma*, it is about motherhood. Bernarda is the matriarch of the family, Poncia is her elderly maid, Adela is the youngest and most beautiful daughter and Martirio is a slightly older sister who distinctly lacks her sister's beauty.

ACTIVITY   Try to identify a subtext in this extract and how that subtext is communicated to an audience.

PONCIA:	Bernarda!
BERNARDA:	What's happening?
PONCIA:	Librada's daughter, the unmarried one, had a child and no one knows whose it is!
ADELA:	A child?
PONCIA:	And to hide her shame she killed it and hid it under the rocks, but the dogs, with more heart than most Christians, dug it out and, as though directed by the hand of God, left it at her door. Now they want to kill her. They're dragging her through the streets – and down the paths and across the olive groves the men are coming, shouting so the fields shake.
BERNARDA:	Yes, let them all come with olive whips and hoe handles – let them all come and kill her!
ADELA:	No, not to kill her!
MARTIRIO:	Yes – and let us go out too!
BERNARDA:	And whoever loses her decency pay for it! *(Outside a woman's shriek and a great clamour is heard.)*
ADELA:	Let her escape! Don't you go out!
MARTIRIO:	*(looking at Adela)* Let her pay what she owes!
BERNARDA:	*(at the archway)* Finish her before the guards come! Hot coals in the place where she sinned!
ADELA:	*(holding her belly)* No! No!
BERNARDA:	Kill her! Kill her!

Curtain to Act 2

[Lorca, F., *Three Tragedies: Blood Wedding, Yerma, The House of Bernarda Alba*, Penguin, 1961. pp.185–186]

Everyone in the scene except Adela wants Librada's daughter to die for what she has done. This is the information given to us. The subtext tells us more about the situation. Be aware that the reading of a subtext will be *subjective* and every reader may see something slightly different, so be sure that you acknowledge this in your writing. It will significantly help if you substantiate all comments.

'The subtext indicates that the family enjoy the prospect of the forthcoming violent death in a rather perverted manner. Bernarda's choice of weapons are particularly unpleasant in a violent and sexual way: "let them all come with olive whips and hoe handles"; "Hot coals in the place where she sinned". The sadistic pleasure in the killing is enforced by Martirio's desire to share in the spectacle: "...let us go out too". The scene grows to an almost hysterical climax with the primitive cry of "Kill her! Kill her!" All this could lead us to suspect some hidden sexuality in the women, who appear to be erotically excited by the murder to come. We do not simply see a group of women anxious for moral justice.

'In addition, Adela's desire to prevent the attack seems full of subtextual meaning. Martirio appears to be aware of her sister's thought processes, as she pointedly looks at Adela when she says, "Let her pay what she owes!" There is a feeling of glee in Martirio's words. Adela is strident and forceful in her pleas. Each of her speeches is monosyllabic and sharp and after the first question each concludes with exclamation marks. When she holds her own belly, as if in sympathy for the daughter of Librada, we wonder why; Lorca leaves us with some hints about Adela's own sexual relations. It could even be possible to believe that she is, or has been, illicitly pregnant, like Librada's daughter.'

The subtextual meaning is not always easy to identify, but close analysis of the text will help. By a subtextual analysis of this section, we have gained further indications of the characterisation of all the women, but particularly Martirio and Adela.

It is also worth remembering that it is often the individual director's reading of the subtext that distinguishes one production from another.

PRESENTING CHARACTERS

Realising the character on stage completes the characterisation

Questions concerning character will directly or indirectly ask you to discuss how the character could be interpreted. It would be difficult therefore to answer a question about a character without referring to the *realisation* of that character.

It is important to remember that you will need to plan the presentation of that character *in a production of the play or extract*. This implies that you are approaching the text as a blueprint for performance and that you see this character in the light of the whole production. This is important and is relevant even if you are only considering an extract rather than a full text. There is little point in having a clear idea of how you would like to stage the text and which particular themes you wish to emphasise in your production and then deciding on an interpretation of one particular character that is alien to this conception. Characterisation should be part of your coherent realisation of the text.

For discussing the realisation of a character, you will have to refer to the techniques of acting and you may want to consider the following:

- Action
- Body movements
- Gesture
- Proxemics
- Facial expression
- Tone/type of voice
- Pace of speech
- Volume

- Extra detail that might be relevant; for example, make-up, use of costume, use of props and so on.

This is only a checklist. Attempting to run through the whole list would show a lack of sensitivity to the particular playtext. When you are discussing the playing of a character, you should draw on the needs of the role first rather than adopt a 'checklist' approach within a response. These categories are only here for guidance. Perhaps they are self-evident categories but it is worth examining them a little further and suggesting vocabulary that could be useful if you are asked to describe the presentation of characterisation.

ACTION, BODY MOVEMENT AND GESTURE

What kind of actions is the character likely to take at particular moments? Does s/he move with fluency, speed, awkwardly, slowly, with purpose, haphazardly, determinedly, unsteadily, with ferocity, smoothly, wearily, in an uncoordinated manner, at a medium pace, unhurriedly, calmly, in a hurry, with excitement, arrogantly, with self-awareness, and/or timidly, for example? Are his or her actions sudden, premeditated, casual, natural, forced, threatening, expansive, exaggerated, violent, fussy, nervous, constant, limited, controlled, minimal, wild, thoughtless, economical? What kind of gestures does the character use at different points in the play? The slight raising of a hand may have a wealth of meaning at the appropriate moment, for example. What is the natural posture for the character? Does the character slouch, stand with shoulders back, hold him or herself still and straight, rarely keep still, keep their hands in front of their chest, for example? Is there a particular reason for a character to adopt a form of movement or posture? (For example, Arturo Ui adopts the actions, gestures and voice of Hitler in Scene 6 of Brecht's *The Resistible Rise of Arturo Ui*. Brecht is deliberately eliding Ui with Hitler to make a political point.)

Choosing the appropriate vocabulary to describe these aspects of a character is an important part of writing about presenting characters. The terms above may just act as joggers. The use of metaphors and similes can be helpful as well. For example, 'She would move slowly and hesitantly but determinedly towards the girl at this point, like a wild animal moving towards some distant prey'.

PROXEMICS

The term **proxemics** refers to the positioning of people in relation to each other and the use of interpersonal space. We study the significance of that positioning and grouping to find out about the relationships between people. Proxemics can be extended to include the positioning of the cast in relation to the audience and the use of space in the 'auditorium' section of the theatre.

Kinesics is the study of movement and gesture; useful for indicating character

Clearly, proxemics is closely related to other elements of non-verbal communication, such as gestures, posture, facial expression and appearance. The word that describes the study of movement and gesture is **kinesics.** Whilst it is an awkward word to use, it is worth recognising that there is a formal term for such a study. If *kinesics* is the study of movement and gesture (or body motion), a *kinesthetic sense* is required for movement, balance, changing positions and so on. It is a word often used in contemporary dance.

Both these terms involve the patterns of stage movement. This may be a more important consideration for a director or designer than an actor, but it is still something an actor would be expected to consider. For example, if you chart the movement pattern of your character in one particular scene, does it represent your relationship to other characters in the text? The patterns of stage movement can reveal a number of different facets about the characters and his or her relationships.

In addition, the dynamic of a theatre piece can be established through attention to proxemics. In Peter Brook's seminal production of *A Midsummer Night's Dream* in the early 1970s, the four lovers played the quarrel scene (Act 3 Scene 2) in a style that would seem to be more at home in a modern DV8 production. They flung themselves at each other as if they were physical acrobats. This acrobatic style and innovative use of space (including trapezes) permeated the whole production and gave the work a ground-breaking zest, vigour and energy (see p.381).

FACIAL EXPRESSION

Difficult to discuss out of context, yet there is some value in considering this aspect of interpreting a character. It is too easy to describe a character's facial expression as 'normal'. For example, 'At this point in the scene, Arturo Ui's face is normal'. This does not help us visualise your interpretation of the character. Again, it is a matter of locating appropriate descriptions. Is the character's facial expression still, mobile, smiling expansively, smiling tentatively, frowning, grimacing with pain, slightly sneering, smug, angry, tight, calm, excited, gentle, at ease, faintly quizzical, furious? Can you describe individual features to help give an appropriate picture? Sometimes this is difficult to achieve without resorting to cliché ('Her eyes would shine at this point') but it is worth pursuing. Is it worth noting a shift in facial expression?

TONE/TYPE OF VOICE, PACE OF SPEECH AND VOLUME

Is the voice high, medium or low pitched? Is there a particular timbre to the voice for a particular reason? Are there any vocal mannerisms such as a tendency to overemphasise the start of sentences? (If so, why?) Are there particular nuances of phrasing (and why)? What tone of voice does the character use at particular moments of the play? Is it a tone that is indifferent, buoyant, cheerful, snide, reassuring, nervous, unsure, timid, wistful, excited, hopeful, inquisitive, prying, calming, friendly, distant, withdrawn, interested, questioning, depressed, doleful, for example? Does the character speak with an accent or dialect? What does this denote? What is the character's pace of speaking? Does s/he speak fast, slowly, at an average rate? Is the pace measured or changeable? Is there a moment in a scene where the pace increases or slows down? Why? How does the character's pace fit in with that of the others in the scene? Does s/he speak with confidence and assurance? Does s/he command attention through the power of the voice or is the vocal contribution comparatively inconspicuous? Does the character appear to be thinking about what they are saying or do the words come out apparently spontaneously? Does the volume change at all? Does the character speak particularly quietly (within the needs of the venue of course) or does s/he shout at all? What does this tell us?

EXTRA DETAIL

Again, this is an area that overlaps with design and/or directing. As an actor, however, there may be particular additional features to the presentation of the character you might want to refer to. For example, does the character carry a prop of some kind that they use constantly? Does the character use a part of his or her costume for some purpose? Does the character brush his or her hair often? This is entirely dependent upon the play and the character of course. As an actor, you would want to consider the costume and make-up of the character. There are several good books that offer comprehensive details about clothes across the centuries and stage make-up. (See the bibliography at the end of Part 1.) In addition, we touch on this briefly in the 'Approaching the text as a designer' section.

Using a variety of practical exercises will help with developing characterisation

So far, we have not suggested methods of *arriving* at the presentation of character, e.g. practical exercises that can help 'find' the characterisation. Certain ideas are suggested in section 1.1.3 under 'Approaching text as a director' (see pp.47–53). In addition, there are a number of books that offer more detailed advice on acting for developing characters. For Advanced Level work, you should be engaging with practical work that does not just rely on traditional characterisation methods (e.g. neo-Stanislavski techniques). Many performance courses teach physical methods of developing characters now, such as 'finding the centre of energy for the character'. You will need to consider such methods in writing about and preparing for portraying a character. It is worth remembering that today's acting style is rooted in 'identifying' with the character. However, this might not be at all appropriate for portraying characters from certain playtexts. As Wallis and Shepherd say in their book *Studying Plays* (p.24): 'Different

Be aware of the need for different performance registers

sorts of dramatic script invite or assume different registers of performance. And what is invited or assumed is a matter not only of the type of play (say, farce or tragedy), but also the prevailing theatrical conventions.' They suggest the following as a list of varying performance registers:

Presentation
Narration
Demonstration
Representation
Imitation
Impersonation
Identification
Realisation
Possession

(Wallis, M. and Shepherd, S. *Studying Plays*, Arnold, 1998. p.24)

It is useful, therefore, to consider the appropriate performance register for the genre and theatrical conventions implicit in the text you are studying. All your preparation work will be tempered by these considerations. The performance registers 'identification' and 'impersonation' are perhaps the registers most familiar to theatre students of the early 21st century. This has developed from Stanislavski and the American Method and now can be seen in soap operas and films. However, it is unlikely that you will be thinking about minute psychological details of performance if you are performing a Restoration comedy, for example, or if you are performing with the Brazilian physical performance group De La Guarda.

CHARACTER STUDY FOR HEDDA GABLER

Below we give an example of a character study for Hedda Gabler from Ibsen's play of that name. If you are adopting an analytical approach to characterisation (sometimes done for an identification or impersonation performance register) this can be a useful and efficient method of doing a character study. The character study is selective; it would be difficult to be comprehensive with such a key figure as Hedda. If you are studying the play, you may wish to address other characteristics instead of, or as well as, the ones suggested below.

The third column is a form of notating possible interpretations of moments in the text. Often, you are required to explain how you would interpret a part in a *written* form. This grid *cannot replace* a lengthy, collaborative, practical rehearsal period, which is how the realisation of a character should be developed. It can act as a supportive summary, however. As such, it shows only selected glimpses of a practical interpretation that would be coherent and rounded. Its purpose is to act as a reminder of practical work and to be used for written explanations.

We have taken into account: the character's own words and actions, other characters' words and actions, stage directions, subtext (see above, pp.26). All references are taken from the popular Methuen edition, first published in 1965, *Ibsen Plays: Two*, translated by Meyer.

Brief facts about Hedda	She is 29, the daughter of General Gabler. She is 'handsome' and from an aristocratic lineage. She has been married to Tesman for nearly six months at the start of the play.
Character overview	– longs to defy convention; – uses her aristocratic status as power; – forceful and demanding; – her father's daughter, not her husband's wife; – takes pleasure in the outrageous and dramatic (including sex), but often vicariously (there is a sense of the binary virgin/whore in Hedda; she is a mixture of the two); – wishes to stay safe within society's bounds; fears scandal; – lonely; – intelligent, witty and talented but all this is underused; – selfish and callous; – frustrated, bored, trapped; – commands physical admiration; – jealous at times; – devious; – charming when she chooses; – non-maternal. The following charts engage with some of these characteristics.

Characteristic	Evidence from the text	Thoughts on the interpretation of one example
Forceful and demanding	p.244 Bertha: '... you should have seen all the things madam made me unpack before she'd go to bed!' p.261 Hedda pushes Mrs Elvsted down into the armchair. pp.294–6 Hedda attempts to get Loevborg to drink alcohol	pp. 294–6 (Hedda attempts to get Loevborg to drink alcohol) This section is a clear example of the lengths Hedda will take simply to demonstrate her power over Loevborg. She offers Mrs Elvsted as a metaphorical sacrifice. She moves from a veiled request to egocentric persuasion [Hedda: (*looks into his eyes*) But if I want you to.] to destroying Mrs Elvsted's confidences in order to get him to drink – just because she wants to prove she can. This journey can be demonstrated physically and vocally. Her vocal tone can shift as she moves from one stage to another – perhaps using a casual, lightly pitched tone at the start and a faintly smug, sarcastic tone towards the end as she suggests that Loevborg is unmanly because he won't drink. Physically, she can move from an apparent casual quality as she appears to be about to pour a drink at the outset of the section, to a focused proximity to Loevborg as she attempts pointedly to use her personal influence. In the final section, she could move away from him, incorporating the distant two men in her vision, as if she is daring him to meet their standards.
Selfish, callous	p.246 Tesman: 'We were so sorry we couldn't give you a lift. But you saw how it was – Hedda had so much luggage – and she insisted on having it all with her.' p.271 Hedda [on hearing of a potential lack of earnings]: 'I can't allow this to alter my plans.' [A new writing desk subsequently appears.] pp.253/254 Knowing it isn't, Hedda suggests that Aunt Juju's hat may be an old hat belonging to the maid just to insult her.	pp253/254 [The hat incident] Hedda confesses to Judge Brack later in the play that she deliberately suggested the hat was the maid's. Therefore the incident should be played such that the audience recognise Hedda's callousness. Hedda should be showing signs of barely concealed boredom earlier in the scene in order that the rudeness about the hat can be seen as Hedda's intolerance of Aunt Juju's visit finally becoming evident. The stage directions have already indicated that Hedda is moving around the room and can't settle. Tesman follows her towards the table; her irritation with him (clutching his slippers) can be shown by her overtly turning physically away, at that point seeing the hat on the chair. The audience can see a slight cold smile before and as she comments on the hat, but Tesman or his aunt can't see the smile. This would clarify for the audience her knowledge about the true owner. As she speaks she should speak with irritation, arrogance and contempt in her voice. Afterwards, having 'recognised' that the hat is Aunt Juju's, her voice should not be that sympathetic. Indeed, the vocal quality would *lack* sympathy and still be just slightly bored.

Characteristic	Evidence from the text	Thoughts on the interpretation of one example
		Physically, she would make no attempt to move closer to Aunt Juju, as if in an apologetic manner. A stillness by the table would produce distance. When she is drawn to say 'Very pretty and charming' she may well have moved away altogether, as if no longer interested in the scene. Despite the negative attitude, however, she would maintain the barest semblance of manners and hospitality as society would demand this.
Frustrated, bored, trapped	p.255 [stage directions] *Meanwhile Hedda walks up and down the room, raising her arms and clenching her fist as though in desperation. Then she throws aside the curtains* . . . p.275 Hedda [talking of her honeymoon]: 'Well it's all right for him. But for me! Oh no, my dear Judge. I've been bored to death.' p.332 Hedda: 'Not free. Still not free!'	p.332 ['Not free. Still not free!'] Hedda has considered Judge Brack's offer of an extra-marital affair earlier in the play. However, now he has information about her that could be spread to 'society', she is completely in his power and that changes the balance in their relationship. In addition, she hasn't gained the mental 'freedom' that controlling the death of Loevborg should have given her. Instead of a kind of high-flown ecstasy, she is in the mundane world of sordid affairs. It is as she says these words ('Still not free') and the following 'No. I couldn't bear that. No.' that many directors and actresses place her decision to kill herself. This is entirely feasible as the remainder of her speeches in the play are strikingly lightweight – as if she has already made up her mind what to do. With this in mind, interpreting these few words becomes crucial. (To plan for this one moment without making it part of a coherent, fully developed characterisation would be ineffective, of course.) Hedda's facial expression, eyes and body position have to communicate to the audience that she has finally recognised she is trapped. A passionate move followed by a demonstration of tautness might demonstrate this (such as visibly gripping a chair back after rising swiftly and suddenly). Alternatively, an immense, tight stillness and an amused, almost cynical, smile could communicate Hedda's final 'knowledge' and her entrapment. Vocally, the audience need to hear her sense of despair and resignation – yet almost resolution when she moves on to say 'No. I couldn't bear that.' There can be a sense of finality and, almost, bravery in the tone and pitch. Perhaps each word is spoken separately: 'Still – not – free!' to add emphasis and weight to the moment.

Characteristic	Evidence from the text	Thoughts on the interpretation of one example
Takes pleasure in the outrageous and dramatic (including sex), often vicariously	p.266 Mrs Elvsted [obviously talking about Hedda]: 'He [Loevborg] said when he left her she tried to shoot him with a pistol.' p.271 Hedda: 'How exciting, Tesman. It'll be a kind of duel, by Jove.' p.272 Hedda suggests that she can still amuse herself with her pistols. p.273 Hedda 'playfully' shoots at Judge Brack. p.291/292 We hear of the past 'secret' friendship between Hedda and Loevborg and the questions about sex that Hedda had asked him. p.298 Hedda: 'He'll [Loevborg] be here. I can see him. With a crown of vine leaves in his hair.' p.317 Hedda: 'Do it beautifully, Eilert Loevborg.' (i.e. kill himself beautifully.) p.328 Hedda: 'I only know that Eilert Loevborg has had the courage to live according to his own principles. And now, at last, he's done something big! Something beautiful! To have the courage and the will to rise from the feast of life so early.'	p.298 (Hedda: 'He'll [Loevborg will] be here. I can see him. With a crown of vine leaves in his hair.') Hedda's image of Loevborg with a crown of vine leaves is one she held when they knew each other before. Loevborg tells us this on p.316. The image is complex and is not clearly explained in the text. We can assume that there are religious connotations with Christ dying with vine leaves. Hedda's need for the passionate and dramatic is entwined with a religious fervour at times and the image of the wild, unconventional Loevborg as a living icon to Hedda is possible. However, the crown of leaves was a pre-Christian symbol as well. As William Archer says (quoted in Meyer's introduction) '[T]his [the image of the vine leaves] is a very obvious image or symbol of the beautiful, the ideal, aspect of bacchic elation and revelry . . .'. The links with pre-Christian ritual and bacchanalian rites match Hedda's words 'Burning and unashamed' (p.298) as if Loevborg is seen by her as a young pagan God. Yet she only lives this vicariously; she does not have the courage to cross the line of respectability. The first mention of this image should contain something of the above therefore! We have to hear and see Hedda simmering and excited as she envisages this symbol of sexuality, dramatic power, freedom, breaker of conventions – this young God. All her own pent-up sexuality, which she has been unable to satisfy with the staid Tesman, is invested in Loevborg. In addition, she is highly charged with the thought of having power over Loevborg again. There is a heady quality to her words and behaviour for the remainder of the scene. It would be difficult to perform this line with Hedda speaking it to Mrs Elvsted. She needs to be isolated in her own dreams and a physical isolation on stage would support this. There has to be the sense that she is wrapped in her own world. Perhaps she is looking up, as if in adulation of a figure above her. Depending upon the emphasis in characterisation, it might be appropriate to draw out the suppressed sexuality in Hedda by having her holding her own body tightly, or moving her hands down her waist and thighs.

Characteristic	Evidence from the text	Thoughts on the interpretation of one example
		Her voice and eyes need to be in a state of near-ecstasy. The voice would be full of power and excitement, relishing every word that is spoken and speaking as if pronouncing a momentous announcement. Hedda's face and eyes should be vivid and alive, full of vigour and energy. The overall picture should be one of intense, ecstatic passion.
Wishes to stay safe within society's bounds	p.277 Brack: 'Why not jump out and stretch your legs a little, Mrs Hedda?' Hedda: 'I'm not the jumping sort.' [They are referring to an extra-marital affair.] p.292 Loevborg: 'Oh why didn't you do it? Why didn't you shoot me dead? As you threatened to!' Hedda: 'I was afraid. Of the scandal.' Loevborg: 'Yes, Hedda. You're a coward at heart.' Hedda: 'A dreadful coward. . . .' p.294 Hedda: 'Yes. Courage. Yes. If only one had that –' Loevborg: 'Yes?' Hedda: 'One might be able to live. In spite of everything.' p.331 Brack: 'There'll be a scandal, Hedda.' Hedda: 'A scandal!' Brack: 'Yes, a scandal. The thing you're so frightened of. . . .'	p.294 (Hedda: 'Yes. Courage. Yes. If only one had that –' Loevborg: 'Yes?' Hedda: 'One might be able to live. In spite of everything.') There are more obvious examples to choose in this section, but this extract gives the opportunity of showing Hedda in a more thoughtful mood. Loevborg has just been praising Mrs Elvsted (who is present) for her courage in friendship. Hedda picks up the point. (It is not long after the conversation about shooting Loevborg on p.292.) Hedda should be seen as reflective and musing here. Perhaps there is a wryness in her manner and speech as if to say 'What could I do/have done – if I just had more courage?' She has been married for nearly six months to someone who bores her completely. The tinge of bitterness and regret should be evident in the 'One might be able to live. In spite of everything.' She has missed chances of excitement and drama because she has wished to remain safe. A calm face moving to a grimace would help show the range of feelings she experiences. Certainly, a wry quality in the way she moves her head and speaks in this extract would help the audience understand the layers of meaning. It would be worth trying her looking at Loevborg for these words as if they both know what she means by this; they both understand that Hedda lacked courage once before. However, it could work just as well with Hedda looking away from her companions, as if communicating with herself.

CHARACTER TREE FOR *HEDDA GABLER*

In addition to a straightforward character study, as above, you might find it useful to undertake a character tree. Here, you identify the main themes within the plot and draw up a grid that charts each main character's function and contribution to the themes. Where the protagonist is so closely aligned to the themes, as is the case with Hedda Gabler, it would be pointless to put her in the grid; she represents many of the key themes. Here is an example of such a tree based on just two key themes in *Hedda Gabler*.

	Tesman	Aunt Juju	Judge Brack	Eilert Loevborg	Mrs Elvsted
The draw of the wild vs. safety (society's codes)	Represents safety, boredom and harmlessness. He reproduces rather than innovates (e.g. Loevborg's manuscript).	She is a traditionalist and represents the bourgeois, maidenly female keeping well within society's codes.	Offers the seamier, rather sordid, yet vaguely exciting aspect of 'the safe'. He is *not* 'the wild', however.	Loevborg represents 'the wild' to Hedda. Crucially, however, he does not live up to expectations so she is not allowed to exult fully on the wild, therefore.	She fluctuates between the two and appears, to Hedda, to almost have tamed the wild, bringing it into safety. Hedda rejects this.
Frustration for women	Represents the self-innocent side of a patriarchal society.	Fulfils the role of the forgotten woman with little to offer except 'caring' services.	Represents the fully aware side of patriarchal society, but intent on maintaining women's servile place.	Offers a different, more equal, place for women with his unconventionality.	Represents another frustrated woman but seeking to address this within society's codes.

WRITING ABOUT CHARACTER

When you are writing about a character for an examination, you would be advised to be selective and pick key moments to substantiate your character evaluation and presentation. If you have extensive character studies, as for Hedda Gabler above, you will only be able to select the most important aspects of the character. The grid above comprises only notes, of course. For an examination paper, you will be expected to write a full essay.

It is possible to write extensively, even if you are writing about a character in an unseen extract rather than a full text. Take, for example, Douglas Dobson in the extract from *All Things Bright and Beautiful* on p.20. It would be possible to undertake a short character study by focusing on this extract alone.

'Douglas is an uncaring, single-minded official who is preoccupied with bureaucracy. We see the small-minded officiousness of his character in his first speech. The speech consists of a number of short, sharp monosyllabic words, which indicate a forceful, aggressive style. The dominant words in this speech are virtually the only long ones: ''authority'', ''authority'' again and ''official notification''. It is as if he can only use polysyllabic words if they have been fed to him as part of his job; he seems only capable of thinking as far as the ''official authority'' will let him. In addition, there is a negative quality about him which we sense enjoys people's misfortunes. This is seen clearly on analysing the speech, which contains a number of negative words and phrases – ''no'', ''none . . . anybody'', ''Not''.'

So far, you have embarked on a straightforward character study. At this point, you might wish to talk about interpretation. You might well continue:

'As an actor playing the part, I would wish to emphasise the small-minded, uncaring, officious nature of Douglas in this scene. To do this, I would firstly concentrate on the way the lines were spoken.

'I envisage Douglas as naturally having a Northern accent, as he appears to be from the area. However, I would attempt to speak with a poor version of Received Pronunciation (R.P.) as if I was trying to hide my origins, believing that R.P. symbolises status. This would demonstrate that Douglas thinks of himself as someone with power who is better than Queenie, Albert and family: an officious petty bureaucrat. The final speech about the disabled woman and the man who wants a garden would be delivered in ''hysterical'' tones. A hard-edged, laughing voice would indicate the lack of care with which Douglas operates. I would build this to a crescendo on ''Dig it up . . .'', as if he feels his line is some sort of clever aphorism and is the highlight of the conversation; he sees himself as important and witty.'

In this way, you are interpreting the part of Douglas as if you were an actor. You are using the voice as your base, although you might well go on to describe gestures, facial expressions, posture and so on. You have looked at the type of voice used, the tone and the range of volume.

Practise writing about character interpretation from shorter extracts

If so much detail can be gleaned from such a short extract, it is possible to see how much can be written about a character from a full text. As a stage towards this, look at a longer extract now and a specific question concerning characterisation and language to explain more fully the points made in this section.

The following extract is from *Translations* by Brian Friel. It is set in Ireland in 1833, in a disused barn which is used as an informal school. Hugh is the master of the school; Owen, his younger son, works with a section of the English army who are making a map of the area. Doalty, Bridget, Sarah and Jimmy are adults at the 'school'. (Jimmy is fluent in classics; his speech 'Nonne Latine loquitur?' is in Latin and asks if the soldiers can speak Latin.) Manus is Hugh's older son who helps his father in the school.

The text is written in English but most of the Irish characters are speaking Irish and only Hugh and Owen understand English. When Owen translates, he is speaking in Irish.

(OWEN enters with LANCEY and YOLLAND. CAPTAIN LANCEY is middle-aged; a small, crisp officer, expert in his field as cartographer but uneasy with people – especially civilians, especially these foreign civilians. His skill is with deeds, not words.

LIEUTENANT YOLLAND is in his late twenties/early thirties. He is tall and thin and gangling, blond hair, a shy, awkward manner. A soldier by accident.)

OWEN: Here we are. Captain Lancey – my father.

LANCEY: Good evening.

(HUGH becomes expansive, almost courtly, with his visitors.)

HUGH: You and I have already met, sir.

LANCEY: Yes.

OWEN: And Lieutenant Yolland – both Royal Engineers – my father.

HUGH: You're very welcome, gentlemen.

YOLLAND: How do you do.

HUGH: *Gaudeo vos hic adesse.*

OWEN: And I'll make no other introductions except that these are some of the people of Baile Beag and – what? – well you're among the best people in Ireland now. *(He pauses to allow LANCEY to speak. . . LANCEY does not.)* Would you like to say a few words, Captain?

HUGH: What about a drop, sir?

LANCEY: A what?

HUGH: Perhaps a modest refreshment? A little sampling of our own aqua vitae?

LANCEY: No, no.

HUGH: Later perhaps when . . .

LANCEY: I'll say what I have to say, if I may, and as briefly as possible. Do they speak *any* English, Roland?

OWEN: Don't worry. I'll translate.

LANCEY: I see. *(He clears his throat. He speaks as if he were addressing children – a shade too loudly and enunciating excessively.)* You may have seen me – seen me – working in this section – section? – working. We are here – here – in this place – you understand? – to make a map – a map – a map and –

JIMMY: *Nonne Latine loquitur?*

(HUGH holds up a restraining hand.)

HUGH: James.

LANCEY: *(To JIMMY)* I do not speak Gaelic, sir. *(He looks at OWEN.)*

OWEN: Carry on.

LANCEY: A map is a representation on paper – a picture – you understand picture? – a paper picture – showing, representing this country – yes? – showing your country in miniature – a scaled drawing on paper of – of – of – *(Suddenly DOALTY sniggers. Then BRIDGET. Then SARAH. OWEN leaps in quickly.)*

OWEN: It might be better if you assume they understand you –

LANCEY: Yes?

OWEN: And I'll translate as you go along.

LANCEY: I see. Yes. Very well. Perhaps you're right. Well. What we are doing is this. *(He looks at OWEN. OWEN nods reassuringly.)* His Majesty's government has ordered the first ever comprehensive survey of this entire country – a general triangulation which will embrace detailed hydrographic and topographic information and which will be executed to a scale of six inches to the English mile.

HUGH:	*(Pouring a drink)* Excellent – excellent.
	(LANCEY looks at OWEN.)
OWEN:	A new map is being made of the whole country.
	(LANCEY looks to OWEN: Is that all? OWEN smiles reassuringly and indicates to proceed.)
LANCEY:	This enormous task has been embarked on so that the military authorities will be equipped with up-to-date and accurate information on every corner of this part of the Empire.
OWEN:	The job is being done by soldiers because they are skilled in this work.
LANCEY:	And also so that the entire basis of land valuation can be reassessed for purposes of more equitable taxation.
OWEN:	This new map will take the place of the estate-agent's map so that from now on you will know exactly what is yours in law.
LANCEY:	In conclusion I wish to quote two brief extracts from the white paper which is our governing charter: *(Reads)* 'All former surveys of Ireland originated in forfeiture and violent transfer of property; the present survey has for its object the relief which can be afforded to the proprietors and occupiers of land from unequal taxation.'
OWEN:	The captain hopes that the public will cooperate with the sappers and that the new map will mean that taxes are reduced.
HUGH:	A worthy enterprise – *opus honestum*! And Extract B?
LANCEY:	'Ireland is privileged. No such survey is being undertaken in England. So this survey cannot but be received as proof of the disposition of this government to advance the interests of Ireland.' My sentiments, too.
OWEN:	This survey demonstrates the government's interest in Ireland and the captain thanks you for listening so attentively to him.
HUGH:	Our pleasure, Captain.

[Friel, Brian, *Translations*, Faber and Faber, 1981.]

ACTIVITY With specific reference to this scene, explain how, as an actor, you would interpret the role of Lancey. Use your wider performance experience to help you.

The above is a typical question that you might be asked if you were given this passage as an unseen extract to analyse and comment upon. With little variation, it could be used as a basic question for a full text you have studied as well. Obviously, the answer for a full text would be significantly more detailed and comprehensive.

The remainder of this section is used to suggest ways of approaching the question.

GENERAL POINTS Your first task is to make an instant analysis – what does the question want? You are attempting to use the text to assess the character of Lancey and to help you find an interpretation. In addition, you are asked to use your wider experience to help in the answer.

What do you notice immediately about the text with particular reference to Lancey? His first speeches to the group are hesitant; there is repetition and a number of dashes, which indicate pauses. Some of the characters giggle at how he is speaking. The stage directions give an indication of how Brian Friel envisages these speeches being said; for example, '*He speaks as if he were addressing children.*' The later speeches are comparatively long and convoluted, with a number of technical words concerning cartography (the making of maps). They are contrasted with Owen's succinct translations. He quotes from a government or army document ('our governing charter'). Lancey seeks reassurance or support from Owen by looking at him on a number of occasions.

Looking more closely at the scene, you should keep in mind the points you have just noted and work to develop and expand them. At this stage you should start to think about the points made on pp.00–00; in other words you should look at the character's own words, the character's own actions, other characters' words, other characters' actions, stage directions and the subtext.

Remember to look for *key examples*. Responding to short extracts demands a swift response; you will not have time to go into as much detail as you might wish. It would make sense to underline quickly examples of text that you feel would be useful to justify character analysis. You can then use these few underlinings as the substance for the main part of your answer. If the extract is part of a full play you are studying, make additional notes referring to the full play.

Remember also to consider **text**, **production** and **reception**. This question has already helped you here as it has asked for 'interpretation'. From the start, you know that you will be answering from an actor's (or director's) point of view and this will automatically keep you thinking about **production** and **reception**.

FRAMEWORK

You must form a framework to ensure you cover the question. A framework for this question might be:

1. Give a brief overview of the character.
2. Go through these major characteristics, one at a time, picking out key examples from the text which illustrate them. Explain how these examples justify your decisions about characterisation.
3. Take some of those key examples and explain how to present them to interpret that character. In each point, use an example from your own experience as a performer to enhance and support what you have said.
4. Summarise.

Alternatively, you might want to run sections 2 and 3 together so that you are demonstrating the interpretation alongside each characteristic.

A DETAILED ANALYSIS

1. A brief overview of character

The first section will be brief and acts as an introduction to the answer. It might read:

'We are given several clues in the text to assist in an interpretation of Lancey. The stage directions immediately suggest that he will be ill at ease with the folk of Baile Beag, ''. . . uneasy with people . . .'', and the subsequent scene proves this. He appears stiff, condescending at times and unsure of himself and his surroundings. He fails to gain the sympathy of the audience from the outset.'

For a full text answer, you might want to bring in general information about the role of the army in Ireland at that time which you might have acquired through background research, thus giving a context for the character of Lancey and the difficulties of his position.

2. Examples of main characteristics

Part of your second section might read:

> 'Some of the Irish people make every effort to make Lancey welcome. Hugh offers him a drink and attempts to cover any embarrassment arising from Jimmy's use of Latin. Yet Lancey cannot unbend. He refuses Hugh's offer in hurried monosyllables: "No, no." He appears rather rude by referring to the people as "they" in his fifth speech and the emphasis on the word "*any*" implies that the Irish are to be pitied for not speaking English. (This adds irony to Jimmy's Latin question as clearly Lancey is unfamiliar with one of the classic languages.) His defensiveness, which arises from the insecurity of his position, comes out in irritation and condescension. His first speeches to the gathering are almost a parody of the traditional English attitude to foreigners.'

A later part of section 2 might be:

> 'Friel's use of bathos adds to the audience's impression of Lancey's inadequacies. His long and unnecessarily complicated speech about the "comprehensive survey" is made particularly ridiculous by Owen's apt summary, "A new map is being made of the whole country." This happens frequently and Lancey even uses bathos himself in his last speech. He uses the grand quote from the government charter and then makes the trivial comment, "My sentiments, too." This use of bathos makes Lancey seem self-important and the audience finds it difficult to sympathise with him. The sniggering of Doalty, Bridget and Sarah is quite understandable.'

In an answer on the full text, it would be important to trace the character's *development* through the text. Therefore, the examples used would cover the whole play, or at least all the parts in which the character appears.

3. Interpretation and your experience

You may have decided to run sections 2 and 3 together in your answer so that interpretation immediately follows characterisation at each stage. Whichever order you choose, when you are writing about interpretation make use of the points made under 'Presenting characters' on pp.31–2. Picking up on the character analysis above and the importance of integrating your wider theatrical experience you might write something like this:

> 'Brian Friel's piece is clearly written in a naturalistic style. The conversation and the setting indicate this. I would want to explore the character with this in mind, therefore. The piece reminds me of another Irish text, Conor MacPherson's *The Weir* which I saw in London. The delicate shifts in tension throughout this extract of *Translations* are similar to those in *The Weir*; this would help me understand how to replicate the ebb and flow of Lancey's dialogue. I would be aiming for a naturalistic performance, like those in *The Weir*.

'It would be possible to demonstrate the condescension and rudeness of Lancey's character in his fifth speech. Firstly, he interrupts Hugh; I would emphasise his rudeness and insensitive behaviour by abruptly turning my back on Hugh as I start the speech. The phrase "and as briefly as possible" would be said firmly and loudly, giving it authority and weight. This will help make the audience more aware of the irony when Lancey *doesn't* speak briefly at all; in fact he is longwinded and confusing.

'As he says, "Do they speak *any* English, Roland?" I would want to be frowning with annoyance and speaking with irritation, not bothering to lower my voice. Speaking at a normal pitch adds to the insult to the locals, as Hugh patently *does* speak English. The frown would show the audience that he believes they are at fault for not speaking English rather than him at fault for not speaking Irish.

'When we undertook a project on feminist theatre, I played the role of Ada in Maureen Duffy's play *Rites*. Ada is the exceptionally domineering ruler of her kingdom - a set of women's lavatories at an underground station. She was a bitter, disillusioned, insecure, middle-aged prostitute and, in preparation for the role, I worked on creating this combination of insecurity and anger where everyone else seems to be at fault but you. One of the exercises I found most useful was to externally physicalise huge emotions (e.g. lust, anger) with only 5 seconds preparation. We videoed these and when we replayed the exercise, we could see certain "instant" expressions that were usable. We took some of these and "naturalised" them but retained the essence of the emotion. This kind of exercise would be very useful for learning how to communicate Lancey's internal frustration.'

We have only given examples for parts of an answer to the question, **'With specific reference to this scene explain how, as an actor, you would interpret the role of Lancey. Use your wider performance experience to help you.'** Clearly, there is more to add.

It may be useful to take note of the following points that we have addressed in answering this question:

- We have referred to **text, production** and **reception**; there are several references to the expected response from the audience, i.e. reception.

- The examples show that we are answering from the viewpoint of an **actor**.

- Text analysis has been interwoven with analysis of characterisation.

- Text analysis has made use of 'things immediately noticed', for example the length and type of sentences (see pp.72–3). In addition, further terms have been used, notably bathos, irony, monosyllabic, parody and pause (see pp.74–81).

- The analysis of characterisation has made use of the character's own words, the words of others, the actions of others and stage directions (see p.26). *Key* examples have been used.

- Suggestions about interpreting the character have been made, including the use of a number of acting techniques, as listed above on pp.32–4.

- Your 'wider performance experience' has been included.

- A framework for answering the question has been suggested.

APPROACHING THE TEXT AS A DIRECTOR

Directing is mainly about interpreting the playtext . . .

There is an important thread that runs through this section on directing. This is the notion of **interpretation**. Theatre is about text, production and reception; the text has to be *interpreted* to be produced and subsequently received by the audience. This is so for full playtexts and extracts.

As a director of a text, the first thing you have to do is to judge the meaning and sense of a text. The first part of Section 1.1.3 (pp.15–24), 'Finding the meaning', is *particularly relevant* to directors therefore and should be considered as the first step in approaching the text as a director. Once you have come to a decision about appropriate meanings in the text, you use this judgement to make decisions about the visual look of the piece, its pace, its emphasis and many other areas. You are *interpreting* and *producing* the extract.

It is particularly worth remembering the idea of 'seeing and hearing' the text in production as you read the script. This will produce a holistic approach to the text that will automatically take in all the elements of presentation. You will 'hear' the way the lines are spoken; you will 'see' the set, movement, facial expressions, props, etc. It becomes *one* production in your mind and you will find that you are placing your own variation of interpretation on to the text/blueprint. You should even be seeing the audience and bearing them in mind as you mentally develop your own production. What reception do you want your production to be given?

... after identifying your audience

You should remember at all times that the essence of studying and understanding theatre is how a director and/or company decides to interpret a text. You have to become that company – or at least its director or one of its actors. You have to interpret the text so that it becomes a production and you have to consider how you want the audience to receive that interpretation and realisation. You should always ask "For whom is this production? *Who are* the audience?" The answer to this will guide all your subsequent decisions. You should decide this before proceeding further.

One of the main roles for a director is to draw the best performances from his or her acting company and to work collaboratively with a designer. In particular, it is the director's task to identify the meaning of a playtext and to lead the company into visualising and practically realising the text. Additionally, the director will consider the appropriate venue and audience for the playtext. It is important, therefore, to consider *all three* of the 'Approaching the text' sections in Part 1.

This section draws together the various points in Part 1 into a logical sequence for a directing student approaching a playtext.

There are several aspects of the production to work upon in rehearsals

The following is a list of areas that a director and company might be interested in addressing in rehearsal. It is unlikely that all these will be relevant to your particular play or extract; you, as director, would decide what you wished to concentrate upon according to the text.

- To explore the **themes** of the piece, identifying and amplifying the author's intentions.

- Taking this further, to work on the **author's intentions** and the **directorial interpretation** where the latter is going to take a particular perspective on the play.

- To explore the **characterisation** and **relationships**.

- To gain an understanding of the background **context** of the play – period, place, social history, political environment etc.

- If there is a clear **style** to the piece, rehearsal work might explore the style itself; this could include work on language. For example, if the piece was of a distinctly melodramatic nature with long, rhetorical speeches, the method of speaking this language would be useful background work.

- The playtext may require academic and practical **research into theatre practitioners** who have developed a particular method or style of work.

- Work around **pace**, the building of **tension**, and **atmosphere** might be useful.

- If you, as director, have decided to set the piece in an unusual environment, such as an open-air theatre, rehearsal work could include particular kinds of **vocal training**.

- It would be important to work on any **special performance techniques** that might be required, for example physical theatre, singing, audience participation techniques.

When you are writing about the direction process, clearly it is not -enough to say, for example, 'I would want to explore the themes of the playtext with the company' or, if you are writing in retrospect, 'I explored the themes of the playtext with the company'. First, you would need to identify the methods you deem to be most appropriate for exploring the themes. Secondly, you would need to discuss the results, or expected results of these activities.

Below, we give a few examples of such activities for the list given above. These are only *examples* and you should recognise that attempting to use the same activities without variation would show a lack of understanding of the needs of particular pieces of theatre. You must be selective, according to the demands of the text. It is worth building up a store of such activities to which you can refer if appropriate.

For work on full texts, you will need to work out carefully how you would rehearse the play. You should establish which of the above areas might be addressed in a rehearsal period and you should experiment with certain exercises with your group. The results of these exercises are worth noting; it may be useful to refer to these in an answer on rehearsing the text.

For unseen extracts, you need to be able to select instantly certain exercises that would be appropriate for the extract.

THEMES   Examples of rehearsal and background activities:

i) Identify the themes first through brainstorming and other methods. Try the following activities to explore them further and gain a broader understanding of the author's preoccupations.

ii) Improvise around the theme, developing pieces that address the same issues but in a different time, with different people and so on. For example, if you are addressing the theme of ambition in *Macbeth*, you might ask your company to develop an improvised scenario set in a 20th-century multinational business where one person is caught up with an ambition to lead the organisation. Such improvisation work encourages a broader understanding of a key theme and allows the cast access to the emotional framework underlying ambition.

iii) Carry out background research into the themes, if relevant. For example, Caryl Churchill's *Vinegar Tom* is about how poverty, poor conditions and discontent led to people hounding others for their misfortune in 17th-century England (see the *Vinegar Tom* extract, pp.21–2). Parallels are deliberately drawn to modern times. For background research it would be interesting to look up statistics about poverty at that time and today and crime figures concerning racial attacks.

iv) Divide the play into Units and Objectives. Read the section about Stanislavski's Unit and Objectives on p.243. Divide the play up according to 'theme' objectives rather than the more normal Stanislavskian 'character' objectives. Similarly, you might want to identify a 'super-objective' theme. This will help identify particular sections that focus on specific themes.

DIRECTORIAL INTERPRETATION

Having identified the author's intention to communicate a certain message, as a director you may want to realise the text with a particular emphasis on specific issues. You may choose to give the text an unusual interpretation; you may even select a new setting to support this. Any such variance would be worked on in the rehearsal period. Work with the actors can also focus on script experimentation, for example trying a different emphasis on certain lines, giving certain moments in the script more weight by stillness and pauses, etc. This allows the director to find the appropriate slant on lines and words to match her or his particular interpretation of the text.

Establishing the directorial interpretation is one of the major tasks of a director, as we indicated in the opening to this section. *All* the following subsections ('Characterisation and relationships' to 'Special performance techniques') would relate to this chosen interpretation. In addition, the design of the production is crucial to support the directorial interpretation. With this in mind, a director should carefully consider the design concept (see the '**Approaching the text as a Designer**' section, pp. 53).

CHARACTER-ISATION AND RELATIONSHIPS

Characterisation can be one of the key methods of realising the directorial interpretation in a performance of the playtext.

Certain rehearsal techniques are helpful in creating a background for the character and developing an understanding of that person. This is not *always* appropriate, as some texts do not present fully developed and psychologically deconstructed characters. These activities may also be overused and become clichéd. It is important to justify fully the choice of activity and assess its value for the actors.

You should remember that basic warm-ups, both physical and vocal, and group exercises always form a sound base for practical work. The group dynamics are most important; many of the following exercises will help here at least.

i) 'Hot seating', i.e. asking somebody in role questions about themselves. The questions can centre on how the character perceives his or her relationship with other characters within the play. (This is one of the most popular techniques and should be suggested circumspectly.)

ii) 'Thought tracking', i.e. speaking as somebody's thoughts as they enact a situation. This could be whilst they enact a piece of the text or improvise around the text.

iii) 'Abstract images', i.e. putting into an abstract image a character's emotions or state of mind or the relationship between characters. This would give the actor playing the part a visual and perhaps aural image about the character's feelings to keep in mind. For example, if a character is feeling a sense of frustrated anger, the group can form an image of what they think the essence of that emotion might look like if it was interpreted visually. This might have a central 'body', tightly coiled up, with a number of jagged, spiky edges composed of people's arms and legs. A vocal sound could be added which would match this visual image: taut, sharp, unpleasant cries perhaps.

iv) 'Conscience alley': the whole company form an alley-way for the character to walk down and speak out loud all the possible thoughts the character might have at a particularly crucial moment in the text.

v) Stanislavskian methods can also form a good basis for character development. For example:

- Emotion memory – or variations upon this (see p.244)

- 'If' and the Given Circumstance (see p.241)

- Units and Objectives (see p.243). Establishing a 'through line of action' for the character (or Super-Objective) would be particularly useful.

vi) Work on the subtext of the scene can help actors to understand the characters and their relationships within the text. The company can perform the *sub*text rather than the written text. This would mean speaking a character's actual thoughts where this differed from the spoken text.

vii) Drawing up a character study would provide a thorough background for an actor. There is an example of this on pp.35–40.

viii) An actor could work on specific moments of the text that are important for the particular character, rehearsing different methods of presenting the subtext of the moment.

ix) In contemporary theatre, many companies work physically on developing characterisation. For a comprehensive account of such work, see Chapter 3, 'Directing', in Mackey, S. ed., *Practical Theatre*, Stanley Thornes, 1997. In this chapter, a number of contemporary directors describe their methods of practice. In addition, there are a number of texts in the bibliography on p.135 below that offer useful exercises. See, in particular, Johnstone's *Impro* and *Impro for Storytellers* and Boal's *Games for Actors and Non-Actors*.

CONTEXT Understanding the context of the play will include knowing about the life of the time, the social conditions, the political environment and the cultural background. This is covered comprehensively on pp.102–12.

Examples of rehearsal and background activities:

i) Background research – e.g. reading, museums, interviews, internet websites, viewing documentaries, etc. followed by brainstorming sessions.

ii) Improvisations set in the period and concerning a number of different aspects of the society; the actors will use information gained in their background research.

STYLE OR GENRE Examples of rehearsal and background activities:

i) Carry out background research into the author's period of writing and her or his influences. Read critical texts (e.g. books, chapters, introductions) that debate the work and its genre.

ii) Read other plays of a similar period and within the same genre. This is covered in detail on pp.119–26.

iii) Read plays of a different style, perhaps from a previous period, simply to draw comparisons and recognise how the style of writing changed.

iv) View other productions that use a similar style.

v) Experiment with the script in the same way as for the directorial interpretation. Finding the right speech patterns, movements and gestures will enable you, as the director, to realise the text in the appropriate style. For example, plays that are satirical in style, or witty, are likely to use wordplay and puns. A particular sharpness of diction to enable rapid yet enunciated speech would be appropriate for the style of play. Training and experimentation would take place during the rehearsal period.

vi) Certain texts would need extensive work on style at the outset of rehearsals. For example, if you were producing a Restoration comedy such as Wycherley's *The Country Wife*, the performance style is crucial. Even the different positions in which a fan is held would need to be known, as there was a recognised 'code of the fan' in the Restoration period.

THEATRE PRACTITIONER RESEARCH When you have researched the context of the playtext, you may recognise that you have to, or wish to, work with the ideas and practice of a particular theatre practitioner. For example, if you were working on Theatre Workshop's *Oh! What a Lovely War*, you would almost certainly want to understand Brecht's work (see pp.292–330). Alternatively, if you were going to direct Weiss's *Marat/Sade*, you may look at Artaud (see pp.256–291). Even if there is not an obvious connection between a text and a practitioner, you may choose to work with a particular practitioner in mind. Grotowski's 'poor theatre' (see pp.348–351) has been popularised over the years and can be adapted and extended for many different texts. An understanding of the work of *many* practitioners will encourage you to experiment further with your own directing.

PACE, TENSION AND ATMOSPHERE

As a director, you may wish to spend some time finding the appropriate pace and rhythm for the play; in addition, there will be particular moments of tension that need careful building. Experimenting with speech patterns, rhythms and different emphases will help you and your company find the right sense of pace for the play. The following exercises are examples to help you experiment with pace.

i) Stand opposite your co-actor and speak the lines to each other from some distance apart, gradually moving closer together as you speak; the pace and tension will alter as you move.

ii) With your co-actor, jog round the room holding on to each other, with your breathing synchronised. Speak the script, slowing down and speeding up, changing the emphasis in sentences and so on as you jog. This makes you aware of the rhythms and patterns within the speeches.

iii) Experiment with the script, for example doing speed runs (speaking at a gabble pace) or cueing runs (just speaking cue lines, thus giving emphasis to the pace of the 'hand-over' of lines).

iv) Such exercises will automatically assist with tension and atmosphere. However, creating tension and atmosphere demands a more holistic approach to directing. You may not initially recognise the atmosphere that you wish to create. It is quite appropriate that this arises during the rehearsal process. Then, tension and atmosphere can be enhanced through other elements of performance such as stillness or activity on stage, lighting and sound effects. Even temperature can be considered! In Buzz Goodbody's 1975 production of *Hamlet* at The Other Place in Stratford, the entrance of Fortinbras at the end of the play was made through opening doors from the outside of the theatre. A cold draught was created and accompanied his entrance. The chilling effect added to the atmosphere of dread and hopelessness as Hamlet (Ben Kingsley) lay dying.

v) Beware of clichés when you are creating tension and atmosphere. You may feel that the sudden switch to red light at a moment of high tension would help you achieve your effect. However, this is a mightily overused theatrical cliché.

VOCAL TRAINING

This would be worth highlighting if you had stated that you wanted the production to take place in an unusual setting, such as an open-air space or a circus arena, for example, or if the production called for a particular use of voice. For example, *Metamorphosis*, by Stephen Berkoff, demands experimentation with vocal techniques to establish the expressionistic world of the Samsas.

Particular training on accents and dialects would take place with the use of prerecorded tapes and building up the use of the accent or dialect in improvisation.

A number of traditional voice exercises can help actors to develop well-projected voices. These will assist breathing, diaphragm usage, enunciation of vowels and consonants and projection. (See Chapter 1 of *Practical Theatre*, ed. S. Mackey, Stanley Thornes, 1997.)

SPECIAL PERFORMANCE TECHNIQUES

These would entirely depend on the text. You would simply need to be aware of rehearsal techniques in case the script called for unusual skills. This would also depend upon your interpretation of the script. For example, a group from De Montfort University (then Leicester Polytechnic) performed Molière's *The Hypochondriac* at the Edinburgh Fringe in 1990. Normally bewigged and stately in appearance, this production was a glorious piece of physical theatre, with the actors playing not only the cast but also a snooker table, a tiger rug and even a pencil sharpener, whilst bringing enormous energy and physicality to the piece. Such an approach would require some specialist physical theatre training.

The rest of Part 1, particularly 'Finding the meaning', should be considered as part of 'Approaching the text as a director'. It contains important information for a student director. The above is a *framework* for approaching directing. Listed in the bibliography at the end of Part 1 are some good 'hands-on' texts that give advice about the actual day-to-day process and pragmatics of directing, for example McCaffery's *Directing a Play*; Taylor's *Directing Plays*; Miles-Brown's *Directing Drama*.

APROACHING THE TEXT AS A DESIGNER

Students of drama and theatre studies need to have some understanding of how to approach a text as a designer. Some students will want to specialise in this area. When considering **text**, **production** and **reception**, the design of the production is of importance. However, all areas of theatre design have their own particular specialist areas. We can only give a broad overview of theatre design, sufficient for students who do not need to be specialists in this area. The bibliography on pp.136–7 gives a range of specialist texts.

Having knowledge of performance spaces and theatre language is obviously important. Therefore, sections 1.1.1 and 1.1.2 ('Performance spaces' and 'Stage terms') should be considered in conjunction with this section.

'Approaching the text as a designer' looks at the notion of an overall design concept, general considerations, set, costume and lighting design.

AN OVERALL DESIGN CONCEPT

Design should be an integral part of the production process

The design concept should be part of a production from the outset. The director works in conjunction with the designer and together they shape the piece. If you were discussing design, you would tie the design into a production concept, that is an overall vision of the production aligned to an interpretation of the playtext.

A clear example of this was the enormously popular Lloyd Webber rock opera, *Cats*. John Napier, the designer, and Trevor Nunn, the director, conceived a production where the cats lived in their own somewhat seedy, downbeat world, full of emotions, trials and tribulations. The cats had moments of triumph, fear and hope, just as humans do. Their world was an intriguing and original reflection of our own, and we, the audience, caught glimpses of ourselves and our world in the cats' behaviour and their physical world.

Integrating the design with
the production concept is vital

It was important that the *design* concept integrated fully with this production concept. The cats' world had to be complete and fully represented on stage. So the design team created an environment that was viewed from the cats' perspective. Huge scrap-metal food cans, broken tennis racquets, lorry tyres and even a car bonnet, together with countless other items of junk, formed the cats' territory. All objects were outsize, of course. This dilapidated scrapyard acted as a cats' playground, full of nooks and crannies, swinging ropes and hidden entrances. The environment spilled out into the auditorium making the whole theatre one enormous tip.

The costumes, make-up, lighting and sound design were all integrated into the creating of a dramatic piece. The cats' skin-tight costumes were often faded and sometimes positively scraggy, with the make-up an extension of the costume. The lighting was a technical masterpiece, providing shady corners, chill nights and quasi-spacecraft journeys. All the elements of design were part of the whole design conception, which in turn was part of the whole production conception. The production aimed to give us an image of the cats' seedy world; this world was then transcended through moments of joy, pathos, cunning and magic as demonstrated in T.S. Eliot's original poems. *Cats* was an allegory for our own lives.

The design and the direction were finely interwoven – the show was conceived with the help of the designer. There was no sense of the design team simply 'servicing' the realised text; they were an integral part of the creation from conception to realisation. Whilst the musical/rock opera as a genre could be criticised, the design concept of *Cats* has been broadly and warmly praised.

Developing an overall vision
of the play is important

If you are responding to a text by discussing its design, you must focus on the *whole* design concept. This is not just about your ability to draw diagrams of costumes or scale plans of sets; it is more to do with swiftly developing an overall vision for the extract or play that enhances or even guides the directorial interpretation. It is important to 'see and hear' the text in your mind when reading it initially. This process of 'seeing and hearing' should incorporate all the design elements – lighting, costume, sound, make-up and props. It takes practice and imagination to do this.

A designer will consider a
number of aspects when
creating the design concept
...

A design concept is likely to reflect **the themes, the genre, the period** (the social and cultural context), **the reception** and **the atmosphere** of the text. This is not a comprehensive list, nor would all these necessarily be relevant to the design. However, many of them will interrelate as you think through an overall design concept.

... the themes ...

We have already discussed **themes** and the meaning of the play. (See pp.15–24.) A designer would be expected to consider these as key to interpreting the text. Having identified the key theme/s and after discussion with the director, you would consider how strongly these are to be realised in the visual and aural design of the text. The **designer's lexicon** below would help you here.

... the genre ...

The **genre** is similarly important. For example, if the extract or play appears to be naturalistic in dialogue and genre, you as the designer may well choose to emphasise this naturalism through all the design aspects (naturalistic, imitative set; costumes absolutely of the period; naturalistic make-up with very little allowance for stage light; lighting at all times suggesting the time of day, weather). You will recognise that to do this would enhance the naturalism of the dialogue; it allows the delicate interplay between the characters to be a focus of the production, as the audience will be associating a strong naturalistic design with the subtlety of naturalistic dialogue.

Alternatively, the designer might deliberately choose to create a visual environment that is stark and surreal, justifying it by the desire to concentrate purely on one central issue in the text, for example the inner sense of isolation of each character. Thus the set might be a white box with the audience inside the box and the two characters dressed in bodystockings. The light is raw white and the performance is conducted within the box as a form of physical acrobatics, the actors using the audience as objects to hide behind, confront, protect etc, depending on the particular moment of isolation for each character. The overall concept would be one of harsh, bright surreality.

This is an extreme example but such things do happen. At the 1989 LIFT (London International Festival of Theatre), the East German director Matthias Langhoff directed Strindberg's *Miss Julie*, which is actually subtitled *A Naturalistic Play*, as a surreal nightmare. He was highlighting the psychodrama and erotic fantasy elements in Strindberg's play. Miss Julie was a white-faced sex doll with false breasts, wearing a ballgown with huge balloons attached. The highly expressionistic set had sloping floors and puce walls. As one Miss Julie left the set at the end to commit suicide, another came in, suggesting that the cycle would begin again. The director deliberately moved away from Strindberg's naturalistic intentions because he chose to emphasise certain issues in the text that were most appropriately expressed through expressionism and the surreal.

... the period ...   The **period**, or the social and historical background, is going to be very important in some texts. Clearly, you must research the look of the period: architecture, furniture, clothes and any other relevant visuals (e.g. guns in 1930s–40s America for *Arturo Ui*). If the text demands that you re-create that time, and this has been agreed as appropriate with the director, then authenticity will be important in your final design decisions.

... (including the cultural and political climate ...   Another aspect of period research is the cultural and political climate. This could influence the mood and atmosphere of the design. The hedonism and decadence of 1930s Berlin, with its developing Nazi oppression, could well be a decisive factor in your design for the musical *Cabaret*, for example. (See pp.102–28 for further suggestions on support research.)

... and the forms of staging at the time a text was written) ...   In addition, you might also take account of the forms of staging at the time the text was written to help you understand it and to consider how this might affect your designs. In the Elizabethan stage, 'beneath' the stage represented hell and the top canopy above the thrust was painted as the heavens. The witches in *Macbeth* could well have emerged from the trap in the stage, therefore. In Restoration theatres, the DS area was used extensively for direct contact with the audience. In Victorian melodramas, the external scenes would take the whole stage and the interiors would be played in front of the 'first flats' whilst major scene changes took place behind. In the medieval period, the mystery plays would have been played on 'stations' or wagons; the contact with the audience would have been exceptionally close. This knowledge may well affect your reading of the text.

... audience reception ...

The audience **reception** must be briefly considered. For whom is the production? What will their expectations be? Where is the venue? The answers to these questions may not take much time but they do give a boundary to your thinking and you should take them into account.

... and the desired atmosphere

The **atmosphere** is a broad term and hard to qualify. It is all the above (theme/s, genre and period) yet it is more than that as well. It is the *feeling* of a playtext. A **designer's lexicon** may help you with this.

A designer's lexicon will include terms such as: **colour, tone, resonance, texture, line, rhythm** (fluidity), **pitch** (e.g. bold, shallow), **focus** (e.g. positioning), **shape, perspective** (and depth of field), **proportion** (scale), **contrast, word scenery**. This is a way of breaking down the visual, spatial and aural elements that designers have to consider. So, having decided on the themes, the genre of the text, the period and the audience reception of the play, you can think more comprehensively about designing. These terms enable a designer to gain a sensitive, coherent, all-encompassing *feel* for the production that can then be interpreted in the various design disciplines. The way to use these terms is to take a particular text and start to ask yourself questions (as a designer). It is useful not to tie these responses down to set, costume, music and so on, but to keep them 'open'. Once you have responded to the designer's lexicon, then you can start making decisions.

- What range of **colours** comes to mind when thinking of the play? If I am studying *The Beggar's Opera*, for example, I might think of browns, greys and blacks with the occasional flash of cheap, bright colours such as red.

- Associated with colour, what is the **tone** of the piece? You might say that the tone of the same play is dingy, murky, begrimed but with some clear tones that are not tinged with dirt.

- **Resonance** is a difficult word to describe. Perhaps it is easier to contrast two texts. Take as an example, Brecht's *Arturo Ui* and Ibsen's *Hedda Gabler*. The Brecht play resonates with speed, action and pace interspersed with nervous, double-dealing tension. It has an air of the superficial, of parody and it resonates accordingly. *Hedda Gabler* is measured, controlled and ordered with the sense of something seething under the surface. The vibrations are deep and resounding.

- What is the **texture** of the piece? If we think of *A Midsummer Night's Dream*, the texture could be interpreted in many different ways. It is possible to think about the natural textures of the wood – the crinkled leaves and the bark of the trees – to give an insight into the design concept. Alternatively, you might want to consider the translucent web and fabric of Victorian paintings of fairies. (A 1997 production in London, designed by Julian Crouch, used sticky backed tape (Sellotape) as the main design ingredient.) You could arrive at 'texture' in another way by considering words such as rough, smooth, jagged, harsh, pitted, mottled. These might give you an insight into the text.

- Deciding on the **line** of a production is easier. Immediately start thinking of curved, straight, dotted, spirals, broken, continuous lines and then decide which of these images is appropriate for the text you are studying.

- What are the **rhythms** of the piece? Chekhov's *The Three Sisters* has a complicated rhythmic structure. The rhythms are gentle and fluid at one moment and then there are bursts of barely disguised staccato.

- By **pitch**, we are referring to the density of the text. Do you see the play as bold and sharp, as shallow and faded, as firm and stated, as fluttering and distant?

- A designer considers **focus**. What is the focus of the play? Is it a theme, a symbolic object, an area of space? How can this be reflected in the design elements e.g. the set, the lighting and the audience, even.

- **Shape** is a useful term. What shapes come to mind when you think of the text? If you are looking at *The Trojan Women*, you might think of tall, vast, magisterial shapes that have been broken down. You might think of shapeless bundles. You might think of scattered pieces of broken shapes lying on the ground. If you are considering Gogol's *The Government Inspector*, squat, rather compressed squares come to mind.

- **Contrast** asks you to consider any strong variations within the text. Are you looking to deliberately establish contrast? Is it implicit in the text? For example, in *West Side Story* the contrast between the Jets and the Sharks, the two rival gangs, is etched into the text. The music supports this and any designer would look carefully at how to bring out contrast in set design, lighting, costume, make-up and props. The contrasts might be described as jagged, steel blues, pale, modern (Jets) and smooth, purples, dark, traditional (Sharks).

- **Perspective** and **proportion** bring us nearer to the practicalities of designing. A designer would consider the perspective of the playing space and the appropriate selection of perspective for the text. The depth of field is important here. How much distance do you want the audience to see? In Stoppard's *Arcadia*, the play uses the landscaped gardens of the 18th and 19th centuries as the setting for the action, to be seen beyond the interior set. It would be absolutely necessary for the distant perspective to be seen, therefore. The scale and proportion are a matter of choice. The designer may choose to play around with these for a particular reason e.g. *Cats* mentioned above.

- **Space** is crucial. How does a set utilise the space effectively? What *is* the fictional space? (A living room? A wood? A beach? An otherworldly space?) Does the space *signify* anything? Is there private space for each individual (see part of the review of *The Weir* on pp.170–81) and public space within the fictional space on stage? What is the relationship between the actors' space and the audience's space? How is the space enhanced by the other design elements (sound, lighting, costume for example)?

- Look for **word scenery**. This is when the dialogue helps you by indicating the feel of the setting. (This is not the stage directions, which can often tell you exactly what the set must look like. However, many designers move away from this.) Wallis and Shepherd (*Studying Plays*, p.131) use an example from *A Midsummer Night's Dream* where Titania invites Bottom to 'sit thee down upon this flow'ry bed' to explain this. We know that in Shakespeare's theatre, there would not have been a 'flow'ry bed' but the words have given us the flavour of the setting.

Having brainstormed all the terms in the lexicon, making notes or diagrams accordingly, you should have a coherent *feel* for the design of the text. It may be that you are not going to use precise points. For example, you may have thought about dotted, spiralling downward **lines** for *The Three Sisters*. It is unlikely that you would use this precisely in your set or costume design, but it has added to the 'flavour' of your design thinking.

ACTIVITY   Look at the following piece of script and see if you can decide upon an overall design concept. You are not trying to be too specific here. Do not draw out set designs, for example; discuss an overall framework for the extract, much as we have done above for *Cats* and *Miss Julie*. The play is a form of documentary drama (with strong overtones of Brechtian satire) about the First World War. The actors are dressed as pierrots.

Justify your thoughts with reference to the themes, the genre, the period, the reception and the atmosphere, probably using elements of the designer's lexicon.

Alternatively, take a full playtext that you are studying (e.g. Bond's *Restoration*, Casey's *Shadow of a Gunman*, Weiss's *Marat/Sade*, Jonson's *Volpone*, any Shakespeare or Greek text, Gay's *The Beggar's Opera*) instead of the extract. Similarly, write about your overall design concept, justifying this with reference to the themes, the genre, the period, the atmosphere and the reception, probably using elements of the designer's lexicon.

NEWSPANEL:	AUG 4 BRITAIN DECLARES WAR ON GERMANY.
M.C.:	[Master of Ceremonies] Well, that's the end of Part One of the War Game.

(The band plays a chorus of 'We don't want to lose you', during which the pierrots go off one by one, as slides of the coming of war in different countries are shown, ending up with the Kitchener poster.)

Slide sequence:
Slide 5: British civilian volunteers, marching in column of fours from recruiting office.
Slide 6: Street parade of civilians led by young boys, one with Union Jack and playing the bagpipes.
Slide 7: Crowd of German civilians cheering a military parade.
Slide 8: Another parade of British civilians being led by young boys, one with Union Jack, another playing a drum.
Slide 9: Young British girls dancing in the streets.

Slide 10: Crowd of British volunteers outside a recruiting office.
Slide 11: Eton schoolboys marching with rifles at the slope.
Slide 12: Poster of Kitchener pointing, with caption 'Your Country Needs You'.

(The girls sing a verse and chorus of 'We don't want to lose you'.)

(The band plays a half-chorus of the song. Mime tableau of Belgium at bay, Germany threatening with a bayonet.)

M.C.:   Gallant little Belgium.

(During the last chorus of the song there is a mime of recruiting. The men hand in their pierrot hats and kiss the girls goodbye, marching off behind the screen. They re-emerge wearing uniform caps and march off saluting.)

NEWSPANEL: **COURAGE WILL BRING US VICTORY.**

BAND: *Cavalry charge music*

(Six men, wearing the capes and caps of the French cavalry enter upstage, riding imaginary horses.)

STANDARD-BEARER: Bonjour, mes amis.
FRENCH SOLDIER: Bonjour, mon capitaine.
STANDARD-BEARER: Il fait beau pour la chasse ... Vive la Republique!
FRENCH OFFICER: En avant!

(They gallop downstage. There is a sound of gunfire: an ambush. They retreat.)

STANDARD-BEARER: Maintenant, mes amis!
FRENCH OFFICER: Ah oui.
STANDARD-BEARER: Pour la gloire.
FRENCH OFFICER: Charge!

BAND: *Part of the Marseillaise*

(The cavalry charge. There is a sound of machine-gun fire and whinnying horses. The men are killed and collapse. They hold their poses, standing, sitting or lying while a girl singer enters.)

NEWSPANEL: **GERMANS HELD AT LIEGE ... LONDON WILD WITH JOY**

[Theatre Workshop, *Oh What a Lovely War* (1963), Methuen, 1965. pp.23–24]

This section has offered a *framework* for considering design. In the bibliography there are texts that give a hands-on, practical approach to design. In particular, Kimber and Wood's *Stages in Design: Assignments for the Performing Arts* offers an incremental approach to design through a number of practical design assignments.

Approaching the text as a designer, therefore, requires you to consider a design concept. It is this that should influence the 'individual' areas of design. As a designer, you would be responsible for *all* areas of design: set, costume, props, lighting and design. In reality, there are often specialists in these areas who would work with the overall designer to realise his or her whole concept. However, the next sections offer information and guidelines for a designer in some of the individual design areas.

SET DESIGN   This section can be built into work on the overall design concept or it can be used to address particular questions on *set* design.

As with the overall design concept, a set design will have to consider **the themes, the genre, the period**, the possible **reception** and **the atmosphere** of the playtext. Your answer will be based on justifying the decisions you make taking all these into consideration.

Read the following extract, which we will use as a basis for analysis.

(SCENE: *The dining room of the Beauregard Private Hotel, near Bournemouth. It is small, rather bare and quite unpretentious. A door at back leads into the lounge, a swing door upstage R. into the kitchen, and another downstage R. into the hall and the rest of the hotel. Windows L. are curtained at the moment, for it is a winter evening, about seven o'clock, and the guests are at dinner. Each sits at a small separate table . . .)*

MABEL:	Were you medaillon or goulash?
LADY MATHESON:	*(Correctly accenting)* Medaillon.
MABEL:	Sorry. I thought you were goulash.
	(She stumps with the unwanted goulash to the kitchen door.)
LADY MATHESON:	It was probably my fault.
MABEL:	*(Gloomily)* I dare say.
	(She passes on to MISS MEACHAM.*)*
	Now, you *were* goulash, weren't you, Miss Meacham?
MISS MEACHAM:	*(Deep in her book)* What? Oh yes, Mabel. Thank you.
MABEL:	*(Serving her)* And what to follow – the mousse angelic, or the turnover?
MISS MEACHAM:	Which do you think?
MABEL:	Turnover.
MISS MEACHAM:	Turnover then.
	(MABEL drifts away.)
MRS RAILTON-BELL:	I think cook's acquiring a little lighter touch with her pastry, don't you think?
MISS MEACHAM:	Not judging by the tarts we had at tea yesterday. Cannon balls.
MRS RAILTON-BELL:	Did you think so? I quite liked them. I much preferred them to those pink cakes on Tuesday.
MISS MEACHAM:	I didn't mind the pink cakes. The tarts gave me the collywobbles. I had the most terrible dreams.
MRS RAILTON-BELL:	*(With a faint smile)* I thought you were always having dreams.
MISS MEACHAM:	Oh these weren't my proper dreams. Not the ones I make myself dream. These were just horrible, pointless nightmares. Cosh boys and things. *(After a slight pause)* I talked to Louis XV on Thursday night.
MRS RAILTON-BELL:	*(Plainly humouring her)* Did you indeed dear?
MISS MEACHAM:	The goulash's rather good. I think you made a mistake

[Rattigan, Terence, *Separate Tables*, Hamish Hamilton, 1955.]

ACTIVITY   We suggest focusing on the following question; it provides a general basis for discussion:

Give your ideas for a suitable setting for this scene from *Separate Tables*, making explicit reference to your wider theatrical experience.

We give you a tight structure below, which you might find too restrictive. You are likely to want to move on from such a schematic method once you have gained some experience. However, these are useful pointers for any question on set design.

FRAMEWORK

1. What do you, as a designer, judge to be the overall characteristics of the extract, i.e. **theme, genre, period, atmosphere**?
2. What type of performance venue is appropriate for what kind of audience?
3. What does the set look like? Set plan/diagram. (This is the major section to address.)
4. How does this design relate to **the themes, the genre, the period, the atmosphere**?

Throughout all four sections, use your own experience to support and enhance your response.

A DETAILED ANALYSIS

1. Overall characteristics

It is important to find a hook upon which to hang your ideas for the set design. This must originate in the concerns of the text (the theme, style, genre etc.). You should always identify these first, and it is convenient to start your answer in such a way. Make sure you read the stage directions at the start of the extract, or throughout the full play, thoroughly; these are often crucial in helping you decide upon the set.

With the *Separate Tables* extract, you might state the concerns of the extract like this:

> 'The play seems to be highlighting the isolation of a number of individuals living in a hotel. They share a dining room and conversations, but they don't share tables; even the conversations appear desultory and lacking in depth. The dining room seems uninviting and lacking in warmth; we wonder at the circumstances that brought these people to this hotel in which they appear to live. We can assume the play had a contemporary setting as there is nothing to suggest otherwise; it is likely to be the 1950s.'

2. Performance venue

Identifying an appropriate performance venue demonstrates a broad understanding of the theatrical process. Placing your set design in an appropriate space shows that you can see your ideas in context.

For this extract you might decide on the following:

> 'The setting and dialogue appear to be naturalistic. As a director I would wish to enhance this sense of naturalism in the set design. I would deliberately want to put the set in a proscenium arch theatre so that we could work in a traditional box set with the arch as the 'fourth wall' of the dining room. Proscenium arch theatres would have been the most familiar form of staging in the 1950s and I would like to capture the time as much as possible. In addition, I want the audience to feel slightly removed from the characters, just as they are slightly removed from each other.'

3. Set design

Next you must clarify your set design. This should be sketched out, however roughly. It is far easier to convey what you mean with drawings, supporting these with written text. Whilst you will be short of time, it is worth spending a few minutes quickly drafting your ideas. Labels help and save a lot of time in writing out in full text what each object is.

For the *Separate Tables* set, you might draw something like this:

Figure 1.10

We have added to the scene where we can, bearing in mind that the directions said it was 'rather bare and unpretentious'.

4. Justification of the design

Your task is to justify your design briefly, relating it to your overall intentions as designer, and to make appropriate references to your theatrical knowledge.

This would be the longest section of your answer. One part of this might read:

> 'When the doors open, background flats depict the adjoining rooms. For example, when the swing door to the kitchen is swung open, the audience can see part of the 1950s kitchen, complete with full shelves, cupboards etc. This attention to detail is to reinforce the overall style of the piece. As a

designer, I have decided to keep to a naturalistic style as most appropriate for the text; therefore, the set should be completely within the conventions of naturalism. Suggesting the rooms offstage will clearly assist this.

'This "close naturalism" is rooted in the late 19th century with the work of Zola, Strindberg and others. It was Strindberg who said in his preface to *Miss Julie*, "When one has only one set, one is entitled to demand that it be realistic". He suggested rooms offstage for *Miss Julie*; I am taking that idea.'

This is only *one* example of justifying an aspect of the design and using your broader knowledge. You should also point to more thematic concerns. For example, the positioning of the tables might reflect the occupants' desire for conversation yet also their need to maintain privacy.

Have a rough knowledge of domestic settings from the 20th century

For unseen extracts, you will not be expected to have a detailed knowledge of furniture, room fashions and clothes for every century. However, you would be expected to have a general knowledge: for example, there would not be a computer or a video in someone's living room in the 1960s. You may not know what would be in a 1950s kitchen, but you can write such things as 'shelves' and 'cupboards' or 'cooker' reasonably safely. For questions on full texts, you *would* be expected to have done your research and to know the furnishings and decor of the period in which the play is set.

Research for full texts more comprehensively

ACTIVITY

Re-read a text you know well. Take particular note of the stage directions that refer to the set such as entrances and exits, and any words spoken by the characters that refer to the set in any way. Use a similar framework to the one on p.61 to answer this question:

What set would you design to help you realise the meaning in the play?

COSTUME AND MAKE-UP DESIGN

As with set design, you will have to consider **the themes, the genre, the period, audience reception** and **the atmosphere** of the piece.

For unseen extracts, you are not expected to be a costume specialist, but a basic knowledge of fashion might be useful. It is worth looking through a book on clothes or costumes in the 19th and 20th centuries to pick up the following information:

- hemlines for women
- waistlines for women
- trousers for women; were they acceptable?
- trouser widths for women and men
- particular use of accessories, e.g. hats
- hairstyles for women and men, e.g. length of hair
- unusual amounts of make-up used, e.g. heavy eyeliner for women.

Have a rough understanding of 20th-century fashion

Appropriate books are suggested below, p.136. It is well worth having some idea of the decades' changing fashions; with this knowledge and some understanding of how a costume should reflect the character, you will be well equipped to answer questions on costume. However, it may be that although an extract was written in the 19th or 20th century, the text is set in a previous century. You then have to decide whether you wish to play the text in comparatively modern dress, or whether you feel you can attempt a design using costumes of the time.

Research fashion for full texts more comprehensively

For your full texts, you are expected to have researched the fashion of the time and to have identified appropriate costumes for the individual characters.

In general, whilst it is useful to have a knowledge of costumes, the most important area of costume design is to relate the costume to the overall design concept and to the character involved. For example, if you are studying Euripides' *The Trojan Women*, you may decide to costume the piece in late 20th-century, mid-European dress as you have made the directorial decision to draw strong links to the Kosovo conflict at the end of the 20th century. (The production of Sophocles' *Antigone* at the Old Vic, autumn, 1999, did something similar.) You would then need to consider how the individual (or chorus) designs can represent the characters within that concept.

The same can be said for make-up. In the 1990s, the use of make-up became less fashionable in the theatre. However, it is worth having some very basic knowledge about make-up for general use, such as foundation. Refer to one of the good make-up books recommended on p.136. In addition, you ought to be aware of the use of make-up for a more expressionistic purpose, as Miss Julie's white face mentioned on p.55.

If make-up is important in your full text, research it.

For your study of full texts, you should decide whether any of the characters should wear particular make-up. This is particularly relevant for genres such as Restoration comedy, where make-up was fashionable for men and women. In addition, you should consider the implications of make-up for texts such as *Metamorphosis* by Berkoff. Because Berkoff's original style favoured the use of white make-up, you would have to make some decisions about its use yourself.

Read the following extract from David Campton's *The Cagebirds*.

This short play is set in a 'room with a large locked door. Several Ladies sit or stand around the room.' There are eight characters, six of whom seem to inhabit this room. These are 'The Long-Tongued Gossip', 'The Mirror-Eye'd Gazer', 'The Medicated Gloom', 'The Regular Thump', 'The Constant Twitting' and 'The Great Guzzle'. They are looked after, or guarded, by 'The Mistress'. A note at the beginning of the play states: 'Although no character is based on a specific bird, they could have bird-like characteristics, particularly in movement. Bird-like appendages could be translated into human terms: there need be no beaks or plumage, but a long beak, for instance, could be indicated by a walking-stick, or extravagant plumage by a fan.'

(The Guzzle and The Gazer appear to converse with each other. In ping-pong dialogue one makes a statement and the other seems to respond to it. It just happens that they are talking about different subjects.)

GUZZLE: Gravy is most important.
GAZER: Oh, indeed. Never back-brush too hard.

GUZZLE: Dark brown and smooth it should be.

GAZER: That's what I tell them. There's no point in spending a small fortune on a permanent if you brush it all out again.

GUZZLE: Exactly. How can bumps get into gravy? Criminal carelessness.

GAZER: Not that I expect a permanent to be too permanent.

GUZZLE: No, indeed. There's no excuse for lumps.

GAZER: This year's fashion is next year's old hat. But I have such fine hair.

GUZZLE: Even in times of economic stress my gravy was exemplary.

GAZER: Mine is like spun gossamer.

GUZZLE: Speaking as a consumer.

GAZER: Bobby pins tomorrow.

GUZZLE: A gravy user.

GAZER: With gossamer.

GUZZLE: Gravy.

GAZER: What there is of it.

TWITTING: I was never given to opinions.

[Campton, David, The *Cagebirds*, Samuel French, 1976. p.3]

ACTIVITY   Answer this question using the given framework.

How would you want The Gazer to appear? Refer to costume and make-up and to your wider theatrical experience.

FRAMEWORK   1. What do you, as a designer, judge to be the overall concerns of the extract, i.e. **theme, genre, period, atmosphere?**

2. What do you see as the key features of this character?

3. What do the costume and make-up look like? (You will need to include a diagram or sketch.)

4. How does this design relate to **the character, the themes, the genre** and/ or **the period?**

Throughout all four sections, use your own experience to support and enhance your response. (See pp.45–6 for examples of bringing in 'wider theatrical experience'.)

We suggest that you use these four points as a structure for your comments as we have done on p.61. You may find certain areas difficult to address, such as the period of the piece. Don't be put off by this; if the period is not clear, you may not wish to refer to it, or you may find a point in it being somewhat timeless.

The diagram or sketch need only be basic. It can be labelled, which will make it easier to refer to the various features in other parts of your answer.

LIGHTING DESIGN   When considering lighting design, you will be aware that you should be lighting the set, the costumed actors, the props, make-up and so on. Therefore, as part of a coherent design concept, ideas for lighting the production should refer to these elements. As with other design areas you will also have to consider **the themes, the genre** and **the atmosphere** of the extract. The **period** and **audience reception** may also be important.

Knowledge of a few lighting terms would be useful, although again you are not expected to be an expert. These terms will help you in addressing a lighting question:

Types of light

- Fresnel – gives a soft edge to the light
- Profile – gives a hard, firm edge to the lit area
- Follow spot – useful for highlighting one character
- Flood – floods an area with light.

You would be advised to become familiar with the particular names of the lights available to you in your own performance space, e.g. parcan, silhouette, and so on.

A 'state'

A lighting 'state' refers to a set of lights that are up to particular levels. When you move to another state, different lights or different levels will be up.

Crossfade

When one state is gradually replaced with another; this can be done as quickly as you wish.

Preset

When one state is already set up and waiting on the lighting board. All you have to do is to take down the existing state and move to the preset state.

Gels

The coloured material placed in front of lights to provide colour. This material used to be made out of gelatine, thus the term gel.

There are hundreds of colours of lighting gels. It is worthwhile getting a sample colour set from a stage-lighting firm and just noting a few names of colours. For example:

- steel – a pale blue useful for a colder atmosphere
- straw – a pale yellow frequently used for warmer atmospheres.

Strong primary colours are rarely used in naturalistic productions. They are more suitable for musicals or pantomime.

Gobo

Metal (or similar material) that is cut out and shaped. This is then placed in front of the lantern and can produce shapes or patterns. A popular example is a gobo cut to create a dappled light for a woodland effect.

Barndoor

A device with four shutters that slots into the front of a **fresnel** lamp. It prevents spill of light and gives the fresnel a firm edge. It can be rotated so that the 'edge' to the light can be directed.

The above list is not comprehensive, but it should give you some ideas. Questions that deal with lighting on its own are unusual. You may well find that you refer to lighting as part of **staging** overall or as part of a question on **technical effects**. An extract or play would have to be particularly suitable for such a question; the *Separate Tables* example would not be a likely technical effects question, for example. *The Cagebirds* extract, however, might be more interesting.

Read this extract from the play as well as the one on pp.64–5. The Mistress has brought a new character into the cage/room. She is The Wild One, who tries to persuade the others to leave the room with her after she has broken the lock. The ladies resist.

WILD ONE:	The earth and its abundance is waiting for you. This way. This way. There. *(The Guzzle reaches the door. She peers out. Then she shrieks, and runs back to the group.)* What am I doing here? You're not worth saving.
GUZZLE:	Too much. Too many. Too big. Too far.
WILD ONE:	You could stretch your wings and fly. But you cling to your cage. Why? Why? Why?
GOSSIP:	Naturally, as I said to her – knowing where that story came from . . . *(She pauses, then carries on in a different voice. The words come slowly, almost painfully, as though dragged from her; and the rest of the speech she alternates between her usual babble and this unusual speech. The effect is of two people talking.)* Who – would – feed – us – out – there? . . . A likely tale, as I told her at the time . . . Who – would – clothe – us – and – change – our – bathwater? . . . As if I hadn't known the whole family from the cradle on, as if she didn't know . . . Who – would – protect – and – shelter – us – out – there?
WILD ONE:	Out there you can take care of yourselves. Come and go as you please. This is a prison.
GOSSIP:	Our – prison.
THUMP:	Ours.
GLOOM:	Ours.
GOSSIP:	If – this – is – a – prison – it – is – well – kept – and – clean.
WILD ONE:	A prison is a prison. All prisons should be destroyed. All cages broken open.
GOSSIP:	This – is – what – we – are – used – to. This – is – our – home.
THUMP:	Ours.
GLOOM:	Ours.
GUZZLE:	Ours.
WILD ONE:	That's only what a cage has done to you. You'll sing a different song when you're over the fields and under the sky.
GOSSIP:	We – shall – stay.
WILD ONE:	No. I'll take you from this place if I have to burn it down. I'll march you lot to freedom, or die in the attempt.
GOSSIP:	Die.
GLOOM:	Die.
THUMP:	Die.
GUZZLE:	Die.
GAZER:	Die.
	(They form a semicircle round The Wild One.)
MISTRESS:	*(off)* Who opened the door?

WILD ONE:	Too late, she's coming back.
TWITTING:	She's come back. She's come back. She's come back.
WILD ONE:	She's not important. She can die. There are seven of us to one of her. And I opened the door for you. Kill her and you'll all be free. Kill her!
	(The Ladies close in around The Wild One until she is hidden.)
	Kill her and follow me! Kill her and destroy this cage! Kill –
	(She ends with a choking cry.)
	Silence.
	(The Mistress appears in the doorway.)
MISTRESS:	Who opened the door?
	(The Ladies scatter, leaving The Thump, who has her hands around The Wild One's neck. The Thump releases The Wild One, who slumps to the ground.)
THUMP:	*(moving away)* There's too much violence in the newspapers these days.

[Ibid. pp.23–25]

ACTIVITY   From your knowledge of the two extracts, answer the following question, as a designer:

Give your ideas for technical effects that might be used to enhance this scene, referring to your wider theatrical experience to support your answer.

FRAMEWORK   1. What do you, as a designer, judge to be the overall concerns of the extract (i.e. **theme, genre, atmosphere**) at this particular moment?
2. *Briefly* state a setting for the extract and explain it.
3. Describe the technical effects (lighting, sound, use of props?) and how they are used. (This is the major part of the answer.)
4. How does this enhance the dramatic moment?

In sections 3 and 4 particularly, you will bring in your own experience. (See pp.45–6 for examples of bringing in 'wider theatrical experience'.)

The four points above are only *suggestions* for a framework. You may find a completely different structure, of course; don't let yourself be confined by this one.

This particular play, *The Cagebirds*, gives quite a wide scope for interpretation; the technical effects for this scene are therefore very much open to your own creativity. *Separate Tables* is less of an experimental piece. A similar question using that extract would make different demands upon you. The technical considerations would arise out of the design decisions, which in turn arise out of a naturalistic text, where the staging should be based on what looks real. With such a text, the question is likely to be different.

ACTIVITY   Re-read the *Separate Tables* extract or a naturalistic text that you know. Answer this question:

What technical considerations would have to be addressed for this text? Refer to your wider theatrical experience.

Use and adapt the framework given above, if appropriate.

OTHER DESIGN CONSIDERATIONS

Be aware of further technical elements that could be useful in staging a text

For this section, it is enough to be *aware* of other possible staging areas, such as **properties** and **sound**. As with make-up, costume and lighting, questions would only call for ideas relating to these if the text was appropriate.

Specialist knowledge in areas such as properties and sound is not necessarily required for questions on unseen extracts. On the whole it is enough to be creative in your ideas and to ensure they are related to the text and justified. Similarly, you need not be totally familiar with specialist jargon for *general* questions on effects for your full texts. For example, *Macbeth* could raise an interesting discussion of technical effects which would make good use of sound (referring to the first witches' scene):

> 'As we gradually become aware of the witches on stage, I would want the auditorium to be filled with a quiet, insistent recorded sound. This is the sound of a gentle bubbling, combined with the faint rustle of whispering voices. The bubbling could be taken literally by the audience as the bubbling in the cauldron, or it could be hinting at the bubbling molten rock, deep in the earth's core, suggesting that the witches inhabit the unknown regions of the planet. The whispering is representative of the impact their words will have on Macbeth; they will remain as instant whispers at the back of his mind. Overall, the effect should be quite eerie and strangely threatening. Because it surrounds the audience, they will feel that threat for Macbeth.'

This kind of answer is adequate for general questions; there is no reference to any technical sound jargon here. However, you should have some specialist knowledge of technical areas if you are hoping to answer a specific technical question for productions of full texts. If your design for a full text incorporated particular use of sound, you might want to discuss the use of specialist equipment. For example, if you wanted to underpin your production throughout with multi-layered pre-recorded sound and music, you might wish to refer to some of the following:

- digital multi-tracking (on computer or on an individual unit);
- use of DAT tape or minidisc;
- 'sampling' – recording and manipulating sound;
- editing software e.g. Sound Forge.

See Walne's *Sound for the Theatre* in the bibliography (p.137) for further information.

If you have specialised in a technical area such as sound at any point in your studies, you would be wise to consider bringing this experience into other areas of your course, not just in answers on full texts, for example when responding to unseen extracts; undertaking performance analysis.

For your full texts you will be expected to have a clear understanding of the type and nature of **prop** you would require. The period is important and you should have researched appropriately; the nature of the prop will reflect other design decisions.

For example, you might decide as director/designer for Ibsen's *A Doll's House* that the set will reflect the rather quaint, pretty rooms that might be seen in a doll's house of the 1880s. (The play was written in 1879.) The whole design concept would be based upon Torvald's perception of his wife as a doll. This could be carried through to the props. The macaroons that Nora takes out of her bag at the beginning of Act 1 could be particularly dainty and decorated in pink and white. At this point in the play, Nora is very much the dutiful doll; such a prop would be entirely appropriate and in keeping with the whole design concept.

For unseen extracts, you will wish to refer only to key props and will not be exhaustive.

1.2 *Textual analysis*

1.2.0 INTRODUCTION

In one sense, this could be considered the starting point of any work on playtexts. However, we wanted to emphasise the practical implications of working on playtexts first; we have ordered the sections to highlight this. Textual analysis (and background research) is crucial, of course, to studying and producing drama texts but it is sometimes easy to lose track of the ultimate point of a playtext: the production.

However, it is now important to engage with the language of the text itself and understand how to draw meaning from it. At the same time, the process of interpreting and realising the textual language practically will be addressed.

1.2.1 GENERAL APPROACH TO THE LANGUAGE OF TEXT

Language here is taken to mean the words in the text. A more general use of the term occurs when referring to the 'language of the theatre', which can include set, lighting, costumes and the other elements that go into making a complete production. However, this section looks specifically at words.

The following are some principles to bear in mind when looking at language in texts:

- Language is used as a means of communication. This communication is not simply between the characters on stage. Language communicates to an audience and sends out signals to us.

- From the language we can draw conclusions about **themes** and **issues, character, style, genre, tone, atmosphere** and **plot.**

- On the whole, the language in a play makes sense to us, we can understand what the characters are talking about. Sometimes we can't; some expressionistic and absurd plays deliberately make no(n)sense.

- Most late 19th- and 20th-century texts are written in prose; occasionally a playwright writes in verse for a particular reason. The use of prose has developed from the great naturalist writers, Ibsen, Chekhov and Strindberg, at the end of the nineteenth century. In previous centuries, blank and rhyming verse was frequently used.

- No language in a playtext is *natural*, although it can be natural*istic*. Dramatic language is always contrived, even if originally based on improvisation work and however much it resembles real life.

- There is always a reason or purpose behind the dramatist's selection of language.

- **Analysing the language of a text is the surest method of progressing to intelligent and sensitive understanding about the text.**

SHAPE OF SPEECHES

What do you notice immediately in any new scenes that you are reading? For example:

- Are there abnormally long or short speeches?

- Are many speeches interrupted by another character?

- Is the scene in verse or prose?

The shape of the speeches can immediately raise useful questions

What do the answers to the above tell you immediately? For example, if one character has speeches that are significantly longer than those of the other character(s), this could show that he or she is clearly the dominant character in the scene. The dramatist may be using one character as a mouthpiece for his or her own beliefs. Alternatively, he or she might be attention-seeking or just boring.

If speeches are interrupted, why? The dramatist could be trying to recreate a pattern of naturalistic, fast-moving conversation, or one character could be impatient.

If the extract is in verse, why? In some periods of drama, playwrights used verse as the conventional way of writing dramatic scripts: the Elizabethan and Jacobean era is a classic example. If you are working on a set text, it would be important to understand *why* this was the convention and how it enhanced the theatre of the time. (For further details about the use of verse in theatre history, see pp.108–15 in Mayne and Shuttleworth's *Considering Drama*, Hodder and Stoughton, 1986.) There are very few 20th-century dramatic texts written entirely in verse. Some will have passages of verse or song in them, however, and it is important to consider why they might be there.

Verse can intensify and/or encapsulate

Verse is not necessarily poetry; it could be described as highly patterned writing. Just as songs are a stylised medium for communication, so is verse. Certain ideas or feelings cannot be described in prose because they would seem incongruous. However, by moving into another convention – verse – the playwright persuades the audience to accept them. This is achieved by removing us one step away from the naturalistic into an artificial, almost fantasy world. The extract from *Vinegar Tom* on pp.21–2 is a good example: the song is a commentary where the cast come out of character temporarily into an artificial world.

Verse is a polished form of dramatic writing and this can intensify the drama. We allow verse to have enormous rhetorical power, whether the whole text is written in verse or only parts. In 20th-century drama it is often used to summarise and encapsulate an issue, and it can do this very effectively. For example, the first act of *All Things Bright and Beautiful* finishes with Albert and Queenie's permanently offstage son singing the hymn of that name. The last four lines we hear intensify the authors' message about the lack of care given to housing poorer people, with hard-edged irony:

The rich man in his castle,
The poor man at the gate.
He made them high and lowly,
Each to his own estate...

On this occasion, the verse is well known. Original verse can perform the same function (as in the *Vinegar Tom* extract pp.21–2.)

SENTENCES   For example:

- Do the sentences make sense and are they long, short or a mixture?

- Are some sentences full of long or short words?

- Do the sentences state facts, give commands, acquiesce with the previous speaker, question?

- Are the words in the sentences indicative of a country or region of a country?

If the sentences make sense, are they particularly well formed and grammatically correct? This might indicate the education and background of the character. If the sentences aren't complete, can this tell us something about the style that the dramatist is employing? Is there an attempt to recreate the haphazard dialogue of real life, for example? Is the syntax (the arrangement of the words) confused or orderly? If confused, why?

If the sentences have a number of complicated words in them, does this indicate a highly patterned style of writing, elevated from real life? Does it show us that this particular character lives and works in an environment where the spoken word is revered and valued, or is the character showing off, for example? Is he or she using words correctly?

Briefly look at the content of some sentences in any playtext. Are they 'constative' or 'performative' utterances? Constative utterances simply state facts, including agreeing with a previous fact. Performative utterances give commands, ask questions, name something and so on; they are taking a more proactive stance. What does this tell us about the individual speakers – and their relationship?

Regional or dialect words in sentences could be hard to identify, although the extract may be preceded by a description of the place in which the text is set. Even if you cannot explain the meaning or origin of a dialect word, the fact that a character speaks in dialect is important: the author is setting the character in context.

PAUSES OR   Are there any? If there aren't any obvious pauses or silences written into
SILENCES   the stage directions, are there implicit pauses within the speeches? (This is something that might not be instantly evident.) If there are obvious pauses or silences, why? What can this immediately tell us?

You need to be alert to the various implications of such breaks in the flow of the text. Does it mean that some of the characters are hesitant in this situation? Is there an awkwardness between the characters? Is one person reticent? Is the author attempting to portray a realistic world where people do intersperse speech with silence?

ACTIVITY   Take a page from a text that you are studying. Look at the text with the headings 'Shape of speeches', 'Sentences' and 'Pauses or silences' in mind. Choose one of these areas: **themes and issues, character, style, genre, tone, atmosphere** or **plot**. Draw some conclusions about the area of your choice based simply on the shape of the speeches, the type of sentences and any pauses or silences written into the script.

LANGUAGE TERMS

Language terms are the basic tools to use when analysing texts

For further analysis of playtexts you will need **language terms.** Below is a list of such terms. These will give you a firm base for studying and analysing text.

Rather than just produce a list with brief explanations, we have given further suggestions about how you might use these terms. In this way, you will begin to recognise how they may help you in responding to texts whilst considering production and reception.

We suggest a cumulative approach to learning these terms. With this in mind, some are asterisked. These are the more obvious and you should engage with them immediately. Any text extract can be used as a basis for practising the use of some terms.

Some of these terms do not strictly apply to 'language', for example anti-hero and protagonist. However, they are of use as terms specific to dramatic texts; they also appear in the glossary on pp.409–11.

Allegory
Using a parallel to symbolise the real meaning. Classic examples are the parables in the Bible. It is a form of extended **metaphor**.

If a playwright uses an allegory it is likely that he or she has a reason for not wishing to say something in a straightforward manner. It is worth questioning why this might be.

If a character uses allegories in a long speech, again it is worth analysing why. Does the character enjoy testing her or his companion(s)? Is he or she trying to say something but only able to do so obliquely? There may be many more reasons. How should the allegory be delivered? For example, should the speech be spoken in clipped tones as if the character is hiding a real meaning?

Be aware that a whole play can be an allegory. If this is the case, detailed consideration should be given to the direction and interpretation of the text to draw the audience's attention to the underlying intentions of the dramatist.

Alliteration
Two or more words close together that begin with the same letter(s).

This is a common figure of speech which is quite easy to recognise: for example, 'When I saw Priya, she looked cheery, chubby and chunky.' However, just recognising alliteration is pointless; it has to be worth commenting upon. It may be that the speaker is merely showing off by using alliteration to impress her or his audience. Alternatively, it could be that the speaker is deliberately trying to create a particular feeling in her or his companions by the choice of words. With this example, the speaker would clearly want the listeners to gain a pleasant, warm and positive impression of Priya. The alliterative 'ch' sounds are pleasing to the ear and lively in tone. The actor speaking the lines should ensure they are spoken with that warmth in his or her voice.

Antagonist

A character who acts in opposition to the **protagonist**. Generally, an adversary to the main character.

Anti-hero

A **protagonist** but one who displays the less pleasant characteristics of human beings. One of the most famous anti-heroes in modern drama is Jimmy Porter in John Osborne's *Look Back in Anger* (1956).

As with many of these terms, using a word such as anti-hero demonstrates the student's familiarity with the appropriate dramatic terminology. It also makes writing swift answers much easier; for example,

> 'Jimmy appears to be something of an anti-hero; his manners are offensive, his attitude is aggressive and he makes no attempt to lighten the atmosphere when Alison reappears in the last scene.'

This tells the reader a lot in a relatively short space of time. Compare the above to this: 'Jimmy is not a typical hero. He does not have all the things about him that we expect of a hero. Yet he is obviously the central character. His manners are offensive, his attitude is aggressive and he makes no attempt...'

Knowing the language helps keep your writing concise and meaningful.

Aphorism

A sharply coined expression; pithy and clever.

It is difficult to give examples, as generally the expression would only be recognised as an aphorism because of the preceding context. The works of Stoppard and Wilde are full of aphorisms, however. Here, Rosencrantz and Guildenstern are alone on stage and appear to have nothing to do to occupy their time:

> Rosencrantz: Shouldn't we be doing something – constructive?
> Guildenstern: What did you have in mind? . . . A short, blunt human pyramid . . . ? [Aphorism]
>
> Stoppard, Tom, *Rosencrantz and Guildenstern are Dead*

You would be expected to identify why such figures of speech are being used. In this example, the two **protagonists** are caught in a 'no man's land' and verbal banter is their main method of passing time. Wordplay is prominent throughout the text; this aphorism is one of many such sharp comments. You should consider how the actor playing Guildenstern would deliver the line to enhance the aphorism: an overtone of false innocence or a hard, ironic edge to the voice?

Aside ★

Anything from a short phrase to a lengthy speech which is intended for the audience's hearing but not for those on stage. This may be spoken directly to the audience or simply out of the other characters' hearing. Certain *genres* of drama make more use of asides than others, for example melodrama, farce, Restoration comedy. However, asides also occur in more serious drama.

Even if there is no stage direction indicating that a character is speaking an aside, one could be included as a method of enhancing the humour or secrecy of a particular moment.

Bathos

Anti-climax. Most clearly recognised in comedy, although found in serious work as well: 'I want to fly to the moon, sail round the world, climb Mount Everest and – crawl into bed.'

Bathos is often used by a playwright deliberately to reduce the audience's level of expectation; we are suddenly brought down to a sense of humdrum reality.

As well as identifying bathos, further points can be made, for example:

> 'Tom's comic nature is most visible in the middle of Act 2. The author uses the comic device of bathos to make this clear: "... – and crawl into bed" is typical of Tom's sense of humour and would further irritate Sarah, who has a more serious manner. The actor would speak most of the line building up energy and volume, only to let the line fall away at the end.'

The manner in which bathos is presented is crucial to its effect.

A whole play might end with bathos. This is a popular technique with some modern comedy writers such as Ben Elton or Lee Hall.

Catharsis

From Aristotle, this refers to a 'purification' of the emotions by watching great drama or tragedy. You were supposed to feel as if you had released the emotions by almost sharing in the emotional experience of the characters on stage. Brecht strongly opposed this kind of vicarious experience in the theatre as it led to passivity.

Chorus ★

A character or group of characters who comment on the action, providing a summary and a narrative link. In the original Greek theatre, the Chorus acted as the group who discussed events with the **protagonist**. The Chorus may be played by one actor or by a group, who do not have to speak in unison.

Cliché ★

A phrase or saying that is over-used and has become trivial and hackneyed. Examples are many and sometimes run together: 'At the end of the day, when all's said and done, every cloud's got a silver lining.'

The author will have a reason for determining on her or his characters speaking in clichés. This is what you need to address – *why* this should be so. Is the author defining a type? Is there a class issue? Is the author indicating a lack of stimulus in the character's life or perhaps a lack of will to move beyond talking in clichés? Is the author ridiculing the audience, intimating that this is the kind of language the audience would understand? If you are responding to a text from the perspective of a director, actor or designer, it then becomes important to explain how (and how far) this feature is emphasised in the realisation of the text. How does the actor speak the cliché to emphasise the triviality of his or her conversation? Can 'cliché' become the focus for the set design?

Denouement★

The final moments of the plot to which everything has been leading. The twists and turns of the narrative are unravelled. It does not necessarily mean that there has been a final resolution, but that is the usual consequence of the denouement.

Dialogue ★

A conversation between two or more people.

The *nature* of the dialogue is the important aspect to concentrate upon. For example:

> 'The dialogue in Act 1 demonstrates that the two characters are barely interested in each other. Harry only engages in a two-way conversation once; this is when he responds to Sarah's question about the weather. Throughout the rest of the short episode, his remarks are virtually directed to himself. As a director, I would wish to emphasise Harry's reclusive nature by . . .'

Diction ★

The rendition of words, particularly referring to clear or poor pronunciation.

This term is useful when discussing actors' performances, particularly for some texts; if the text has a character such as Lady Bracknell, Wilde's archetype of the upper classes in *The Importance of Being Earnest*, then it might be pertinent to refer to the actor's diction. In this instance, some traditional voice workshops might assist the actor to achieve clear, refined diction.

Duologue ★

A scene in a play which consists of two actors holding a dialogue. This tends to be a clear-cut episode rather than a couple of speeches in the middle of a scene.

Epilogue ★

A final section of a play which often acts as a summary or 'coda' to the main play. It can encourage the audience to leave the theatre space considering some key theme or aspect of the play. For classic examples of epilogues, see Shakespeare's *A Midsummer Night's Dream* or *As You Like It*.

It is worth considering to what extent an epilogue summarises the preceding scene(s) or the whole play and, if not, why not. Is there a reason for the author deliberately to point the audience away from the key issues in the play? If the epilogue does refer to, or in some sense comment upon, the issues raised in the play, how effectively can it be staged to reflect these issues fully ?

Epigram

Similar to aphorism. Epigrams are short and witty and tend to signal a final comment on the situation or provide a sharp summary on the preceding conversation. If an author writes using a number of epigrams, he or she would be said to be writing in an epigrammatic style.

Oscar Wilde is the most famous dramatist who delights in writing in an epigrammatic style. For example: 'The English country gentleman galloping after a fox – the unspeakable in full pursuit of the uneatable' (*Lady Windermere's Fan*).

Euphemism

This is a figure of speech where the speaker substitutes a more pleasant or sensitive phrase for a direct or blunt one. Examples might be: 'He passed on last month' instead of 'He died last month'; 'Could you tell me where the smallest room is?' instead of 'Could you tell me where the lavatory is?'

If a character uses euphemisms, it would be worth mentioning. Perhaps there is something rather coy about him or her, or even pretentious. Sometimes, a euphemism is used as a form of wit, where the speaker deliberately uses a less straightforward word or phrase because it is amusing. The actor speaking the lines would be expected to emphasise the purpose behind using the euphemism in his or her voice and mannerisms.

Hubris

A flaw associated with Greek protagonists. It refers to an arrogance, conceit or insolence that provokes (or, at very best, ignores the coming of) disaster and tragedy. Pentheus in Euripides' *The Bacchae* is one example; Oedipus is another although he does not have so much *hubris*. Macbeth is a Shakespearian example. *Hubris* would be used, particularly in association with discussing the plot narrative and who or what intitiates it.

Irony ★

A figure of speech where the implied meaning behind the words spoken is different to the actual words. Sometimes irony can be sarcastic, particularly when praising something but meaning the opposite. Irony also refers to the difference between expected and actual outcomes. *Dramatic* irony is addressed in detail later (see pp.90–1).

Metaphor ★

Where one thing is described in terms of something else; it is equated to it. Metaphors can consist of just one word or sentence or can be extended.

Imagine that a person is discussing their forthcoming marriage with his or her partner: 'When we embark on this voyage of discovery, there are bound to be many difficult seas and uncharted lands, but I know that it will be an exciting and very happy journey.'

If a character uses metaphors, this is worth noting. To think metaphorically is quite an advanced thought process. It means that the person is able to assimilate information, process it and think of parallels that effectively mirror the thought or information.

Monologue ★
A single lengthy speech, made when other people are present in the scene. (See **soliloquy**.)

Monosyllabic ★
Speaking in monosyllables, i.e. words of one syllable.

This is easy to recognise. If a character speaks mainly in monosyllables, it is worth you commenting upon this. Why? Is the character angry and speaking quickly? Is the character shy and quiet? Does he or she lack language skills? Is he or she surly?

When you are discussing how to interpret the part, you would want to consider how this monosyllabic character would speak to emphasise the nature of his or her frame of mind. For example, if the person is using monsyllables because of surliness, you could write:

> 'The speeches would be spoken with a tone of irritation in the voice and a coldness which show that she does not wish to take part in this conversation at all. The words are clipped and spoken briefly; there is a sense of dismissal in the tone used.'

Non-sequitur
Something that does not follow from the previous thing said. Literally it refers to something that is not in sequence:

'I found your behaviour very worrying tonight.'
'Have you seen the price of bread nowadays? It's frightening.'

Here, the second character starts a new line of thought. Again, the important point is *why* the subject has not been followed through. This could be because the first sentence hasn't been heard. It could be because the second character doesn't want to discuss the subject. It could be because the second character enjoys annoying the first and knows that such changes of subject do just that. There are a number of reasons that are possible and which would be clear when you are familiar with the whole text. The way the lines were spoken would help clarify the intention, of course, and you would want to consider how the lines would be said.

Paradox
Where there appears to be a contradiction although there might be valid reasoning behind it. For example: 'For us to live, she has to die.' For a further example, see the extract from *Lady Windermere's Fan*, p.87.

Parody
Something that mocks a given style of writing by taking key characteristics of that original and using these in a more trivial manner and with a less substantial subject matter; parody often exaggerates these features of the original.

Henry Fielding's play *The Life and Death of Tom Thumb the Great* is also entitled *A Tragedy of Tragedies*, indicating that it is a parody of the tragedies of the 17th and early 18th centuries. Such ludicrous figures as Princess Huncamunca and Queen Dolabella are passionately in love with the diminutive Tom Thumb. Huncamunca even says, at one point, 'Oh Tom Thumb, Tom Thumb, wherefore art thou Tom Thumb?' – a direct parody of *Romeo and Juliet*. The conventions of tragedy are used for a ridiculous purpose.

Polysyllabic ★
Speaking in polysyllables, i.e. words of many syllables.

Prologue ★
The introductory section to a play which acts as an entry into the piece for the audience. See its counterpart, **Epilogue**, above. Again see Shakespeare for many examples, e.g. *Romeo and Juliet, Henry V*.

Protagonist ★
The principal character in a play. The protagonist is the person who initiates the action, directly or indirectly. Some plays do not have protagonists, as no one character stands out. The word is derived from the Greek meaning 'first actor'.

Obvious examples are Oedipus, Hamlet and Macbeth. As with **Anti-hero** (see above), using this term clearly identifies the character and acts as a coded shorthand.

Pun ★
A form of word-play, based on similar-sounding words, or words with more than one meaning. This is usually done as a form of wit, for example, 'This is the third time running he's gone out with someone called Helen; I suppose it's a case of troy, troy and troy again.'

Recognising puns will help clarify the style of the piece. The delivery of such word-play would be important in order to stress the comic nature of the script, and you should consider tone of voice, facial expression and other acting techniques in that delivery.

Rhetoric ★
A style of speech that is particularly elaborate and eloquent. This is often used to persuade the listener(s) to the speaker's way of thinking. Key politicians' speeches are often described as full of rhetoric.

Again, it would be worth suggesting a method of delivery to enhance the rhetoric. Would the speaker be most successful using a declamatory style of speech and gesture? Should the speech be underplayed, allowing the words to drop innocuously into the listeners' ears without additional force from the speaker?

Satire
A satirical speech or play is when wit, irony, ridicule and other forms of humour are used to highlight vice or folly in a person or a society. See p.86 for further discussion of satire.

Simile ★

This is a figure of speech where one characteristic of a person or thing is emphasised by a comparison with something whose main characteristic that is. For example: 'as gentle as a lamb'; 'as black as night'.

See **Metaphor** above for further thoughts about the use of such figures of speech.

Soliloquy ★

A single lengthy speech, made when no other characters are on stage.

Understatement ★

A statement which falls short of fully describing the matter. For example, on the break up of a marriage: 'I think we've got one or two little problems.'

If a character uses understatements, there are likely to be reasons that are worth mentioning. For example, is the character living in an unreal world, where the true magnitude of difficult situations doesn't impinge upon him or her? Is the character using a dry, or wry, sense of humour? Is the speaker trying to lessen the impact for another character?

ACTIVITIES Look back at the *Vinegar Tom* extract on pp.21–2. Look at the descriptions above of non-sequitur, allegory, epilogue, dialogue and paradox. How could you use these terms in describing the extract? Find specific examples where possible. Apart from recognising the use of these terms, what is their particular significance here? How could the *dialogue* be realised in performance?

Take a few pages of a full-length play and go through it identifying as many different terms, and their use, as possible. Again, don't just be content with recognising them; comment on their significance and think about how this could be realised on stage, as we have done above.

1.2.2 FURTHER ANALYSIS OF TEXTS

This section takes a more detailed approach to analysing and realising texts.

If the purpose of drama is to entertain and to enlighten, then the playwright will employ a number of devices to achieve those results. The director, designer and actor will draw on these in the practical realisation of the text. Such devices are used to convey the meaning of the text and it is important to be able to recognise *where* they occur and *how* they convey meaning. This section looks at devices such as **humour, wit** and **satire, dramatic irony, symbols** and **imagery, plot, mood** and **atmosphere, pace, tension** and **climax**.

Inevitably, these devices will be closely linked with language and characterisation; we have made the point on several occasions that all aspects of drama should be considered holistically. The subdivisions we have employed are simply a way of breaking down this whole into manageable parts.

HUMOUR

That quality of action, speech, or writing, which excites amusement; oddity, comicality. The faculty of perceiving what is ludicrous or amusing, or of expressing it; jocose imagination or treatment of a subject. (Less purely intellectual than *wit*, and often allied to pathos.)

[*The Shorter Oxford English Dictionary*]

Humour can include wit, irony and satire, of course.

HUMOROUS PLAYS

There are many types of humorous plays

It is not appropriate here to delve into the vast and diverse array of humorous plays or **comedies** that have existed since Greek times – and before. (The word comedy is derived from the Greek *komos*, meaning revel.) However, it may be of interest to be reminded of the different *genres* that *broadly* come under the banner of humorous plays/comedies:

- Greek and Roman comedies
- Early English comedy – some mystery plays
- *Commedia dell'Arte*
- Romantic comedy
- Comedy of Manners
- Satirical comedy
- Restoration comedy
- Sentimental comedy
- Burlesque
- Farce
- Pantomime
- Black comedy
- Theatre of the Absurd.

The bibliography on page 137 gives sources of further information on these types of play. (See the Banks and Marson text, for example.)

Some of these can be sub-divided again (for example Restoration comedy into comedy of humours, character or manners); some recur in different centuries (comedy of manners); some aren't terribly humorous at all (Theatre of the Absurd). However, this list gives you some idea of the extent of the subject 'humorous plays'.

Each dramatist will have a different purpose for writing a humorous play

There may be as many purposes in writing a humorous play as there are humorous plays in existence. The dramatist recognises that humour is an effective method of conveying a story, message, theme or character to an audience. Thus each individual would have a different purpose for writing in a humorous style. For instance, Oscar Wilde wrote his comedy of manners called *The Importance of Being Earnest* (1895) in order to satirise society, whereas Henry Fielding wrote the burlesque called *The Tragedy of Tragedies* or *The Life and Death of Tom Thumb the Great* in 1739 to satirise dramatic writing. Both were written to entertain and enlighten, however.

There is no set 'form' to comedies

Just as the use and purpose of humour varies, similarly the composition and content of comedies will vary. This can be shown through two extreme examples. The anarchic fringe comedy of the late 20th century is characterised by its *lack* of format. It can vary from one-person stand-up routines in crowded, smoke-filled pubs to the motor-bike and chainsaw mayhem of Archaos, the human circus, complete with circus tent. Compare this to Greek comedy. F.L. Lucas (*Greek Drama for the Common Reader*) suggests that Greek comedy followed a very clear format:

1. Some character has a bright idea: a man thinks of stopping the war by flying to heaven on a dung-beetle, or a woman tries to stop it by organising a women's sexual strike.
2. A Chorus, sympathetic or hostile, enters.
3. There follows a set debate about the proposal.
4. The Chorus turns and addresses the audience directly (a *parabasis*), perhaps a relic of the mockeries flung at bystanders by the old phallic mummers.
5. A series of farcical episodes arises from putting the original idea into practice.
6. All ends in a scene of revelling such as a feast or a wedding: a further relic of primitive merrymaking.

[Quoted in Banks, R.A. and Marson, P. *Drama and Theatre Arts* (2nd edn), Hodder and Stoughton, 1998. pp.72–3.]

Comedies are thus extremely diverse in purpose, content and form. Dramatists use humour for a number of different reasons and to talk of 'humorous plays' is to cover a vast area of dramatic texts.

THE USE OF HUMOUR FOR PARTICULAR EFFECT

Why does an author turn to humour at particular moments? Is it simply to raise a laugh?

A classic example of using a humorous episode occurs in Shakespeare's *Macbeth*. The drunken porter 'entertains' the audience at a crucial moment in the play, just after Macbeth has murdered Duncan, the king. He makes 'in-jokes' with the audience, he urinates and he procrastinates about opening the castle gates to some importunate knocking. He can be extremely funny.

The scene has many purposes:

● It is a bridge in time, allowing the principal actors time to cleanse the 'blood' off their hands; this practical purpose is often forgotten.

● Comic interludes or codas have their roots in ancient drama (for instance the satyr plays after Greek tragedies). Shakespeare was using an ancient tradition which the audience might recognise.

● It acts as relief from tension for the audience.

● It is funny and entertains the audience.

● It is symbolic; the porter's words are relevant to the themes of the play, so the comedy acts as a reinforcement of the message through another style.

● The insistent knocking cannot be avoided; the audience recognises this and feels an impending sense of doom, so the speech acts as a prologue to the rest of the play. The fact that this prologue-speech is humorous adds a tinge of irony.

If you understand all the uses of this humorous interlude, it becomes easier to identify uses of humour in other plays.

The following is an extract from *Singer* by Peter Flannery. This epic play parallels the life and times of Rachman, the notorious racketeer landlord of the 1950s. Before looking at the extract, it is important to know that there has been one traumatic scene before this one: the prologue, set in a concentration camp in World War II. It has introduced Singer (Rachman) and his nephew, Stefan, as they try to survive and to outwit fellow prisoners and German guards alike. The prologue has also introduced a character called Manik, a fellow prisoner, whom Singer has been forced to hit on the head under the orders of a German guard. A terrible and forceful scene, that prologue is followed shortly afterwards by the scene below.

This extract is set at Southampton Docks. A chorus (one person) has introduced the setting and explained that the war is over. The German concentration camp refugees have disembarked onto the dock, met by immigration officials.

IMMIGRATION OFFICIAL:	Does any of you speak English?
	(Most of them look at him uncomprehending.)
STEFAN:	Say words. Little words.
SINGER:	My daughter!
	Oh my duck's hat!
	Fled with a Christian!
	Oh my duck's hat and my daughter!
	William Shakespeare.
IMM. OFF.:	Ah! Well, look, try to listen carefully to what I'm saying; you may be expecting to simply walk off the docks and into normal life here in England.
	(MANIK raises his hand.)
	Yes?
MANIK:	California ist einer grosser Fische.
IMM. OFF.:	I'm sorry.
MANIK:	California . . . is a big fish.
IMM. OFF.:	Yes. This is England. You were *expecting* England, weren't you?
MANIK:	California ist einer grosser Fische, das unts verschlukt.
	(MANIK makes a big gulp. The others think he's barely sane.)
IMM. OFF.:	I'm sorry.
MANIK:	I'm in the groove, Joe.
SINGER:	He's 'meshuge'. Hit head. 'Meshuge'.
IMM. OFF:	Ah! Is he now?
	(IMMIGRATION OFFICIAL looks at his paperwork, to see if there is any note of this.)
	(To MANIK) You are . . . ?
STEFAN:	He's with us. He go with us. Us.
IMM. OFF.:	Well some of you will be going to Slough initially. Slough.
REFUGEES:	*(Muttering)* Slow. Slow.
IMM. OFF.:	Into a camp. Until we can sort you out; and others to Kirkcudbright.

[Flannery, Peter, *Singer*, Nick Hern Books, 1989. p.10]

ACTIVITY You would find it useful to analyse why Flannery uses the humour he does in the same way that we have discussed the porter scene in *Macbeth*. Think about what is humorous, why it is so and how Flannery communicates that humour.

VISUAL HUMOUR

Be aware of the possibilities of **visual** comic moments. Words can often be combined with the visual to make the joke, or the humour can simply be visual.

Television and film comedy makes particularly good use of visual humour. The old spoof film *Airplane* is a classic example; much of the comedy comes from the visual element. For example, at one point a flight tower worker yells for an Air Israel plane to be moved, as it is blocking a runway. The camera shot then moves to the huge jet which is wearing traditional Israeli headwear around the whole of its pilots' cabin. The humour comes from that instant camera shot and the incongruity of an aeroplane 'wearing' a hat etc.

Another classic example of visual, and sick, humour is in an old sketch from *Not the Nine O'Clock News*. Mel Smith is blind; he walks up to a pedestrian crossing and presses the button, waiting to hear the signal to cross. Next to him, Rowan Atkinson's watch alarm then sounds, which makes a noise similar to the 'beep' of the pedestrian crossing. The blind Mel Smith walks off the pavement.

There are uncountable examples to give. Be aware of such visual humour in a theatre text and also how such jokes might be presented.

Here are three extracts from texts which give rise to visual comedy and humour:

A beam of wood now enters through the door. At its far end, supporting it at the crossbar, is a WOMAN IN ARMOR. *There is a crucifix on her breastplate. Evidently what she is carrying is simply another crucifix. Only the one she is carrying is well over seven feet long. In attempting to enter the room the crossbar of the crucifix slams into the doorframe and catches fast.*

[Kopit, Arthur, *Chamber Music* (1963), Methuen, 1969.]

CECILY:	. . . May I offer you some tea, Miss Fairfax?
GWENDOLEN:	*(with elaborate politeness)* Thank you. *(Aside.)* Detestable girl! But I require tea!
CECILY:	*(sweetly)* Sugar?
GWENDOLEN:	*(Superciliously)* No, thank you. Sugar is not fashionable any more. *(CECILY looks angrily at her, takes up the tongs and puts four lumps of sugar into the cup.)*

[Wilde, Oscar, *The Importance of Being Earnest* (1895), Heinemann Educational, 1970.]

(GUIL *positions himself next to* ROS, *a few feet away, so that they are covering one side of the stage, facing the opposite side.* GUIL *unfastens his belt.* ROS *does the same. They join the two belts, and hold them taut between them.* ROS's *trousers slide slowly down.)*

[Stoppard, Tom, *Rosencrantz and Guildenstern are Dead*, Faber and Faber, 1967.]

ACTIVITY   How could the visual humour in these scenes be enhanced in performance? Answer this question referring to the three extracts above..

The stage directions are quite detailed already, so you would be expected to concentrate on additional points to *enhance* the realisation of the text on stage. You should think about vocal exclamations, facial expressions, speed and style of movement, possible reactions from other characters and so on.

WIT AND SATIRE

Inevitably, we have already incorporated wit within humour. It is a particularly intellectual form of humour, however, concentrating on a sharpness of mind that is usually demonstrated in speech. Humour need not be word-based (see 'Visual humour', for example, above), but wit usually is. The list of language terms on pp.74–81 has already defined words associated with 'wit' (see: Aphorism, Bathos, Epigram, Irony, Metaphor, Parody, Pun, Satire, Simile).

These terms are useful for describing a witty remark or sequence in a playtext. The *purpose* of such wit would then be discussed.

There are particular dramatists of whom we think when we talk of 'witty' plays . Coward, Shaw (up to a point), Stoppard, Orton, Ayckbourn and Godber (again, up to a point) are a selection from the 20th century. These dramatists have employed wit as a method of conveying their meaning to the audience. Others from previous centuries include Aristophanes (ancient Greek), Shakespeare (late 16th to early 17th century), Molière (mid to late 1600s, French), Wycherley, Congreve (both late 1600s), Goldsmith, Sheridan (both late 1700s) and Wilde (very late 19th century).

Wit is frequently seen in satirical plays

In some of these instances, the wit becomes satirical. For example, Ayckbourn satirises the middle classes of the late 20th century; Wilde does the same for the upper classes of the turn of the century. Both playwrights ridicule the follies of their targets. Both make their audience wince as recognition takes place, and allow that audience to sit in judgement on the characters, often realising that we are judging ourselves. However, Wilde is much sharper, more epigrammatic and literary, lending a certain distance to the self-realisation, whereas in Ayckbourn's plays it creeps up and overtakes us. Satire, as a style, can be far tougher than this; television's *Spitting Image* in the late 20th century was a prime example of the cutting and ruthless satire of modern times.

The following brief extract is an example of Wilde's work. We have added notes to particular sections to demonstrate where wit is most clearly seen and where any figures of speech or particular devices are used. The notes are in square brackets.

In this scene in *Lady Windermere's Fan*, the Duchess of Berwick has attempted to tell Lady Windermere that her husband, Lord Windermere, is having an affair.

DUCHESS OF BERWICK:	[. . . .] And now, my dear child, I must go, as we are dining out. **[Bathos]** And mind you don't take this little aberration of Windermere's too much to heart. **[Understatement – 'little aberration' is referring to an affair!; irony – 'too much to heart', as it will be Lady Windermere's heart that will be badly affected.]** Just take him abroad, and he'll come back to you all right. **[This hard-headed, flippant comment is a paradox. To get him back, you take him away.]**
[. . . .] LADY WINDER-MERE:	It is very kind of you, Duchess, to come and tell me all this. But I can't believe that my husband is untrue to me.
DUCHESS OF BERWICK:	Pretty child! I was like that once. **[Patronising and gaily cynical.]** Now I know that all men are monsters. **[Metaphor – men as monsters. The lack of concern for the nature of men is something that Wilde uses often as a source for wit and humour.]** (LADY WINDERMERE *rings bell.*) The only thing to do is to feed the wretches well. **[Understatement; almost bathos – that's what to do if your husband is having an affair! The humour would partly arise from the audience of the day feeling a slight truth in the idea of men liking comforts.]** A good cook does wonders, and that I know you have. My dear Margaret, you are not going to cry? **[Swift change of subject and alarm at the possibility of emotion being shown. A jibe at the upper classes for hiding all genuine feeling. Actor's facial expressions would help greatly.]**
LADY WINDERMERE:	You needn't be afraid, Duchess, I never cry. **[Emphasises the jibe.]**
DUCHESS OF BERWICK:	That's quite right, dear. Crying is the refuge of plain women but the ruin of pretty ones. **[Epigram. Clinches this section of the scene.]**

[Wilde, Oscar, *Lady Windermere's Fan* (1892), Methuen, 1962. pp.12–13]

In addition to **satire**, there are other forms of **wit**. For example, Stoppard's wit verges on the absurd at times. His plays deal with a wide variety of topics, from the nothingness of existence in *Rosencrantz and Guildenstern Are Dead* to Lenin and Dadaism in *Travesties* and entropy, physics, metaphysics and neo-Romanticism (amongst other topics) in *Arcadia*. His hallmark is intellectual wordplay; puns and aphorisms abound.

For what purpose does a dramatist employ wit? How does wit affect us? What is the intended audience response?

Audiences enjoy wit

Wit is, on the whole, admired. In the great period of Restoration comedy, wit was considered to be most important in high-quality theatre; playwrights were greatly admired for their intellectual prowess. Even now, most audiences enjoy the use of clever language and word-play. We admire the author or deliverer. Popular television programmes of the 1980s and 1990s have proved this: *Whose Line Is It Anyway?*, *Have I Got News For You* and *They Think It's All Over* are examples of highly popular, improvisation-based programmes which rely on the use of the participants' wit. The sharp comments, swiftly contrived phrases and abrasive wit have proved to be a most successful formula for good viewing figures. Playwrights expect that same appreciation for a witty text. Our minds *enjoy* the challenge of understanding the quickness of comment and astute observation and we feel a sense of intellectual complicity with the writer; in an understated way, we admire the dramatist and the work and we are *receptive* to the text.

Wit can determine a character

Wit is also used to demonstrate character, of course. A character using quick, clever words is likely to have a quick, clever mind. A brief look at any of Shakespeare's fools illustrates this.

Wit can highlight a theme in a play

Wit could also be used to reflect the message of a play. A satirical wit is clearly intended to ridicule society, or a section of society. A witty style which is full of riddles and absurdity could be reflecting a message that points to the absurdity of existence and the ironies of life.

Wit can enhance the plot puzzle for the audience

The presentation of a storyline to the audience can be a further reason for using a particular kind of wit. Semi-hidden, craftily phrased, puzzling comments, which hint at plot details, can keep the audience in suspense and anticipation. This very gradual build-up of audience awareness is popular in dramatic texts. It is almost as if the dramatist is engaged in a game with the audience. Of course, the increase of audience knowledge need not employ 'wit' as such, but a piquancy is added to the game of 'working out what is going on' if there is an edge to the unfolding comments. Anthony Shaffer's *Sleuth* is a fine example here.

The following examples are from different plays which consist of witty dialogue.

DEBBIE:	Charlotte tell you about Ben?
HENRY:	No.
DEBBIE:	This is his shirt. **[Non-sequitur and bathos. We don't expect this rather down-to-earth comment.]**
HENRY:	Oh yes? Can I meet him?
DEBBIE:	He travels.
HENRY:	A salesman?
DEBBIE:	Fairground. **[Bathos]** You wouldn't approve.
HENRY:	Well ... swings and roundabouts. **[Pun]**

[Stoppard, Tom, *The Real Thing*, Faber & Faber, 1982.]

GERALDINE:	What is Mrs Prentice like, doctor? I've heard so many stories about her.
PRENTICE:	My wife is a nymphomaniac. Consequently, like the Holy Grail, she's ardently sought after by young men. **[The use of the metaphor adds to the sex-based humour. Also an epigram.]**

[Orton, Joe, *What the Butler Saw* (1969), Eyre Methuen, 1976.]

PADRE:	Sir! The Entertainments Officer is dead.
ERPINGHAM:	*(to* RILEY*)*. Remind me to send one of our Class A (Highest Employee) wreaths to his next of kin. **[Sick/black humour]**

[Orton, Joe, *The Erpingham Camp* (1967), Eyre Methuen 1976.]

ARCHIE:	With the best will in the world I can't give the Chair of Logic to a man who relies on nasal intuition. **[Incongruity of the sentence leads to humour.]**

[Stoppard, Tom, *Jumpers*, Faber & Faber, 1972.]

ACTIVITY Take one of the plays that you are studying that contains humour. Answer the following question '**If you were directing this play, how would you convey the humour to the audience?**' Use the following framework.

1. Write a brief introduction. This simply tells us what is going to be in the following paragraphs. It gives us the order of your answer.
2. Put the humour into the context of the play. In other words, is it constant? Is it only in certain scenes? Is it associated with certain moments? Once you have done that, say what kind of humour it is. Verbal, visual, both? Are particular characters humorous? On what is the humour based? Literary wit? Misunderstandings? Knockabout farce? You may want to draw in the background to the play (see 'Support research', section 1.3 of Part 1) to support your comments here. For example, if you were talking about Gogol's *The Government Inspector*, Jonson's *Volpone*, Gay's *The Beggar's Opera* or Shakespeare's *Twelfth Night* or *A Midsummer Night's Dream*, you would want to refer to the conventions of the period and the placing of this work within such conventions.
3. Identify any holistic approach you might take to the humour. For example, would you try to reflect it in the choice of design for the production? Would you adopt a particular style of production e.g. slick and fast paced? Explain this fully.
4. Select certain comic moments in the whole playtext and explain that you are using them as examples. Say why you have selected these examples. Trace through the examples, analysing the humour and describing how it could be realised or enhanced in performance. (This will be the major section of your answer and will take several paragraphs.)
5. Summarise your response.

The following paragraphs are examples of writing for the fourth part of the framework:

Re-read the Singer extract (p.84). Part of your response might read:

'Singer knows only a little English and part of the humour arises from the uselessness of the Shakespeare quote that he knows. They have just arrived in England for a new life; Shakespeare is far removed from the practical problems that they are likely to confront. I would therefore emphasise the humour by asking the actor playing Singer to step forward and ''declaim'' these lines in a mock theatrical manner. This heightens the ridiculous (in other words, humorous) side of the situation for the audience as the theatrical style of delivery would emphasise that the lines are irrelevant for everyday life. Manik's comments about California are particularly unreal and unrelated to the present situation. To emphasise the humour, these should be spoken with deadly seriousness and with a sense of importance in the actor's voice.'

The *Lady Windermere's Fan* extract (p.87); part of your response might read

'The humour for the audience in this scene would arise from the sharpness of the verbal wit. Therefore, the method of delivering speeches is important. The line "Just take him abroad, and he'll come back to you" should be said with a slightly dismissive air, as if the Duchess sees the affair as of little consequence. I would ask her to speak with a tone of condescending humour in her voice. To emphasise the witty paradox in the sentence, I would ask her to gesture with her hand into the distance for the first part of the sentence and bring her fingers scuttling back for the second part.'

The *The Erpingham Camp* extract (p.89); part of your response might read

'Erpingham's total lack of concern for the Entertainments Officer is the source of the black humour in this extract. This insensitivity can be enhanced by speaking in a rather monotonous, business-like tone; I would probably speak in the same voice I used in his previous speech. This would demonstrate Erpingham's inability to be at all moved by the occurrence. In addition, I would look at Riley in a disdainful manner.'

DRAMATIC IRONY

Dramatic irony arises when the audience knows more than the protagonist

Dramatic irony makes use of the audience. The audience knows something of which one or more of the characters is unaware. In this way, we are in complicity with the dramatist. Shakespeare is a master of such irony. In *Macbeth*, we know that the English forces have hewn down branches of Birnam Wood as they advance on Macbeth's castle, Dunsinane. We also know that Macbeth believes himself to be safe, as the witches have prophesied that he will be so until Birnam Wood comes to Dunsinane. When it appears as if the wood is indeed advancing on Dunsinane, we have greater knowledge than Macbeth and await his reaction. This is dramatic irony. Dramatic tension is produced through such irony. It generally needs time for information to be given to the audience to allow the irony of the situation to take place. In *Macbeth* we hear the witches' prophecy in one scene, some scenes later the soldiers are told to hew down the branches and in yet another scene, Macbeth hears that Birnam Wood is moving.

Dramatic irony is extended when a character makes a remark that we know is inappropriate

Dramatic irony also exists when a character says or does something that we as audience know is inappropriate because we are in fuller possession of the facts than the character. When Duncan arrives at the Macbeths' castle in Inverness, we know that the Macbeths have started to plan his death. On his arrival, the first words Duncan says are:

This castle hath a pleasant seat; the air
Nimbly and sweetly recommends itself
Unto our gentle senses.

There is a weight of dramatic irony in this speech as we believe that the castle is far from having a 'pleasant seat' for Duncan and the 'air' may soon be rent with the cries of murder.

Dramatic irony adds tension and a sense of involvement for the audience

What is the purpose of dramatic irony? First, as stated above, it adds to the dramatic tension of the play, thus ensuring the audience's close attention and creating a more powerful impact. As an extension of this, we become involved with the character, caring about his or her actions because we have been given a wider knowledge. We are allowed a sense of ownership of the character. Paradoxically, we also act as a judge because of this knowledge.

Dramatic irony can symbolise the lack of control and knowledge we have in life

Secondly, dramatic irony can symbolise a situation in the life of a character where he or she has little control over his or her destiny or actions. You could take this further by suggesting that dramatic irony is a method of showing the audience that we are not really in control of our lives. This would be taking the device too far, however, for many plays.

Dramatic irony can highlight folly; often used in comedy

Thirdly, dramatic irony can be used to particularly good effect in comedy. The audience may be aware of 'the truth' of a situation and watches a hypocrite or deceiver become entangled in an 'untruth'. Because of our greater knowledge, we can see the character's true motives. In this situation, the dramatist is likely to be using dramatic irony to highlight the folly and deceit in human nature.

SYMBOLS AND IMAGERY

Look for symbols and imagery in the playtext

Dramatists frequently make use of symbols and imagery. These can richly support the impact and effectiveness of a play, allowing directors the opportunity to enhance the meaning of a playtext through drawing out the imagery or symbols in production.

For example, at the end of Strindberg's *Miss Julie*, Miss Julie collects her caged bird ready for her flight from her father's house with his man-servant, Jean. The caged bird is a symbol of Julie, trapped by her background, circumstances and genes (Strindberg's nod at determinism). Jean kills the bird rather than let her take it. When Julie exits, alone, the death of the bird is symbolic of the death of Julie's dreams and illusions and, we assume, of her real death that is about to take place by suicide.

Symbols can be purely visual

Symbols can be more lighthearted. In the Natural Theatre Company's *One Lump or Two?* at the Edinburgh Fringe Festival in 1999, the protagonist, Lady Margaret, persuaded various members of the audience to make paper doilies. Performed in the Holyrood Suite within the five-star Balmoral Hotel, the whole piece was a satirical pastiche of the British upper classes and the paper doily was a symbol of their flimsy, elegant lifestyle.

In Phelim MacDermott's *70, Hill Lane* (various venues, 1997), there was no set. Instead, sticky-backed tape was used to mark out different parts of the houses he lived in such as his own flat, his family's house and so on. Two fellow members of the company were responsible for unpeeling the tape and holding it in place until it was time to change the *mise-en-scène*. In addition to framing the work in the most original style, the tape symbolised the transience of his existence and that of the people in his autobiographical story.

In *Hedda Gabler*, Ibsen uses the pistols as a symbol of Hedda's father as well as an image of death. Ibsen used symbolism heavily, particularly in his last plays, although even in the early *A Doll's House*, Nora's offstage children symbolise her role as a submissive housewife and the door slam at the end of the play is a symbol of her independence.

The image of Alison, and then Helena, ironing in Osborne's *Look Back in Anger* supports one of the play's underpinning themes: Jimmy's destructive need to attack the middle classes and bring them to his own level. This repeated image of a tedious, everyday activity emphasises the 'new social realism' style of the play.

One image can underpin a whole production

Shakespeare's texts are full of imagery. Pictures are painted with words. Enobarbus's image of Cleopatra in her barge, in *Antony and Cleopatra*, immediately gives us a world of decadent splendour ruled by a beautiful and powerful queen. This image is extended through most of the play. Directors, designers and actors often use certain images to guide their interpretation of a Shakespeare play. One famous example was Anthony Sher's eponymous Richard III at Stratford in 1984. Sher took a reference to Richard as a bottled spider (spoken by Queen Margaret) and from this he created a scuttling black creature wielding two crutches as if they were a natural extension of his arms. This image of Richard as a spider dominated the whole production.

It is important to identify any strong use of symbols or imagery in the texts you are studying. Using these in planning a production can significantly affect the interpretation, design and performances of a text.

PLOT

Recognising the plot or storyline is second nature to us

We are all well acquainted with noting the plot of drama. Virtually every story we have heard since we could understand language has had some form of plot and we learn to identify plot quickly. Too often, we regard a piece of drama as unworthy simply because the plot is not clear to us.

Never retell the plot

However, there is rarely any reason to discuss the plot in isolation. If you are involved in critical writing you will doubtless realise that 'plot-telling' is superfluous and guaranteed to irritate your readers. You must always assume that your reader is fully acquainted with the plot of a play or extract and you should never waste valuable time giving them a useless recap.

You will probably be anxious to understand the plot as quickly as possible. This is natural, but there is a chance that you may *not* understand it, either because it is obscure or because there is no 'plot' as such to discover. However, it is highly unlikely that a full-length play would be *entirely* lacking in plot.

Assuming that you have identified some form of storyline, this should be referred to only in connection with *another* aspect of the playtext. For example, you may be discussing the presentation of one particular character:

'Gus will be frightened at this point. He has been angry and frustrated earlier, particularly with the nonsensical scraps of paper arriving in the dumbwaiter. Facing Ben, who holds the gun, the frustration and anger will be replaced by a deep fear. I would want to show this by his complete lack of movement after entering.'

The plot has been mentioned – the scraps of paper in the dumbwaiter earlier in the play – but only in relation to Gus's character.

Epic and dramatic are useful terms for describing plot

You should bear in mind the terms *epic* and *dramatic* when discussing the plot.

Essentially, the term *epic* theatre refers to episodic drama where the audience is not given an incremental storyline – one that builds up in the most usual narrative manner. The audience sees instead a series of possibly unconnected scenes. Epic theatre is often associated with the work of Brecht (see p.304).

This technique is established in the theatre today; some playwrights create work in a quasi-epic style. Some television and film drama is recognisably epic, but on the whole audiences are still more used to the dramatic, incrementally narrative format, as exemplified by soap opera.

It would be important to recognise the implications of an epic-style extract. If we take Caryl Churchill's writing as an example, she often expects the audience to make connections through experiencing a number of different scenes which focus on the same event or theme. She clearly wants us to form opinions from a multi-layered perspective. For others who have been influenced by Brecht's style of theatre, see pp.323–6.

Dramatic theatre on the other hand gives an incremental storyline, in other words a plot which builds upon the previous section of the story and then builds again – in increments. Most theatre follows a dramatic or incrementally narrative shape.

You should identify whether there is a single plot line, sub plots or multiple, equally weighted plot lines. This will help you understand the meaning of the playtext; the weight given to particular plot lines will show you where the dramatist's interests lie. In addition, as a director, designer or actor, you should be clear about these so that the stage realisation of the text is given the appropriate emphasis.

Consider 'male' and 'female' plot structures

You may also want to consider 'male' plot structures and 'female' plot structures. It has been suggested that Western theatre has been dominated by linear narratives with clear closures or endings and that these are 'male' ways of thinking. Feminist theatre practitioners have sought to address this in recent years, writing in different structures. (See Aston, E., *An Introduction to Feminism and Theatre*, Routledge, 1994.) Certainly it is worth looking at Caryl Churchill's *Cloud Nine* as an example of challenging dramatic conventions.

A 'french scene analysis' can help you identify important points in a plot structure

One useful and thorough method of becoming familiar with the plot and, in consequence, the importance of certain characters within that plot, is to undertake what is called a 'french scene analysis'. By adding certain subheadings of your own, and key quotes from each section, you are familiarising yourself most thoroughly with the plot *and* the meaning of the playtext. You are able to recognise instantly not only the practicalities of cast members in individual sections, but, more importantly, the rhythm and structure of the play. By this we mean: the weighting of the presence of certain characters, the frequency of their appearance, the combinations of characters, the 'key' lines or essence of each section, the trajectory of the narrative, who thrusts the narrative forward and so on.

French scene analysis for scenes from A Midsummer Night's Dream

	Act 2 Scene 2							Act 3 Scene 1						Act 3 Scene 2								
	a	b	c	d	e	f	g	a	b	c	d	e	f	a	b	c	d	e	f	g	h	i
Theseus																						
Hippolyta																						
Egeus																						
Hermia			✓	N	N	N	✓								✓				✓			✓
Lysander			✓	N	N	✓											✓	✓	✓		✓	N
Demetrius				✓											✓	N		✓	✓		✓	N
Helena					✓	✓											✓	✓	✓			✓
Philostrate																						
Oberon		✓												✓	N	✓	N	N	N	✓		
Titania	✓	N	N	N	N	N	N	N	N	N	N	✓	✓									
Puck			✓						✓		✓			✓	N	✓	N	N	N	✓	✓	✓
Peaseblossom	✓												✓									
Cobweb	✓												✓									
Moth	✓												✓									
Mustardseed	✓												✓									
Quince								✓	✓	✓	✓											
Bottom								✓	✓		✓	✓	✓									
Flute								✓	✓	✓	✓											
Snout								✓	✓	✓	✓											
Snug								✓	✓	✓	✓											
Starveling								✓	✓	✓	✓											

✓ = active in all or most of the scene.

N = Non-speaking. Often this means that the characters are not seen by others in the scene e.g. they are sleeping and out of sight.

2.2a Titania is sung to sleep. 'You spotted snakes with double tongue'.

2.2b Oberon, solo, squeezes love-in-idleness juice on Titania's eyes. 'Wake when some vile thing is nigh'.

2.2c Hermia and Lysander are exhausted from their flight. They settle to sleep. 'Lie further off, in human modesty'.

2.2d Puck anoints Lysander (by mistake). 'When thou wakest ...'.

2.2e Demetrius in and out; running from Helena.

2.2f Lysander wakes to see – and fall in love with – Helena. She runs off in disbelief; he follows. 'Wherefore was I to this keen mockery born?'

2.2g Hermia solo. Wakes to find Lysander gone; leaves to find him. 'Either death or you I'll find immediately'.

3.1a The beginning of the rehearsals. Solving the production problems! 'Some man or other must present Wall'.

3.1b Puck spying on rehearsals. 'What hempen homespuns have we swaggering here'. Bottom staggers off.

3.1c Rehearsal continues.

3.1d Bottom returns with the ass's head on. Chaos as the others come in and out and Puck adds to it. 'I see their knavery! This is to make an ass of me'.

3.1e Titania wakes and falls in love with Bottom, complete with head. 'So is mine eye enthralled to thy shape'.

3.1f The fairies are told to serve Bottom by Titania. 'Be kind and courteous to this gentleman'.

3.2a Puck tells Oberon the news about Titania and Bottom. Oberon is delighted. 'Titania waked and straightway loved an ass'.

3.2b Demetrius still in love with Hermia and following her as she seeks Lysander. She goes off angrily and he remains – to sleep. 'Out dog! Out cur! Thou drivest me past the bounds / Of maiden's patience'.

3.2c Oberon berates Puck for anointing the wrong man. Oberon anoints Demetrius. Puck goes to get Helena.

3.2d The start of the big 'lovers' quarrel' scene. Lysander apparently in love with Helena. 'Why should you think that I should woo in scorn?'

3.2e Demetrius wakes and joins in. 'O Helen, goddess, nymph, perfect, divine – '

3.2f Hermia arrives. The battle between the girls. 'O me, you juggler, you canker-blossom, / You thief of love ...'.

3.2g Oberon again blames Puck and sets in place the restoration of order. '... and all things shall be peace'.

3.2h Puck pretends to be each of the male lovers, egging them on to fight. Gets them to lie down near each other to sleep.

3.2i The girls arrive separately; they too fall asleep. All is ready for the restoration of order. 'On the ground/Sleep sound./ I'll apply/ To your eye, /Gentle lover, remedy'.

By doing this, you are well prepared for examination work. You have studied the text in detail to fill in the grid and you have had to summarise each scene and select appropriate quotations. All this adds to your knowledge base considerably. In addition, this french scene analysis throws up some interesting points that might be useful for practical decisions about the production of the text by a director, designer and/or actor. Your choice of production concept may be affected because the following strike you:

- There is *no* section here without one of the fairies in it (even if it is just Titania sleeping). Directors have used this 'ever-presence' of the fairies as a major motif in productions.
- There are few sections without a 'non-speaking' character present. Someone is either asleep or observing. This sense of never being alone reinforces the wood as a theatrical device for making private matters public.
- The ticks in the lovers' boxes move and change frequently. This mirrors the chaotic, erratic relationships taking place, contrasting with the solid set of ticks for the stolid mechanicals.
- Puck is a constantly returning presence – the fetcher and carrier.
- The selection of 'key' quotes was done with only the particular scene in mind – they seemed key to that scene. Yet if you look at them, they are virtually all to do with love and deception – key themes in the play.

MOOD AND ATMOSPHERE, PACE, TENSION AND CLIMAX

How do these rather nebulous, intangible terms relate to dramatic texts? How are you likely to use them or respond to them? What do they actually *mean*?

The Shorter Oxford English Dictionary suggests a number of definitions. We have selected the ones that seem most appropriate for reference to a piece of theatre:

Mood – a frame of mind or state of feelings
Atmosphere – mental or moral environment; a supposed outer envelope of effective influence surrounding various bodies
Pace – rate of movement in general; speed, velocity (rapidity of motion or action).
Tension – a straining, or strained condition, of the mind, feelings or nerves
Climax – gradation, 'ascending series', culmination.

*These terms are all part of the **meaning** of a play*

For dramatic purposes, mood and atmosphere are virtually interchangeable. Tension, pace and climax are connected, but they do not refer to exactly the same thing. All these areas are interwoven with the themes and ideas that a dramatist intends to communicate. All the elements of a play interrelate and support each other to create *meaning*.

When you are referring to these terms, ensure you relate them directly to the text

Because these terms are somewhat vague and intangible, it is important that you immediately relate them to hard examples from the text. If you attempt to *define* any term in an abstract manner, you will be in danger of classic 'waffle'. You must hang the term(s) on to evidence from the text to give substance to your comments. In this way you are *describing* the terms rather than *defining* them. This is the most appropriate method of addressing mood, atmosphere, pace, tension and climax

To be able to *describe* these terms, you will have to recognise how the dramatist realises them in the text. This will be through speech or stage directions. If you look at the extract from *All Things Bright and Beautiful* on p.20, you will be able to find places in the text where the dramatists give pointers to the mood, atmosphere, pace, tension and climax.

Queenie speaks 'formally' and Douglas 'officially' at the beginning of the scene. This indicates a constrained, formal **mood/atmosphere**. The speeches support this; Queenie speaks in a precise manner, full of tight politeness: '...we've been under the impression ... We've been given to understand ...'. **Tension** builds suddenly out of this constrained atmosphere because Albert 'walks menacingly' and tears up a document. The word 'menacingly' immediately implies tension. The tension is then maintained at the same pitch because Albert does not suddenly burst out; instead he speaks quite rationally and then 'walks calmly back'. The dramatists are indicating that they want the same level of tension maintained until Douglas's burst of 'hysterical amusement'. (This would also be affected by directorial interpretation.)

You could use the same examples from the text to describe the **pace** of the scene at this point. The pace noticeably alters with Douglas's speech. The style of writing is different: he speaks in short, sometimes unfinished sentences and exclamation marks are used frequently. We can tell from this that the speech should be spoken in a fast, staccato manner; the *pace* has increased significantly. The **climax** is reached with Douglas's final line 'You're in flats now!' The information has been building in the scene and the tension has increased to this mini climax.

This analysis of just a few lines from the extract shows you how clearly the dramatist signals the mood, atmosphere, pace, tension and climax to the audience. It demonstrates also how *changes* in mood, atmosphere, pace, tension and climax can be detected in the script, through changes in the style of writing. Dramatists frequently change the mood, atmosphere, pace, tension and climax; it is part of creating interesting and vibrant dramatic texts.

It is important to find useful vocabulary to help with descriptions of mood etc. Look at the few lines from *Equus* on p.27. If you were discussing the *tension* in this scene, you would have to ensure that you were referring closely to the script and using appropriate words of description. For example:

> 'There is a significant level of tension in this short scene, mainly instigated by Alan. Alan "slams about" and speaks in short, sharp sentences which are indicated by their length and the use of exclamation marks. Dysart seems to be attempting to reduce the tension by saying "I'm sorry" at the outset and by responding directly and calmly to Alan's question; his sentences do not have exclamation marks and the words are economical and rather flat. He fails to release the tension, however, because Alan moves towards him "hostilely". Alan is clearly angry and increases the tension of the scene by making this aggressive move.'

ACTIVITIES   Re-read the extract from *Vinegar Tom* on pp.21–2, up to the song *Something to Burn*. Describe the mood or atmosphere of the piece, referring closely to the text, as we have done with the *Equus* example above.

Take a playtext you are studying. Describe how the playwright builds to a climax at one particular point in the play.

Pace is the most difficult term and it is easy to mistake the things that create the pace of a scene

Of the five terms, *pace* is the most difficult to describe. It is therefore worth spending longer looking at what this term might mean. Often interchangeable with 'tempo', pace is clearly concerned with the speed and rapidity of the scene or extract. However, there is more to discuss than just the speed with which the lines are delivered.

Also, pace is *not* just about speeding up or slowing down cues (see Glossary). In fact, the speed of the cues should simply match the pace of the rest of the scene.

The pace is set by a number of other factors, for example:

- the language and style of writing (including the length of speeches and sentences; see pp.72–3)
- the rapidity of movement and action on stage
- the speed of gestures
- the rapidity of changing facial expressions
- the sheer weight of numbers and their co-ordination (people who move as a synchronised group have a different effect on pace to people who move entirely individually; the pace is usually speeded up when groups are synchronised, unless they are deliberately synchronised to move particularly slowly, of course)
- speed of voice and clarity of enunciation (deliberately forced enunciation can slow the pace)

Individual speeches can vary in pace, just as whole scenes do, obviously. Often the dramatist indicates the pace of the speech in the words themselves. A classic example is from *Macbeth*:

> Tomorrow, and tomorrow, and tomorrow,
> Creeps in this petty pace from day to day
>
> (Act 5 scene v lines 19–20)

The repetition alone indicates a sense of tedium and lack of inspiration; it would be difficult to speak the lines with zest with so many words repeated. In addition there is a series of long vowel sounds, which forces an actor to maintain a slower pace. The long vowel at the end of 'tomorrow' makes it particularly difficult to move swiftly on to the next word.

You will see from the list above that pace and tempo are determined more by the *production* of the text than by the text itself, although, as the *Macbeth* example shows, the text can be important. This is the case for *all* the terms in this section. Therefore, to describe the mood, atmosphere and so on fully, you will need to engage with the realisation of the text and as a **director, actor or designer** you will be expected to suggest how to realise these elements.

For example, if we take the *All Things Bright and Beautiful* extract again:

'The actor playing Douglas should initiate the increase of pace as he embarks on his first long speech. He should pause in astonishment as he watches Albert walk "calmly back", with a look of disbelief on his face. The pause is lengthened so that there is stillness after Albert stops walking. Then Douglas should speak his first two words in a stunned, shocked, quiet voice, staring fixedly at Albert: "What the –". Thus he would maintain the same level of pace and tension that Albert has created with his move, actions and speech. There is then a radical alteration in pace as Douglas reacts in "hysterical amusement", shouting "you're all in flats, man!" This needs to be spoken vociferously, with a sense of it bursting out of him. There is a mixture of mock disbelief and anger in his voice and he barely pauses for breath. His arm and hand gestures are similarly slightly uncontrolled as he "draws" the flats hurriedly in the air. The pace is suddenly increased here, which has a bulldozer effect; it's as if Douglas is flattening the Hesseltines' hopes by speaking and gesturing in a fast, relentless manner.'

You may also want to use other theatrical elements to help you realise the mood, atmosphere etc. The information on design, lighting and other aspects of production will be of assistance here (see pp.53–70). It may be worth looking at these before attempting to try the exercise below. An answer which includes reference to technical areas (for a hypothetical play) might read:

'The set for this scene is painted predominantly in dull greys and browns. It is clear that the atmosphere is depressing and lacking in vitality. To further emphasise this, the lanterns used would be fresnels without barn doors which will give the audience the impression of a woolly indecisiveness; there is no finite "edge" to the set. In addition, the gels would be a pale yellow so that the room appears stale and uninviting. These technical aspects would support the overall dismal, hopeless atmosphere created by the author's language.'

Similarly, technical aspects of the theatre can help you realise a *change* of mood, atmosphere etc. For example:

'By cross-fading the lighting state from a predominantly steel blue general cover to a straw-coloured focus on centre stage, the audience will become aware of the tension altering. Matching the gentler words taking place between the two characters, the mood perceptibly changes. It is less fraught and more relaxed.'

The following extract is from *The Visit*, written by Duerrenmatt and adapted by Valency. Claire Zachanassian has returned to visit Gullen after leaving many years ago, when she was in her late teens. She is now very wealthy and the townspeople hope that she will donate money to the town to help restore its prosperity; it is in a state of some dilapidation. They hope for as much as one million marks and are giving a banquet in Claire's honour.

BURGOMASTER:	. . . And you, gracious lady, whom we remember as a golden-haired – *(He looks at her.)* – little red-haired sprite romping about our peaceful streets – on your way to school – which of us does not treasure your memory? *(He pokes nervously at his notebook.)* We well remember your scholarly attainments –
TEACHER:	Yes.
BURGOMASTER:	Natural history – Extraordinary sense of justice. And above all, your supreme generosity. *(Great applause.)* We shall never forget how you once spent the whole of your little savings to buy a sack of potatoes for a poor starving widow who was in need of food. *(The* CHILDREN *serve wine.)* Gracious lady, ladies and gentlemen, today our little Clara has become the world-famous Claire Zachanassian who has founded hospitals, soup-kitchens, charitable institutes, art-projects, libraries, nurseries, and schools, and now that she has at last once more returned to the town of her birth, sadly fallen as it is, I say in the name of all her loving friends who have sorely missed her: Long live our Clara!
ALL:	Long live our Clara!
	(Cheers and applause. [SOUND CUE no. 14.])
CLAIRE:	*(Rises.)* Mr Burgomaster. Fellow townsmen. I am greatly moved by the nature of your welcome and the disinterested joy which you have manifested on the occasion of my visit to my native town. I was not quite the lovely child the Burgomaster described in his gracious address.
BURGOMASTER:	Too modest, Madame.
CLAIRE:	In school I was beaten –
TEACHER:	Not by me.
CLAIRE:	And the sack of potatoes which I presented to Widow Boll, I stole with the help of Anton Schill, not to save the old trull from starvation but so that for once I might sleep with Anton in a real bed instead of under the trees in the forest. *(The* TOWNSPEOPLE *look grave, embarrassed.)* Nevertheless I shall try to deserve your good opinion. In memory of the seventeen years I spent among you, I am prepared to hand over as a gift to the town of Gullen the sum of one billion marks. Five hundred million to the town and five hundred million to be divided up per capita among the citizens. *(There is a moment of dead silence.)*
BURGOMASTER:	A billion marks?
CLAIRE:	On one condition. *(Sits.)*
	(Suddenly a movement of uncontrollable joy breaks out. PEOPLE *jump on chairs, dance about, yell excitedly. The* ATHLETES *turn handsprings in front of the speaker's table.)*
SCHILL:	Oh Clara, you astonishing, incredible, magnificent woman! What a heart! What a gesture! Oh – my little witch! *(He kisses her hand.)*
BURGOMASTER:	*(Comes Down Centre and holds up his hand for order.)* Quiet! Quiet please! On one condition, the gracious lady said. Now Madame, may we know what that condition is?
CLAIRE:	I will tell you. In exchange for my billion marks, I want justice. *(Silence.)*
BURGOMASTER:	Justice, Madame?
CLAIRE:	I wish to buy justice.
BURGOMASTER:	But justice cannot be bought, Madame.
CLAIRE:	Everything can be bought.
BURGOMASTER:	I don't understand at all.

CLAIRE: Bobby, step forward.

BOBBY: (*Crosses Centre. He takes off his dark glasses and turns his face with a solemn air.*) Does anyone here present recognise me?

FRAU SCHILL: Hofer! Hofer!

ALL: Who? What's that?

TEACHER: (*Rises and takes a step toward him.*) Not Chief Magistrate Hofer who was on the Governing Board?

BOBBY: Exactly. (*TEACHER returns to his place.*) Chief Magistrate Hofer. When Madame Zachanassian was a girl, I was presiding judge at the criminal court of Gullen. I served there until twenty-five years ago when Madame Zachanassian offered me the opportunity of entering her service as butler. I accepted. You may consider it a strange employment for a member of the magistracy, but the salary –

CLAIRE: (*Bangs mallet on table.*) Come to the point.

BOBBY: You have heard Madame Zachanassian's offer. She will give you a billion marks – when you have undone the injustice that she suffered at your hands here in Gullen as a girl. (*ALL murmur.*)

BURGOMASTER: Injustice at our hands? Impossible!

BOBBY: Anton Schill –

SCHILL: Yes?

BOBBY: Kindly stand.

SCHILL: (*Rises. He smiles, as if puzzled. He shrugs.*) Yes?

BOBBY: In those days, a bastardy case was tried before me. Madame Claire Zachanassian, at that time called Clara Wascher, charged you with being the father of her illegitimate child. (*Silence.*) You denied the charge. And produced two witnesses in your support.

SCHILL: That's ancient history. An absurd business. We were children. Who remembers?

[The scene continues until Claire explains that her condition for giving the vast sum of money is that she wants the life of Anton Schill.]

[Duerrenmatt, F., adapted by Valency, M., *The Visit*, Samuel French, 1958. pp.33–36]

ACTIVITY   Trace the changes in mood, pace and tension in this passage and give examples of how you would realise these in performance. Refer to additional theatrical knowledge where relevant.

GENERAL POINTS   You could approach this question by addressing mood, pace and tension separately. However, your answer would be more theatrically coherent if you analysed the text chronologically, identifying the changes in mood, pace and tension as they occur. In this way you will not fall into the trap of forming arbitrary divisions between these three closely linked elements.

FRAMEWORK   1. Discuss the opening section up to '(*Cheers and applause...*)', suggesting how the prevailing mood, pace and tension would be realised, e.g. through the use of sound, lighting, movement, gesture, facial expression and so on. Each of the following sections would then be described using similar methods and particularly noting the *change* from the previous section.

2. Take the next section up until Claire sits.
3. The next section could be taken to end a few lines later when Claire says, 'I want justice. (*Silence.*)'
4. The remainder of the text constitutes the last section.
5. Summary (for Set Texts).

A DETAILED ANALYSIS   An example of your response to section 3 might read:

'The stillness which envelops the stage as Claire sits erupts into noise, activity and excitement. There is a dramatic change of mood from apprehensive hope and exaggerated politeness to "uncontrollable joy" and a sense of wild relief; the population have ignored Claire's pregnant statement: "On one condition". The pace increases rapidly at this point although the Burgomaster slows it down again after the lengthy outburst of delight. The tension alters swiftly in this short section: it is released instantly as the crowd reacts spontaneously, but it builds up again until a key moment of tension when Claire announces her condition, "I want justice".

'The actors' movements will be of particular importance in realising these alterations in mood, pace and tension, although technical aspects, such as lighting, will also add impact. To emphasise the outburst from the citizens, a moment's pause after Claire sits would act as a useful contrast; noise into complete silence is more effective. After the pause I would want to follow the suggestions in the stage directions, with every actor quickly and energetically breaking from her or his still position to a sequence of movements. This would be capped by the synchronised activities of the athletes, giving the whole scene a sense of ritual – like praising the gods for their bounty and goodness.

'In addition, I would want the lighting state to alter. If there were lights on stage, perhaps as part of the setting for the town's celebrations, it would be possible for some of the actors to move to them and start swinging them around, giving the effect of coloured spotlights sweeping the celebrations. (I saw this done at an Edinburgh Fringe production to great effect.) As well as adding to the sense of excitement and jubilation for the audience by having the *actors* operating the lanterns, the emphasis is on the townspeople being responsible for their own actions; this is a thread that is picked up later in the scene as Claire wants them to initiate justice to get the financial reward.'

ACTIVITY   Take a text that you are studying, e.g. Gay's *The Beggar's Opera*, and identify about five pages in the text where you recognise there are particular mood shifts, tension, perhaps a mini climax and so on. Answer the following question:

How would you direct this scene/these scenes to bring out the different moods and tension for an audience?

1.3 *Support research*

1.3.0 INTRODUCTION

To be in a position to stage a production of a text, a director, actor or designer would be expected to embark on a certain amount of research. This research would follow a number of different directions. In this section, we outline appropriate areas for background research and give examples of the information that might result.

We have suggested three areas of research for *any* set text; these should be combined to give you a thorough and comprehensive knowledge to support your understanding of the playtext itself. These three areas are: **the social and cultural context; the theatrical background; plays of a similar time, genre or theme**.

Be selective in the areas of background research that you undertake; ensure that it is relevant to the text

Be aware that not all texts will require equal emphasis on the different types of background research. For example, you may spend more time looking at plays of a similar time and/or genre for some 20th-century texts than the social and cultural context. This could be because the latter does not seem so relevant. Alternatively, you may spend little time looking at other 18th-century plays when studying Sheridan's *The Rivals*, but you would find it fruitful to research the dramatic background; the influence of earlier Comedies of Manners would help your understanding of the play. So do not feel that you must cover each area of research exhaustively. It entirely depends on the particular text that you are studying.

This chapter cannot give you all the information you would need for the *particular* text that you are studying, of course. What we can do is to explain the *sorts* of information you need through certain examples. In other words, we are giving you frameworks for study.

1.3.1 THE SOCIAL AND CULTURAL CONTEXT

The context will have influenced the writing of the play and will help us understand the audiences of the time

To understand a text fully, you will need to address the period in which the play was created. You will need to become aware of the events and social issues of the time, the politics of that society, its ethics, its cultural background and its preoccupations. All these will have contributed to the creation of the text in some way, and as part of your research you should be able to place the dramatist in his or her historical environment in order to establish some of his or her influences. In addition, the **reception** of a play is one third of the theatre process and an understanding of the original audience and its preoccupations allows us some idea of that audience's likely reception.

It is only in our modern society, and by that we mean roughly the last two thirds of the 20th century, that theatre has come to represent a rather formal, esoteric 'Culture'. In previous centuries, and in widely differing civilisations, drama was a part of, and mirrored, the culture and the society of the times. Drama and the way of life of the people have always been closely linked, from the time when drama was a form of religious festival or ceremony. Even today, when theatres are not at the centre of the entertainment and enlightenment business, many dramatists are fully engaged with mirroring society and seeking changes in it, particularly through the medium of television.

To understand a play, therefore, you have to address the culture that created that play and playwright and the society in which the audience lived.

We will take two examples of British theatre to demonstrate what we mean here: the Elizabethan period and the 19th century. In each example there are *key areas* which are investigated. These are:

- **Events and social issues**
- **Politics**
- **Ethics**
- **Cultural background and preoccupations**.

These headings provide a framework that could be followed for any set text. However, such headings might alter according to the text and period you are studying. You may find that education could be a possible major area to consider, or law and order, or living conditions, for example; the text should suggest to you appropriate areas of social and historical research.

Be aware of the sources for such research. Depending on the period, these might be:

- internet sites (although the veracity of these can be questionable)
- history textbooks
- newspapers – for text or pictures
- diaries and biographies of people living at the time
- photographs
- fiction – novels, poetry and films
- journals
- television reports
- paintings
- books on period clothes
- other art forms – dances, music?
- maps – for geographical understanding
- appropriate museums

The examples below represent two slightly different models of social and historical research. The first, on the Elizabethan period, addresses the events, social issues and ethics without much reference to the texts of the time. The second example, the nineteenth century, interweaves the history with the drama of the period. You may find either method appropriate, but it is likely to depend upon the set text studied. In the 19th and early 20th centuries playtexts were particularly closely linked with the social events of the time; indeed, the playwrights *chose* to write about such issues. In the Elizabethan period, theatre was less obviously connected with the social context. When you study one specific text, you can more easily choose an appropriate form of research.

EXAMPLE 1 – ELIZABETHAN ENGLAND

This would be particularly useful for the plays of Shakespeare and his contemporaries: Marlow, Jonson and Kyd, for example.

The Elizabethan era saw the change from feudal to Renaissance society

The Elizabethan period can roughly be delimited by the years of Queen Elizabeth's reign, 1558–1603. This period marked a distinct change from the life of the Middle Ages: a change from the feudal system to the Renaissance. Shakespeare and his contemporaries were Elizabethan (and Jacobean) writers and would have been influenced by such changes taking place.

The feudal system was autocratic and absolute

What did these changes mean? The feudal system was a carefully structured hierarchical system that had operated in the Middle Ages. It was a time of absolute and, seemingly, unchanging autocracy; the people were ruled by powerful individuals who were not democratically elected but who ruled by hereditary right, unquestioned by the masses. From the king to the lord of the manor, rulers were in place because their fathers had been rulers. Property laws were organised around those with a wealthy and noble heritage; the people could live or grow food only on common ground or on the Lord's ground in return for various taxes and duties. The state was decentralised, with great power in the hands of individual lords and landowners, which included the Church. Looking at the times in retrospect, the feudal era was remarkably straightforward. There was no education for the masses and the wealthy ruled without question; even the morality of the country was guided by them.

Morality was fixed

The feudal system encouraged a form of group morality that was fostered by the Church and the secular powers. The value systems were based on strong religious influences; the masses were the sheep and the Church leaders were the shepherds. There was a common notion of what was right and everyone understood the same moral code. There was little to change people's belief systems: values were fundamental and absolute.

If this was the feudal era, what of the Renaissance? Renaissance means new birth. The term 'Renaissance man' has become synonymous with individualism, humanism and liberalism. (Women played very little part in public life; it is appropriate to say Renaissance *man*.) But what brought about these changes to the prevailing attitudes?

New worlds were discovered, expanding the physical and mental horizons of the Elizabethans

In the sixteenth century, the world was physically changing: new lands were discovered and the picture of the world was altered accordingly. Renaissance man realised that Europe was not the total extent of the world and his foundations were shaken as a result. Added to this came an increase in scientific research and scientific discoveries, making people question how the physical world worked.

A sense of change from ordered, predestined lives to an emphasis on individuality

The old systems of morality were becoming unstable. As new cultures were encountered, completely different codes of behaviour impinged upon Renaissance Europe. There was a growing sense of change and

Renaissance people had to learn to adapt to a new world. The knowledge of widely differing civilisations did not necessarily lead to the Elizabethans *accepting* those cultures, but it did bring about a basic and fundamental questioning of the nature of man and the purpose of existence. The focus on the individual as, in some sense, more responsible for his or her actions took over from the predestined, ordered lives of the feudal past.

Religious changes unsettled the population

Religious change also had some impact on the alterations that were taking place in Elizabethan society. The move to Protestantism that came with Elizabeth's rule decreased the ritual that surrounded the Catholic mass and replaced it with a direct and individualistic approach to God. For many, the ornate rituals of the Catholic church were part of the key moments of existence – birth, marriage and death. The removal of these rituals left an uneasy gap in people's lives. In addition, the constant changes of state religion, from Henry VIII's Reformation, back to the Catholicism of Mary I and then to Elizabethan Protestantism, accompanied by the persecution of people because of their beliefs, was a major source of instability in the sixteenth century.

Trade increased

Extended geographical horizons opened up new areas and routes for trade and the Elizabethan age saw the rise of a whole new class of people – the merchant class. The new trading possibilities provided enormous potential for wealth as well as bringing changes to an insular culture. The merchants made money; this was the first time anyone outside the aristocracy and the Church had become wealthy. The rise of the professional and merchant classes inevitably altered some of the long-held feudal beliefs about who should rule the country. Previously, aristocratic status had equated to power. Now the developing upper middle classes saw that earned money could also give them influence. Much changed and the removal of a seemingly pre-ordained hierarchical system was the result. The localised autocracies of feudal times gave way to a more centralised state government. This in turn encouraged the merchant and professional classes to increase mining and manufacture at home as well as to explore and exploit overseas lands. Thus there was an expansion of the 'ruling' class as a result of this growth in the wealth, status and power of the upper middle classes.

The wealthy trading classes recognised that money could mean power

The artistic and cultural world expanded

The arts and culture prospered during the Renaissance. One of the key reasons for this was, again, the expansion of physical horizons; more travel led to an increase in artistic and cultural exchange with European artists. Inevitably, the wealth of resources for English artists and intellectuals grew. So whilst Elizabethan man was being forced to alter his understanding in the light of completely alien cultures, the expansion of travel opportunities for the merchant classes meant that much broader cultural resources were available to help him do so.

Education was in demand

Meanwhile, there was a growing demand for educated administrators, from the newly forming professional classes, to support trade. This coincided with the desire of the wealthy social elite to be well educated. It is estimated that in the early 17th century two and a half per cent of young men were educated to university level. This was not to be matched until the 20th century. The basic level of education and literacy also increased for many ordinary people. The printing press, probably the most important long-term influence on literacy, produced

Basic literacy improved for the middle classes

books from the late 15th century onwards. Trade guilds made basic literacy a pre-requisite for entry into apprenticeships, so that the signing of one's name and the ability to read became a necessity. Ten thousand copies of *The ABC and Little Catechism*, a reading primer, were sold in 1585. Whilst this growth of literacy skills was mainly in the professional classes, it still represented a significant increase.

CONCLUSION   This is a brief and possibly simplistic overview of the social and historical background to Elizabethan England. Clearly, there is far more that could be researched in greater detail. You could look specifically at the impact of travel on the Elizabethans' consciousness, or at the firm Protestant rule of Elizabeth and how that would have affected the playwrights of the time. The choice of particular areas of research would depend upon the play and playwright under analysis. For example, if you were studying one of Shakespeare's tragedies, you could use the information on social and political change above. Fintan O'Toole makes this point, using a poem by John Donne, who wrote in this period:

> 'Tis all in pieces, all coherence gone;
> All just supply and all relation:
> Prince, subject, father, son, are things forgot,
> For every man alone that he hath got
> To be a Phoenix and that then can be
> None of that kind of which he is but he.
>
> Donne, *The First Anniversary*

O'Toole goes on:

> Looking at his and Shakespeare's England, Donne saw a world in which all order and coherence had fallen apart, in which the hierarchy of relations both within the state and within the family was breaking down, in which men were getting the idea that they were uniquely their own invention rather than the product of their place and status within a highly stratified society. His poem could also have been an exact description of Shakespeare's tragedies, of the inter-related breakdown of family and state in each of them, of the Phoenix-like Lear and Hamlet and Macbeth and Othello, each believing that he is a self-made man, that he owes his individuality not to his status but to his free will. Their tragedy is that their world is not yet quite like that, that the pull of order and hierarchy is still very strong, not least within their own minds.
>
> [O'Toole, F., *No More Heroes: A Radical Guide to Shakespeare*, Raven Arts Press, 1990. p. 20]

It is useful to summarise as follows:

- **Events and social issues** – New worlds being discovered; growth of merchant classes.

- **Politics** – Growth of a middle class with wealth and therefore power; hierarchical feudal system breaking up.

- **Ethics** – Old Catholic morality shifting as Renaissance man becomes more individualistic and reliant on self; less automatic acceptance of traditional values.

- **Cultural background and preoccupations** – Instability as old, permanent systems become clearly impermanent; new ideas about responsibility for one's own fate and less reliance on established systems as awareness of new cultures affected population.

EXAMPLE 2 – 19TH-CENTURY ENGLAND

Research on this period is particularly useful for two different types of drama: melodrama and the more serious or 'new' drama that followed it. Melodrama was popular for roughly the whole of the 19th century; the 'new' drama of Galsworthy, Shaw and Granville-Barker was written in approximately the first 20 years of this century. It is useful to understand the social and historical background in order to see the origins of these two types of drama.

To study the historical background of the theatre period from the early 19th century to the early 20th century, it is important to go back to the end of the 18th century.

It was around this time that the Industrial Revolution began in Britain. The country was transformed from a rural, agricultural society to an urban, industrialised one. For example, the population of London trebled between 1811 and 1851. In 1800, just as the Industrial Revolution was blossoming, 20 per cent of the population lived in towns. A hundred years later, 77 per cent of the population lived in towns.

The Industrial Revolution had a major impact on society

Prior to the Industrial Revolution cottage industries had flourished, with cloth-making and other work being undertaken in rural homes. In addition, the majority of the people still worked on the land. With increasing mechanisation, however, fewer people could find a living on the land; similarly, cottage industries were needed less as the new factories were built to take machines. These machines produced cloth far more quickly and cheaply than individuals in their homes. Factories were built in towns and so people moved to the towns to find work.

Charles Dickens's novel *Hard Times* describes such a town:

> It was a town of red brick, or of brick that would have allowed it; but as matters stood it was a town of unnatural red and black like the painted face of a savage. It was a town of machinery and tall chimneys, out of which interminable serpents of smoke trailed themselves for ever and ever, and never got uncoiled. It had a black canal in it, and a river that ran purple with ill-smelling dye, and vast piles of building full of windows where there was a rattling and a trembling all day long, and where the piston of the steam-engine worked monotonously up and down like the head of an elephant in a state of melancholy madness. It contained several large streets all very like one another, and many small streets still more like one another, inhabited by people equally like one another, who all went in and out at the same hours, with the same sound upon the same pavements, to do the same work, and to whom every day was the same as yesterday and tomorrow, and every year the counterpart of the last and the next.

Poverty and anonymity led to a demand for excitement

These towns provided a mass market for entertainment. Condemned to anonymity in life and work, struggling on the borderline of poverty and starvation, people, not surprisingly, sought excitement, forgetfulness and the vision of a better world through their entertainment.

Playwrights turned to sensationalism, patriotism and spectacle as sources for entertainment. The resulting melodramas were nautical, Gothic, oriental or domestic in flavour. They tackled subjects that appealed to the mass audiences because they provided escape into an exciting and idealistically straightforward world. British victories, particularly at sea, proved popular source material, appealing to the patriotic instincts of the people. Further material was provided by Gothic novels, with mysterious castles and dark forests, highly stereotyped oriental settings with Arabian wrongdoings, and 'domestic' villainy: any crime would be eagerly snatched up and turned into a hack script overnight. The murder of Maria Marten in a rural barn or the supposed killings performed by the London barber Sweeney Todd were examples.

Melodramas consisted of a world of absolutes: good versus evil. Frequently the oppressed and poor were portrayed as the good, the wealthy and aristocratic as the bad. Other key characteristics of the form were strong stereotypes, or stock characters, who were easily identifiable by the audience, music to demonstrate emotion, much visual spectacle, fast pace and large amounts of action, happy endings, a high moral tone and rapid alternation between scenes of different types, for example comic and tragic. The audiences enjoyed the simplicity of the storylines, the accessible characters, the excitement of the spectacle and, most importantly, a world where the oppressed good triumphed over the wealthy bad and gained a reward. This form of easily digestible, formulaic entertainment, where life could be slotted into readily understandable blocks, relieved the bleakness, tedium, injustice and poverty of the city population's everyday existence.

The sheer size of audiences also helped shape the direction of drama. They drove the upper classes out because of their numbers and because of their demand for cheap, instant entertainment. The upper classes moved to the opera houses, preferring the more rarified operatic entertainment, together with the occasional witty, elegant comedy by Sheridan or more literary Shakespearian play, and were not seen back in the popular theatres in any number until later in the 19th century. The large numbers demanded larger theatres. At its largest, Drury Lane held well over 3,500 people, with a stage that was 30 metres deep. The effect on the style of performance was dramatic. To fill the auditorium, subtlety of voice and gesture was sacrificed and this helped establish the exaggerated form of acting associated with melodrama.

However, although melodrama lasted as a popular form for over a hundred years, eventually the tides of taste altered. The writers themselves felt the need for change; the hack melodramatists evolved into playwrights concerned with more complex issues and interested in presenting reality on stage, through both the form and the content of their plays. Tom Robertson is one early example of these playwrights; plays such as *Caste* (1867) portrayed a more lifelike situation, which dealt with class problems, in quasi-naturalistic sets. Such plays as these set the scene for social and political writers such as Galsworthy, Granville-Barker and Shaw. Like Robertson, they moved away from sensational and spectacular settings, favouring the naturalism that was becoming popular in other parts of Europe, for example in the work of Ibsen.

However, it was not just the *form* of the theatre that altered; the new dramatists adapted the form because the *content* required a different form. These dramatists wished to tackle social and political issues in order to draw attention to current injustices and ills and thus to promote reform. Such content clearly called for a theatrical style that matched the serious nature of the issues; a move away from sensational melodrama was necessary. In addition, this development reflected the needs of an increasingly educated audience, which was less downtrodden and more socially aware.

Social reform was needed and the dramatists took up these issues

The mass movement to the cities during the Industrial Revolution had led to appalling living conditions, as described by Charles Dickens above. The beginning of the 20th century saw a strong shift in public consciousness as the insanitary and overcrowded conditions in most cities were recognised as being unacceptable in a civilised society. The plight of the poor, the role of capitalism and the new socialist values current in some parts of Europe engaged the attention of many who wished to change and improve the lives of the British populace. Limited political reform had led the way in the middle of the 19th century (two major reform acts affecting the constitution of parliament); some social reform had also taken place, such as the reduction of working hours and laws against allowing young children to work. The cry was now for further social reform. This encompassed both the socialists' cries for health care and the Suffragette movement demanding a rightful place for women in society. Running parallel with the rise of the socialist movement was the gradual decline of the British Empire; the shouts for democracy and humanitarian treatment for all – whatever their class, creed or gender – were being heard with increasing amounts of sympathy in many quarters. It was this voice, the voice of the social reformer, that could be heard in the new dramatists of the day.

The plays of the time reflected the social ideals

The new progressive theatre shocked its audiences. The zeal of the social reformer, tackling society's ills, became the tone of the dramatist; the middle and upper classes (who had started to return to the theatre as the huge, rowdy, predominantly working-class melodrama audiences retreated) found that they were confronted with topical issues on stage. Galsworthy's *Strife* (1909) looked at the long-term effects of a strike on the chairman of the board and the strike leader. His *The Skin Game* (1920) portrayed the aristocracy, who were determined to hold on to power above the industrial capitalist classes. Granville-Barker similarly tackled 'modern' issues. *The Madras House* (1910) looks at the role of women in society and *Waste* (1907) was banned by the censor as it dealt with a politician's affair, leading to abortion and death. Shaw followed the same lines; he was a key figure in the rising Labour movement and brought his passionate socialist beliefs and his dramatist's skill together in his plays. His topics were often controversial. *Mrs Warren's Profession* (1902) looked at prostitution and *Major Barbara* (1905) has at its centre the contemporary problems of poverty and wealth; the philosophy behind charity is explored. Shaw (1856–1950) was a prolific playwright, writing over 50 plays, and had a profound influence on the British theatre and, indeed, British democracy. All the dramatists of this time were much influenced by socialist ideals; the deprivation of the working classes and the transfer of power to the masses through the unions were part of this agenda.

CONCLUSION   As you can see, a study of the social and historical background of the melodrama period and the early 20th-century 'new' writers gives a clear cultural context for these periods of theatre. The genre of melodrama was driven by social conditions leading to audience need. The new writers in turn were driven by social conscience and new theatrical genres; Stanislavski, Ibsen and the European naturalists informed their style. The Labour movement and the growing social conscience among the middle classes informed their content.

A summary of this research could be:

- **Events and social issues** – The Industrial Revolution; poverty of the masses and the need for entertainment. Poor living conditions leading to social reform.

- **Politics** – Middle classes and capitalists with far more power; emergence of the Labour Party and socialist reformers.

- **Ethics** – The masses wanted a world of moral absolutes; the later socialist reformers were indignant about the treatment of the poor.

- **Cultural background and preoccupations** – The shift from a rural society to an industrialised society; the divide between rich and poor.

USING YOUR RESEARCH

These are only examples of the kind of historical research upon which you might choose to embark. The period and type of play you are studying will determine that research. However, it would be useful to follow the guidelines laid out for you above as the events and social issues, the politics, the ethics, the cultural background and the pre-occupations of any period would influence its playwrights.

Use of this information will depend upon individual points under discussion

How would such information be used? It is impossible to give any generalised recommendations for this; it would entirely depend upon the particular point you wished to make about the set text. It is only possible to give examples from specific plays. For example:

What points would you consider if you were playing the role of Hamlet?

Your answer would rely heavily upon a character study of Hamlet. (See pp.26–40 for further details about such character studies.) However, you might choose to frame your response by referring to the cultural context of the play as a significant factor in your interpretation of the role. If this is the case, you could write something like this before embarking on the main section of your response :

'Hamlet displays the signs of a powerful young man who has lost the main foundations on which his whole existence was based. His seeming vacillation in killing his uncle, Claudius, is not merely procrastination. We feel that he is unsure and hesitant about *everything* at this point, including all his relationships.

'We sense that Hamlet symbolises something of the Elizabethan times. Not only is he a deeply complex, interesting and finely drawn character, but he also represents the instability and hesitancy of the times. The Elizabethan period acted as a bridge between the Middle Ages and the Renaissance. The stable, autocratic society of the feudal system was being replaced by the expanding horizons and shifting values of the Renaissance. Such a change inevitably led to uncertainty when the traditional, accepted beliefs of English society were being challenged by new and different cultures. This sense of change and lack of certainty could be emphasised in the portrayal of Hamlet.'

This is an example of using your research when the question does not openly ask for such information. However, there is a danger of falling into the trap of recalling facts irrelevantly without closely referring them to the question. There is certainly no point in using your research without a reason; you will merely irritate your reader. However, the ability to link the set text with its context is important. You are showing a full understanding of text, production and reception because you are demonstrating an awareness of the prevailing climate in which the play was produced and the preoccupations of the original audience.

Without asking directly for an awareness of the social and historical background to a text, some questions might be more clearly open to the introduction of such knowledge. For example:

If you were to direct a production of *Major Barbara*, how would you emphasise the central issues of the play in performance?

You may well decide to refer to the prevailing social problems of the day in answering this question. Part of your answer might read:

'Shaw was a strong and active socialist all his life and *Major Barbara* reflects his socialist views. The turn of the century marked a time when the plight of the socially deprived, particularly in the major cities, was being voiced with increasing vigour. Growing numbers of the more liberal and humanitarian middle classes, of whom Barbara Undershaft is an example, were becoming deeply concerned about such poverty. Overcrowding, slum-like housing and illness had been brought about by the surge of people moving to cities at the time of the Industrial Revolution during the early 19th century. Critics of society had been busy for many years; now key playwrights added their voices.

'Shaw's central themes in this play are not just poverty and charity, as represented by the Salvation Army personnel, e.g. 'Major' Barbara. He moves on from this and debates the paradoxical position of capitalism *providing* that charity and the morality behind this. In this play, this paradox is heightened because the wealth that provides the charity is gained from the manufacture of weapons. Shaw questions the ethics of this and in doing so joins the debate about poverty and the methods of handling this that was current in the early 1900s.

'These are the central issues in the play that I would choose to emphasise in a production of the text. There are various methods of achieving this emphasis . . .'

BIBLIOGRAPHY

It is difficult to recommend specific texts here as there are so many different periods to consider. In addition, there are few theatre books which fully take into account the historical context. It is likely that research will have to take in history textbooks as well as theatre books.

You would be well advised to scour a good academic bookshop (or library) for recently written texts on your particular period. Certain periods are better covered than others. For example, huge numbers of books have been written about Shakespeare's work and times. For an approach which incorporates the social context of the time, look out for books by Lisa Jardine, Graham Holderness, John Drakakis or Terence Hawkes, for example.

1.3.2 THE THEATRICAL BACKGROUND

All theatre is set within the context of an ongoing tradition and may broadly be said to be either a reflection of or a reaction to it.

Dramatists are always influenced by recent theatrical practice. The predominant form of theatre production, the content of plays and the typical style in which they are written will influence any playwright and affect his or her own work. For some, this influence is minimal; for others, the mode of the time inspires them and they endeavour to develop the influence in their own writing; for yet others, there is a deliberate reaction against the current mode or genre.

Discussing a play in its theatrical context gives the text more meaning

It is important that you understand the particular *theatrical background* to the text you are studying. It then becomes possible to recognise influences on the writing of your set text, or even attempts by the dramatist to react against the predominant mode of writing. When you are discussing the text you are then able to treat the play as part of a broader context, commenting upon recent dramatic history, rather than discussing the play as if it existed in a theatrical vacuum.

It is important to study the playwright's background as well as the theatrical background

In addition to this you will want to research **the life and works of the dramatist** you are studying. We have not attempted to undertake such a task here because even a framework is superfluous. Most texts have a straightforward introduction, which will give a brief biography and highlight the most relevant details about the playwright. It is particularly important that you are able to place a specific text in the context of the playwright's life and works. For example, if you were studying *A Doll's House*, it would be useful to know that Ibsen's wife, Susannah, was a feminist and that he had been criticised by a female Norwegian novelist for his poor treatment of women in his early plays. The sympathetic approach to Nora in *A Doll's House* begins to have meaning when you understand something of Ibsen's history.

A framework for research into theatrical background

Theatrical background research should identify the key issues which are relevant for the tradition from which the set text that you are studying emerged. When researching the background for any playtext, you should be looking for **dominant styles or genres, subject matter, key influential practitioners,** and **a reflection of society's preoccupations.**

This list should act as a guide. If you look at the following example you will recognise that we have broadly covered these themes.

EXAMPLE – LATE 18TH- AND 19TH-CENTURY EUROPEAN THEATRE

If you were studying a set text by a playwright such as Ibsen, Chekhov or Strindberg, some understanding of theatre in late 18th- and 19th-century Europe would be useful. These three great playwrights had writing careers spanning the years 1850–1905. Ibsen (1828–1906) was Norwegian (although he spent much of his writing life in Italy) and has become known as the father of modern drama because of his use of realism; Chekhov (1860–1904) was the temperamental Russian who is frequently associated with Stanislavski's Moscow Art Theatre; Strindberg (1849–1912) was a Swede and encompassed both extremes of naturalism and expressionism in his work.

Whilst these men were by no means the only good European playwrights of the time, they were probably the best and certainly they are now the best known. Their work was considered progressive, new and radical. To comprehend fully the impact that such writers' plays had on the theatrical world, the recent dramatic background would need to be understood.

ROMANTICISM

Romanticism, in all its guises, dominated the artistic world in Europe in the late 18th and early 19th centuries

The Romantic period had a number of characteristics; these centred around freedom and intensity of expression and the celebration of self and art

In the broadest terms, the Romantic movement swept through Europe from the late 18th century into the 19th century. There were great social and political changes at this time; most notable was the French Revolution of 1789. This bloodbath, in which the King and Queen and many of the aristocracy (and large numbers of ordinary people) were guillotined, had far-reaching effects. The cry of the Revolution had been 'Liberty, Equality and Fraternity' and this search for political and social freedom resonated across Europe until the middle of the 19th century.

In many ways, the Romantic movement was the successor of the 'Enlightenment' in the first half of the 18th century. The Enlightenment, or Age of Reason, encouraged the belief that people were closely connected with nature, that they were reasoning and rational beings and that they should be free of political or religious oppression. The progressive and liberal views of the Enlightenment rationalists led directly to the French Revolution. The Romantics developed some of these characteristics, but they were in direct opposition to the *rationalist* side of the Enlightenment. The intensity of individual experience was of far more importance. Artists of the Romantic period, as it became known, were concerned with the working classes, the humble peasant rather than the noble and possibly aristocratic hero. The uncertainty and irrationality of humans and their existence were favourite themes and an unfettered individualism characterised the arts of the Romantic decades. There was a lack of rules and regulation; inmost feelings were given expression and humans' closeness to nature was explored. Incorporated into this intensity was often an exaltation of emotion, religion and the supernatural.

> . . . romanticism is best characterized by its idealist celebration of the self, by its respect for the transcendental, and by its conviction of the power of the imagination and of the supreme value of art.
>
> [Flew, A. (ed.), *A Dictionary of Philosophy*, Pan, 1970. p.307]

The real essence of the Romantic period is not to be found in theatre; Goethe and Schiller came nearest to being Romantic dramatists and their work has nowhere near the resonance of other artists. Romanticism is at its best in the other arts, particularly music (Schubert and Schumann), poetry (Byron, Wordsworth, Shelley) and art (Delacroix). Perhaps theatre is too literal a medium to encompass the 'idealist celebration of self'; these characteristics of Romanticism are more easily realised in those arts that have more freedom of expression.

The Germanic states and France provided the centre of continental Europe's theatrical activity in this period. Artistic activity in other European countries reflected the movements in these countries.

The Sturm und Drang movement of the 1770s was an early brief form of Romanticism

Theatre in Germany in the 1770s briefly became known as the *Sturm und Drang* (Storm and Stress) movement. Although it did not last, the movement is symptomatic of the times. Advocates of *Sturm und Drang* chose to idealise the early Middle Ages. This was part of a desire to escape from the politics of the day, with its autocratic state kings and princes, and return to what they believed were the freer days of the past. They saw the early Middle Ages as a time of romance and sensation and of comparative freedom. (In fact, these early feudal times were grossly misinterpreted by the intellectual Romantics, who relied on some literature and much imagination for their sources.) The Gothic novel, full of villains, castles and strange events, was a typical by-product of the *Sturm und Drang* times. The plays used extravagant language and topics.

Goethe and Schiller were the giants of German theatre

Two names emerged as German theatre progressed from the Storm and Stress days and the late Enlightenment to the full Romantic era: Goethe (1749–1832) and Schiller (1759–1805). While certainly Goethe claimed to dislike the chief characteristics of the disordered Romantics, both he and Schiller nonetheless belonged to the genre. In fact, many would consider Goethe's *Faust* as the most typical of Romantic drama.

Goethe wrote of such things as an honourable robber knight fighting tyrannical rulers (*Gotz von Berlichingen*, 1773), the revolt of the Netherlands against Spain, with the hero dying for the sake of his humanitarian and honourable actions (*Egmont*, 1788), and of course Faust, the man who makes a pact with the devil for material wealth (*Faust, Part 1*, 1808; *Part 2*, published 1833). In this vast verse play, tragedy and farce exist side by side and Faust is redeemed in the end.

Schiller's plays, such as *The Robbers* (1782), the *Wallenstein* trilogy (1798–9), and *Mary Stuart* (1800), have similar Romantic characteristics to Goethe's. They concentrate on the rights of the individual, containing powerful language and lengthy poetic speeches. His first play, *The Robbers*, had a dedication, 'Against tyrants'. He, like Goethe, tried to combine popular and serious drama and attempted both political and poetic plays. His work was rapturously received.

The plays of the German Romantics are not successful in the Britain of the late 20th and early 21st centuries

Today we would find these authors excessive in their use of language and heightened emotions. There is a melodramatic quality to the writing that is not to the modern taste. While their theme, the conflicts of the soul and the relationship between feeling and reason, has some appeal, the florid style of writing does not. Both dramatists opposed any naturalistic tendency in the theatre; there is a strong romantic quality to the work which negates any possibility of producing the pieces with overtones of present-day naturalism. However, Goethe's *Faust* was staged at the Lyric, Hammersmith, in 1988 in a very successful production, with Simon Callow as Faust. The staging included acrobatic actors using a huge curved iron bridge, trapeze ropes, a glass bubble and water tanks.

In later years, German Romanticism drifted into sensational melodrama, as was also the case in France and England; the later Romantics lacked the skill of the earlier dramatists. This indicates both a gradual decline of inspiration and ability and also the dictates of an audience who relished the straightforward, instantly accessible diet offered by pure melodrama.

French Romantic drama lacked the same quality as German

France's Romantic drama followed a less distinguished path than Germany's. Whilst one might think that the Revolution would have been a source of inspiration, there are very few French dramatists of note in this time. Such massive political instability seems not to have encouraged playwriting.

The names that are best known are Pixerecourt (1773–1844), who wrote profusely but not terribly well and concentrated on melodramas; Victor Hugo (1802–85), who was predominantly a novelist, but whose *Hernani* was a classic Romantic play of epic proportions with sweeping verse; Dumas and de Musset, although again their plays verged on melodrama (de Musset's less so than Dumas's.)

It is worth noting that there are other varieties of French drama that also form part of the dramatic scene of the 19th century: the well-made play and farce.

THE WELL-MADE PLAY

The well-made play proved popular with the bourgeois classes for its aesthetic neatness

This form of theatre was developed in France predominantly by Eugene Scribe (1791–1861). These plays appealed to the rising bourgeois classes; they were carefully and systematically constructed and staged with elegance. However, they lacked complexity of characterisation and their literary content was thin. The style ranged from tragedy to comedy. Scribe wrote over 300 plays. Sardou (1831–1908) was another prolific writer of the style.

In the first act of a well-made play, the initial situation was introduced. This was developed in the second and sometimes third act. The third or fourth act contained the climax or denouement and the piece was completed in the fifth, ensuring all loose ends were tied up. Whilst other playwrights have used this form, including Shakespeare for example, the well-made plays are particularly contrived and indeed written to a 'format'. There is a neatness and tidiness about the way they are developed that is constrictive. Some well-made plays took historical subjects, but most focused upon contemporary bourgeois society; the themes were trivial.

Inevitably this extremely tight structure meant that the plot became preeminent. Whilst it was aesthetically pleasing to have such neat drama, characters were forced to speak lines that were essentially only there to keep the shape of the play intact and characterisation was weak as a result. The plays were often unconvincing. The well-made plays lacked the force of both Romantic drama and the great naturalistic plays to come.

FARCE   This was another popular form of theatre in France (and England) in the 19th century. Farce consists of unsubtle physical and verbal comedy. It flourishes in a moral community because it is anarchical, relying on overturning widely accepted values. The chief characteristics of farce are sexual misadventure, flirtation, verbal abuse and comic despair, which frequently lead to instant decisions and spontaneous action.

The most prolific and famous French farce writers were Feydeau (1862–1921) and Labiche (1815–1888). Labiche wrote nearly sixty plays and helped write about 100 others. Not surprisingly, the plays lack originality and concentrate on reworking old jokes. His most famous is *An Italian Straw Hat* (1851).

Feydeau was the originator of bedroom farces, the descendants of which can still be seen occasionally in London today.

> Feydeau's middle period plays are the archetype of French farce. The principal characters are Parisian bourgeois, their major driving force is extra-connubial lust, and the basic source of the humour is their ever more desperate attempts to avoid being found out. Although no respectable married woman is ever seduced by her husband's best friend, it is not for want of trying on either side. The plots seem to have been constructed by a mad watchmaker, but the status quo is always restored at the end.
>
> [Griffiths, T.R. and Woddis, C., *Theatre Guide* (2nd edn), Bloomsbury, 1991. p.107]

NATURALISM, THE FREE THEATRE AND THE RUSSIAN SCENE
Theatre alters according to the changes in society

As society changes, theatre moves with it, reflecting its needs. So as the excesses and passion of the Romantic movement began to dwindle, the theatre assumed a different tone. A society's preoccupation with survival tends to lead to unrealistic and epic drama about life and death, with simplistic values. When society becomes more preoccupied with the *quality* of life rather than life itself, so the theatre becomes less exaggerated and more concerned with debating the realities of living.

The declamatory style of the early 19th century was moderated, and the words written by novelists and playwrights in the later part of the century were used for expressing the realities of everyday existence; prose took over from verse. Settings and costumes became more associated with reality and scenery often represented real environments.

Naturalism stemmed from a desire to understand further the workings of the human mind

The naturalistic novels of the 19th century led the way for dramatists such as Chekhov, Ibsen and Strindberg. Novelists such as Dickens, Balzac and Flaubert sought to show the real world in their writing. The French novelist Emile Zola (1840–1902) provided the basis for succeeding naturalists in the theatre and in literature, particularly in his preface to *Thérèse Raquin* (1873). Here he advocated that the theatre should be closer to reality and should adopt some of the ideas behind the latest experimental science. Human nature should be scientifically analysed and the arts should present the findings of such analysis, showing the spiritual and emotional reality of human beings. He argued that both Romanticism, with its Gothic happenings, and the bourgeois plays of unconvincing sentiment should be replaced by the new naturalism.

Zola's words were, knowingly or not, adopted by many dramatists. At around the same time, the word psychiatry (with its derivatives) was being introduced to society and emphasis was being placed on the importance of the human psyche. A short time after Zola wrote *Thérèse Raquin*, Sigmund Freud's theories began to alter the way people saw the workings of the human mind. Freud (1856–1939) was immensely important, and the stress on psychoanalysis came to dominate the culture of the western world in the 20th century.

Freud's theories affected the arts and culture

These waves of change were felt right across Europe, including the Scandinavian countries and Russia. A new mode of thinking was in the air of Europe, extending right to its edges. The gradual growth of the study of social sciences, together with the presence of more detailed human analysis in the naturalistic novel, all had their effect on the Russian and Scandinavian theatres, producing playwrights such as Ibsen and Strindberg. Perhaps because the focus of Romantic culture had been in France and Germany, the more remote countries were more susceptible to new ideas and changes in the cultural fashion. However, the new writing remained on the 'fringe' for many years and was not taken up by mainstream French and German theatres.

The 'new' writing remained on the fringe

The new naturalist drama was radically different to Romanticism, melodrama, the well-made play or farce. The speech of the people was used, complete with colloquialisms and pauses. Everyday matters were discussed, as well as topical issues; this was completely different to the remote, heightened, fanciful world of the Romantics. There was no requirement for happy endings, in fact quite the reverse: Miss Julie exits to kill herself (Strindberg's *Miss Julie*), Nora leaves her husband (Ibsen's *A Doll's House*) and Hedda shoots herself (Ibsen's *Hedda Gabler*). Often, a play had no satisfactory conclusion, and the audience were left with the impression that life would go on (usually not particularly happily) outside the play. People's lives were not and could not be packaged into five carefully wrapped acts (as in the well-made plays). The plays addressed topical and controversial issues, which helped prevent their entry into mainstream French and German theatres. Divorce, venereal disease, sex and the class war were topics handled with integrity by the writers but found unsuitable by many mainstream theatres.

Naturalism worked against 'packaging' people's lives

Russia, meanwhile, was dominated by the cultures of Germany and France in the 18th and 19th centuries. French and German were considered to be the languages of cultured and educated people, and many literate Russians chose to speak them. The Tsars were repressive and censorship was harsh, conditions which did not encourage theatrical experimentation.

As in England and France, the wealth of talent in the arts lay with the novelists, notably Turgenev, Dostoevsky and Tolstoy. The novel escapes censorship more easily than the theatre and here artists found expression. Nonetheless, the century saw some fine writing of comic drama by Gogol (*The Government Inspector*, 1842) and Ostrovsky. In addition, both Turgenev and Tolstoy tried their hand at drama, the most well known being Turgenev's *A Month in the Country* (written in 1850, performed in 1872), a delicate play about a woman in love with her daughter's tutor.

This was a quite naturalistic piece and can be seen as a forerunner of Chekhov.

In the 19th century, Russian theatre's main strength was its actors, the best known being Stanislavski's inspiration, Mikhail Shchepkin (1788–1863). Shchepkin was a fine actor who held the truth of the part to be of prime importance (see pp.246–7). These actors often played the classics and plays from France and Germany. It was Anton Chekhov (and Stanislavski, with whom Chekhov worked for a while) who built upon the gradually developing strength of the performance and fully revitalised the tradition of Russian theatre. For a fuller account of this period in Russian theatre which helps give a background to Chekhov particularly, see pp.233–4.

SUMMARY OF KEY POINTS

- **Dominant styles or genres** – Romanticism, well-made plays, farce, naturalism, realism.

- **Subject matter** – Heroic deeds, closeness to nature, liberty and political freedom (Romanticism), human nature.

- **Key practitioners** – Lessing, Goethe, Schiller (German Romanticism); Scribe (French well-made play); Feydeau (French farce); Zola, Antoine, Strindberg, Ibsen, Chekhov (broadly naturalism).

- **Reflection of society's preoccupations** – Liberty, equality and fraternity were idealised in the Romantic period; ludicrous escape from morality (French farce); concerns of everyday life and topical issues in naturalism.

USING YOUR RESEARCH

There is no set pattern for the use of theatrical background research

Having successfully carried out this research, how can you use it when responding to set texts? As with social and cultural research, it is difficult to generalise; the use for the information will entirely depend upon the text and the particular point you wish to make about it.

For example, you might be discussing the power of a particular Ibsen play and how that power was achieved. As well as discussing the use of language and other details gleaned from textual analysis, together with subject matter and methods of presentation, you might refer to the dramatic background in some way. You could briefly mention the earlier Romantic period (and/or other styles) from which the naturalists wished to escape. For example:

'. . . So instead of dramatising the noble deeds of a humanitarian soldier hero as the German Romantic, Schiller, did at the end of the preceding century, Ibsen chose to address the issue of women's status, which had more relevance to the society of the day. The exaggerated and heightened style and subject matter of the Romantics had lasted through the 19th century in the guise of hack melodramas. The move from such Gothic fantasy to the concerns of everyday life written and performed in a naturalistic manner had a tremendous impact, not surprisingly. The resulting power of plays such as *A Doll's House* and *Hedda Gabler* was so strong that the plays were discussed in sermons or newspapers at the time.'

Again, it is most important that the information you use is *relevant*. It is always tempting to 'show off' knowledge, but this will count against you. It is highly unlikely that the information that you research on the social, cultural and theatrical background would ever be used specifically for a whole question. It is far more likely that you would bring in such information to support or frame an answer. It is here that you can demonstrate your breadth and depth of theatrical understanding, but *only* within the context of the question.

1.3.3 PLAYS OF A SIMILAR TIME, GENRE OR THEME

Within reason, it is worthwhile taking the trouble to get to know plays that have something in common with the one you are studying. This will extend your knowledge of the period, genre, theme and/or author and allows you to make firmer judgements about the play under scrutiny.

Of course, it is impossible to give suggestions of further reading for all the texts that might be studied. Instead, we have taken a few key examples from major periods in theatre history and explained what you might look for in other plays that could help your understanding of the selected text.

Before you take this any further, it is worth understanding what we mean by the term 'genre'. A genre is a loose collection of plays that share a number of conventions: their construction might be similar, as might their use of certain devices, their language and/or characterisation and their subject matter or issues. They are of the same 'family species'.

It is important that you identify any clear conventions belonging to a genre to which your text belongs. For example, there are particular conventions associated with the genre of Revenge Tragedy. These are:

- five acts, as laid down by Seneca (Roman, 3BC–AD65) in his original rules of tragedy

- the desire for revenge

- Italianate, or Southern European, settings

- the action takes place behind closed doors, in private worlds

- order is restored at the end of the play

- the notion of what it is to be a courtier is usually highlighted

- ghosts, death, skulls and madness all feature.

You might like to explore this idea further by identifying the conventions belonging to a television genre such as soap opera or detective series.

At the end of the following tables, we summarise the criteria for selecting relevant accompanying texts; this should help you make choices for your own text. A good theatre dictionary is invaluable for helping make such selections. (See suggestions on p.138.)

Selected text	Further texts to consider	Reasons for considering this further text	Additional comments
Sophocles, *Antigone* (c.441BC)	Sophocles, *Oedipus Rex* (c.429BC); *Oedipus at Colonus* (406BC)	These are the plays that complete the immediate Oedipus cycle. The enormity of the tragedy is more impressive when all the plays are considered.	It is worth getting different translations of *Antigone* to distinguish variations.
	Aeschylus, *The Oresteian Trilogy* (458BC)	One of the few other surviving Greek tragedies. Useful to gain a broader perspective of Greek tragedy.	Tony Harrison's adaptation of *The Oresteia* for The National Theatre in 1981 is excellent.
	Berkoff, S., *Greek* (1979)	Berkoff uses the Oedipus legend, shifting it ironically from heightened nobility to blaspheming working class, to comment aggressively on women (particularly mothers) and marriage. An updated version of the myth with strong messages for the modern audience.	
	Euripides, *The Trojan Women* (c.415BC)	Euripides wrote many of his plays with women as the focus (as Antigone); this is a particularly harrowing and tragic work about the effects of the Trojan War on women.	See also *Medea* (431BC) and *The Bacchae* (c.405BC).
	Cocteau, J., *La Machine Infernale* (The Infernal Machine) (1934)	Another version of the Oedipus myth.	
Anon., *Everyman* (c.1500) An English medieval morality play	Anon., *The Castle of Perseverance* (early 15th century)	This is another of the 15th-century medieval morality plays of which *Everyman* is the classic example. Both use allegory to make their point; this is primarily to teach morality.	
	Eliot, T.S., *Murder in the Cathedral* (1935)	This difficult verse drama is supposed to have used medieval plays, particularly *Everyman*, as its inspiration. It is useful to recognise a (fairly) modern play influenced by such an old play.	
	Any of the Mystery Cycles – York, Chester or Wakefield (c.15th century)	These were the most popular form of theatre of the day. Performed by the mysteries (the craft guilds) they 'taught' the Bible to the illiterate masses on wagons in town squares. They are closely linked with the morality plays, as they consist of Bible stories. Useful for understanding the audience's expectation of theatre at the time.	Tony Harrison's adaptation of *The Mysteries* was performed in promenade style at the National Theatre between 1977 and 1985. A very accessible modern update.

Selected text	Further texts to consider	Reasons for considering this further text	Additional comments
Middleton, T. and Rowley, W., *The Changeling* **(1622)**	Webster, J., *The Duchess of Malfi* (1613); Tourneur, *The Revenger's Tragedy,* (1606); Middleton, *Women Beware Women* (1621); Ford, *'Tis Pity She's a Whore* (1632)	All these plays have the typical features of revenge tragedies (see p.119 for a list of these characteristics).	Other revenge tragedies from the Jacobean period would be appropriate.
	Shakespeare, *Measure for Measure* (1604)	Has a similar theme of a (potentially) tragic woman who is the victim of an unstable moral world.	
Wycherley, W., *The Country Wife* **(1675)**	Other Restoration plays e.g. Congreve's *The Way of the World* (1700)	There is a strong similarity of style between all the Restoration comedies, with their satire and robust comedy focusing on the hypocrisy surrounding sex and position in society.	
	Bond, E., *Restoration* (1981)	Here the playwright takes the themes and many of the conventions of the Restoration. The relevance is for a modern audience, however.	
	Wilde, O., *The Importance of Being Earnest* (1895)	Wycherley's play is essentially a Comedy of Manners. So is Wilde's but from another era.	See *The School for Scandal*, below, for another Comedy of Manners.
	Jonson, B. *Volpone,* (1605)	An earlier Jacobean comedy; the subject matter concerns the greed of society and the style is similarly satirical. In this play, all the characters are based on animals.	Worth looking at the more recent Berkoff's *Metamorphosis* (1969) and the Capek brothers' *The Insect Play* (1922) for other plays that use animals (insects) as a metaphor for the human world – and all its faults.
Sheridan, R.B., *The Rivals* **(1775)**	Sheridan, R.B., *The School for Scandal* (1777)	This is Sheridan's most famous play (and the best).	
	Goldsmith, O., *She Stoops to Conquer* (1773)	Goldsmith is the only other playwright of the period who is still played today. This piece is written in a similar style to Sheridan's – a Comedy of Manners.	

Selected text	Further texts to consider	Reasons for considering this further text	Additional comments
	Wycherley, W., *The Country Wife* (1675) [see above] Farquhar, G., *The Beaux Stratagem* (1707)	Both these plays are an earlier version of the same genre and deal with similar subject matters – the differences between town and country society.	
	Gay, J., *The Beggar's Opera* (1728)	One of the only other notable plays of the 18th century. This is also a satire but of a much more boisterous style owing much to the conventions of ballad operas.	Gay's play broke with the stolid sentimental dramas of his time, just as Sheridan forged new ground towards the end of the century.
Gogol, N., *The Government Inspector* (1836)	Pushkin, *Boris Godunov* (1825)	This play was banned for thirty years but it was one of the only worthwhile plays written of the period.	Read any early melodrama to understand the 'traditional' kind of drama on the Russian stage in the early 19th century.
	Chekhov's one-act farces	Chekhov's style in these farces follows something of Gogol's (even more apparent in his play *Marriage* (1842) than in *The Government Inspector*).	
	Ibsen's *Pillars of Society* (1877), Fo, D. *Accidental Death of an Anarchist* (1970), and Flannery, P., *Our Friends in the North* (1982)	All these texts explore the same theme of corruption in local governments and society.	
Wilde, O., *The Importance of Being Earnest* (1895)	See Wycherley, Sheridan and Goldsmith, all mentioned above, for further Comedies of Manners.		
	One of Noel Coward's plays such as *Private Lives* (1930)	Coward follows the same line as Wilde. His sardonic approach to the lives of the upper classes comes close to Wilde, as does his use of epigrams and wit.	
	One of Joe Orton's plays such as *Entertaining Mr Sloane* (1964)	Orton had the same arch humour as Wilde and Coward and similarly soaked his work in sharpness and wit. His plays are far more outrageous – as suits the time in which they were written.	

Selected text	Further texts to consider	Reasons for considering this further text	Additional comments
	Stoppard, T., *Travesties* (1974)	*Travesties* takes much of the structure of *Importance*. It also takes some of the lines, particularly the Gwendolen and Cecily scene.	
Ibsen, H., *Hedda Gabler* (1890)	Ibsen, H., *A Doll's House* (1879)	*A Doll's House* is another of Ibsen's plays that focuses particularly on the sense of imprisonment for a woman. It is also a truly great play.	It is worth reading more of Ibsen's work, particularly plays of the middle period e.g. *Ghosts* (1881), *An Enemy of the People* (1882), or *The Wild Duck* (1884).
	Strindberg, A., *Miss Julie* (1888) or *The Father* (1887)	Strindberg denied, rather ineffectually, that he was influenced by Ibsen's writing. *Miss Julie* and *The Father* are his best naturalistic dramas and take a very different perspective on gender issues.	
	Shaw, G.B., *Mrs Warren's Profession* (1902)	Shaw acknowledges the influence of Ibsen.	
	Caryl Churchill, *Vinegar Tom* (1976); *Top Girls* (1982); Franca Rame, *A Woman Alone* (1977); *Waking Up* (1977); Claire Luckham, *Trafford Tanzi* (1980); Ntozake Shange, *for colored girls who have considered suicide when the rainbow is enuf* (1974)	Various more recent plays which deal with women's issues sympathetically. They incorporate a number of associated topical concerns about class and race as well.	
Chekhov, A., *Three Sisters* (1901)	Ibsen, H., *The Wild Duck* (1884)	Chekhov liked Ibsen's work and was doubtless influenced by him. He said that *The Wild Duck* was his favourite play.	
	Chekhov, A., *The Cherry Orchard* (1904)	All Chekhov's plays contain the sense of decay and self-perpetuating frustration. This is another fine example.	
	Matura, M. *Trinidad Sisters* (1988)	This rewrite of *Three Sisters* looks at the consuming power of the mother country, Trinidad, on the black sisters Irene, Olga and Marsha.	

Selected text	Further texts to consider	Reasons for considering this further text	Additional comments
O'Casey, S., *Shadow of a Gunman* (1923)	O'Casey, S., *Juno and the Paycock* (1924) and *The Plough and the Stars* (1926)	Both these plays are set inside Irish tenement blocks also and both address the effect of the Irish troubles in the 1920s on Dublin's residents. They are slightly more mature than *Gunman*	It is worth reading something by J.M. Synge e.g. *The Playboy of the Western World* (1907) to understand the recent context of Irish writing. Also see W.B.Yeats's work such as the *Cuchulain* plays for a further contrast.
	Friel, B., *Freedom of the City* (1973)	A more contemporary play (and on Northern Ireland) concerning the Troubles and the effects on a group of civil rights protesters.	
	Finnegan, S., *Act of Union* (1980)	Another recent Irish play on the effect of the Troubles on Belfast residents.	Also worth looking at the work of Anne Devlin.
Brecht, B., *The Resistible Rise of Arturo Ui* (1941)	Brecht, B., *The Measures Taken* (1930) and *Mother Courage and her Children* (1941)	These are two plays that offer very different Brechtian writing (even though *Mother Courage* was the same year). *Measures* is a didactic piece and *Mother Courage* is epic.	Both these texts also offer a view on the individual and politics.
	Theatre Workshop, *Oh What A Lovely War* (1963)	This is one of the best examples of Brecht-influenced texts available and we can see Brechtian techniques in use here.	
	Hampton, C., *Tales from Hollywood* (1982)	This play looks at European exiles in Hollywood at the time of *Ui*. Brecht appears as an unsympathetic character.	
Miller, A., *Death of a Salesman* (1949)	Miller, A., *The Crucible* (1953)	Whilst *Death of a Salesman* attacks American capitalism, pointing to the destruction it causes, *The Crucible* attacks the American communist 'witchhunts' in the 1950s by taking the witchhunts of the 17th century as its story. Both plays harshly condemn society.	
	Mamet, D., *Glengarry Glen Ross* (1983)	This play also attacks the American dream and shows us something of the reality behind the hype.	
	Wilson, A., *Fences* (1985)	This black American playwright has written a play similar to Miller's in that it implicitly criticises 1950s America. This time it is centred on racial issues.	

Selected text	Further texts to consider	Reasons for considering this further text	Additional comments
Beckett, S., *Waiting for Godot* (1955)	A Eugene Ionesco play such as *The Bald Prima Donna* (1950)	A further example of what has become known as the Theatre of the Absurd. Whilst it is inappropriate to characterise Beckett's work too firmly, the Absurd is a useful catch-all.	Also read Beckett's *Endgame* (1957) and/or *Happy Days* (1961).
	A Jean Genet play e.g. *The Maids* (1946)	Genet too has been placed into the same genre. His plays are even darker than Beckett's.	
	Stoppard, T., *Rosencrantz and Guildenstern Are Dead* (1966)	Stoppard's play is clearly influenced by Beckett's. The irrationality of existence for two men waiting for somebody or some people to arrive forms the central focus of both plays. Stoppard's play is an extension of the Absurd.	
Osborne, J., *Look Back in Anger* (1956)	Any of the plays of that time by the other 'angry young men': Try Wesker's *Chicken Soup with Barley* (1958); Arden's *Live Like Pigs* (1958); Waterhouse and Hall's *All Things Bright and Beautiful* (1962)	All these plays show the new social realism in the theatre where playwrights were kicking against society.	It is worth reading some of the social realism of the early 20th century as well, such as plays by Ibsen, Galsworthy and Shaw.
	Osborne, J., *The Entertainer* (1957)	Also looking at the moral decline and stupor of British life; a better play, in fact.	
	Osborne, J., *Dejavu* (1991)	The 'sequel' to *Look Back in Anger*. The protagonist Jimmy Porter is a generation older. Worth a glimpse.	
Weiss, P., *The Persecution and Assassination of Jean-Paul Marat as Performed by the Inmates of the Asylum of Charenton under the Direction of the Marquis de Sade (Marat/Sade)* (1964)	Artaud, A., *The Jet of Blood* (1925)	Weiss was heavily influenced by Artaud; this was particularly evident in the original Peter Brook production of the play for the RSC. It is worth reading this extraordinary four-page play therefore.	In addition, obviously it is worth becoming familiar with the theories and practice of Artaud (see pp.256–91) and Brook (see pp.363–408).
	Look at the work of contemporary directors Robert Wilson and Robert le Page.	These directors work in the same scale as Weiss.	

Selected text	Further texts to consider	Reasons for considering this further text	Additional comments
	Mnouchkine, A. (of Theatre de Soleil), *1789*, (1970)	This is the most important play about the French Revolution in recent years.	
	The works of Arden and Osborne for example (see above).	Worth looking at to understand another, and more conventional, aspect of British theatre of the period.	Edward Bond is another dramatist worth reading. Writing at the time, there is a similar sense of pushing boundaries by showing violence e.g. in *Saved* (1965).

Note that we have deliberately not included any of Shakespeare's plays, as the list would be so long. For any Shakespeare it is worth reading a Marlowe play, e.g. *Dr Faustus* (c.1588) or *Edward II* (c.1592), and a Jonson, e.g. *Volpone* (1605) or *The Alchemist* (1610). Particular Shakespeares would clearly point to other relevant plays. For example, if you were studying *The Merchant of Venice*, you would want to read Marlowe's *The Jew of Malta* (c.1589); if you were studying *Hamlet*, you would be well advised to read something from the Revenge Tragedy genre, such as Kyd's *The Spanish Tragedy* (1587) or Tourneur's *The Revenger's Tragedy* (1606).

SELECTING RELEVANT ACCOMPANYING TEXTS

Plays of a similar style or genre and the same period
By making comparisons with plays of a similar genre and period you will become increasingly aware of how the writer of the specific text you are studying reflects and manipulates the accepted conventions of a dramatic genre or style.

In the table above for example, several selections were from the same genre and period: see Webster's *The Duchess of Malfi* (1613) and the suggested revenge tragedies. These all use the same conventions and themes including death, revenge, lust, villainy, even hewn-off parts of the body. See also Beckett's *Waiting for Godot* and other plays from the Theatre of the Absurd genre.

Plays of a similar style or genre from a different period
These would share conventions, as above, but would come from a different time. This is not very common, however.

For example, in the table above see Wilde's *The Importance of Being Earnest* and the references to other Comedies of Manners across the centuries.

Plays with the same story
Again, this is not a frequent happening, but reading another playwright's treatment of the same story in a completely different setting can highlight facets of your text that you had not focused upon before.

Examples of this might be Sophocles' *Oedipus* trilogy and Berkoff's *Greek*, or Chekhov's *Three Sisters* and Matura's *Trinidad Sisters*.

Plays with a similar theme

It is quite common for dramatists to address similar themes. This can broaden your understanding of dominant issues which have recurred throughout the centuries. It is particularly useful to demonstrate your awareness of such cross-fertilisation, as it will make it clear that you are not regarding your text in isolation.

Ibsen's *A Doll's House* or *Hedda Gabler* and more recent plays such as Luckham's *Trafford Tanzi* are good examples of plays that are related in this way.

USING YOUR RESEARCH

As with all background research, information concerning similar texts will only be used in particular circumstances. However, drawing comparisons with other texts and being able to analyse and evaluate that comparison will demonstrate that you have a thorough and impressive awareness of modes of theatre. This question is an example of where such information might be useful:

Which do you consider to be the most significant themes of Ibsen's *Hedda Gabler*? Discuss how these might be interpreted in performance.

One part of your response might read:

> 'The theme of feminism or the subordinate role of women in society is central to Ibsen's play. Hedda's final decision to shoot herself to escape from male oppression (Tesman's and Brack's) was appalling to many of the play's audience when it was first produced and the presence of such female behaviour on the stage was thought to be shocking. Whilst Ibsen had highlighted this cause in *A Doll's House* in 1879, for example, other playwrights of the time resented his championing of the female cause. Strindberg's *The Father* of 1887 gives us a very different perspective on the place of women in marriage; here we are shown a wife, Laura, who destroys her husband. The status of women was clearly a significant theme at the end of the 19th century.'

You might select other themes to discuss in addition to this. You would then, of course, move on to discussing how the theme can be recognised in the text and suggest methods for realising this in performance.

This is an example of using knowledge of contemporary plays with a similar theme. Another opportunity would occur if the question asked you to identify the function of certain characters in the text. If the text belonged to a clear *genre*, where the characters always had particular functions, such as melodrama, you could briefly discuss the general function of such characters within the genre as a whole, with specific reference to similar texts. For example, in discussing the function of the hero, William, in Jarrold's *Black Eye'd Susan*, you could refer to the similar role of Mark Ingestre in *Sweeney Todd, the Demon Barber of Fleet Street*. A hero in melodrama is a young man of extreme good looks who has a number of functions. He is in love with the heroine yet often parted from her, thus provoking her to impassioned, emotional speeches; he is the enemy of the archetypal villain; he is enormously moral, making lengthy speeches supporting this; he is usually patriotic to the extreme, encouraging the audience to follow suit. Both William and Mark Ingestre match this description fully; there are plenty of examples from both texts which could support your response about the hero's (and thus William's) function in the play.

1.3.4 SUMMARY

There is one further area of background research that may be of use to you and which touches upon all three areas identified in this section. Depending on the period you are studying, it may well be worth your while researching the **physical theatre spaces** and **methods of staging** that were contemporary with the play. For example, if you are studying a text from the ancient Greek period, you will need to be fully conversant with the conventions of Greek theatres, including use of the orchestra, skene, episkene, masks, actor and chorus and the various other elements appropriate to the original staging of Greek theatre.

You will need to make decisions about the staging of your set text. With a period text, part of this process will include a consideration of the staging of the day. You will need to demonstrate that you are aware of the staging conventions the playwright had in mind and that you have decided whether or not to follow them. Your decision for this choice of staging would have to be justified, of course.

In addition, if the period is distinctive in its particular methods of staging, it is quite likely that you will be asked a question specifically about the staging of the day. This is most appropriate for the major periods of world theatre, namely Greek and Roman theatre, mystery cycles, Elizabethan, Restoration, Victorian and modern theatre. There are many straightforward theatre staging texts to help in this research. See the bibliography on pp.135–8, particularly at the end of the 'Support Research' section.

All background research is valuable. It is time-consuming and demanding, but it adds significantly to the breadth and depth of your responses concerning set texts. To study a set text in isolation is rather like trying to describe one particular tree without ever having seen another one. How would you know if it was tall, bushy, shady, and so on? A full description and understanding needs to include comparisons to other trees (plays). If you work through your text using textual analysis methods and developing fully rounded character studies, you could well achieve adequate answers. They will not necessarily demonstrate a comprehensive understanding of the theatrical process, however, as you will not be discussing the text in its context.

For all these elements of research, it is essential that you do not include information at random: rather use none at all than be irrelevant. Questions on full texts have to be tightly structured and focused; as soon as you attempt simply to show off your knowledge without any focus, you will be submitting a weak answer.

1.4 *Final activities and questions*

ACTIVITIES Using a text you are studying:

Decide what the major concerns of the playwright are. For example, are there clear themes and issues? Does he or she wish to pinpoint an injustice in society? Is a 'message' hidden or overt? Are the characters important? Does the dramatist wish the relationship between the characters to be of key importance in the play?

Decide whether you would wish to produce the play echoing all the concerns of the playwright or whether you would focus upon *particular* concerns more than others. You may wish to concentrate on an unusual viewpoint of the text, but this *must* be fully justified. Consider the audience when you are making these decisions. Who are they? Are they likely to appreciate your interpretation – whether you are picking up the authorial voice or taking your own line?

Does all, or any of, your background research have an impact upon this decision? How? If not, why not? For example, will you stage it as if in the time it was written? (This will take account of other plays of the time, methods of staging, etc.) What influence does the context that informed the writer have on *your* production?

Now consider staging the play. Justify all your responses to the following questions, using the text as far as possible:

- What is your choice of performance venue and why?
- What is your overall design concept and why?
- Design and draw up your set plan(s). Explain your decisions.
- Is there an overall costume theme? Design some of the major costumes and draw these. Explain your decisions.
- Make notes for the lighting of the piece. Discuss your choices.
- Are there any special technical effects? Where and why?
- Is there any other important aspect of staging, e.g. props, sound, make-up?

Select particular moments in the play which could be used to highlight your interpretation. These may be very short – only a few lines. Rehearse these using others to play the characters. Consider the proxemics, the blocking, actions, gestures, facial expressions, use of voice and pace. Describe this afterwards in written form.

Select one or two key characters (if characterisation is important in your text). Find key moments in the text for those characters and rehearse these moments, as above. Write this up as a particular instance of how to interpret one character.

Devise rehearsal sessions to explore the themes, the directorial interpretation, the characters, the background context, the style, the pace and tension and vocal work, where these are particularly appropriate for your text. Write these up.

By working in this way, you will be continually addressing the text as a blueprint for performance. You will then find that you are responding to questions from a theatrical perspective and not a literary perspective; this is most important.

We can only give very broad frameworks here without specific reference to texts. For further guidance on particular texts, see the sample material published each year by the various examination boards or their Marking Schemes, which refer to answers from the previous year's examination. (In addition, these are extremely useful for understanding central issues about the plays that are not always found in critical textbooks.)

Below we give three typical questions and a possible structure for each answer. Please be aware that there would be many alternative answers; these are not prescriptive.

The dots are in place of the name of the text; it should be possible to insert the name of one of your set texts here.

ACTIVITY   **Discuss the value of undertaking historical background research for directing a production of . . . .**

POINTS TO CONSIDER
- You are asked to respond as a *director*; this means you must have a coherent picture of a production of the text.

- Do you need to use all the types of historical research? Justify the areas you do need.

- Beware of just *listing* the research appropriate to the play. The key words are *discuss the value*. In other words, you must say how you would use such research.

- Remember to refer your points to the play in performance; it is too easy for this to become an English Literature or History answer, otherwise.

A DETAILED ANALYSIS

Introduction
Comment on why historical research is important for a historical text (theatre as a sign of the times, theatrical staging methods, overall understanding of the period, etc.).

Main body
For each section in the main body of the essay, take a specific area of historical research. For each section explain:

- what type of information would be relevant
- where this information could be found

- how you would use it as a director
- what it would bring to the overall production.

For example, one area of historical research might be **research into housing details, style of furniture, etc.**

- This information could be found in paintings, descriptions and diagrams in history books, descriptions in novels, appropriate museums.
- The research could be used for work with the designer and company in creating an authentic setting within the possibilities of your chosen venue. Refer to stage directions and hints in the script that provide clues to the setting, i.e. link your research with the script.
- This would help the overall production by clearly indicating to the audience the surroundings and atmosphere of the times.

Another area of historical research might be **research into major world events that preoccupied the society of the period.**

- This information could be found in newspapers (if appropriate), diaries and original documents in history books.
- It could be used for improvisation work with the actors to help them understand some of the concerns of their characters; for programme notes to inform the audience of the author's context; and to help the company understand some of the references in the text (use relevant quotes here).
- It would underpin the production with the preoccupations of the author.

This format would continue for subsequent sections, suggesting a different type of research in each section.

Conclusion

Explain why you have chosen only certain areas of research (this will depend very much upon your text.) Point out the problems of doing this production *without* such research. You might change tack by suggesting that another approach to the text might require no historical research, for example if the production was taken completely out of its context. Could this be justified?

ACTIVITY   **Discuss the effectiveness of the author's dramatic methods in.......**

POINTS TO CONSIDER

- Refer closely to the text for your response.
- Think as broadly as you can about that rather elusive term, 'dramatic methods'. It simply means everything the author writes that makes the play a piece of drama. For example: approach (e.g. naturalistic, expressionistic); particular key moments of intensity; the form of characterisation; the use of language (natural, absurd, poetic); the author's suggestions for set, lighting, costumes and/or technical effects; unusual ideas given (e.g. the projected slides and tickertape board in *Oh! What A Lovely War*, or the choreographed movements in some of Berkoff's plays); the use of the subject matter. These suggested 'dramatic methods' will make more sense when you relate them to a play; it is likely that only some of them will be relevant.

- Discuss how the author's dramatic methods would be realised in production.

- Consider what impact they will have upon the audience. There is no point in just saying they are there; you are asked to discuss the *effectiveness*. You can't do this without reference to expected audience reception.

- Be selective about the 'dramatic methods'. You may not be able to include everything; this will depend upon the play.

A DETAILED *Introduction*
ANALYSIS Describe how you believe the dramatist wanted to affect his or her audience. Suggest the key dramatic methods he or she uses to accomplish this (see suggestions under 'Points to consider' above).

Main body
In each section of the main body of the essay, take one form of dramatic method. For each one, explain:
- what the dramatic method is
- where we see it in the text
- how this could be realised effectively
- how you would want the audience to respond
- how this interrelates with the whole text or contributes to the whole.

For example, one dramatic method might be the absurd nature of the dialogue.
- Give some particularly striking examples of such dialogue from the text.
- Describe how this could be emphasised on stage – by tone of voice, gesture, etc. (You may have time to describe only one or two examples.)
- Describe what you would expect the audience to assume or pick up from these examples of performed text.
- How does the absurd dialogue function within the whole play? Is the author making a general comment about the absurdity of existence? (This is entirely dependent upon the play, of course.)

Another dramatic method might be particular moments of intensity.
- Give a couple of examples from the text and select one to discuss.
- Describe *some* of the staging of this moment to enhance the intensity, e.g. proxemics, pauses and silences, levels of voice.
- Describe the expected audience reaction.
- Put the moment of intensity into its context in the rest of the play. For example, does the dramatist use moments of tension sparingly and if so, why? Alternatively, do these occur fairly regularly within the overall structure of the play? What is the resulting effect?

This format would continue for subsequent sections, suggesting a different dramatic method in each section.

Conclusion
Give your thoughts about the interweaving of topic, themes or issues with dramatic methods. Do the two (content and form) match? It would be useful to bring in a quote, perhaps from a newspaper review or a

critical text, giving an overarching comment about the play that would be an appropriate summary.

ACTIVITY   **Select one character from....... Discuss the challenges of playing this character and explain how you would develop the role.**

POINTS TO CONSIDER
- Select a particularly significant and challenging character to make your answer more meaningful.
- Approach this from the perspective of the actor.
- Remember to discuss the role as part of a whole production.

A DETAILED ANALYSIS

Introduction
State which character you have chosen and *why* you have made this decision. What does this character bring to the play and why do you think she or he is particularly challenging? In other words, what *function* does the character have in the play?

Further introduction
What are your own production objectives and how does this character fit into these objectives?

Main body
Describe the specific challenges of the role, particularly in the light of your stated directorial interpretation. For example, the character acts as a catalyst; provides a sounding board; speaks with the author's voice on certain issues; is the chief initiator of certain action; acts as an observer and commentator; has a number of awkward relationships; is the most respected and humane of the characters in the play; has a difficult physical and/or vocal role; has to mature noticeably; has little detail within the text upon which to build a characterisation; is presented in a different style to most other characters (e.g. symbolic or surreal in a mainly naturalistic world), etc. This will entirely depend upon the text and the character.

Use examples from the text at all times, explaining how each aspect of the character is represented through the words and actions used.

Describe the various rehearsal techniques you would use to help you address these challenges. You may not be able to discuss all the points you have made above; be selective, but justify this selection. An example of a rehearsal technique for a role which is the voice of the author might be:

> 'I would improvise being on a tea chest at Speakers' Corner in Hyde Park and having to talk in a running stream about the views that my character (and the author, we assume) holds. This would require me to expand beyond the words in the text and form a well-rounded argument, particularly if the rest of the company act as agitators and hecklers. My conviction should become evident as the exercise continues.'

The question asks how you would *develop* the role. You should therefore devise rehearsal methods that suggest a build-up, both according to the most important aspects of the role and also leading up to the production.

This might involve moving from improvisation work to script work to final rehearsal suggestions, if appropriate.

Give one or two examples of moments in the text explaining how you would actually perform them as a result of the development of the role.

Conclusion

Describe how you would want the audience to react to this character as a result of this preparation work and within the production concept. Add appropriate quotes about the character (perhaps from another character, a critical text or a review) to support your own view of the role.

1.5 *Bibliography for Exploring texts*

PRESENTING THEATRE

Acting and directing

Mackey, S. (ed.), *Practical Theatre: A Post-16 Approach*, Stanley Thornes, 1997.
Has particular chapters on, for example, acting, directing and design. Provides a number of practical activities to engage with these areas.

McCafferey, M. A., *Phaidon Theatre Manual – Directing A Play*, Phaidon, 1988.

Miles-Brown, J., *Directing Drama*, London, Peter Owen Ltd, 1994 (reprinted with revisions).

Taylor, D., *Directing Plays*, A & C Black, 1996.
These four texts are at the appropriate level. They have a similar content as they look at the history and context of directors and the process of directing, including methods of directing. They each have different advantages. They work with fairly traditional directing methods but offer a solid, rigorous hands-on base for student directors.

Auslander, Philip, *From Acting to Performance: Essays in Modernism and Postmodernism*, Routledge, 1997.
This is an academic text that charts theatre practice from the 1960s to the 1980s. It includes reference to the work of Artaud, Brook, Grotowski *et al.* May be helpful to teachers, particularly the first chapter.

Boal, A., *Games for Actors and Non-Actors*, Routledge, 1992.
Johnstone, K. *Impro*, Methuen, !982.
These two are classic improvisation texts helpful for exercises to use as a director or actor.

Johnstone, K. *Impro for Storytellers*, Faber and Faber, 1999.
The latest book from this master of improvisation. Not as usesful as the first but grounded in his understanding of the art of improvisation.

Johnston, Chris, *House of Games: Making Theatre from Everyday Life*, Nick Hern Books Ltd, 1998.
Another very useful improvisation book with a number of traditional and new drama exercises within a clear, thoughtful analysis of improvisation.

Hagen, U., *Respect for Acting*, Macmillan, 1973.
A classic acting text. Still excellent.

Design
This is a comprehensive bibliography. If you were to buy only one text from each design area, we suggest the ones asterisked.

Buchman, H., *Stage Make-Up*, Watson-Guptill Publications, 1989.
A classic text on make-up.

Carlson, V. and Carlson, S., *Professional Lighting Handbook* (2nd edition), Focal Press 1991.
One up from the Reid stage-lighting book, this is as it says – a professional text. Therefore, only really useful as a reference book for those students who are following a specialist stage-lighting route.

★**Corey, I.,** *The Face is a Canvas: The Design and Techniques of Theatrical Makeup*, Anchorage Press, 1990.
Exactly as it says!

★**Coult, T. and Kershaw, B.,** *Engineers of the Imagination: The Welfare State Handbook* (2nd edition), Methuen, 1996.
Excellent book for large-scale, unusual craft design and making.

Goodwin, J., *British Theatre Design: The Modern Age*, Weidenfield and Nicolson, 1989.
Excellent for pictures; not so good on theory.

Hoggett, C., *Stage Crafts*, A & C Black, 1978.
Solid, reliable text on set, props etc. but out of date.

★**James, T.,** *The Prop Builder's Molding and Casting Handbook*, Betterway Books, 1989.
Quite precise. Useful to have available for those who are interested in prop-making.

Kaye, D. and Lebrecht, J., *Sound and Music for the Theatre*, Back Stage, 1992.
Reliable, detailed book.

★**Kimber, K. and Wood, D.,** *Stages in Design: Assignments for the Performing Arts*, Hodder and Stoughton, 1994.
Very good for an introductory hands-on approach for students in all design areas.

★**Mayer, D.,** *Costume and Make Up*, Phaidon, 1993.
Sensible, good book to have available.

Motley, *Designing and Making Stage Costumes*, Herbert Press, 1992.
Still the classic costume text.

Pilbrow, R., *Stage Lighting*, Nick Herne Books, 1993.
Another good lighting book.

★**Reid, F.,** *Designing for the Theatre: Costumes, Props, Settings, Lighting*, A & C Black, 1989.
Small book, quite hands on. Gives a reasonable grounding of an approach to stage design.

★**Reid, F.** *The Stage Lighting Handbook*, (5th edition) A & C Black, 1996.
This is still the classic stage-lighting book. Regularly updated, it provides a solid introduction to lighting.

Rumsey, F. and McCormick, T., *Sound and Recording: An Introduction* (3rd edition), Focal Press, 1997.
A very dense text indeed. This would be appropriate only for sound specialists.

Visual History of Costume series, Batsford, 1992.
Looks at costumes century by century. A swift way of understanding the changing fashions.

★Walne, G., *Sound for the Theatre*, A & C Black, 1990.
Still a good book despite changes in technology.

FINDING THE MEANING AND TEXTUAL ANALYSIS

(See the dictionaries below, also, particularly the Pavis.)
Griffiths, M. and Hemming C., *A Sense of the Dramatic*, Collins Educational, 1984.
Useful for unseen extracts. May have to get it via a second-hand system.

Mabley, E., *Dramatic Construction: An Outline of Basic Principles*, Chilton Books, 1972.
(Contains sections on *Oedipus*, *The School for Scandal*, *The Cherry Orchard*, *Juno and the Paycock*, *Godot*, *Marat/Sade* and others.) For text analysis and understanding of dramatic structure – unbeatable. Very thorough and detailed.

Mayne, A. and Shuttleworth, J., *Considering Drama*, Hodder and Stoughton, 1986.
General drama book addressing a range of aspects including 'dramatic irony', 'staging', 'interpretation', 'the conventions of drama'. Quite long-winded.

Wallis, M. and Shepherd, S., *Studying Plays*, Arnold, 1998.
Excellent book for teachers, although really an undergraduate text.

SUPPORT RESEARCH

Foulkes, R., *Teach Yourself Theatre*, Hodder and Stoughton, 1999.
This is a highly accessible, slim book that charts the history of theatre in a user-friendly style. It is a brief version of the Banks book (see below) and would be a useful reference for all theatre students. It looks at each period of theatre history brusquely locating key figures, styles and companies in their context.

All the following are good for overviews of theatre history:
Banks, R. A. and Marson, P., *Drama and Theatre Arts* (2nd edition), Hodder and Stoughton, 1998.
Still pretty thorough but very much rooted in theatre and not so much in the cultural context.

Brockett, O. G., *History of Theatre* (6th edition), Allyn and Bacon, 1991.
Has a broader view – American. Covers a great deal.

Cottrell, T., *Evolving Stages: A Layman's Guide to 20th-Century Theatre*, The Bristol Press, 1991.
As it says!

Shepherd, S. and Womack, P., *English Drama: A Cultural History*, Blackwell, 1996.
At last, a book that overtly places theatre in its cultural context. It is a university text so it is best used and filtered by teachers for the particular period studied.

Southern, R., *The Seven Ages of the Theatre*, Faber and Faber, 1962.
Very old now but the first sections on ritual and the growth of the player are still good.

Styan, J., *Modern Drama in Theory and Practice*, 3 vols, Cambridge University Press, 1981.
Still excellent for the first three-quarters of the 20th century.

Wickham, G., *A History of the Theatre* (2nd edition), Phaidon, 1992.
Still the best. Also bears in mind the cultural context of theatre – more so than many others. If you buy only one, make it this one.

Leacroft, R. and Leacroft, H., *Theatre and Playhouse: An Illustrated Survey of Theatre Building from Ancient Greece to the Present Day*, Methuen, 1984.

Oenslager, D., *Stage Design: Four Centuries of Scenic Invention*, Thames and Hudson, 1975.

Southern, R., *Changeable Scenery: Its Origin and Development in the British Theatre*, Faber and Faber, 1952.

These three books will all help with the history of theatre architecture, design and staging. Most specifications now ask for a knowledge of this area and it is not always easy to find. These three, even though they are old, are very useful May have to be borrowed from the British Library.

For further research into past stagings of particular texts (as required by the EdExcel specification), we advise you to contact the Education Department at the Covent Garden Theatre Museum. The museum has archives of past productions across the centuries.

DICTIONARIES

Griffiths, T. R. and Woddis, C., *Bloomsbury Theatre Guide* (2nd edition), Bloomsbury Publishing, 1991.
Excellent.

Hartnoll, P. and Found, P., *The Concise Oxford Companion to the Theatre*, Oxford University Press, 1992.
Perfectly solid.

Pavis, P., *Dictionary of the Theatre: Terms, Concepts and Analysis* (trans. Shantz, C.), University of Toronto Press, 1998.
Useful for a range of theatre terms from Abstraction, Absurd and Acts to Pantomine, Parabasis and Parable to Well-Made Play, Women's Theatre and Word Scenery. Highly recommended!

Banham, M., *The Cambridge Guide to Theatre* (2nd edition), Cambridge University Press, 1995.
Another very good theatre dictionary to have available.

PART 2

Reviewing Productions

2.0 *Introduction*

Analysis of contemporary
productions should
demonstrate a full
understanding of text,
production and reception

An understanding of theatre revolves around a full appreciation of **text, production** and **reception**. You will have addressed this in relation to presenting theatre and textual analysis, discussing your own ideas for the production and anticipated reception of certain texts. To demonstrate a comprehensive theatrical understanding, you need to be able to analyse and comment critically upon theatre in performance.

You will need to develop a
distinct system for
performance analysis

Analysing theatre performances for examination purposes will be very different from just going to the theatre. You will be writing detailed critical analysis, which requires a far more rigorous process than simply watching a production. This system will be different from the procedure followed by any other group of people going to the theatre, such as the average theatre-goer, the academic literary critic and even the theatre critic.

You will develop and use this system specifically for writing such detailed analysis. However, the habit of analysis that you form will stay with you to some extent and will affect your future theatre-going. You will retain much of your critical faculty and will be able to appreciate fully all aspects of a theatre production because you have gained an analytical eye. (Remember that this may refer to a positive analysis just as much as to a negative analysis.) Equally important, you will gain insights into the nature of theatre and what is possible in the production of plays that will help you in other aspects of your work on theatre.

A basic rule for watching theatre productions is to remain open-minded and to keep your critical faculties awake to receive all sorts of different messages from the production. In this context you are responding as the **receiver** of the text and the production. You need to be open to that reception. You need to be awake – literally – and quick to take in the various signals that the production team are sending to the audience.

Be alert and prepared when
analysing productions

In addition, you need to be able to differentiate between **text** and **production**. A particular move or action with a prop may impress you in the performance you are watching and you may feel that this moment has summed up the character's attitude in the scene. You may attribute this to the **production**, whereas in fact this action is already suggested by the dramatist in the **text**. To recognise this sort of fine detail, you clearly need to be alert and *prepared*, i.e. you will need to know the text, where one exists.

This part of the book introduces you to the process of approaching performance analysis, suggests a system to enable that analysis to take place and gives you examples of notes in response to this system. Therefore Part 2 comprises:

2.1 Analysing productions

2.2 A system for performance analysis

2.3 Sample notes using the system

2.4 Questions and suggested frameworks for answers on contemporary productions

2.1 *Analysing productions*

Allow time to build up performance analysis skills

There are various methods of approaching work on contemporary productions. Here we suggest just one possibility, which can be followed fully or in part. Whatever method you choose for theatre performance analysis, it is wise to allow a gradual and incremental build up of experience and to ensure that you review several different productions. Because there appears to be no 'subject matter' or syllabus to cover, it is easy for this area to appear insubstantial.

Below, we give a step-by-step guide to approaching the analysis of contemporary productions. Steps **1–7** lead up to and include the first production you see; on page 146 we give you some general points to consider after your visit.

STEP 1

If there is a production that is common to your group, that every person has seen (or even in which they have participated), take this as a production to discuss. Otherwise, a television play would be acceptable for this initial discussion. (Note that television plays are *not* acceptable for a full review.) You may choose to discuss a production of one of your set texts for this exercise, as you will be familiar with the text, which is useful. (Again, it is inadvisable to choose a production of a set text for your examination response as it signifies a limitation of experience.)

ACTIVITIES

Discuss the purpose of theatre, as suggested in the general introduction of this book (pp.xi–xiii), with this production in mind and using it as a focus. For example, how far does the dramatist seek to entertain and enlighten us? What are the main themes of the piece?

Then move on to discussing the *interpretation* of the text. This is why it is a good idea to know the text first. How does the production help you to interpret the text? Does it bring out certain aspects of the text more than others? How does it do this – by emphasis of speech? Certain actions? Lighting emphasis? Set design?

STEP 2

Whether the production is a circus, a piece of street theatre or a Shakespeare play performed in a traditional thrust-stage theatre, it will use certain elements of performance to signal meaning to an audience, and these need to be identified.

The various elements of production are explained in section 2.2. It is worth becoming familiar with the topics covered in section 2.2 at this stage. These are:

2.2.1   The place of performance
2.2.2   The performance space
2.2.3   The audience space and the actors' space
2.2.4   The set
2.2.5   Lighting
2.2.6   Sound
2.2.7   Costume
2.2.8   The actor and his/her performance
2.2.9   The text/non-text and directorial interpretation
2.2.10   Overall impact and audience reception
2.2.11   Future performance analysis

ACTIVITIES   Understanding the notion of signalling meaning to the audience through elements of production can best be achieved by taking a short piece of script and directing it yourself. It is unlikely that you will have all the possible elements of production available to you. You may be reliant upon the actors' performance. It is still possible to interpret a text, however, and to justify your decisions about blocking, positions, tone of voice and so on.

Then make decisions about how you would direct a full realisation if this were possible, for example what the set would look like, lighting options, the position of the audience, the type of theatre space, the costumes. Explain what you are attempting to convey with each of these elements.

STEP 3

For the first production that you analyse, you may find it best to see a good production of an accessible text. It is often easier to analyse the production if it has a clear directorial slant. (This latter is not always possible, of course.)

ACTIVITIES   Read the playtext of a production that you are going to see in the theatre. As a group, discuss possible methods of staging the text that would highlight certain themes. For example, how do you think the set should look? What overall impact would you expect an audience to receive and is there anything that would particularly help this, such as use of music?

Note key 'moments' in the text to look out for in the production you are intending to visit.

STEP 4

It is often useful to have some help in identifying the directorial objectives or interpretation of the text. Sometimes these cannot be clearly understood just from seeing the show, particularly when you are new to analysing theatre. It can help to get some confirmation of the director's line of thinking. Sometimes programmes help, by giving you quotes or short articles that highlight the intentions of the production. If it is a piece of street theatre or something else non-traditional, however, this might be impossible. (This is one reason why it is sensible to see something relatively conventional for your first piece of analysis.)

ACTIVITIES   Try to organise a discussion with the director. This could be extremely difficult, but it is worth trying. (Depending upon the production, you may decide it would be better to meet after seeing the play, as your questions will be more informed. If this is the case, it is worth allowing yourself the interval, if there is one, or some minutes after the show to frame some pertinent questions.) Try to find out what the director is hoping to achieve. If the piece is directed as a co-operative venture, you will want to speak to some, or all, of the company, because there will not be a single director. Occasionally, theatre companies arrange just such question and answer sessions as a 'special'.

Approach a discussion with the director or company from an analytical viewpoint. Assess their stated aims in terms of what you observe from the production.

STEP 5

Before you watch the production, it is worth allocating particular areas from the system outlined in section 2.2 to different people in your group so that each person does not have too much to concentrate upon in this first piece of analysis. Thoroughly read the topic in 2.2 which you are allocated. As we point out, this is not so much a questionnaire as a guide to help you read the signals of the production.

ACTIVITIES   As you watch the production, you are likely to find it useful to have a notepad and pen to scribble notes on the production element that you have selected. (For examples of such notes, see pp.156–62.) Most conventional theatres still operate with the auditorium in blackout during the performance; this makes note-taking quite difficult but you soon adapt to writing 'blind'. However, it would be impossible to retain in your head all the points of which you become aware during the performance. Try to be aware of other audience members and be as discreet as possible.

Whilst you are making notes about one specific element of production, it is also worth noting other things that particularly strike you.

STEP 6

ACTIVITY   When you meet as a group, discuss all the elements of production, adding to your notes any comments that other people have to offer about your area of analysis.

Whilst this is a useful method of working at the initial stages of performance analysis, you would be ill-advised to have a 'group response' (i.e.

one that is devised collaboratively) for any future productions. The examination demands an individual response; you will want to ensure that you develop *your own* views in your notes.

STEP 7

It is important that your 'first impression' notes are rewritten. Although you only have one aspect of the production to write about from this first visit, it is still worth practising the rewriting process. These rewritten notes will take into consideration your *reflection* upon the piece: your thoughts about *why* certain things were done in a particular way and what effect this had upon the audience. An example of *rewritten* notes is on pp.163–70.

ACTIVITY   Write up your notes as suggested here. Add appropriate quotes from the text that support your points. These quotes can be from stage directions as well as the text.

SEEING FURTHER PERFORMANCES

You will now be in a position to see further theatre performances. On the next occasion, you should cover more, if not all, of the system in section 2.2 in your note-taking. You will want to be familiar with all the topics in section 2.2 at this point. An example of the type of notes that you would take while sitting in the theatre, covering most aspects of the production, can be seen on pp.156–62. Occasionally, you might decide to select only certain aspects of the production to analyse if they are particularly prominent. It is worth making your notes as comprehensive as possible, and as ordered as possible, so that you can decipher them easily for the next stage – rewriting.

It is important that your notes are rewritten in a logical order, as you will need to be able to refer to them rapidly in the examination. You may want to work with a system of colour coding for certain elements. It is certainly worth separating your notes into sections, such as directorial interpretation, lighting, sound and music, performance, use of language (for a new play/piece of theatre), costumes, set, proxemics, overall impact/audience reception. As stated in step 7 above, these rewritten notes will take into consideration your *reflection* upon the piece. You must attempt to identify the thinking behind all the production decisions and explain the audience reception. There are examples of *rewritten* notes on pp.163–70 and 170–81.

Move on to seeing non-text-based theatre or new plays where it is not possible to pre-read the script. This offers you different challenges. You will find that **text** and **production** become indistinguishable and that you are not concentrating on 'directorial interpretation' but attempting to assess the overall 'piece objectives'. An example of this is given for *The Street of Crocodiles* on pp.167–9.

Ensure that you see *at least* four pieces of theatre that are suitable for the examination. The more you see, the greater the choice of question you will have. For instance, if one question asks you about the impact of lighting on two shows that you have seen, but only one (or even none) of the productions you have seen had anything out of the ordinary in the way of lighting, then you have limited your options.

In addition, the more theatre you see, the more understanding you will gain of the theatrical process from the viewpoint of a **receiver**. You will find that it is only by the time that you see your second or third production that you are really beginning to be finely tuned to the nuances of analysing performances. Consequently, your later review notes will be better.

Try to see a wide *variety* of theatre. This entirely depends upon the area in which you live, of course, but you should try to see a certain amount of experimental or fringe theatre as well as the more standard repertory theatre. If fringe theatre is difficult to see, it would be worth trying to get to the Edinburgh Fringe Festival in August/September or arts centres in regional cities and towns that act as touring fringe venues. You might also try to go to something like the National Student Drama Festival in April, where you can experience about 16 productions in a week. Even if some of this work is difficult to review, it helps your own practical work and your broad understanding of theatre.

It is also worth having one review from a more unusual theatre event such as a circus or a piece of performance art or community theatre.

Eventually, you will gain experience of turning these notes into focused essays (see pp.182–5). However, do not take essays you have written into the examination or try to adapt them to a new essay title. You are far better advised to approach each question with fresh ideas, selecting relevant parts of your notes to illustrate your answers, and avoiding a generalised review.

2.2 *A system for performance analysis*

2.2.0 INTRODUCTION

Sitting in the near dark, scribbling away, trying to make sense of what you are seeing, hearing and feeling, can be a daunting prospect. To simplify matters it would seem to be sensible for you to refer to a checklist of things to look for. Unfortunately, this is not a feasible way to evaluate the performance once you are in the theatre (and answering questions in a pre-planned sequence is no way to enjoy a performance experience).

This system gives you a structure for performance analysis

In this section we suggest a **system of performance analysis**: a very structured set of guidelines with which you can become familiar. By familiarising yourself with the questions in the system *before* you see the production, in conjunction with any other pre-reading or discussion (see section 2.1), you will find it easier to focus on particular aspects of the production during the performance.

You will arrive at your own order for taking notes

One of the main problems with any checklist like this is the order in which it is arranged. As you sit taking notes you will inevitably arrive at your own order, which can then be re-structured and expanded later. So we have taken what we consider the clearest pathway, knowing that at any one moment you will be drawing on any of the sub-headings for help.

You need to develop your findings later

For example, we start with the theatre or place of performance, as you will probably arrive in time to take in the total environment of the production. As the performance begins, you may note what the set looks like before you note a detail of an actor's costume. However, you should feel free to write down thoughts as they occur, knowing that you will want to work on your findings later.

Select one aspect upon which to concentrate, if appropriate

If you know the text in advance, or have discussed the production with the director, you might decide ahead of time to concentrate on a particular area, for example character performances in *The Seagull*. Otherwise, you might choose to see the production again if you feel there might have been one particular area upon which you would wish to comment in detail. Be wary, however, of having too many different sets of notes which all concentrate on the same thing, such as technical effects.

The questions are meant as starting points. You can develop them further on your own.

2.2.1 THE PLACE OF PERFORMANCE

QUESTIONS TO CONSIDER

In what building did the performance take place? Was it a purpose-built theatre? Or was it a building that used to have another function? Does the building have a history; is it part of the social life of the community?

These are very specific questions aimed at one type of performance, one that would take place indoors. But what of other forms?

For street or open air theatre you might need to examine the environment:

QUESTIONS TO CONSIDER

Is it in a town centre? Is it in a park or the countryside? What effect did this have on you as an audience and more particularly the actors?

Make more than a yes/no response

Wherever it occurs the place of performance should generate some comment. **This is true for all the questions: all of them will need to be developed beyond a 'yes' or 'no' answer.**

QUESTIONS TO CONSIDER

How does this affect your view of the whole experience? Can you make a cross-reference to another aspect of the analysis?

2.2.2 THE PERFORMANCE SPACE

You should look at the theatre and the performance space separately

You should aim to separate this from the theatre, as usually you will pass from a foyer into the performance space itself, but again there will be notable exceptions, and you can find interesting things to say about the formal or informal ways an audience enters the performers' space. For example, going to a circus, you might buy your tickets in the open air and then be led into a temporary structure to see the show. This is a very different experience from entering a dark auditorium and is worth commenting on.

The means of entering the space is important

The way in which you enter the space is worth a lot of attention, since, as an audience, we tend to take it for granted. You would find it helpful to take some time in analysing this moment, as it can affect your whole attitude to the rest of the experience.

QUESTIONS TO CONSIDER

What effect does the 'feel' of the theatre have? What colour is the auditorium, if there is one? How does this affect your feeling of being in the place for performance? How does the actors' area relate to the audience area? How far/near are you to the actors' area? Is there any visible lighting equipment? If you are standing, will you be able to see/hear the actors? If you are in the open air, what time of day is it? What is the weather like? How do all these factors affect you?

Look very carefully at the architecture of the place for performance and how its physical properties have been used. There is a lot of difference between the 19th-century gilt of the Theatre Royal, Drury Lane, in London and the high-tech look of the Royal Exchange in Manchester.

QUESTIONS TO CONSIDER

What are the conditions that you notice first? Is the curtain raised and can you see the set? Are the actors visible? What are they doing? Is there someone literally drumming up support, asking you to gather at a particular point? Are the clowns chasing each other round the arena? Have you been given something to read? Have you bought a programme?

The flavour of an event can be established even before the performance begins

All these conditions will give you a flavour of the event you are to witness, and may make you feel welcome or otherwise. They can radically influence the way you receive the performance, and you will need to make them part of your evaluation.

2.2.3   THE AUDIENCE SPACE AND THE ACTORS' SPACE

There are no clear-cut conventions for performance space

This is one of the most fascinating and also most difficult aspects of evaluating a performance, since there are no preconceived conditions. Conventions have been so different in periods of theatre history, and we seem to be living through a time when any of them is considered appropriate, from a Greek arena to a street corner. There is no one conventional relationship to discuss.

There are, however, a number of specific areas to look for here, all of which relate to people's distance from one another and the distance an actor is from the audience. We have already referred to a convenient word to summarise these concerns: **proxemics** (see pp.32–3).

Proxemics can be extended to include looking at the way buildings, space, actors, their audiences and the staging relate one to the other. We want to look at these two elements:
• how the audience is collected together
• how the actor is separated from the audience.

In each case we need to look at how this is different in what we call **formal** and **informal** conditions.

The formal audience is a unit

In **formal space** the audience is seated as a unit, in rows facing in the same direction, and the intention is that everyone receives basically the same performance. It is also usually in the dark.

The informal audience may have a variety of experiences

In **informal space** the audience can be split up, forming units that don't necessarily see a performance from the same viewpoint. For example, in a circus one bank of the audience is looking at the other, with the performers in between; in promenade performances, several different parts of the action may be taking place in different areas of the space.

These examples show what a variety of experience you might be having, and you should be able to discuss this.

How does the formal/informal space affect the way the audience behaves? How does this affect the way the actors behave? What are the main means of communication? How is it different sitting in the dark to standing in daylight?

The actor and formal space

These different ways of positioning an audience have a very dynamic effect on the relationship with the actor. In **formal** space the actor has well-defined means to keep him or her separate from the audience, such as:

- a raised platform
- a curtain
- a proscenium arch
- being in the light.

These means reinforce the way she or he communicates.

The actor and informal space

In **informal** space the actor may:

- be on the same level
- have no architectural barrier
- be as close as he or she likes
- be in the same light.

There are no clear expressions of separation, no boundaries except those that we might subconsciously erect for ourselves to keep the actor at a distance.

**QUESTIONS
TO CONSIDER**
Is the performance space appropriate or not? What are the advantages and disadvantages of informal or formal spaces in the production you are analysing? Why is the circus in the round? What shape is a street theatre performance, if it has one? How does this affect the perfomance?

2.2.4 THE SET

A word list and a rough sketch are useful

It is important to make notes on points that occur to you as you first see the set. Try starting with a list of words, for example cold, warm, real, fantasy. Try making a sketch of the set if you have time. It doesn't matter how rough this is – it will help you remember features to discuss at a later date.

During the performance or in an interval you may be able to write further about the role of the set in the overall production concept, and how it changes, or is made to change, by the interaction of other elements, which might include the actors, machinery, lighting or visible stage managers.

If you have read the play before going to the performance, part of the fun is seeing how far the designer's (and director's) result differs from what you imagined.

If possible, try to talk to the designer or director. You will find this a very useful exercise and it will help you compare the process of their decision-making with the end result.

Is the set representational, i.e. naturalistic? Does it have three walls, with the audience forming the fourth? Is there more than one set? Or, if it is theatre in the round, is the floor the most important factor? What is shown and what do we infer from what is not shown? What is implied as an off-stage world? If there is furniture, how has it been selected to tell us more about the play/characters? Is it contemporary to the play? If not, why not, do you think? What is the importance of colour, form and texture? What meanings do they convey?

2.2.5 LIGHTING

Lighting has different functions in different types of performance

Like all aspects of design, this has a huge influence on the overall impression you receive, and it can play a very active part in the performance. In circus, musical theatre, ballet and opera, it usually has a very different function from that in a 'straight' play.

Lighting has a very particular function in theatre, since it can both enhance a set or actor and at the same time act as a great mood changer. In a fully mounted production, for example at the Royal National Theatre, there can be a great number of lighting cues which go largely unrecognised by the audience. These subtle changes help to enhance the flavour of the scenes and the overall mood of the production.

It would be helpful to make yourself familiar with some of the functions of lighting equipment and you can do this by referring to pp.65–6 and books on the subject. If the hardware is visible, and some of it usually is, look at how different lanterns have particular jobs to do.

Be familiar with the equipment

In proscenium arch theatres lighting usually remains in much the same place, but in other venues it can move around and you might be able to see who controls the changes, or even see people who have responsibilities for individual lanterns, such as a follow spot.

Can you see the source of illumination? Are there follow spots, as in a musical? How is the lighting arranged to focus your attention on the play? Does it have a naturalistic function, i.e. are you conscious of it or not? Or does it play an active part in the way the text is interpreted? How does it change the atmosphere/mood of the performance? Does it have colour and if so, why? Does it suggest time passing? What is the value of a blackout? A slow fade? How/why does the lighting state change? What effect does the lighting have on *your* perception of the performance?

2.2.6 SOUND

Sound can be an integral part of the performance

In recent years some theatre has begun to use recorded sound, almost like a film soundtrack, and of course in musical theatre the majority of the text might be sung to music. However, by **sound** we mean more than a musical accompaniment.

We can divide sound up into various categories which will help with analysis:

- onstage, related to a character: the rattle of coins in a pocket
- offstage, related to the imagined world: a doorbell
- recorded sound, music or effects that are outside the text.

It is worth noting these different types of sound as you watch the performance.

Music can evoke atmosphere and expectation

In all cases, sound plays a large part in suggestion and in the creation of expectation. More than any other element it can evoke atmospheres and moods by direct appeal to our imagination and senses.

QUESTIONS TO CONSIDER

What is the source of the sound? What is its purpose? Is it natural, i.e. does it spring from the text? Or is it abstract, i.e. making a mood or atmosphere more explicit? Is it live or recorded? What does it convey about the offstage world? If it is music, what function does it have? How is it used to support the singers (if there are any)? In circus, how does it function to support the 'acts'?

2.2.7 COSTUME

Costume denotes character

Seen onstage, costume plays a vital part in our understanding of a character's age, social class and rank and, most importantly, the production's attitude to the character. On the simplest level, kings wear crowns, soldiers wear uniforms, poor people dress in rags; the simple is often a good starting point. However, costume, like all the other design elements, depends on an overall design concept, and this comes from collaboration.

Design concepts come from collaboration

The best costume decisions are made by the designer and director with the direct involvement of the actor, since it is he or she who will be living in the clothes for the period of the performance. There may be hours of discussion before a decision is made, so when you analyse this aspect of design, be on the look out for how you think the final result may have been reached. If you have read the text beforehand, you may already have formulated a design concept and thought about appropriate costuming. With reference to your own decision-making process, try to understand the decisions the professional designers would have taken.

QUESTIONS TO CONSIDER

What is the relationship of the costumes to the overall design concept? What is their relationship to the characters? Do they indicate a social order? Are they formal or informal? Are they 'in period' and what does that mean? Are they making a comment on the period? Are they fantastic? Do they represent conventions, e.g. a dame in a pantomime? How does the choice of colour or texture help us to an understanding and/or identification of character? What is each costume's relationship to any other? Are conventions mixed?

2.2.8 THE ACTOR AND HIS/HER PERFORMANCE

The actor carries a huge responsibility

You probably wouldn't argue with the statement that we often go to the theatre to see and enjoy the 'acting'. This makes the actor a hugely important member of the team, because she or he carries much of the responsibility for the interpretation of the director's overall conception (see 2.2.9).

Try to be familiar with the text

We assume that over a period of rehearsal, actor and director have agreed on the production concept and we are therefore seeing the outcome of a process. If you are familiar with the text, analysing the interpretation will be a more fascinating experience than if you are coming to it for the first time. Some people talk of having seen *Hamlet* as many as ten times and never getting bored.

The actors' main task is to communicate the meaning of the play

The actors have the main job of communicating the meaning of the play to you. How they do this and how successful they are, or not, is the basis of your analysis. To talk about 'good' and 'bad' acting is not useful, however. After a few visits to performances you will become more perceptive in your evaluation of an actor's skill.

Talk to the actors if you get a chance: most enjoy talking about their work and it will give you an insight into their job and what they found were the challenges they had to overcome. Reading the critics' reviews and interviews can give you an insight into the way interpretation can be evaluated.

QUESTIONS TO CONSIDER

What is the relationship between each individual performer and other members of the cast? Does one actor play more than one part? How are they differentiated? What is the relationship between spoken text and physical movement or gesture? If there is no text, how is meaning conveyed? How is the voice used? Is there a dialect or accent? If so, why? What about facial expressions? Can you detect particular manipulation of the text in terms of emphasis and pauses for effect? Do these work? How?

What are the spatial relationships between the actors? What are their relationships to the set? Do/don't they acknowledge the audience? If so, why and how? If there is a 'star' actor how does this influence expectation before and evaluation after the performance? How do you think this has influenced the choice of text/role? Is the actor a solo as well as a company performer?

Do the actors have more than one function? In what ways are they used as story-tellers? What are the different modes of communication? How do these link with the actor and his text? Can you categorise the acting style, e.g. Brechtian?

2.2.9 THE TEXT/NON-TEXT AND DIRECTORIAL INTERPRETATION

In section 2.1 we suggest that this aspect of analysis should be the first to be written up. However, it is logical for it to be one of the later points of your analysis when you are actually in the theatre.

Be familiar with the text as this will improve your analysis

Whenever you can, you should make yourself familiar with the text before you go to a performance. Although you will hope to enjoy a performance, and part of that enjoyment is not knowing what to expect, for this exercise a knowledge of what you are about to see can improve your analysis immeasurably.

Text is a blueprint for performance

So much that appears on the page bears little or no relation to what will happen in performance. A text is merely a blueprint for the event. If you have a knowledge of the starting point, however, you will have a key to how the director and his or her collaborators have arrived at their interpretation. This is the importance of **production** in the 'text, production and reception' equation. It is worth discussing the text and finding different areas of emphasis before seeing it in production; what aspects of the text would *you* choose to highlight to an audience and how could this be achieved?

If the text is not available as it has not been published, or has only just been published, try to get a copy as soon as possible after seeing the performance. You will be working retrospectively, but it will still help.

Some performances have no text

You may well go to performances that have no text, or very little. Here you will be principally concerned with physicality and how this relates to meaning. How you notate this can be interesting; for example, you could try drawing stick people to remind you of a strong or striking moment.

Subtext is very important

Remember to write down any moments when the subtext seems more important than the text. (See pp.29–31 for further details about subtext.) These can be very vivid and sometimes more memorable than lots of dialogue. A look, a pause, a silence or a laugh can convey more than words.

Discuss what you didn't understand

As we have suggested, try to talk to the director as this will give you an insight into how the production was conceived. You may not be able to interpret the whole production from one performance, so try to go more than once. What you *didn't* understand can be a good source for discussion and debate.

The programme can be useful for understanding the interpretation

In addition, the programme can often be illuminating. Even if programmes are expensive, it is worth sharing. The sample notes on *The Street of Crocodiles* in section 2.3 rely heavily upon assistance from the programme, for example.

QUESTIONS TO CONSIDER

What interpretative choices have been made? What aspects of the performance tell you anything about these decisions? Where is this to be seen? Through the actors' performances? The setting; lighting; costumes? The dramatic pace? When, why and how?

What is spoken and what is implied? Is there a subtext? Does the text belong to a genre? Is there a plot? How is it structured? What part does any plot play in the action? How is the story told? Is it by words alone?

Is the text in translation? Has this affected the interpretation?

What is the thematic relationship between the text and the visual imagery? Is the text supported or questioned by the imagery? Give examples and possible explanations.

Was the work devised by the company? Was it group led? At what points do you think the actors made an input to the process? How has this affected the end result?

2.2.10 OVERALL IMPACT AND AUDIENCE RECEPTION

Summarise all your points and comment on the overall impression

This is the section where you can make a summary, taking the most important points from all the other sections and adding any further comments that sum up your overall impression of the piece.

It might be useful to note down those images you retained from the performance. The images are often more vivid and last longer than the words, and are part of the afterlife of the event. They can be important in contributing to your comments on the 'overall impact'. You may remember one striking image which summarised the whole essence of the piece; this image may well remain with you and influence your thinking in the future. For example, the stoning of the baby in Edward Bond's *Saved* (1965) can be staged extremely powerfully, so that you remember it for many years and recognise it as a devastating comment on the deprivation in certain areas of modern British society.

Have a discussion immediately after the performance

In your role as part of an audience, the moments after a performance can be just as interesting as the event. Try to make space for a little discussion immediately; it is useful to note first impressions. (These may change on reflection.) It also helps you fix your thoughts and compare them with other people's.

Audience response is important

Remember to note down the audience's responses to specific moments, and compare these with your own. Note whether the audience response changes the actors' performance in any way, and if the audience's response itself changes during the play.

Be constructively critical

Don't be tempted to dismiss a performance. Anything you see is worth your considered attention. If you have not enjoyed the theatrical event because you haven't understood it, discuss it to help you find the meaning in the piece. Your meaningful analysis will both give you pleasure and strengthen the way you look at this unique art form.

QUESTIONS TO CONSIDER

How have you been helped towards an interpretation of meaning? By reading the text before the performance; by reading any critical writing about the work; by discussion; by reading reviews about the performance; by reading a programme? Were you helped towards an analysis by an audio/video tape recording of the performance? What in the performance didn't make sense to you or wasn't communicated clearly enough? Was this fact important or not?

What was your role as spectator? Were you interested or bored? How did the audience as a whole react? What are the most important aural and visual moments that you retain? How did you *feel* at the end of the performance? Would you remember this production for particular reasons? Is there likely to be any long-term impact? Go back to your notes some time later and respond to the production retrospectively.

2.2.11 FUTURE PERFORMANCE ANALYSIS

It is worth taking the time to improve your own 'system' before you return to another theatrical event. You will probably find areas that haven't been covered in this system, particularly relating to unusual events.

QUESTIONS TO CONSIDER   What were the problems of analysing the performance? How could you change the procedures for future reference?

Figure 2.1 suggests one way in which you could remind yourself of the different elements of performance analysis.

You would not expect to use all the headings all the time, but a 'spider-gram' is a useful way of noting your first reactions when discussing a piece of theatre.

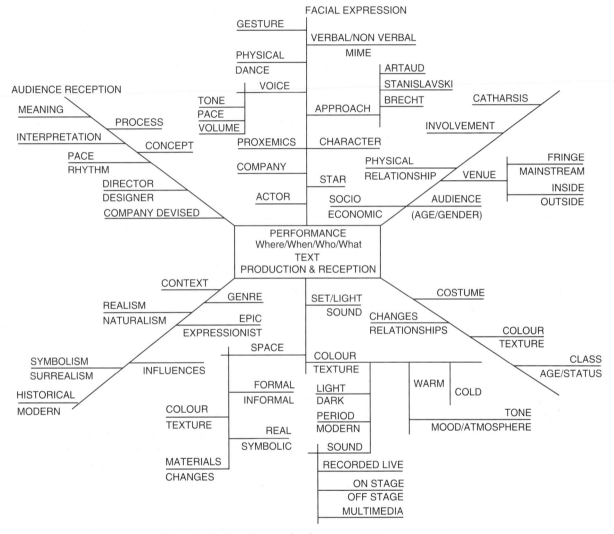

Figure 2.1   The elements of performance analysis

BIBLIOGRAPHY

Aston, E. & Savona, G.	*Theatre as Sign System*	Routledge, 1991
Esslin, M.	*The Field of Drama*	Methuen, 1987
Wardle, I.	*Theatre Criticism*	Routledge, 1992
Pavis, P.	*Theatre Analysis, Some Questions and a Questionnaire*	New Theatre Quarterly, No. 2, 1985

2.3 *Sample notes using the system*

These notes follow the system outlined in section 2.2, with relation to two productions staged in 1994. They give you an idea of the sort of notes that you might consider writing, but are not comprehensive.

As mentioned in section 2.1, you will make two different sets of performance analysis notes. The first will be the rough notes that you make in the theatre during the performance. The second will be written when you have reflected upon the production further and will attempt to make a coherent picture of the production. At this stage you will edit out extraneous detail and expand more relevant areas.

The first example below illustrates the *first stage*, that is rough notes taken whilst at the theatre. The notes on *The Seagull* are broadly based and do not focus on any particular part of the system given in 2.2. Whilst this would suffice to answer some questions in an examination, you would be well advised to concentrate on *detailed* notes in appropriate areas. For example, you might have wished to make exhaustive notes on two or three characters in the production of *The Seagull* discussed below. The play is ideal for character studies and the rather traditional production would support this.

The other examples, on *The Street of Crocodiles* and *The Weir*, gives you a selection of *second stage* notes; in other words, they have been rewritten after reflection and show further understanding of aspects of the production. Here, we give analysis of particular elements of the productions – e.g. the performance space, the set, the text/non-text and directorial interpretation and the overall impact in *The Street of Crocodiles*. It is likely that you would have taken extensive notes for *all* aspects of these productions, of course; they are certainly worthy of such detail.

EXAMPLE 1 – THE SEAGULL

This production of *The Seagull* was part of the repertoire at the Royal National Theatre, London. This is an established classic play, produced by Britain's national company; it is therefore a reasonably conventional choice.

Here we give examples of the way you might record a production *before* you shape it into a coherent report. These notes have been made under headings; you might find it possible to operate like this in a theatre, or alternatively you might have to scribble your notes in any order.

Figure 2.2   A scene from *The Seagull*, The Royal National Theatre, London, 1994.

Figure 2.3   Dame Judi Dench as Arkadina in *The Seagull*, 1994.

Title: *The Seagull* by Anton Chekhov, directed by John Caird
Venue: The Royal National Theatre, London – Olivier Auditorium
Company: Resident company
Date: 10.9.94

PLACE OF PERFORMANCE

- The Royal National Theatre, on the South Bank of the Thames, part of a complex of buildings that includes other places for performance.

- A draughty approach from Waterloo Underground until the theatre is reached. Ugly concrete walkways.

- Once inside the foyer space it is light and warm. Music is live. People are sitting and listening.

- The Olivier Auditorium is on a different level, by stairs and lift. A standby ticket means a seat at the fixed price of £10. Prior knowledge suggests that the auditorium will not be 'sold out'; there is no queue and a ticket is available. This would normally be full price: £22.00.

- Lots of people in the gathering space by the bookshop, in the shop itself and by the bar. Restaurants are full. Room to circulate, no sense of rush. No real sense of occasion. 'Curtain up' is 7.15pm, which is earlier than West End theatre. This is deliberate, to catch people who work in London.

- Programmes can be bought in advance from the bookshop outside the auditorium. They are £1.80.

PROGRAMME

- Twenty pages. Twelve pages actually devoted to this production, including extensive theatre biographies of the company, director and designers. Worth having if you can afford the price.

- Free cast list available.

- The overall feel is that the play is a 'classic'. Most of the information is about Chekhov and the first production (1898). Quotes from his letters. Good illustrations. A new translation from a literal version. Article by Pam Gems (translator) on the difficulties of the job.

- Very good photographs of the company in performance, mostly in close-up. No pictures of the set. 'Stars', i.e two leading actors, have full page photos.

- Artist drawings of the cast in rehearsal throughout the text.

- No statement by the director or designer.

- Cast and credit list has a landscape with the bare branch of a tree as a background. The tree proves to be a motif from the design concept.

THE PERFORMANCE SPACE (AND ACTOR'S AND AUDIENCE SPACE)

- Olivier stage has no curtain. The auditorium is best described with reference to its Greek origin. Curving rows of (purple) seats facing a circular stage. It is 'formal space' with no crossing of the boundary between actor and audience.

- It is very large. Rather forbidding. Probably the largest stage for 'straight theatre' in the UK?

- The lit set is in full view. A chance to take in this aspect of the production. Stage is empty. No music.

- The set is dominated by huge sky cloth (cyclorama) and the lake, referred to in stage directions. Placed in the semi-foreground is the temporary stage for the play that will take place in Act 1.

- Overall impression created by the bare branches of framing trees is cold and gloomy.

- Set strongly backlit, with gobos focused on the floor to create the impression of foliage.

- Auditorium fills up quickly, with an expectant audience. Stalls are full – rest of the auditorium half empty. The seat is stage right. Very good view.

THE SET
- As a 'classic', the playtext is available for study before the production, though not in this version. So there are preconceptions as to the way it might be designed, acted and directed.

- The dominant first impression of cold and winter (see above) can only be deliberate. But it runs counter to the suggestion in the text of Act 1 of a summer evening. Also the programme/poster image suggests summer.

- Later in the play, particularly in Act 4 the coldness image becomes appropriate. But from Act 1 we are stuck with it.

- Beginning of the play is a very complex technical sequence, designed to focus us immediately into Chekhov's world. Crossover here into directorial interpretation. The first moments are important and very laden with information.

- House lights and set light go to black, music begins – dreamy (flute?) with echo. Cast enter in blackout and blue backlight reveals them in silhouette. They begin to move slowly and fill the stage. They end standing each in their own spotlight. Listening(?) to a woman singing a folksong as if in the distance. More echo.

- A huge picture frame (almost the width of the stage) descends upstage. The sound of hammering by the men erecting the little temporary theatre – lights to full, text begins.

- Two things not understood at this point: actors moving in a seeming dream, and the huge picture frame. This proves to be the first of four, which accumulate as the play progresses. For Act 2 the frame has a garden statue within it, and for Acts 3 and 4 furniture. Items descend as part of the frames from the flies.

- Actors cross the frame to enter. Why are they 'framed'? The very definite rectangle probably works best from centre seats, doesn't read very well from the side. Frame is used to suggest the important locked doors in Act 4.

- By the end there are four frames, filling a good proportion of the upstage area.

- The lake is very important: it looks like quite a complex effect. Lighting plays a large part in giving it a shimmer. It gets smaller in each act and disappears at the end. As a symbol of the loss of the 'magic'? This is achieved by closing a solid ellipse from the sides. Why? Our distance from it? Its importance in the lives of the people? It's a symbol, like the seagull. A rather mechanical way of making a point.

- Frames disappear at the end, lake disappears and cast repeat opening motif. The set is very dominant in the structure and meaning/interpretation of this production.

- Furniture moving on and off is done by cast of servants or by the characters. Kept to the minimum: basket chairs, wooden seats. Used outside and inside the house.

- The theatre within the theatre, which is such a potent symbol, gets pushed back at the end of Act 1 and in the final act is seen demolished and with wind blowing its curtains. A symbol of decay. The metaphor of theatre is one of the play's themes.

THE ACTOR AND HIS/HER PERFORMANCE

A difficult section, involving both concentrating on the performance and writing detailed notes on characterisation. Some of these details will probably come together in a post-performance discussion. (You would use the actors' names in your notes.)

- Konstantin. Rather lacking in energy, difficult to hear in Act 1. Not an easy part, has to represent a 'new' generation trying to overturn old ideas (like Chekhov?) and it's written rather on one note. His nervous rhythm in Act 1 gives an indication of his unhappy relationship with his mother. At his best in last act with Nina. A really tragic end to two lives.

- Nina (the seagull). Found her too sharp and loud. Rather breathless energy swamped her innocence. Came across as rather terrified – but of what? Chekhov sketches in her (offstage) parents rather well; this actress gives the impression they rule her life. A rather desperate performance from Act 1 onwards. Impulsive in movement, e.g. kissing Arkadina. In the final scene with Konstantin, the tragedy of her wasted life is movingly conveyed. Stillness and sudden movement are contrasted.

- Arkadina. A star actress playing a star actress. The reason for doing this production? Life and art really are blurred in this instance. There is obvious pleasure in watching one of the world's leading actresses play another, from a different period. A lot of touching her lover Trigorin. Very focused. You feel her intensity through her relationships to others. A 'physical' performance. She and Trigorin end up on the floor at one moment as she embraces him. Uses the whole stage in quite sweeping movements. Not allowed to dominate the play, though. She is off-stage for large chunks of the text. Vocally, by far the most experienced on stage. Can hear every syllable. Uses her eyes. When she focuses we look too. She commands attention.

- Dorn, the doctor. Gives one of the most interesting performances. An experienced actor, he is accomplished. Fascinated with things. Noticed how he manipulates personal props, his pince-nez, his stick. They really belong to his character. He flicks dust from the theatre curtains, picks at an imagined flower. A feeling of control is communicated, and mastery of the stage space. Addresses the audience directly. This is quite a shock, since the play doesn't signal this.

- Polina, wife to the estate manager. Wearing orange. A comic performance, very vivid. Looks miserably unhappy for most of the play. In love with Dorn. Anxiety cripples the character's speech, but she expresses feeling non-verbally. One watches her physicality.

COSTUME

- In period. No sense of updating. Predominantly creams, greys and white to suggest summer. Light fabrics. Darker colours in Act 4.

- Arkadina. Extravagance. Bold colour, mostly red and black. In Act 2 in white. Huge hat. Theatre costume from the period of the play seems to have been the inspiration. Her Act 1 costume is glittery, black jet. Totally inappropriate for the countryside. She has a turban, with a black feather. She plays with a red shawl. She *is* theatre. Costume makes an amusing comment on her profession.

- Konstantin. Begins the play in waistcoat and trousers, wears a Russian peasant shirt for Act 2 when he brings the dead seagull to Nina. His trousers have mud on them. In Act 4 he is in a tight black suit and glasses. Totally transformed. Buttoned down, serious. A good example of costume and character development going together.

- Sorin, Arkadina's brother. By the end of the play in a wheelchair. Subtle changes of jacket and scarves transform the well man into the sick one. From being a bit of a dandy in a cream suit, he ends as invalid in shawls. Detail builds up.

- Quite difficult to record this when viewing the play. Overall impression is how carefully everything has been considered. Colour, i.e. Arkadina's dress, and texture, i.e. Sorin's woolly scarf. The costumes are vital in the development of character. They act as emotional barometers.

LIGHTING

- Very much part of set design, and director's intention. Unobtrusive in this production except for the opening and closing images and the spotlit seagull (see Interpretation).

- The play gets more claustrophobic, as the Acts progress. This was helped by the concentration of warm candlelight in Act 4 as opposed to the sunlit garden in Act 2. There is smoke piped onstage from the start to give the set/lighting an 'atmosphere'.

- Use of gobos becomes apparent when general lighting gives way to an atmospheric moment, in Act 2, when the cast listen to singing from across the lake.

- Lighting hardware is very visible in the Olivier Auditorium. Control is sited in rear stalls. Sound desk is in the open. So that the operator can hear levels and quality?

DIRECTORIAL INTERPRETATION

- As a classic text the play has acquired a lot of baggage over the years, i.e. as a director what am I going to 'do' with this text? There's a lot of critical material about the text, and meaning.

- Lots of opportunity to work on character, probably with Stanislavski's influence. (See pp.225–55)

- A play of moods, but also full of ideas about life/art. The job of a writer. Being an actress and what that means.

- Everyone does something or wants to do something. A kind of yearning to make life meaningful.

- Theatre is a dominant image in the play. Sorin says, 'You can't have life without theatre.' This line comes over very strongly. It seemed to be a key line. Perhaps this explains the frames? A proscenium? Just what the Olivier hasn't got.

- The set has given us a mood which is rather dark and brooding. Despite the sunshine in Act 2 it's the act in which Konstantin kills the seagull for Nina, and it's the act where Trigorin, as the outline for one of his short stories, foretells Nina's fate. It seems that the director wants a tragic mood for this production.

- The visual elements come over very strongly, whether they are to do with character, e.g. the colour of Arkardina's dress, or whether they support and echo the text, e.g. the strongly spotlit dead seagull at the ends of Act 2 and 4. Taking opportunities to express the visual symbols. Is the director tending to over-emphasise the obvious?

- If there is a strong directorial interpretation, it is not obvious, apart from stressing the importance of theatre and life being interwoven. It has as much to do with the atmospheric design as anything else. Despite the text's short length, this production seems very slow and deliberate.

OVERALL IMPACT AND AUDIENCE RECEPTION

Some of these thoughts occur at the time, some afterwards.

- Strange choice of text for this auditorium. Huge, rather bleak visual images, combined with a fairly realist directorial intention. Suspect some actors' performances are just too 'big'. They have to be because of the size of the Olivier.

- It's a dreamy, rather heavily signalled, moody production. Strong visual statements not clear, i.e. the lake getting smaller.

- Chekhov's writing leaves duologues to propel the action. Big set piece scenes. Must need lots of energy to keep it afloat. But this is the quality it lacked. Pauses/silences not filled. Seemed painfully slow in places. Too 'meaningful'.

- A new version of the text helped to give it some life as it was quite colloquial.

- Audience responsive to the humour, and irony of the text. Light relief. The fact that the theatre wasn't full must mean something. The play? The critics? Chekhov?

- There was obvious delight at the end: lots of warm applause and murmers of appreciation.

EXAMPLE 2 – THE STREET OF CROCODILES

This production was devised by the company Théâtre de Complicité, based on the writings and life of Bruno Schulz, a Polish Jew who was killed by the Nazis in 1942. Therefore, there was no published script to read and analyse on first viewing. The notes taken for such a production will be different from those taken for the above example where it was possible to read a playtext beforehand. For example, the section 'directorial interpretation' is irrelevant, as there was no playtext to interpret – it was a devised piece. 'Objectives of the piece' or 'company objectives' makes more sense.

These notes have been rewritten after reflection upon the performance, and they are selective in the areas that are addressed. We have tried to identify the thinking behind everything seen and find a reason for it.

1st Viewing	2nd Viewing
Title: *The Street of Crocodiles*	
Venue: The Young Vic, Waterloo, London.	Queen's Theatre, London
Company: Théâtre de Complicité	
Date: 11.8.94	12.2.99

THE PERFORMANCE SPACE (AND ACTORS' AND AUDIENCE SPACE)

The studio that is the main Young Vic performance space was dark and hazy; clearly the company was attempting to create a certain atmosphere as you walked in. The haziness was created by dry ice and the effect was one of mystery (and dampness from the 'mist'). This was supported by loud, regular dripping. The dripping appeared to be from a tap which was standing proud of the stage DSL. This tap was lit, unlike much of the stage. It was, in fact, a sound effect, amplified and echoed, which faded out after the action started. (It was difficult to establish the meaning of the tap and the dripping.) Very little of the set was visible because of the mist and dim lighting. No actors were visible.

The auditorium was dark, with curtains behind the main banks of seating giving an enclosed feel. It is a traditional theatre space with a thrust stage. The audience was on three sides – again, therefore, we had a feeling of enclosure. The audience was slightly raked up, never too far away from the stage. There was also a higher level – a gallery set back. The audience was divided up into banks of seats. All the seats were bench seats; we felt very close to the next member of the audience! There was a sense of rather oppressive enclosure. This linked in with Schulz's sense of being locked, or enclosed, in his own world. The company may not have selected the venue for this purpose, but they enhanced the sense of enclosure and oppression with the dry ice and ominous dripping sounds.

The theatre was completely full; the ushers had difficulty seating everybody. This set up expectations. We felt it was a popular production. (It had been in London before – at the Royal National – and on a world tour, so obviously it had a good reputation.) The audience was mixed: a cross-section of age, gender, race and probably class. The production must appeal to a wide range of people.

Because the production started life elsewhere, we realised that the piece was not devised with this performance space in mind. The actor–audience relationship was formal. We were not directly part of the performance; it was intended that we should be observers. The production was focused towards the front bank of the audience; quite possibly the side banks did not receive as impressive a show – they must have missed some bits. Perhaps the company did not change its performances enough for different venues. During the show, the performance space was lit, not the auditorium, and the stage is raised; the actors were definitely

Figure 2.4   Rehearsing for *The Street of Crocodiles*, Théâtre de Complicité, 1994.

Figure 2.5   A scene from *The Street of Crocodiles*, 1994.

removed from the audience. The audience barely reacted to the space. We were aware that we had been firmly given the role of 'audience'.

THE SET   See above under 'Performance space' as well.

There was a composite set which seemed to represent the 'library' where Joseph was sorting out books for the Nazis. There were books in many places: USL and USR, above two quasi-entrances and piled on the floor SL. The stage floor was bare. This allowed for its transformation to represent different areas as the show progressed, with just the minimum of furniture brought on and off by the cast.

The tap seemed odd at the opening of the show, but we barely noticed it; it remained in position (DSL) throughout and was actually used later. Cold water was run from it to help some of the characters cool down in the section entitled 'August'.

The back wall was just that, with paint splashed on it, apparently at random. This was barely lit at the beginning of the show.

The set changed to become different 'places', all of which had elements of naturalism but also an abstract and transient feel. For example, the set became a schoolroom and the cast brought on school desks and chairs; these provided an element of naturalism, but they were moved to act as a forest, a shop counter, a dining-room table and perches for birds in the upstairs attic, for example. We grew to expect this constant changing of settings as the show continued. The design was entirely flexible; like the action, it allowed the environment to change fluently and without fuss or attention – it just happened. The cast reshaped the area and moved furniture and props as part of the action. The main effect of this on the audience was to keep them entranced by the action of the show. There were no breaks in the action and the smooth, rapid flow of events added to our feeling of taking part in a dream.

The set supported the underlying concept of the show – it 'migrated' according to the action. For example, one line of books set up high, USL, was brought cascading down at one point, when the setting was being changed. They were all attached and we realised that it was a prop, specifically designed to allow the 'line of books' to fall smoothly. They were then dragged off, as if Joseph was having his past removed.

Most of the distinctive use of the set to support the intentions behind the piece occurred near the beginning. Joseph had a trolley of books and there were a number of other books and pieces of furniture (e.g. a wastepaper bin) that made us realise that we were in a library of some kind. He was flicking through books, discarding some, as ordered by the Nazis. We, the audience, were given clear signs that this was a reasonably conventional setting; we even heard the recorded sound of Nazi jackboots outside.

Then we realised that Schulz was drifting into a dream world of the past. We were instantly removed from reality because the back wall was illuminated and a person was walking *down* the wall, perpendicular to it (using a harness, presumably). The trolley opened and another figure came from that. A further figure came from the wastepaper bin. (None of these figures had been seen before this moment.) Two more crept/ shuffled down the aisle. The bizarre, surreal quality of these actions instantly signalled that we were no longer in the 'normal' world. As an audience, we were transfixed by the wall-walking figure and there was a rustle of amusement and exclamation around the auditorium. We were quickly unsettled and taken into the dream world that comprised the rest of the play.

MAIN SETTINGS

- The library where Joseph works. Books up above entrances USL and USR lit. Books in heaps USL and CL on floor also lit. Trolley brought on by Joseph to DSL. A wastepaper basket US. Lit pleasantly, realistically. A sense of filtered sunlight in a room full of history. Despite the stage being pretty bare, we sense naturalism. Browns and dull reds. Slightly dingy feel. This was the only 'real' setting; all the others were in Joseph's dream world of memories.

- The cast became swooping birds, using books and a rustling sound to portray this. They used the whole stage. Uniform colours – browns, blacks, blues. This colour scheme was used throughout unless for a particular reason.

- The forest. The cast used chairs and themselves to become a forest, holding chairs up above their heads. 'Forest' sounds – birds, crickets, etc. They were scattered around the stage. Joseph used the trees for a 'hide and seek' game, dodging around them.

- The schoolroom. The cast brought chairs into rows and columns. Single, old-fashioned school desks were brought on by the cast as well. They used them for the 'lessons'. Bright lighting, presumably to represent the vividness of Joseph's memories.

- The shop of Joseph's father. The cast were mannequins and customers. The desks were moved by the cast to a long row, like a shop counter. Huge stretches of material were used as goods (material) in the shop. Towards the end of the show, one fantastically large piece of white material was unravelled from the back wall (set on a roll, USL, on the back wall, about four metres high). The white material represented a number of ideas – Joseph's father/God spreading his words, the sea for the parting of the waves for the children of Israel, the greed for cloth of the customers of the shop, a huge net to catch all the father's birds. The white in the middle of the dull colour scheme acted as a powerfully bright 'force'.

- The family dining room. The desks were moved to become one big table. Various members of the cast become members of the family at dinner.

SOUND

The constantly changing 'extended images' or 'scenes' were accompanied by continual sound, which enveloped the audience and played on our aural senses just as the action played on our visual ones. This sound was an essential part of successfully communicating the *feel* of the scene. The sounds were many and varied.

The characters spoke in English, German, central European languages, French and Spanish (or Italian?); we felt we were in a no man's land of mixed languages and yet everybody understood each other.

Music evoked the season and atmosphere. For example, there was heavy, luscious music in the summer scene entitled 'August'. The music evoked a sleepy, decadent atmosphere and the languid quality was enhanced by the slow echoing of Joseph's word 'Mother', as if the air was still and the sounds hung in the air, barely moving.

Occasionally there were vaguely naturalistic sounds which were appropriate but extended: for example, the larger-than-life buzzing for the wasps in 'August'. Another example was when the books were thrown down, and therefore rejected, at the beginning of the production. There was an amplified echo to this, almost as if he resented the task he had been set. Sometimes there was a mixture of music and 'noise': for example, the percussion sounds made in the classroom scene by the children doing woodwork. This turned the woodwork class into a ritual, with rhythmic, percussive sounds.

The cast all played live instruments at one point in the performance. This was rather threatening, as there was a cacophony of sound 'following' Joseph, from which he could not escape. Instruments varied from a tambour and castanets to a clarinet, saxophone, violin, ukulele and trumpet.

Sound was crucial to convey mood and atmosphere and was a major factor in the audience's 'entrancement'. It was noticeable that the first time we heard music was as Joseph retreated into his dream world. This was a clear indicator of the move from the real to the surreal.

TEXT/NON-TEXT AND OBJECTIVES OF THE PIECE

This was a difficult piece to understand initially. It did not have much speech and some of that was in other languages. The use of many different languages – French, Spanish, central European languages – acted as a distancing effect. The programme made it clear that there was not going to be a 'straightforward' plot; in fact, quite the opposite. Apart from the protagonist, Joseph, there were few actors who retained the same characters. There were act divisions, but the headings in the programme under each act were confusing – 'Act of Remembrance, The Summoning of the Past' or 'The Age of Genius, The Caliphony from Malabar'. We could not sense any breaks in the performance – it was continuous.

However, the introduction to the page of act divisions did give some explanation of the overall thread of the piece. We were shown parts of Bruno Schulz's life and some of his writings – in reality and/or in dreams. However his biography and his writings were interwoven, so that we could not tell how much of the piece came from Schulz's life and how much from his writings.

Schulz is represented by the protagonist of the piece, Joseph, while the other characters are people from his past and/or his writings. Joseph is killed at the end of the piece by the Nazis, as Schulz was in real life. The beginning and end of the play are the only 'real' moments. The rest is a fusion of memory, dream and imagination, focusing on his past: as a child; as a helper in his father's shop; at dinner with his family; remembering the antagonism between the sultry maid, Adela, and his father – particularly about his father's birds kept in the attic; witnessing his father's incarceration in an asylum; his father's death; trying to run the shop after his father's death; his life as a young schoolteacher. The piece is an example of physical theatre, where the actors take on the roles of people, animals and objects. There is little dialogue; the sound is mainly constructed out of sound effects, music and some words.

The company, Théâtre de Complicité, does not 'pretend that this theatre piece is an all-encompassing interpretation of [Schulz's] work. It is an encounter with his artistry – our response to reading his writings, looking at his drawings, speaking to his nephew Jacob and others who knew him. It is a brush with Schulz's imagination.' (Simon McBurney, director of *The Street of Crocodiles*, writing in the programme.) These therefore are the company objectives.

One thing in the piece gives us the 'key' to understanding the piece fully. Joseph's father repeats one phrase time and time again. It is as if Joseph's (Schulz's) remembrance of his father is encapsulated by one sentence that he spoke, so that in Joseph's mind this sentence has taken on huge amounts of importance. The sentence is: *'The migration of forms is the essence of life.'* This seems to be the core of the production. The programme supports this: 'Father is eternally preoccupied with the mystery of creation, the life that lies sleeping in the weave of a cloth, and with the rare birds he has hatched out in the attic of the house.'

This sense of 'migration of forms' is linked with Joseph's imagination. Events become distorted and altered in his memories of the past; things 'migrate' and change, and certain parts of the past have a special emphasis. Time gets distorted; certain moments seem as though they lasted forever, others hardly existed. *'The Street of Crocodiles'* programme supports this: 'The sensuality of [Schulz's] writing captures those long forgotten smells from the past, with bolts of emotional lightning and an imagination which can transform a stamp album into a religious trauma.' In other words, the way that things can 'migrate' or be distorted, through memory or through imagination, is a central theme of the piece.

There is a clear conceptual line underpinning the whole production, which links content and form. The *content* is about 'transmogrification' (transforming completely – and strangely) or 'migration of form'. We see this in a number of ways in the content of the piece, for example in the preoccupations of the father. In addition, there is the sense that everything from one's past shifts and alters because of the passing of time. Again, from the programme: '[Schulz's writing] embodies the elastic, unmanageable and adhesive qualities of time, time poured like honey, continuously transmogrifying, evaporating, reconstituting in an extraordinary flux of interpenetrating seasons, emotions, colours and atmospheres.'

The content is completely interwoven with the *form*. Théâtre de Complicité work in a distinctive style, using a type of physical theatre. (Some of the company trained at the Lecoq mime school in Paris.) They operate from improvisation and build a piece using movement, rhythms, music, costume, multi-useful props, voice, etc. The dominant characteristic of the work is fluidity and control of movement and an ability to change objects into a number of different things.

This ability to change is used throughout this piece (as in all Complicité's work.) Actors constantly change as well, from character to character and from object to 'chorus'. It is this 'migration of *form*' that is part of the overall conceptual approach of the piece; the 'form' of performance and the 'content' of the production are coherently interwoven. There is a unity of style.

It is this unified concept of transformation, occurring throughout the content and form of the piece, that gives it enormous power. We do not feel that the theatrical elements are separated; every part supports the other, so that the piece appears as a coherent whole. The impact is to make us leave the theatre as if we have been inside someone's dream. Like a dream, the production is full of melting images and strange sounds, but with a base in the real world.

[Note that this section could contain even more detail. If the production is new and devised, it is likely that this section will become lengthy. We are giving only an example of the sort of notes you might write after the production, when you have fully read the programme, considered the performance in retrospect and sorted out the scribbled notes taken whilst watching the piece. You will already have noted details about characterisation, costume etc., which will provide the 'guts' of your notes on specific performance elements. This section is likely to be more intellectual where you are putting forward ideas for a conceptual framework for the piece.]

OVERALL IMPACT AND AUDIENCE RECEPTION   The overriding impression of *The Street of Crocodiles* is of having shared in Schulz's dream world, or the landscape of his imagination. As an audience we felt as if we had been magically entranced. Susan Croft (Lecturer in Creative Arts at Nottingham/Trent University) writes in the programme:

> Bruno Schulz's vision is an immensely theatrical one in which human beings, objects, spaces take on temporary unstable shapes and forms before metamorphosing into new ones. The accent is always on transformation. In 1934, in an interview conducted by correspondence with Witkiewicz, Schulz wrote of his vision of reality and of matter, that it is: 'in a state of perpetual fermentation, germination, potential life. There are no dead, hard, limited objects. Everything spreads beyond its own boundaries, remains but a moment in its given shape, only to abandon it at the first opportunity.'

This is very much what was encapsulated in the production. It seemed to comprise extended images: drawn out, reshaped, made excessive and then altered to become a new image. As in many dreams, we felt part of the piece and yet an outside observer of the visual images at the same time. We were not *in* the dream, but we were on the edge of it.

Mood and atmosphere were the dominating aspect of this production. There was very little clear line of plot, although each scene did take in a portion of Schulz's life. What was more important was the *feel* of the piece. We were constantly reminded of the haziness and vague quality attached to memory. The production seemed to stage someone's life as they would remember it. It did this superbly.

The piece lasted for an hour and 45 minutes, without a break. We were carried along by the sheer beauty of the work. Movement, sound, lighting, props and so on all combined to help create each extended image. The audience seemed spellbound by the piece. We responded as one at several moments. Where there was a wry humour – e.g. the humans becoming different sorts of birds – we all chuckled; where there was a particularly powerful visual moment – e.g. when the white roll of material unravelled to billow across the stage with the father at the head of the sheet like some archaic Moses – we all sat completely still in awe; where there was intense sadness – e.g. when Joseph had been shot and in the form of a baby was passed along the row of his relatives and past acquaintances – we were moved, with a surreptitious tissue coming out in many areas of the auditorium.

EXAMPLE 3 – THE WEIR by CONOR McPHERSON

With a remit to produce new writing, The Royal Court Theatre commissioned this play from the Irish writer Conor McPherson. It was first produced in July, 1997 in the Court's Theatre Upstairs. It has received many plaudits; by our third visit (September, 1999), the cast had changed – some characters twice – and the play and writer had won several awards. As with *The Street of Crocodiles*, we had not read the script before seeing the production for the first time. However, one of the customs with new plays at The Royal Court is to sell the script as part of the programme. The script is available for subsequent perusal therefore.

With a new play, rather than an established text that has been interpreted for a contemporary audience, you will be commenting on the text itself at times, as any professional reviewer would. The previous review on *The Street of Crocodiles* does this also. It might be difficult always to distinguish between the directorial interpretation and the author's new text. It is likely that the writer would have been part of the production team and he would have been consulted about many production decisions anyway. (This is established practice at The Royal Court.) In these circumstances, you will find your notes incorporate comments on the text, therefore, particularly as you try to unpick the meaning of the play.

This set of notes falls between the style of those for *The Seagull* and those for *The Street of Crocodiles*. They are a combination of observations and analytical comments.

Title: *The Weir* by Conor McPherson, directed by Ian Rickson
Venue: The Royal Court (at The Duke Of York's, London)
Company: The Royal Court Theatre
Date: 30.1.99 and 15.9.99 (These notes are combined from the two reviewed productions. Where there is the need to, we have indicated the particular performance.)

TEXT AND DIRECTORIAL OBJECTIVES   What is this play about? What have the director, Ian Rickson, and the writer, McPherson, been attempting to say to us? (In this instance, the programme/script is no help to us in seeking anything other than a direct description of the plot. The back cover says: 'A bar in a remote part of Ireland: the local lads are swapping spooky stories to impress a young woman from Dublin newly moved in to the area. But she turns the tables on them ...'. Having seen the play, this description is almost insulting.)

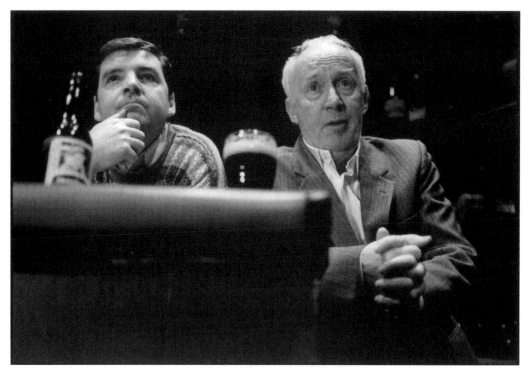

Figure 2.6   Scene from *The Weir*, The Royal Court Theatre.

Figure 2.7   Scene from *The Weir*, The Royal Court Theatre.

The play is set in rural Ireland. The weir of the title is barely mentioned. We find out, briefly, that a weir was built in the area in 1951. It appears to be the last momentous event to have happened in the area. A weir creates both a still, balanced piece of water behind it and a torrent of fast running water the other side. This gives us the clue to the point of the play. There is a clear parallel: the rural area at the centre of the piece is a still backwater; there are swifter-moving places elsewhere. We are being shown a group of people who live in that still backwater for their own reasons. For example, Valerie has actively sought the 'peace and quiet'. (As Jack says, 'You're going to have a peace and quiet overload.') Jack had the opportunity to marry and move to Dublin when a young man but couldn't. ('... an irrational fear that kept me here ... I thought it was a thousand fucking miles away. Hated going up.') Finbar used to live there but he could not take the quiet and moved to the nearby town, Carrick, eighteen years ago. He takes the 'townie' attitude to the rural 'hicks'. The place was a county town in the 16th century but there is nothing of this left except a ruined abbey near by. Even a bypass was built, probably in the 1970s. It is cut off and isolated. The play is about the people who have opted to remain isolated from the mainstream: Brendan, Jack, Jim and now Valerie. Part of Finbar's function in the play is to throw these characters into relief.

There is much in the script to support this symbol of still, unmoving water.

- The men of the area are single; there is no sense of regeneration or new birth. They often talk of the past rather than the future – of their fathers before them – 'Big Finbar' for example.

- Rather like the abbey mentioned, the pub is dilapidated – the beer pump and the Ladies are broken.

- There is no new investment: Brendan will not capitalise on his land and create a caravan park; Jim's house will not be worth much when his mother dies; Jack's garage has barely any business. There is an influx of annual foreign tourists but you realise that they only come to the pub *for* its air of isolation.

- When the locals are together, they speak in restricted codes of language – they know what each other means without having to complete sentences or phrases. They have repeated, ritualistic expressions such as 'a small one' (for a tot of whiskey) and 'Good luck' as they drink.

- The locals are wary of 'blow ins', people who pass through.

Their society does not move on and there is some jealousy and frustration shown to Finbar from those who have remained. Yet there is peace also. There is a sense of escape, of hiding, of contentment, of a lack of energy to move, of acceptance and/or of complacency. It is a still backwater that serves the needs of the people who have chosen to live there, for a long or a short time. The torrent continues elsewhere. The weir is both a historical moment of significance (the last major excitement) and a symbol or metaphor for the locale and its inhabitants.

The play is about the rippling of the still waters. The action takes place within one apparently 'normal' evening but, as Jack says at the end of the play, 'This has been a strange little evening for me.' Valerie's arrival can be seen as a possible catalyst for change, just as the weir's arrival in 1951 upset the balance of nature, bringing dead birds into the hedgerows and fairies knocking at doors. (Valerie's arrival brings the supernatural even closer with her own story.) Because of her presence, Finbar comes back to the pub after a gap of many years, an old house will be given new life, Jack wears a suit (!), and Jack and Jim will frequent the pub during the tourist weeks (they usually forsake it). The female brings regeneration, perhaps. Certainly, McPherson draws particular attention to the feminine in the male world: Brendan has to search for a bottle of wine for Valerie; she has to use the inside, house toilet as the Ladies is broken; all the men shout 'No' together when she offers to buy a drink; it is Valerie (in an almost stereotypical 'woman-as-carer' role) who locates Brendan's car keys for him at the end of the play. In addition, it is the female, Valerie, who tells the most real, and most heartrending, 'ghost' story in which the mother's link with her child is strongly suggested as spiritual; the female is emphasised as the all-powerful life-giver by McPherson, permanently bound to her progeny even beyond death. The weir controls water; the water supports life.

This is not to suggest that Valerie is a symbolic parallel to the weir – the controller of the source of life; that would be too overt. It is more likely that she is simply the stone or stick that disturbs the water and, perhaps, will make it move. She could move these people towards the torrent and the subsequent upheaval. As *The Observer* critic pointed out, 'McPherson is too tactful a writer to spell out the significance of his title, but he shows, movingly...barriers of reticence and memory being breached' [13.7.97]. McPherson, himself, confirms the purpose of the weir metaphor:

> There is a lot of opposition in the play. The weir, for me, is a dam on a river. On one side you have still water, on the other side is rushing water and that's like a metaphor for the play. Yet again on the one side you've got rationality and lights, the weir is used in electricity, and on the other side you've got the unknown, the torrential upheaval and the supernatural which breaks through.

[*The Irish Post*, 3.10.98]

There are resonances, hints and gentle symbols across the play which give it a rich and complex texture. *The Weir* is anything but a series of 'spooky stories', although McPherson writes some excellent monologues (his previous work has all been monologues), and it is far more than just a dramatic metaphor. It is about 'losing and looking for kindred spirits' [*The Daily Telegraph*, 19.10.98]. It is about human interaction, the gentle ebb and flow of friendship, sympathy and of isolation and loneliness. The company presents us with a gripping and ultimately uplifting picture of humans – their emotions, humour, flaws, wit and companionship – that reminds you why you go to the theatre. Ian Rickson's direction is a masterpiece of subtlety. He has brought out poignancy, pathos, humour and much else that is only hinted at in the text on the page. Words and sentences are given real meaning and the pace is perfect. As John Gross says from *The Sunday Telegraph* 'Ian Rickson, like all the best directors, directs with the art that conceals art. I've no idea exactly what he has done, but the result speaks for itself.' [13.7.97]

THE PLACE OF PERFORMANCE

- The Duke of York's is a classic West End Theatre. The Royal Court moved there as their 'home' theatre in Sloane Square was being refurbished with the help of a Lottery grant. Immediately, this sets up a contradiction. The Royal Court has a long-established reputation for being ground breaking and radical yet here is the company in a highly commercial, West End, traditional venue. The audience look like an 'average' West End audience.

- The theatre had a small, very crowded foyer. A rather genteel entrance, it gives the impression that the venue is for a traditional, middle-class, theatregoing public.

- The crowds indicate that *The Weir* is popular, confirming the press reports on the noticeboards outside.

- The tiny Royal Court Bookshop is most prominently displaying Stanislavski texts. This may be a coincidence but it puts thoughts of naturalism into your mind even before going into the theatre space.

THE PERFORMANCE SPACE (AND ACTORS' AND AUDIENCE SPACE)

- You seem deep in the bowels of the theatre in the stalls. It is an unusually long way down. This actually helps remove us from everyday reality.

- The auditorium is standard, traditional West End. It has three tiers, ornate balconies, red plush-velvet seats and boxes. There is again a deep sense of paradox when thinking of the iconoclasm associated with The Royal Court. This gives a slight sense of unease. The auditorium is dim. Perhaps the production team is trying to hide the fact that they are in a West End theatre!

- Having been advised to sit near the front, we are in Row D. The auditorium is formal. It is a proscenium arch stage and the seats are in rows facing the stage. There is no curtain. We can dimly see the set; it seems as if we are in a fourth wall convention. The signs indicate a piece of naturalism.

- The stage ahead appears to be very slightly raked. That and our proximity to the stage help our immediate engagement with the piece.

- The fly tower above the stage is lit. There is a sense of an outer world beyond the intimate interior of the set (see next section). Even before the piece begins, therefore, we are reminded of the outside world. The set is illuminated only through the reflected fly tower lighting.

- The audience is full and there is an excited sense of anticipation; some people talking in the audience have seen the production before and are highly recommending it to their friends. This sets a positive note just before the piece opens and helps to redress any unease felt earlier.

- There is no interval in this 90-minute play so the auditorium plays little part in affecting the remainder of the production. The lack of interval is a bonus; it is so much easier to become immersed in the theatre piece.

THE SET   (Designer: Rae Smith) As with all productions, we swiftly sketched out a diagram of the set whilst at the theatre to help recall details of the setting.)

There is only one set in the show; all the action takes place in a contemporary Irish pub. We know it is contemporary because of allusions in the text: Jack is clearly in his late fifties yet he was 'about seven' in 1951 when the weir was built; a 1990 bottle of white wine is jokingly described as 'vintage' by Brendan. Despite being contemporary, the bar is old fashioned and lacking in care or style.

- The majority of CSL and USL comprises the bar. The bar and the three, non-matching bar stools against it are tatty. There are bottles with optics and glasses on shelves, with old plastic crates under the shelves. Behind the glasses, at one point, there is a faded newspaper picture of a football team. Whether this was something Brendan (the owner) was once involved with or just a picture of his favoured team from some time ago, the impression is the same – past activity rather than present. There are several old postcards; again, there is the feeling of nothing having changed or moved on for years as there are no *new* postcards. Harp and Guinness are the only selection on pump; the bar has very little stock. There is an old television propped on one of the shelves. It looks suspiciously like an old black and white set; you wonder if it works. Also behind the bar is an old, cheap-looking, bronzed map of Ireland and a very old-fashioned black plastic price board with white letters that you clip into place. There are some old trophies, perhaps football or snooker, behind the bar.

- DSL is a hard-backed chair near the wall. On the wall are pictures of the ruined abbey, the photograph of the opening of the weir and 'the view'. Again these are all old.

- DSR There is a working fireplace with an old stove built into it. The stove is fed in the play. By the fireplace is a dull, cloth-covered, faded armchair and two upright chairs with a small bar table. None of the chairs or tables in the bar match. The armchair has a cushion on it covered in 1970s-style material.

- USR is the entrance, some coat hooks and another small table with two chairs (not used in the production).

The set supports the naturalism of the text. There were several relevant additional points arising from the set and props:

- The wallpaper on the walls has marks where pictures used to be.

- The fire works. When Brendan and Jim open the stove, smoke comes out and you can smell the fire. When Brendan moves the armchair nearer the fire for Valerie near the end of the play, he checks the distance of the heat from the fire with his hands so that it's not too hot.

- There is great play with trying to get the beer pump to work. (It doesn't.)

- Several bottles are opened fresh including a wine bottle, complete with foil around the top.

- Money is carefully counted for the till.

The attention to detail was impressive. This served several purposes.

First, it sent strong signals that the piece was in the genre of naturalism. From the beginning of the evening, the audience had an understanding of the kind of theatre they were watching therefore. It was unlikely that the theatrical *form* was going to challenge us and subconsciously you relax into the familiar naturalistic mode of communication.

Secondly, and closely connected, the audience were encouraged and given every opportunity to enter the fictional world of the people in the bar. Naturalism encourages this and the *quality* of the naturalistic detail in the set and props simply made the journey into the fiction very easy. We were being invited to share this world and vicariously experience the interplay of the characters and their emotions.

Thirdly, the detail in the set, props and their use matched the meticulous quality of the performances. This was a feature of the production /-/ the attention to tiny details. Because of this, the delicacy of the relationships and the emotions were communicated in tiny, subtle ways. This was entirely appropriate for the nature of the text, which presents a fragile web of emotions that needed very gentle handling. Brendan checking the heat from the fire before Valerie sits there is a perfect example of this. You noticed it on the edge of your vision and you were aware of the point of this (the need to care for and cosset Valerie), but it slipped into your understanding without being forced.

TECHNICAL (SOUND AND LIGHT) (Lighting designer: Paule Constable) This would not be a good production to discuss with *particular* reference to technical effects alone. They were strong but they were not an 'obvious' part of the production. The sound and light effects added to the naturalism of the piece throughout the play. There were particular moments worth noting, however:

- The lighting of the fly tower gave a sense of a yawning space outside the bar. Presumably this was to represent the outside world but it was not particularly effective.

- The play opened with a howling wind noise; we hear later in the text that the weather is bad outside. The noise drops after Jack enters the bar. The sound enhances the sense of isolation of the bar and the extreme rural nature of the area.

- Jack walked into a soft spotlight when he first came into the bar. The point of this was not clear. Perhaps we were supposed to suspect that this was going to be 'a strange little evening' for Jack.

- When the ghost stories were being told, the lights dimmed and the wind noise was raised in volume. This was almost too obvious but it did enhance the atmosphere. The part of the stage where Valerie sat remained brighter than the rest. As suggested above, Valerie appeared as a catalyst, as a focus for change; keeping a brighter light on her supported this. Also, the men were telling the stories *to her*, of course.

- When Jack tells his ghost story, the lights have dimmed and he is front lit so that he has a silhouette shadow against the bar. This was particularly noticeable when he was talking about the wind outside the door. Again, the effect added to the atmosphere.

COSTUME (Costume supervisor: Iona Kendrick) As for Technical, above, this would not be a good production to discuss for costume alone. As with all the other elements of the production, however, the costumes were intrinsic to the success of the piece. The costumes had changed for the different casts. Although they were different, both sets of costumes were highly appropriate for the characters. I have selected the most memorable for each character from across the two productions.

Brendan: Shapeless dark shade of trousers. An old lightly patterned sweater in a basic stone colour with blues, browns etc., which you suspect might have been bought from a traditional department store several years earlier. He wears it with a shirt underneath and pushed-up sleeves.
Jack: As indicated in the text, he wore a grey suit, slightly shabby and no tie.
Jim: Pale grey trousers, pale shirt, a dark V-necked buttoned-up cardigan with large diamonds in other colours on the front. These were popular in the late 1970s/early 1980s.
Finbar: Off-white trousers, pale red shirt and a smart textured jacket.
Valerie: Jeans, a smartish soft shirt and a jacket.

Valerie and Finbar are consciously dressed in a more recent style than the others, of course. Finbar's clothes were more showy and, presumably, more expensive. In each production, it was most obvious that his clothes were not appropriate for the bar. Valerie, on the other hand, would have fitted in easily. Jack had put a suit on to show that the locals weren't 'hicks'. Brendan and Jim looked very comfortable in their slightly shabby clothes!

PERFORMANCES   Certain points stood out about the performances:

- All the characters in each performance seen were entirely believable in their parts.

- The effortless *ensemble* performance. This company were playing as an entity with one person easily passing the lead to another whilst the others comprehensively supported every move.

- As noted above, the level of meticulous detail helped convey the complexity of the roles and the emotional ranges needed.

- The 'yarns' were told by the male characters with an edge of self-parody from the characters. Each gave the impression of dismissing the event as impossible at various points, almost laughing at themselves as being ridiculous. Yet, each would then show that they *had* believed the story under the bravado.

- The performances of each character when they were *not* speaking were as powerful as those speaking. The various grunts of agreement and other familiar, everyday sounds and movements of communication added considerably to the effect of life in the bar.

- The use of space was excellent. Each character seemed to have an allotted area on stage. Jim's was the stool UCS and that section of the bar; Jack's was the DSL chair and wall; Brendan's was behind the bar; Valerie and Finbar occupied the DSR chairs and table. An ease of occupancy developed as the evening progressed. It also gave the opportunity for some fascinating proxemics. For example, Valerie told her chilling tale not from her DSR corner but standing in the gap where the bar flap normally sits. Of course, pragmatically this gave her a good centre-stage position for this key moment in her performance but it also supported other points in the piece: Valerie's entry into the men's world (the bar); hers as the central story, because it was the most real and painful; the feeling that she was surrounded and supported by the physical and human occupants of this far-away rural place rather than being on the edge of life in Dublin.

- The pace was rhythmic and lyrical. The production moved from lengthy pauses, particularly in the easy 'locals' section at the beginning to the jabbing near-argument between Finbar and Jack about frightening Valerie.

There were particular 'moments' worth noting:

- Everyone watching Brendan in silence as he poured the glass of white wine for Valerie. When she had sipped this and proclaimed 'It's gorgeous', there was a mini jubilation as the characters smiled, clicked their tongues, physically relaxed and so on. This gave the moment a sense of ritual – a ritualistic welcome for Valerie.

- The silence during Valerie's story was remarkable. The bar seemed completely still and yet you were aware of the deep sympathy being expressed (how?) by these non-moving characters. They all stood at the end of the story, as if in respect for the dead daughter, Niamh.

- The gradual rapport between Brendan and Valerie as the play moved on was delicately performed. There were smiles of recognition to each other (about their companions) and a moment when eyes were held in gentle and grateful friendship just before they went out. This tentative building of a relationship is only just evident in the production – if at all; you think you might be imagining it because you are hoping for it, however subconsciously. Kate Bassett saw it as well: 'McPherson also makes you see that a "ghost" might not be just a figure from a creepy folk tale or a mirage of someone already dead. It could also be the image of a soulmate long dreamed of, of a living person like Valerie who comes to fill a dark, sad gap in the isolated life of someone like Brendan.' [*The Daily Telegraph* 19.10.98]

- Most notable was the *wealth* of tiny details in all the performances at various points in the play:
  - ★ Finbar trying to edge his chair slightly closer to Valerie but she edges away, all performed so slightly that it would easily be missed;
  - ★ With an impatient shake of his head, Brendan waving away the money Jim offers for the small bottle of whiskey he is taking home in a gruff display of friendship;
  - ★ Valerie echoing Finbar's gesture when he says that he has an 'eye for the gap' in the market as if she subconsciously finds Finbar amusing;
  - ★ Valerie sitting forward with her hands together and fingers apart during the first ghost story, controlled and tense.

There were individual performances worth mentioning. We have elected to concentrate on just three of the performances. This is one way of recording the performances rather than undertaking a lengthy analysis of each. By selecting in this way, you are going through a sifting process. In these notes I am recording the performances of Brendan, Jack and Jim in the performance on 30 January 1999. Coyle, Norton and Ahern had been in the cast from the first performance.

Brendan	Brendan Coyle
Jack	Jim Norton
Jim	Kieran Ahern
(Finbar	Dermot Crowley)
(Valerie	Michelle Fairley)

Brendan Coyle was, by turn, lugubrious, taciturn, gentle, amused, patient, understanding, embarrassed, generous, bashful, calm and thoughtful. This was a finely tuned and deeply attractive performance. Coyle was vocally delightful. He used extended sibilance on many occasions, so words were drawn out and left hanging: 'It's intrusive, it's bad manners, it's...'. The 's' was continued on without finishing the rest of the sentence as if it were an irrelevancy. He has a rich Irish voice which was used far less than the other characters (Brendan doesn't have a story to tell) but which resonated round the auditorium. He listened and watched with stillness and concentration. As Benedict Nightingale said in *The Times*, 'is there an actor in London better able to fill silences with brooding emotion? I can't think of one.' [11.7.97] Brendan is the only one who doesn't try to suggest to Valerie that she was mistaken in her story. Coyle was sharp and forceful in his defence of her, speaking with annoyance and impatience, stressing points by thumping the bar: 'She said she knew what it was... But you wouldn't hear someone's voice on the fucking thing, Jim.'

Kieran Ahern's Jim was a gentle, simple man whose life revolved around 'the mammy'. This middle-aged mother's boy with a system for horse racing was the most endearing character on stage. He appears shy and self-conscious at times. At one point he sits on a chair near Valerie, looking hesitant and nervous about doing so until Finbar's suspicious look seems to give him confidence in his own daring. He told his ghost story in a calm manner which developed into disgust at what he'd seen and heard. This was a celibate man speaking with disbelief at evil. His final speech was deeply moving as he plucked up the courage to say to Valerie 'I'm very sorry about what's happened to you.... You enjoy your peace and quiet here now. And we'll see you again. You're very nice....'. Ahern took her hands and spoke without embarrassment in a calm, meaningful and clear voice. His final handshake was a perfect moment of gentlemanly warmth.

Norton as Jack was lively, talkative, cantankerous, short (with Finbar), witty, crafty, caring, lonely, unfulfilled, courageous and sad. If Valerie is the thematic focus of the play, Jack is the dynamic focus. Whether downing 'a small one' or listening to a story, hands deep in his pocket, or skipping across the stage in the middle of a delighted joke, Jim Norton had the audience delighting in his every slight mood change. The most broad-ranging of the characters, he has to reach from jovial excitement to tearful self-anger and regret, and is utterly at ease with all registers. Certain moments were particularly affecting: he carefully pulls his shirt sleeves down so that he looks his best for the visitor; his voice breaks with emotion as he talks of the girl he let get away; the beautiful moment when he says 'Something about your company. Inspiring, ha?' to Valerie with such sincerity in his look to her; the way he covers his mouth with his hands in mock horror after he inadvertently compares Valerie to a 'pile of shite'. This is a superbly crafted performance that communicates layers of complexity in this unfulfilled garage owner.

OVERALL IMPACT AND AUDIENCE RECEPTION

The response to *The Weir* has been exceptional.

This play has more than a touch of Yeats and Synge in it, writers from a hundred years ago. It is a piece of hopeful lyric naturalism in a period of deeply disturbing postmodern texts such as Welsh's *Trainspotting*, Ravenhill's *Shopping and Fucking* and the young suicide victim Sarah Kane's *Blasted and Cleansed*. It is from the same stable – that bastion of new, confrontational, iconoclastic theatre, The Royal Court Theatre. It seems remarkable. However, good, new Irish writing was very popular in London in the late 1990s. Whilst these plays may not have radically challenged form or content in the theatre, they were weighty, thought-provoking, good theatre. The production of *The Weir* was the best of these. It is a combination of fine writing, first-class direction, superb performances and excellent narrative. There are messages and meanings that speak loudly to a contemporary audience about continuity, isolation, fear and, above all, loneliness.

The following extracts help give an impression of the impact of the play. They are taken from a number of reviews written when the play first appeared in 1997 and when it moved to the larger space at The Duke of York's in 1998. These can all be found in the magazine *Theatre Record*. Out bi-weekly, this journal reproduces all the reviews for new productions. For those reviewing and commenting on major productions (not just in London), it is an excellent source.

- McPherson is a natural storyteller, with the confidence to allow his characters to spin strange and elaborate anecdotes and mock themselves while doing so. The cast capture the twilight pub atmosphere exactly, switching from reflective bouts of listening, to sparring, joshing and brooding. [*The Independent on Sunday*, 13.7.97]

- McPherson is also saying something about sexuality and the nature of the Irish imagination, about the residual fear of women.... No praise, in fact, is too high for a play full of the echoing sadness of disappointed lives...The acting is also perfect. Jim Norton beautifully shows how Jack's flinty spryness conceals a sense of lost happiness. [*The Guardian*, 10.7.97]

- Its [*The Weir's*] second achievement is to supply a robust picture of male cosiness and discomfort. ... It's difficult to imagine the details of pub life and camaraderie better evoked or better acted. ...And there is the easy sinking into habitual postures: as each man comes forward to tell his story, the others slump onto bar, table or bench as if bracketed into place. [*The Observer*, 13.7.97]

- While the ghost stories are fun, it is the sense of community and of a sadness kept at bay that lifts the evening into the realm of first-rate drama. [*The Express*, 15.7.97]

- In myriad small ways we are constantly led to reassess our sense of the characters and of the effect they have on one another. ...And as for the acting, a piece as concentrated and tightly knit as this couldn't afford a single only-quite-good performance, and it doesn't get one. Jim Norton is utterly compelling as Jack – talkative and volatile, yet sometimes coming out with a note as deep as Paul Robeson. Gerard Horan (Finbar), Brendan Coyle (Brendan) and Kieran Ahern (Jim) are all flawlessly authentic. Julia Ford (Valerie)... brings to it everything that is called for, in skill and emotional transparency alike. [*The Sunday Telegraph*, 13.7.97]

- McPherson is using something that seems to be a genuine survival in celtic culture, a sense of otherness or mystery that exists in parallel with the banal material world. Thus McPherson makes a critique of Ireland even as he finds something magical surviving. There is nothing particularly musical about these voices, and their language is for the most part crude, yet it is true that the cast play together like a string quintet. The long solo passages are decorated with trills and bass notes of interruption, and there are fine moments of ensemble as the characters square up to each other in anger, or share moments of grief. [*The Sunday Times*, 13.7.97]

- What is it that has inspired most of today's rich crop of Irish play-wrights? Something, surely, akin to what impelled so many of the 19th-century and early 20th-century Russian writers: a sense of what the Russians called *poshlust* – the unimportance of provincial life. For it is in the 'unimportance' of ordinary daily life that the true nature of life becomes most apparent – now petty, now strange; here comic, there pathetic. ...Through a fabric embroidered full of details, the play makes us feel the transitory charm of life even while, no less powerfully, it tells us of life's wastefulness. [*The Financial Times*, 10.7.97]

- The shifts of mood and interplay of character are beautifully caught. So are the small rituals, drinking, the long vistas of boredom, the joshing, the sudden flare-ups, the co-existence in the same person of opposing qualities – tact and tactlessness, jealousy and geniality. [*The Sunday Telegraph*, 18.10.98]

- There isn't a better piece of ensemble acting in London. It's not just the way they talk, it's the way they listen. The move to a bigger stage allows Jim Norton's hilarious portrayal of the feisty, unpredictable Jack to go up several notches. This contrasts beautifully with Brendan Coyle's slow-moving thoughtfulness as the publican. He fills the stage with a watchful strength. [*The Independent on Sunday*, 18.10.98]

For further information on *The Weir*, contact The Royal Court in London for their education pack. Written by Janette Smith, this is an excellent resource for the play.

2.4 *Questions and suggested frameworks for answers on contemporary productions*

Never go into an exam with a prepared essay which you then attempt to adapt to a question. This simply does not work. You should take in comprehensive notes with which you are thoroughly familiar; previous essays will only distract you.

The first example is typical of questions that call for a broad analysis of a production. The second example would require more detailed notes.

ACTIVITY   Discuss *one* play you have seen, commenting on why you found it effective.

POINTS TO CONSIDER

- Decide what you mean by 'effective'; it has to relate to something. Was it effective in relation to the director's intentions, for example?

- Be prepared to discuss the key elements that made it 'effective', for example the style of production, the performances, the design elements, etc. Use your notes closely for this.

- Ensure that you respond from a personal standpoint – 'why *you* found it effective'.

A DETAILED ANALYSIS   State the name of the production, the company performing it (if relevant), the place it was seen and the date on which it was seen.

Introduction

Explain what you think the production was trying to achieve. This might be mainly the directorial interpretation (or company objectives) or it could be a combination of this and the dramatist's intentions. (For example, Théâtre de Complicité were attempting to stage the essence of Bruno Schulz's life and some of his writings, using a particular form of performance style. You would probably mention 'the migration of forms is the essence of life' as a key to the production.)

You should state your position: did you find the play effective? Did *you* feel the aims of the piece were successfully achieved? (For the purposes of this framework, we will assume that you have selected a production which you *did* find effective.)

Main body

These sections will each take an aspect of the production that helped make it such an effective piece. Taking *The Street of Crocodiles* as an example for this framework, these might be the set/props, the physicality of the performances, the use of music and voice and the overall impact.

For each element, you should:

- give detailed examples from the production

- incorporate *your* response to these examples

- explain how this successfully conveys the company's intentions (as summarised in your introduction).

For example, the set/props:

- Give a description of the set at the beginning of the show.

- Explain your response to this; what did you think and feel as you saw it?

- If you haven't already done so, explain how the set fitted in with the overall intentions of the production.

- Discuss the changing of the set later in the show, if appropriate.

- Explain the point of this and whether you felt it enhanced the production's impact.

- Take some of the key props/furniture (e.g. the books, the desks). Give examples of their use.

- Incorporate your reaction/response to this.

- Relate these examples to the overall intentions.

Adapt this procedure for the remaining examples.

Conclusion

Summarise your response by suggesting that other aspects of the production also contributed to its effectiveness. You might mention the programme and finish with an apposite quote. You could bring in a professional critic's response and comment on this – do you agree with him or her? There may be something else about the production that you want to raise: for example, has it had an impact upon you since you saw it? Has the production under discussion helped your understanding of any other theatrical experience you have had? You must feel free to be tangential.

ACTIVITY **Compare the performances of two actors in two contrasting theatre events that you have experienced.**

POINTS TO CONSIDER
- 'Compare' does not mean that one has to be better than the other. You are asked to judge the performances depending upon the requirements of the piece. Your comments will make connections, however. You might discuss the movements of the two – one actor

might move slowly, deliberately and always carefully, which is appropriate for the naturalistic character she is playing, while the other might use expansive, overt gestures and move loosely and in an exaggerated manner. You could point out that each form of movement was appropriate for the style of theatre – one was naturalistic and the other was much closer to symbolism and physical theatre. You *are* comparing and contrasting; you are *not* giving a value judgement, however.

- You need not necessarily talk about *plays*; however, you must choose a theatrical event that has enough characterisation to discuss.

- Only select such a question if your notes have enough detail about characters; you will need to draw upon several examples of the actors' performances.

- Ensure that the productions are contrasting.

A DETAILED ANALYSIS   State the name of the productions, the companies performing them (if relevant), the places they were seen and the dates on which they were seen.

Introduction

Explain why you have chosen these two theatrical events. Briefly describe why they are 'contrasting'. Name the selected characters. Explain your response – did you find one performance successful and one not? Were both successful? (If you choose the former you may find it difficult to avoid *obvious* 'good' and 'bad' descriptions. A more interesting comparison can be drawn from two contrasting performances, both of which you admired or not.)

Main body

To discuss the relevance of the performances, you will have to explain the objectives of each production so that you can place the characters within the context of the overall aims. For example, if you selected Madame Arkadina for one role (from the Royal National Theatre's production of *The Seagull*, as discussed in section 2.3), you would need to place the character in the context of the production. It appears that the director wanted to emphasise the hazy distinctions between life and the theatre in this production, much as Chekhov did. Arkadina epitomised the theatrical, in looks, manner and voice.

By doing this for each character, you are giving the criteria by which you will be judging them. For example, you expect the actress playing Arkadina to be theatrical at certain moments of the play. It is now your task to explain the methods used to produce these effects and the measure of success achieved.

The subsequent sections will depend very much upon the productions chosen. To *compare* two performances you should find common headings and work through these, analysing each performance under each heading, finding similarities and differences and drawing conclusions about the success of each. Such headings will depend upon the productions, but you might choose from the following:

- physicality, including gesture, action, body positions, facial expressions

- voice, including tone, pace, volume, etc.

- key moments in the production where this actor clearly emphasised central concerns of the piece

- key moments in the text where the actor has demonstrated strong elements of the character that you expected

- use of the audience

- ability to fulfil obvious demands from the text, such as a particular physical skill (e.g. hanging off scaffolding as a dung beetle in Berkoff's *Metamorphosis*).

In each section you should deal with both characters. You will need to:

- give examples appropriate to the heading

- discuss them according to the nature of the production

- explain why it was successful, or not.

If the objectives of the two pieces are so different that there are few common headings, you could undertake this question by analysing one character in full and then the other, and comparing them in the conclusion. However, you are in danger of not putting enough 'comparison' into an answer which specifically asks you to 'compare'.

Conclusion
You will want to summarise, perhaps by commenting on the impact each performance had on you at the time and in retrospect. You could draw on the words of others such as critics, commenting on these in terms of your own analysis. Other appropriate comments might refer to the status of the performers: are they well known? If so, were your expectations fulfilled?

PART 3

Key Theatre Practitioners

3.0 *Introduction*

In the first three sections of this book, we have concentrated on a better understanding of how texts are made, and how they can be better understood in performance by you, as audience. We have addressed the **text** from the standpoints of presenting theatre, language and background, and reviewed three actual **productions**.

In this final section we move to a discussion of six **theatre practitioners** whose lives were dominated by their desire for change: change to prevailing theatre practice, which they saw as inhibiting experimentation. Above all, they were all people who took risks, since by challenging outmoded ideas they were forced to provide radical alternatives. We now recognise these as models for our own time.

These ideas, as you will discover, ranged across the whole spectrum of theatre, from Gordon Craig's desire to reform the way plays were designed to Peter Brook's concepts for the redefinition of a performance.

We have chosen these six practitioners because they reflect the widest possible range of theoretical ideas, underpinned by practice; a study of each of them will reveal what their influence has been, and why their work is relevant to the theatre of our own time. (These six are named practitioners in two of the three new UK A/S and A2 Drama and Theatre Studies specification.)

Edward Gordon Craig: see section 3.1

In the early years of the 20th century, **Gordon Craig** redefined ideas about the way a play is staged. He broke away from the 19th-century model in which he had been trained as an actor and began to look at stage space as an architect might design a building. His designs were truly three-dimensional. Using height and depth they allowed the actor to move in and through a space, which could be changed in mood by subtle variations in light.

Stanislavski: see section 3.2

Craig worked with **Stanislavski**, who dedicated his life to changing the way an actor might be trained. He wrote down and published his System, and it is likely that every time you visit the theatre you will be seeing actors who have experienced some aspect of this training. Inevitably, his ideas have been re-interpreted by succeeding generations of directors and actors, but, like all outstanding practitioners, his work still offers us a challenge.

Antonin Artaud: see section 3.3

Antonin Artaud's work can be looked upon as almost out of his time. Had his ideas been taken up and appreciated in his lifetime, the history of the theatre would have been very different. Along with those of other equally innovative practitioners, his theories were responsible for the explosion of alternative theatre after the Second World War. Great directors like Peter Brook took and adapted his radical theories and revitalised theatre with new ideas about the relationship between actor and audience and what constituted a performance. Artaud's lasting influence on the way popular music is presented has meant that his ideas are more pervasive than you might realise.

Bertolt Brecht:
see section 3.4

Brecht is the only playwright out of the six practitioners. However, he was more than that, since he also directed and staged his own plays. If we were to highlight just one important strand in his work it would be his belief that theatre is a collaborative venture. He gave 20th-century theatre the term 'epic' as a means of describing plays and their structure, and he worked from the belief that theatre could be a platform for political change. Brecht is sometimes regarded as the antithesis of Stanislavski, but this would be a very narrow view. For example, his ideas on the art of acting were very different, but that should not place him in opposition. Rather, it should alert us to the fact that these men had complementary ideas which, taken together, reflect the diversity of practice during the 20th century.

Jerzy Grotowski:
see section 3.5

Jerzy Grotowski was hugely influential on any number of fellow practitioners; again and again his name is acknowledged as a truly radical and alternative voice, particularly in the late 1960s, when his ideas were spreading throughout the theatre world. His theories, which are summarised in his concept of *A Poor Theatre*, challenged a post-war bourgeois theatre and led, however indirectly, to the establishment of much avant-garde theatre, which recognised 'poor' as an antidote to 'rich'. In returning to a close study of the actor, he encouraged a move towards rigorous training and the realisation of an actor's potential through self-examination.

Peter Brook:
see section 3.6

Peter Brook is the only living and working practitioner in this section and as such is an ideal example with which to conclude this very selective list. This is primarily because he was so greatly influenced by both Artaud and Grotowski, to name just two sources, and as he stands at the end of one century and the beginning of the next, he is still a working director who continues to strive for what he would term as the universal 'truth'. He in his turn has had an enormous influence on a number of contemporary directors who pay homage to his ideals and ethos.

If we were to isolate just one quality from his work it would be his desire to see theatre as an act of celebration with his expressed objective to 'complete the circle' between the actor and his audience.

Theatre uses all sorts of methods to create meaning; there is no one right prescription. One of the most fascinating aspects of this section is the way in which such diverse opinions are still valid in their different ways. We look to the past to provide us with models of practice: you might agree or disagree with the methods described in Part 3, but simply by studying them and coming to terms with their implications you will have moved towards defining your own views on theatre.

Sections 3.1–3.6 all follow the same pattern. We start with a **chronology** of the life of each practitioner, followed by a brief **biography** which places him in the context of his time.

We have called the central section **Theory and Practice**: this discusses in detail how the practitioner's main ideas were formed and explores their importance to theatre. Two further sections look at those people who were major **influences** on each practitioner, making a major impact on his thinking and development, and how in turn these practitioners had what we term as **followers**. Both of these sections include mini-bibliographies on the subjects covered. We then give a summary of the practitioner's theories, to be considered in relation to the student's own practical work and viewing of other productions.

Finally there are three sections that deal with different aspects of study: a **bibliography** lists books and articles for further reading, there are ideas for relevant **research,** and the final section tackles some **themes** at examination level.

Throughout the text you will find activities that will start you thinking about how to translate theory into practice. Above all, these practitioners were practical people, working in theatre, experimenting, collaborating, writing down their ideas and arguing for theatre, in whatever form, as a vital and meaningful part of all our lives.

3.1 *Edward Gordon Craig (1872–1966)*

Figure 3a Edward Gordon Craig as a young man

3.1.1 A CHRONOLOGY

Father is a noted architect and mother an actress

1872: Born, Stevenage, Herts. His father is Edward William Godwin, the architect, his mother Ellen Terry, the actress. From an early age regularly visits the theatre to see his mother as leading lady in productions by Henry Irving.

1884: At the early age of 12 joins his mother and Irving on a tour of the United States. Is already playing small non-speaking roles in the company's repertoire.

Henry Irving: see section 3.1.4

1889: Begins a career as a full-time actor in Irving's company at the Lyceum Theatre. Works and learns under the watchful eye of 'his second father'.

Herkomer: see section 3.1.4

1892: Attends the lecture given by Herkomer on Scenic Art.

Pryde and Nicholson: see section 3.1.4

1893: Living at Uxbridge. Becomes friends with James Pryde and William Nicholson (The Beggarstaff Brothers). Begins to learn the art of wood engraving.

Makes his first production at Uxbridge of de Musset's *On ne badine avec l'amour*. He designs the scenery and costumes and plays the leading role.

Gives up acting. Publishes a magazine

1897: The end of his life as an actor. In this final year he plays Hamlet in London in his own company. Continues to draw and make wood engravings. Starts to publish a magazine, *The Page* (1898–1901), illustrated with his own work.

Martin Shaw: see section 3.1.4

1898: Meets the conductor Martin Shaw, who introduces Craig to Bach's *St. Matthew Passion*. From this date he works on schemes for its production, which is never to be realised.

Dido and Aeneas: see section 3.1.3

1900, 17–19 May: At the Hampstead Conservatoire of Music (now known as the Embassy Theatre) he directs and designs Purcell's *Dido and Aeneas* (1689). Martin Shaw is the conductor of the Purcell Opera Society, entirely made up of amateur singers.

A specially constructed stage with a low, wide proscenium is built for this production of Purcell's opera, which according to critics set aside 'the worn-out tradition of realism'.

Designs and directs a masque

1901, 25 March: The production transfers to the Coronet Theatre and *The Masque of Love* is added to make a double bill. This second piece is handled more like a ballet. To attract audiences Ellen Terry is persuaded to act in a curtain-raiser, *Nance Oldfield*.

Final production by the Purcell Society

1902, 10 March: At the Great Queen Street Theatre *The Masque of Love* is revived and he directs and designs Handel's *Acis and Galatea* (1721). Craig's ingenious, attractive and economical staging of Handel's opera at an out-of-the-way theatre cannot save the Purcell Opera Society from financial collapse.

A nativity play, again with an amateur cast

17 December: The poet Laurence Housman calls in Craig and Shaw to stage his nativity play, *Bethlehem*. Performances have to be given to private subscribers, as the Lord Chamberlain objects to the presentation of the Holy Family. A special proscenium and auditorium are built in what was then known as the Great Hall of the University of London.

1903, 21 January: At the invitation of his uncle, the actor Fred Terry, he designs scenes for *For Sword or Song*. He considers his scenes mere 'pot-boilers'.

Directs his mother in a play by Ibsen

First visit to Europe

15 April: He designs and directs *The Vikings of Helgeland* by Ibsen. This gloomy play is an artistic success, but most critics feel that Ellen Terry is miscast as the bloodthirsty Amazon, Hjordis, a role she has chosen on her first venture into management. Craig is writing and designing. Travels to Berlin to visit Otto Brahm of the Lessing Theatre. Is invited to design a production there.

23 May: Ellen Terry has always pleased the public as Beatrice in *Much Ado About Nothing*, so this production replaces *The Vikings*. He has to devise a simple and economical set quickly and proves himself capable of doing so. The production goes on tour.

Isadora Duncan: see section 3.1.4
Serlio: see section 3.1.4

1904: Travelling in Europe. Meets and begins to live with the American dancer Isadora Duncan. Is studying Serlio's *Architettura*.

First publication

Berlin: Otto Brahm calls in Craig to design the sets for Otway's play *Venice Preserved*, but they disagree and only two scenes are used. Publishes his collection of essays: *The Art of the Theatre*, in English and German.

Designs are prepared for a number of European productions, but his demand for total control of the staging means that none are used.

Scene: see section 3.1.4

1906, Florence: Craig designs an impressive set for Eleanora Duse's appearance in Ibsen's *Rosmersholm*. Is working on *Scene*, a kinetic (moving) theatre based on Serlio's drawings.

Begins to publish his theatre magazine: *The Mask*

1908: Publishes a theatre magazine, which he calls *The Mask*, from his base in Florence. Uses a disused theatre, the Arena Goldoni, as a workshop/studio. Seldom returns to England during the rest of his life. Agrees to produce *Hamlet* for Stanislavski at the Moscow Art Theatre. Isadora Duncan acts as the go-between.

Yeats: see sections 3.1.3, 3.1.5

1909: Allows W.B. Yeats, the Irish poet and playwright, to use his system of *Screens* in the Abbey Theatre (Dublin) productions of his verse dramas.

Mise-en-scène: see Glossary

1910: Travels to Moscow and spends much of the year on preparations for *Hamlet* in discussion with Stanislavski. A model stage is constructed and the system of *Screens* which will provide the setting is explained. He takes the actors through the mise-en-scène. Two stenographers make a record of these conversations in Russian and English.

Screens are used at the Abbey Theatre

1911: At the Abbey Theatre, Dublin, the *Screens* are tried for the first time, and they remain in use for a number of years. Their success leads Yeats to rewrite his dramas for their use.

The Moscow *Hamlet* uses Screens for the staging

26 December: Moscow Art Theatre *Hamlet*. This famous production – the fruit of three years' work – has far-reaching influences on European

stagecraft. This is the last significant production using Craig's designs and with his involvement that is ever staged. He is 39 years old.

Opens a school in Florence

1913: *Towards a New Theatre* is published in London. Opens a school in his base in Florence. The First World War leads to its abrupt closure.

Continues to develop plans for Bach's oratorio

1914: Begins to build a large-scale model for the staging of Bach's *St. Matthew Passion.*

1915 onwards: Continues to publish *The Mask.* Writes marionette plays. Studies theatre history. Continues to write, and to exhibit his drawings and models in a war-torn Europe (1915–1922).

1919: Publishes *The Theatre Advancing*, another volume of critical essays.

Final production in which he takes a practical role

1926, Copenhagen: Ibsen's early play *The Crown Pretenders* is staged by Danish theatre's two leading actors, the brothers Poulsen, who honour Craig by inviting him to produce it. He creates designs which use architectural motifs, with strong and vibrant colours in the costumes.

1928, New York: Craig has long been interested in producing *Macbeth.* He is persuaded to supply some designs for an American production. He has little confidence in the outcome and produces drawings which he signs 'C.P.B', which stands for 'Craig pot-boiler'.

An edition of *Hamlet* with many striking woodcuts

1930: Publishes a limited edition of *Hamlet* with 75 woodcuts. This forms a permanent record of his thinking on the play and its visual interpretation. Publishes his biography of his mentor: *Henry Irving.* It is considered a perceptive record at first hand of the actor's craft.

1931: Publishes a memoir of his mother: *Ellen Terry and Her Secret Self.*

A final summary of his early years as an actor/designer/director

1957: Publishes *Index to the Story of My Days 1872–1907.*

1966, 29 July: Dies in France aged 94.

This chronology is indebted to:

Leeper, J.   *Edward Gordon Craig*, Penguin, 1948

Innes, C.   *Edward Gordon Craig*, CUP, 1983

3.1.2 A BRIEF BIOGRAPHY

Entirely self-taught

Edward Craig says this about his father Gordon Craig:

> He was lazy in his youth and learned very little, but as he grew older, nature endowed him with extraordinary powers of perception, . . .
>
> [Craig, E.A., 1968. p.19]

Born into a theatrical family

Written after Gordon Craig was safely dead, this brief summary serves very well to introduce his early days. Craig was born into a 'theatrical' family and it is quite clear from all sources that he enjoyed an exceptional childhood. Spoiled by his mother, who was quickly parted from his father, he was abandoned for long periods of time while she returned to her first love – acting.

Extensively influenced by friends

Bearing in mind that Craig had no consistent education as a boy, it is not surprising that he relied on acquaintances and friends to help him shape his ideas. The section on Influences (3.1.4) is especially full for this practitioner, since it was these key people who sustained his growth as an artist of the theatre and who were his true teachers.

Joins his mother as an actor

At the age of 17, Craig was in search of a profession, and it seemed a natural move for him to join his mother, who was at the time Henry Irving's leading lady. In this company he learnt his craft as an actor.

He plays Hamlet as a young man

He often appeared with his mother; being young, talented and very handsome he was an appropriate leading man. Irving, his mentor, cast him in substantial roles, though the part that fascinated him most, Hamlet, he only achieved once he had his own company.

His family support his work

Throughout all his first endeavours as an actor, director and designer, his mother was supportive, lending not only money but on more than one occasion her skills as an actress. It was not until Craig left England more or less for good in 1905 that he severed the strong ties that linked him to his family.

Moves away from acting as a profession

The transition from actor to designer/director was a gradual one, stemming as much from his disenchantment with the current theatre as from a new-found ability to express his thoughts for new design directions on paper.

Success with innovative productions

Taking the bold step to work almost exclusively abroad seems to have been more an accident than a plan. He had enjoyed considerable critical success in Britain with a number of ground-breaking productions, helped enormously by his friend and colleague, the musician Martin Shaw. Their work together with largely amateur companies allowed Craig a huge amount of freedom and he took full advantage of this, trying out new ideas for staging, lighting, costume and choreography.

Working with largely amateur casts

Difficulties working with professional casts

Many of the other productions Craig put on in England featured his mother. She sponsored these and to draw the crowds, who would flock to see her, she also took leading roles. Although he came up with strong and imaginative design ideas, Craig found working with professional actors a difficult challenge, since they were so unused to the innovative designs he produced.

Visits to Europe lead to his taking up permanent residence there

These productions were not successful at the box office and when he was invited to Europe to make some designs for Otto Brahm in Berlin, Craig gradually drifted into the role of a wanderer, making his base in Florence but equally at home in Paris, Berlin and Moscow. His decision was influenced by his falling in love with the dancer Isadora Duncan, who led a similar gypsy existence.

First publication is enormously influential

A period of intense activity in design, production and research came to a conclusion with his book *The Art of the Theatre* in 1905. This confirmed Craig as a force to be reckoned with in theatrical innovation and helped to spread his ideas more readily than any number of collaborations.

The stage director was to be dominant

Direction and design are complementary crafts

Chapters in the book were written as a series of dialogues (see also Stanislavski: *An Actor Prepares*), being in effect a device for the author both to ask and to answer the appropriate questions. The fundamental theme of *The First Dialogue* was to propose the dominance of a single person as director of the drama. Craig was in a particularly strong position to perceive the need for such a person; having worked as both **designer** and **director**, he had knowledge about how one function could powerfully interact with the other.

Setting out a basic philosophy

> ... the Art of the Theatre is neither acting nor the play, it is not scene nor dance, but it consists of **all** the elements of which these things are composed: action, which is the very spirit of acting; words, which are the body of the play; line and colour, which are at the very heart of the scene; rhythm, which is the very essence of dance.
>
> [Quoted in Walton, 1983. p.52]

Isadora Duncan: see section 3.1.4

The dancer Isadora Duncan was a profound influence on Craig. After meeting her he began to express the belief that 'rhythm alone could form the basis of theatrical art'. This conviction led to the series of etchings known as *Scene* (1906) in which a single isolated figure was frozen in dramatic action in abstract settings. The next step was to make the settings move as well, thus creating a truly innovative statement, marrying the technology of theatre to a figure in motion.

A new look for the staging of Shakespeare

Craig was to demonstrate the outcome of this philosophy most fully in his production of *Hamlet* at the Moscow Art Theatre in 1911. With Stanislavski's support, and sometimes incomprehension, he was able to realise his ideas for a kinetic (moving) theatre form linked to the symbolic realisation of the text.

Symbolism: see Glossary

Symbolism was a new movement in the arts at this time and much in vogue in Russia. Essentially it was anti-realistic, appealing to the senses. Thus Craig defined Hamlet in a semi-mystical way as '... a lonely soul in a dark place' [quoted in Styan, J., *Modern Drama in Theory and Practice*, Vol 2. p.18].

> It [the production] scraped away the encrustation of antiquarian, veristic stage business that encumbered the Shakespearian canon; it subordinated the star performance to the total intellectual import of the play and, in doing so, revealed a fresh way of approaching tragedy.
>
> [Senelick, 1982. p.189]

Collaboration was difficult for him

It is ironic that at the height of his powers, Craig felt unable to sustain this momentum. There are as many reasons for this as there are books about him, but the sad fact was that he retreated from most future offers of work, not wishing to compromise or collaborate, two aspects of working in the theatre that are inescapable.

A stage visionary

In many senses, like Artaud (see section 3.3), Craig can be considered as a visionary. He excited and challenged theatre artists of his own generation with what looked like impossible visions.

Drawings that evoked exciting new worlds

His drawings and his books brought these ideas to a receptive Europe, but above all it was his woodcuts, with their deep chiaroscuro, and his etchings that evoked a new world of *The Scene:* a place where anything could and might happen, full of dramatic possibilities. His works provoked simply because of their uncompromising vision.

A potent force for change in 20th-century theatre

Craig continued to write and publish until his death, and he acted as a focus for many younger practitioners, who were influenced by his theory and practice and who metaphorically beat a path to his door to sit at the feet of the master. A prophet in his own lifetime, it was he who provided the imaginative impulse, while others promoted and practised his theory. His theories were to have an incalculable effect on how theatre developed in the 20th century.

3.1.3 THEORY AND PRACTICE

BEGINNINGS

An actor drawn towards design and direction

As an actor, Craig was a consistent and dedicated performer for almost ten years. Steeped in the family profession of acting, he took the decision to leave at no particular moment. It was a gradual process of self-education that drew him away from what had seemed an inevitable path towards a realisation of his own quite different potential.

Beggarstaff Brothers: see section 3.1.4

His meeting with the 'Beggarstaff Brothers' and their subsequent teaching equipped him as a competent artist, able to draw and make woodcuts, and with his wide-ranging reading he rapidly expanded his horizons into visual schemes for new staging.

There were four discernible influences around this time (1897), the first two taken from his reading, the second two by direct contact:
- medieval theatre, with its symbolic and sacred nature; a theatre of archetypes engaged in the re-enactment of Christ's passion
- a production at the open-air Roman theatre in Orange, France, which had been derelict since AD500

Godwin and Herkomer: see section 3.1.4
- the work of his father, Edward Godwin
- the experiments of Hubert Von Herkomer.

[Innes, 1983. p.23]

Medieval theatre as the antithesis of naturalism

Craig saw medieval theatre as the antithesis of naturalism. Performed in the open air from a series of carts which processed round the streets, with the audience in promenade, it was a truly popular theatre form. Visual splendour combined with simple direct language could impress a largely illiterate audience.

The architectural setting of Roman theatre

The theatre at Orange, by contrast, took Craig back to an even older form, where actors in high boots and masks competed for attention with the towering façade of the *scena*. Pierced with doorways and decorated with statuary, this monumental architectural setting with its visual simplicity made a lasting impression on Craig. As he wrote later:

Figure 3.1   Diagrams of Herkomer's model stage.

Once upon a time, stage scenery was architecture. A little later it became imitation architecture; still later it became imitation artificial architecture. Then it lost its head, went quite mad and has been in a lunatic asylum ever since.

[E.G.C., 1913. p.6]

Godwin's approach was not interesting to Craig

The influences of Godwin and Herkomer are touched on in section 3.1.4. That of Godwin has the least direct bearing on Craig's development, despite the fact that he was his father. Craig rescued Godwin from obscurity by publishing his writing in his magazine *The Mask*, but his father's archaeological approach to theatre did not interest him. His own themes were far from any kind of worn-out realism.

Herkomer, by contrast, provided some practical and radical solutions to staging. Although they were of the strictly naturalistic variety, Craig was very influenced by these.

Five key ideas that influenced Craig

Herkomer's key ideas included:

- the abolition of footlights
- projecting clouds on to gauze in front of a blue cyclorama and suggesting infinities with changing levels
- building up the stage floor to create textures and slopes
- a motorised system that could change the proportions of the proscenium
- suggesting that the setting should contribute to the mood of the text.

Abolition of footlights

Projections

An adjustable proscenium

All these themes were radical alternatives to traditional theatre practice, but combined they made for potent new solutions. Footlights were the norm, a leftover from the 18th century where they provided downstage illumination for the actor. Projections were entirely new. Recent advances in the technology of lighting made it possible to focus and control beams of light. A stage that could rise and fall was first installed in the 1880s in New York, but the scheme to create an adjustable proscenium was Herkomer's own, and must have appealed to the artist in Craig. It allowed him to create different ratios with his 'frame'. (See Fig. 3.1)

Herkomer's ideas were absorbed and adapted

Herkomer provided a stimulus for re-thinking methods of staging and by the time Craig came to plan his first productions (1900 onwards) these themes and those of theatres past had become absorbed into his own practice. They resurfaced relatively quickly – altered and changed and harnessed to the way Craig approached his own design.

To sum up:

- The move from acting to design was helped by learning to draw and make woodcuts.
- Themes from the past and ideas from current practitioners focused his thinking.
- New ideas for staging came from study and experiment.

EARLY PRODUCTIONS

These were:

- **1900:** *Dido and Aeneas.* Opera by Purcell (1689). Directed and designed by Craig, with musical direction by Martin Shaw.

- **1901:** *The Masque of Love.* A scenario devised and designed by Craig, adapted from Purcell's *Masque for Dioclesian*, with musical direction by Martin Shaw.

- **1902:** *Acis and Galatea.* Opera by Handel (1721). Directed and designed by Craig, with musical direction by Martin Shaw.

- **1902:** *Bethlehem.* Nativity play by Laurence Housman. Directed and designed by Craig, with musical direction by Martin Shaw.

- **1903:** *The Vikings at Helgeland.* Play by Henrik Ibsen. Directed and designed by Craig, with incidental music by Martin Shaw.

- **1903:** *Much Ado About Nothing* by Shakespeare. Directed and designed by Craig.

In this section, rather than give a detailed account of *all* the productions, we will focus specifically on the ideas that gave them such a distinctive feel and that led to early critical recognition.

DIDO AND AENEAS Craig's meeting with Martin Shaw in 1898 marked the beginning of a personal and professional friendship that unlocked for Craig an amazing creativity. Shaw's interest in early music led him to the creation of the

Figure 3.2   A reconstruction of the staging for *Dido and Aeneas*.

Martin Shaw:
see section 3.1.4

Purcell Society; with Craig involved the Society decided to stage its first opera rather than merely singing it in concert conditions.

Staging of *Dido and Aeneas*:
a concert hall transformed
into a theatre

Against all the odds they found a hall and Craig began the job of transforming it into a theatre. Like most concert halls it had a stepped stage for the orchestra and no proscenium.

> On the front platform I erected a long proscenium, built of eight immensely tall scaffolding poles [...] forming a deep frame, thus, of a rather unusual shape as prosceniums went in those days.
>
> [E.G.C. *Index to the Story of My Days*, 1981. p.228]

Three ideas that owed their
origins to Herkomer

Craig had effectively formed a long rectangle, with an entirely new proscenium ratio, and behind and above this opening had built a lighting bridge. The back wall was concealed by a white cyclorama, in front of which he hung a gauze. There were no footlights, so lanterns were installed on the bridge and concealed in the auditorium to focus on the performers (see Fig. 3.2). All these ideas were traceable to Herkomer's influence.

Very simple staging

Lighting was very subtle

Craig kept the staging very simple since there was no wing space: a throne for Dido, a trellis covered in vines and some poles to suggest the ship masts, all of which could be moved on and off very easily. He worked on the scenes in terms of colour, changing the 'Herkomer' sky with coloured light behind and in front of the gauze, giving the illusion of vastness and distance. At one point the stage floor was covered with a grey cloth from which the witches seemed to appear, bathed in a soft green/blue light. In the final scene Dido, seen against a darkening ultramarine sky, was covered by pink rose petals that descended from above.

Choreography played a large
part in the staging

Craig's choreography was kept on a simple level for his amateur chorus: strong gestural shapes were worked out that even the least experienced could achieve. Costumes were devised from cheap materials that were dyed and painted and that under the lighting appeared richer than they were.

Yeats:
see section 3.1.4

The Irish poet Yeats, who was in the audience, wrote: 'I thought your scenery to *Dido and Aeneas* the only good scenery I ever saw. You have created a new art.' [Quoted in E.G.C., 1981. p.239]

To sum up:

- In his first production as director/designer Craig was drawing on influences from Herkomer and making them his own.

- He was also making his own decisions based on his theories.

- Realism was rejected in favour of simple symbolic visual statements.

- There was emphasis on colour, light and movement to accompany the sung text.

THE MASQUE OF LOVE

Adaptation led to more
freedom of expression

The next collaboration was on the scenario *The Masque of Love*, devised by Craig from another work by Purcell. Because the piece was again musical in origin and had little to recommend it in terms of text, Craig took the bold step of making this almost a ballet.

The Jacobean masque

Audience participation

A masque was a popular form of entertainment in the countryside in Elizabethan times and then became more formalised in the presentations mounted at the court of James I from 1605 onwards. At the conclusion of the spoken/sung and danced text it was usual for the audience, including the king or queen, to join in a final dance.

Movement was a dramatic feature

In Craig's production, movement became the dominant feature, combined with a set and costumes that drew on the folk-dance tradition. Strips of fabric formed a tent-like structure for the setting and this was echoed in the costumes of the chorus, whose ribboned over-dresses moved as they danced to reveal colour on the reverse.

A celebration of 'total theatre'

A cast that included kings, queens, harlequins and pierrots, moving through the pools of light as in a great hall, made for a colourful and celebratory performance style, where all the staging and musical elements blended to make a piece of 'total theatre'.

ACTIVITY   Look at Act 4 scene i of *The Tempest* by Shakespeare, in which Prospero conjures up a masque of classical deities for a blessing on the marriage of his daughter Miranda. Music, song and processions are part of the acted text.

Craig working in musical theatre

It is important to note here that it was musical theatre that first stimulated Craig's imagination, a theatre that used text as only one of its elements and not as the most vital or dominant.

Creative freedom

Craig's work with Shaw and their group of amateur singers enabled him to propose and carry through ideas that more seasoned professionals might well have resisted, and for these first works he was able to develop his ideas as a designer, lighting designer, director and choreographer with total creative freedom.

Other masques were outlined but not produced

The Masque of Love was the only masque devised by Craig that was staged, but from this period of his development there are many drawings and some scenarios that propose other similar entertainments, including *The Masque of London* for which a few drawings were done, and *The Mask of Lunatics*. The most important was *The Masque of Hunger*, in which the masked figure of Grief arrived at a fabulous court to challenge the audience with the body of a dead child. It was a dark and serious piece.

The masque as a form allowed plenty of staging opportunities

There seems to be no doubt that these scenarios challenged Craig artistically and appealed to his sense of a theatre that was more than text-based. They represented a rich and varied opportunity for his visual imagination to work in an unfettered environment.

To sum up:

- The masque offered opportunities for music and dance as well as spoken text.

- Experiments were made, drawing on a 16th-century form, but revised and rethought.

- The overall feel of the productions was light and colourful, with all aspects of staging worked out and controlled.

THE VIKINGS OF HELGELAND

Ibsen's early drama of Norse legendary figures

The final example in this summary of early productions is *The Vikings of Helgeland* (1857), a seldom-performed piece by Ibsen, which took as its theme the Norse tales of mythic heroes and which was considered by some a strangely dark choice for the leading actress of her day. Ellen Terry provided the financial backing and in doing so provided Craig with his first fully professional opportunity.

Not a success

The production was recognised as an artistic success, but too late, as an audience failed to materialise, and it was substituted by Ellen Terry playing her much-loved part of Beatrice in *Much Ado About Nothing*.

An anti-naturalistic setting was devised

Instead of Ibsen's naturalistic stage directions for *The Vikings*, Craig devised a semi-circle of grey drapes or gauze in front of which he could place selected scenic elements. In the first act, a gauze was also stretched across the proscenium, so that subtle changes of light behind the fabric made characters appear and disappear at will across a built-up cliff-top.

The vertical design elements were emphasised

The overwhelming emphasis was on the vertical, the curtain surround pulling the eye upward and so dwarfing the actors. Light, also from above, added to this effect with startlingly dramatic results, especially in the banqueting scene of Act Two.

Costumes and set in tones of grey

Music especially composed

The colours of the costumes were restrained tones of grey, with touches of colour in the huge cloaks. Critics were divided in their remarks about the lighting, some remarking on the half-visible faces and others commenting on its ability to suggest half-seen shapes. The music used appropriately Wagnerian themes, as well as interludes composed by Martin Shaw especially for the play.

Interpretation by a designer/ director

Craig had deliberately chosen a play that allowed him total artistic control; there was no tradition of its production as a classic to get in the way of his interpretation.

While he was entirely responsible for all the elements except the music, the one he had least control of was the acting. Most of the cast, conditioned by their own practice, merely trotted out tired old clichés of style, which went against all that Craig had attempted to achieve.

However a critic remarked positively:

> We see no 'flies', no shaky unconvincing side scenes, no foolish flocculent borders, no staring back-cloths. The impression created is one of real unreality.

> [Quoted in E.A.C., *Gordon Craig, The Story of his Life* 1968. p.173]

The production marked a summing up of his work so far

By the following year Craig was in Europe, but this almost final production had proved to be a culmination of his work so far. He had created an abstract mise-en-scène from a heavily naturalistic text. He had designed, lit and costumed the play with a clear eye for the totality of the production, every element, down to the smallest prop being thought through. Above all, old technologies had been harnessed to new practice, a theme that was to recur in the productive years to come.

To sum up:

- A text had been chosen that gave full rein to creative impulses.
- Simple scenic shapes were placed against a neutral background.
- Lighting played an important part in creating mood.
- The actors were the weak link, bringing old ideas to new theories of style.

DESIGN SCHEMES AND INNOVATIONS

Controversial ideas and theories

We now move on to examine three abstract but influential ideas and schemes that by their inventive and controversial nature placed Craig in the forefront of European theatre practice.

Experience combined with examples from theatre history

These came at a time when Craig was contemplating writing down his theories, and they were derived both from his immediate experience and from his extensive knowledge of theatre history.

STEPS: THE FOUR MOODS (1905)

One of the most common architectural elements to recur in Craig's drawings is that of a staircase or flight of steps. The most often reproduced sequence of drawings, for which he also wrote a commentary, are those he called *Steps: The Four Moods.*

> Among all dreams that the architect has laid upon the earth, I know of no more lovely thing than this flight of steps [. . .] I have often thought how one could give life (not a voice) to these places, using light to a dramatic end [. . .] And so I began with a drama called 'The Steps'.
>
> [Quoted in Walton, 1983. p.108]

Figure 3.3   The first mood

Figure 3.4   The second mood

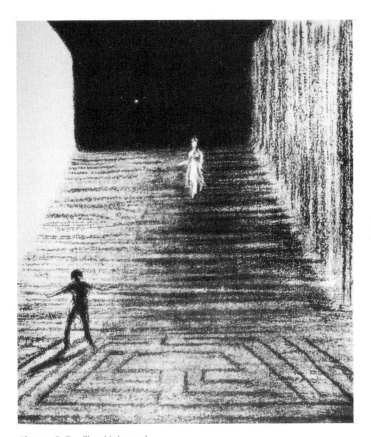

Figure 3.5   The third mood

Figure 3.6 The fourth mood

A drama could be created out of characters related to architectural forms

These drawings stand as an example for Craig's development towards a theatre of architecture and pure movement; he was leaving behind the traditions and technologies of the 19th century and moving towards an abstract modernism, far ahead of its time.

Movement and light

As the subtitle 'Four Moods' suggests, Craig was able to change the mood of a basic flight of steps, ascending between two enclosing walls to an open sky, with subtle changes of light and, above all, with movement.

All the drawings suggest movement, but in the 'second mood' Craig describes them:

> . . . we see many girls and boys jumping about like fireflies. And in the foreground, and farthest from them, I have made the earth respond to their movements. The earth is made to dance.

[Quoted in Walton, 1983. p.110]

Steps as a motif for dramatic action

In all these images there is a suggestion of arrested flight, of action caught and held for a moment by the artist's imagination. They are evocative and suggestive of all kinds of dramatic moments from any number of plays, and like many of Craig's unrealised schemes these motifs appear in any number of projects over the years.

ACTIVITY Find a flight of steps, inside or outside, and photograph or draw a 'dramatic moment' that takes place on them. Make these images in different conditions (light/dark) and see how the steps change in mood, and how this affects the drama. A strong directional light source will make very dramatic statements.

Isadora Duncan and dance

By the time these drawings were titled and published, Craig had met Isadora Duncan, the American dancer who was to play such an influential part in his life. It was she who opened his eyes to the potential for pure movement (as opposed to the rigorous tradition of classical ballet) and showed him how vital it was in the realisation of action on stage.

The importance of music and rhythm

In all Craig's subsequent work the theme of dance and movement became an overriding concern. His work with Martin Shaw had revealed the importance of music and rhythm; the spoken word had been balanced by the silent gesture and accompanied by sound. Now he had discovered movement with all its freedoms. He wrote this to his friend:

> The actors must cease to **speak** and must **move** only, if they want to restore the art to its old place. Acting is Action – Dance the poetry of Action.
>
> [Quoted in E.A.C., *Gordon Craig, The Story of his Life*, 1968. p.199]

To sum up:

- Steps were an architectural form that could be used in abstract dramas.

- Expressive movement was important.

- Strong directional light could change the moods.

THE UBERMAR-IONETTE (1908)

Craig's new-found confidence to express such radical ideas also led to the next development, which was *The Ubermarionette*.

> The actor must go, and in his place comes the inanimate figure – the **Ubermarionette** we may call him, until he has won for himself a better name.
>
> [Quoted in Bablet, 1962. p.105] First written 1908.

Critics were puzzled

This sentence, taken out of context from Craig's essay *The Actor and the Ubermarionette*, led to endless debate as to its exact meaning and how it might be applied to 20th-century theatre.

He certainly touched a raw nerve with critics, who were quick to seize on the notion that actors were to be reduced to the role of a puppet. But this was a narrow view. Craig was moving, as we have seen, towards a notion of almost pure movement. As part of this he was tending to subordinate the role text could play in his theatre. But Craig had been an actor and

An actor must be created to match new theories

with the concept of **Ubermarionette** he was searching for an actor who could match his new ideals. As he wrote to Martin Shaw:

> Today they **impersonate**, tomorrow they **represent** . . . until a new breed can be grown which are like the rest of my thought, hard, clearcut, passionless.
>
> [Quoted in Innes, 1983. p.126]

An actor controlled by a director

What he despised were the 'bad old days' of unspecific performances, with actors left to find their own barnstorming ways through a text. By contrast, he sought an actor who could remain remote from the role, who could represent rather than identify, who could suppress his egoism, who would be pliable for a director to control, and who could fit into an overall scheme.

The actor as masked performer in an anti-realist world

At their most extreme, Craig's ideas suggested that the ultimate actor would be masked and robed, moving through the ceremony of the play as in a ritual. This depersonalised figure could then take its rightful place in the anti-realist world of new texts that would accompany the intended reforms.

ACTIVITY

Work with masks. These can be either full-face or half masks, and you can either make them represent a character or, by painting them a neutral colour, make them abstract. Start with very simple things to do, like meeting each other. It is best to work in mime to begin with; you will then find that your mask begins to be very expressive.

Check in a mirror when you first put the mask on. The image will often give you the beginnings of a character.

Yeats:
see section 3.1.5

The author/director who came closest to this ideal was probably Yeats, who specifically wrote verse dramas in which poetry and movement were dominant, rather than character and motivational subtext.

To sum up:

- An actor was to be depersonalised.

- An actor might be masked and become a ritualised figure.

- The result of this theory was never tested, but it implied anti-realist texts were to be dominant.

SCENE (1907)

This next development complemented and extended the previous two themes, and came from Craig's study of Serlio's *Treatise on Perspective*. The drawing that he found particularly useful was of apparently massive walls laid out on a chess board drawn in perspective, and it prompted Craig to reconsider a theatre of architecture (see Fig. 3.7).

Serlio:
see section 3.1.4

His first influences had included ancient Roman theatre, and using this drawing by Serlio he now developed this into a theory that such apparently abstract spaces could once again be places for action.

Figure 3.7   A drawing by Sebastiano Serlio.

A series of movable blocks controlled by machinery

He began a series of drawings that experimented with raising and lowering the heights of the blocks in sections, and at the same time adding a ceiling that was a mirror image of the floor structure and which could also be raised and lowered. He began to plan a mechanism that could raise and lower these units as required, controlled by one man, the director, from a console in the rear of the auditorium.

A theatre of tableaux

Lighting was devised that could play across these mobile surfaces, changing the mood, while two-dimensional figures rather than living actors would 'hold a characteristic pose for an entire act' [Innes, 1983. p.188]. Innes goes on to suggest that dialogue would be sung or recited offstage as an accompaniment to these silent shapes.

Appia: the view of another practitioner

Another practitioner, Adolphe Appia (1862–1928), working at the same time as Craig, published this statement, which might be taken as a summary of how Craig hoped this project would function:

> The actor no longer walks in front of painted lights and shadows; he is immersed in an atmosphere that is destined for him.
>
> [*How to Reform our Stage Directing*, 1904. Quoted in *Adolphe Appia, Actor/Space/Light*, Calder, 1982]

Light would create shadows, not the painter's brush

In other words, in an ideal theatre the actor would eventually be viewed in a three-dimensional architectural scene in which lighting would mould the forms. The 19th-century practice of painting shadows on the flat scenery would be abolished for ever.

Figure 3.8 *Scene*: a design for movement (1907).

A new medium for making designs

At the same time as these developments were taking place, Craig learned how to use etching as a medium. With this new form he began to develop images of what he called 'moments of arrested motion' (see Figure 3.8).

Towering abstract shapes with figures in action

These exciting and dramatic realisations of abstract and often threatening architectural environments were often reproduced to show towering walls dwarfing the human form, leading to a whole body of criticism that derided their practicality. However, the series also includes some examples where figures dominate the architecture and suggest any number of dramas. Craig would later call these *A Thousand Scenes in One Scene* (1915).

> The scene turns to receive the play of light. These two, scene and light are, as I have said, like two dancers or two singers who are in perfect accord. The scene supplies the simplest form made up of right angles and flat walls and the light runs in and out and all over them.
>
> [E.G.C. 1923. p.25]

Experiments with *Scene* lead to the development of *Screens*

Gradually, as he experimented with *Scene*, Craig found it too restricting and felt it was leading to no useful conclusion. It occurred to him that if the cubes, instead of rising and falling, could open and close like the pages of a book, this would enable actors or technicans to move them, instead of machinery. And so slowly the first phase of the *Screens* began to develop; with them a device was found that would bring years of theoretical planning to a practical conclusion.

ACTIVITY   Make some experiments with light. You can set up simple screens painted a neutral shade or use a white wall. Use a spotlight that can be focused with a gobo (a thin metal sheet cut to project simple shapes). By combining these with colour you can change an abstract space into many environments and moods.

To sum up:

- Three-dimensional abstract shapes provided a setting.
- The setting could be mobile and change the scene while the play progressed.
- Different qualities of light were to be important.
- The system proved too abstract and technically impossible to realise.

SCREENS

Screens have much potential, as moving units

As early as 1907, alongside his work on *Scene*, Craig was experimenting with the system that he would call the *Screens*. Growing out of the inherent inflexibility of the *Scene*, these portable and movable units immediately opened up for Craig an infinite variety of design possibilities, which he was quick to exploit in drawings and models.

Movable screens on castors

By 1908 the *Screens* had grown in sophistication. They were to be made of wood and canvas, much like a conventional stage flat, and painted a light neutral tone. Hinged together, with concealed castors in the base, they could be manipulated across the stage floor and arranged in different and changing configurations.

So pleased was Craig by the idea that he took out a patent which clearly demonstrated how they could function.

ACTIVITY To appreciate fully what Craig had in mind, you can make simple folded card shapes to represent his *Screens*. These can be manipulated in any number of ways. If you make steps to go with them, the result can suggest all sorts of settings. Cut out a figure or two and place them in relation to the *Screens*.

The important thing to remember is that Craig was concerned with scale, the height of his *Screens* in relation to the human figure. If you want to design a set for a text, for example *Hamlet,* make your model to the scale/ratio 1:25. This is the scale used by a theatre designer.

See section 3.2 The next step in his working life was a momentous one. It was Isadora Duncan who, in 1908, on one of her frequent visits to Moscow, recommended Craig to Stanislavski. At this time Stanislavski and the Moscow Art Theatre had been successfully experimenting with new kinds of anti-realist production, in the symbolist manner, then currently very fashionable in Russia. Stanislavski was persuaded to offer Craig the chance to design a production. What he did not foresee was that the process would take three years, that Craig would insist on being credited as joint director and that misunderstandings between the two men would result in a seriously flawed production.

Hamlet becomes the choice for a joint production   With his *Screens* Craig had been experimenting with a scenario for the staging of *Hamlet*, a play and a part that had obsessed him for years. With an apparently 'carte blanche' contract from Stanislavski, he began at once to plan a production for the Moscow Art Theatre, with the *Screens* as the key scenic element (see Fig. 3.9).

Figure 3.9   Set for *Hamlet* (1911).

Craig and Stanislavski at cross purposes	With Craig speaking no Russian and little French and Stanislavski speaking no English, communication between them was impossible without an interpreter. In the best of situations this would have been difficult, but with their widely divergent views on the play, understanding became almost impossible.
Stanislavski aimed for realistic illusion	Stanislavski was totally immersed in his System, which aimed for realistic illusion, and had recently completed a production of *Julius Caesar* in which archaeological reproduction had been a key concept. His experimentations with symbolism were more to do with finding a creative challenge than with any leaning towards anti-realism.
Craig wished for abstract stylisation	Craig, on the other hand, was concerned more with stylisation. The dominance of his protagonist's state of mind was to be expressed in all aspects of the production. The *Screens* could be set to suggest a claustrophobic inner world and then moved in a moment to open out into vistas of light-filled doorways or corridors. The possibilities for a play animated by kinetic settings seemed limitless.
Key moments were successful	In retrospect, many aspects of Craig's intentions were realised. Key moments were astonishing, such as the golden cloak that seemed to cover the stage in Act 1 scene ii, with Hamlet a dark and isolated foreground figure, or the arrival of Fortinbras at the end of the play, like some shining angel, with his banner-carrying troops.
Despite apparent failure, the *Screens* were much copied	But there was much that did not work, including the *Screens*. Stanislavski made much of their failure in *My Life in Art*, much to Craig's anger. It was true that their unwieldy nature led to their being moved behind the house curtain, instead of in full view. Yet it was this element of the production that stayed in people's minds, long after the quarrels of interpretation had diminished.

> By the simplest of means he is able in some mysterious way to evoke almost any sensation of time or space, the scenes even in themselves suggesting variations of human emotion . . .
>
> [Quoted in E.A.C., 1968. p.272]

An innovative production for the 20th century	Craig's disappointment in the production was tempered by the worldwide recognition it achieved. It banished the gloomy, realistic, archaeological, 19th-century model for all time, putting in its place a version that relied on suggestion, movement, light and shade, and the idea that staging by implication could suggest the inner as well as the outer tragedy of its protagonist.

To sum up:

- Flexible moving units could suggest time and place very quickly.

- Lighting was to play an important part in creating mood.

- Anti-naturalistic staging met with antagonism.

- Despite the failure of the production, the theories were much copied.

FINALE

After 1911, Craig lived for another 55 creative years. The tragedy of this time was that apart from one notable exception (see Chronology, 1926) he never again allowed collaboration on any terms and resolutely avoided those opportunities that would undoubtedly have led to further triumphs.

Most of the great directors in Europe wanted to work with him. His work was much copied and adapted, his books read and argued over, but no theatre or set of conditions could attract him to work on the same scale as the Moscow *Hamlet*. If he decided that collaboration would mean compromise, he would have none of it; so, inevitably in an art form that functions on this principle, he was disappointed. Critics have labelled him impossible, demanding and unreasonable. That is probably true, but no more so than for any of the men who are included in this section.

His writings, particularly those in his magazine *The Mask*, which circulated throughout Europe and America, began to spread not just his own ideas, but those he plucked from the past to inform the present. His real triumph was to be a catalyst, changing the way people looked at design and the interpretation of a text. He was a provoker, a self-taught man of the 19th century whose theories can still provoke discussion 90 years after their inception.

In the frontispiece of Janet Leeper's book, published in 1948, Craig contributed, at the age of 76, this typically tongue-in-cheek summary of his work:

> EDWARD GORDON CRAIG PRACTISED SEVERAL CRAFTS. 1889 TO 97 WAS ACTOR. 1893 TO 1926 WAS METTEUR-EN-SCENE I.E. PRODUCED PLAYS AND OPERAS. WAS DESIGNER OF SCENES AND COSTUMES. AND WAS WOOD ENGRAVER. COMPOSED SOME TUNES. WROTE SOME BOOKS. MADE SOME ETCHINGS 1906 TO 12.

> COULD NOT PLAY GOLF. PLAYED FOOTBALL. COULD ROW. NOT SHOOT. COULD NOT COOK. COULD NOT BIND A BOOK. NOR UNDERSTAND BUSINESS. COULD DO NOTHING WITH ELECTRIC WIRES. IS NOT A PRINTER. COULD COMPOSE A PAGE OF TYPE. 1908 TO 15, 1918 TO 19, 1923 TO 29 PUBLISHED THE MASK.

3.1.4 INFLUENCES

TERRY, ELLEN (1847–1928)

A star of the theatre

Supported Craig with money and her talent

Ellen Terry was for 50 years the most sought-after actress of her generation. She spent most of her working life with Irving's company, playing in a number of Shakespeare roles and in the melodramas that continued to be popular. Her son was often her leading man. She supported some of his first efforts at production, lending her prestigious name to these enterprises. Craig writes about her influence in his biography of her:

When I was 16 years old, my mother determined that I should go upon the stage and become an actor: so I was given the name Edward Henry Gordon Craig, and then and there I was christened as such [. . .] Lady Gordon and Henry Irving were my godmother and godfather.

[E.G.C., 1931. p.77]

How Craig came to acquire a stage name

He was about to embark on his apprenticeship as an actor in Irving's company, so a stage name was important. The 'Craig' was adopted because his mother had seen a rock in Scotland called Ailsa Craig and had fancied the name. It is clear that any connection with his natural father Godwin was not going to be by name.

Ellen Terry's magnetic beauty can be best appreciated in the portrait by her first husband, the painter G.F. Watts, which is in the National Portrait Gallery. In later life she married for a final time and virtually retired from the stage.

George Bernard Shaw considered her wasted in Irving's company

Her extensive correspondence with George Bernard Shaw, the great playwright, who considered her talents wasted in Irving's company, was published by him after her death, much to the annoyance of Craig.

Craig, E.G.,   *Ellen Terry, Her Secret Self*, London, 1931

IRVING, HENRY (1838–1905)

Craig was a member of his company

Believe me when I tell you that these Lyceum days were *exciting days*. They were positively worth living, if you chanced to be a member of Irving's company, and they were a full education to a young man wishing to do well towards the stage.

[E.G.C., 1930. p.17]

Very influential in Craig's education

This statement in his biography of Irving sums up Craig's indebtedness to his surrogate father. Not only did he work for this pre-eminent actor-manager of his generation; at the same time Irving encouraged Craig to read, visit museums, draw and discover all those inherent skills that he would develop later in life.

Favoured lavish Shakespeare productions

Irving's greatest period of management was at the Lyceum Theatre from 1878 until 1899, where his repertory consisted mainly of a wide-ranging mix of lavishly mounted revivals of Shakespeare and equally extravagant productions of now little-known texts.

He employed artists, archaeologists, musicians and managers to ensure that every detail of his historical reconstructions was correct and part of an integrated whole.

The first knight of the English theatre, he made the profession respectable

An actor of overwhelming intensity, Irving was not universally admired, but the artistic integrity with which he ran his company eventually led to recognition. His knighthood in 1895 was the first for an actor.

Craig, E.G.,   *Henry Irving,*   Dent, 1930
Irving, L.,   *Henry Irving, The Actor and his World,*   Faber, 1951

GODWIN, EDWARD WILLIAM (1833–86)

Craig's father, a painter, architect and designer

He was the father of Edward Gordon Craig and his sister Edith. Ellen Terry lived with him from 1868 until 1875, after the breakdown of her first marriage to G.F. Watts, the painter.

In the year that Godwin's relationship with Ellen Terry finished he designed her costume as Portia in *The Merchant of Venice*, and later in collaboration with Irving he worked with her again in *The Cup* by Tennyson (1880).

Shakespeare productions as historical reproductions

His great task was to convince popular opinion that accurate archaeological evidence could be used as a source for the plays of Shakespeare. Although he had his detractors, a number of vivid productions attempting historical reconstruction were evidence of his work as a designer and researcher.

Ironically, it was just such historical detail that proved elusive. His attempts to reconstruct the Greek and Roman periods and apply these to Shakespeare's texts were only partially successful, since there was, at that time, little real evidence. But it was a serious and meaningful attempt to rescue Shakespeare in production from the rag-bag of 19th-century theatrical practice.

A friend of Oscar Wilde, the poet and playwright, and a colleague of Whistler the painter, he was one of the most important members of the 'Aesthetic Movement'. Although now largely forgotten he was influential during his lifetime as a reformer of design practice.

> In the case of Craig the legacy from father to son was largely indirect, passed on through the spectacular example of Irving and what he, in turn, had taken from Godwin.
>
> [Stokes, 1972. p.68]

Stokes, J.,   *Resistable Theatres*,   Elek, 1972

HERKOMER, HUBERT VON (1846–1914)

Renowned portrait painter, interested in theatre

Herkomer was born in Bavaria, but his parents settled in England and after a hard struggle he established himself as a magazine illustrator. His attempts at painting in oils quickly brought him fame and by 1878 he was one of the most sought-after society portrait painters.

See section 3.1.3

Craig mentions Herkomer a number of times in *Index to the Story of My Days*, and it was certainly a visit he made to a lecture given by the painter in 1892 that was most influential. In his lecture Herkomer touched on a number of radical and imaginative solutions to staging.

A theatre at the art school in Bushey

Herkomer's financial success as a society portrait painter had allowed him to found an independent art school in Bushey (which was then a little village outside London). It was here, with the help of his students, that he staged experimental theatre productions, which he designed to demonstrate his new ideas.

Audiences travelled to see his experiments

His experiments were based on little more than animated tableaux, but they attracted sophisticated theatre audiences, including Craig, who were fascinated and admiring of his innovative lighting and scenic techniques.

Stokes, J.,   *Resistable Theatres*,   Elek, 1972
Treble, R. & Edwards, L.M.,   *A Passion for Work*,   Watford Museum, 1982

SERLIO, SEBASTIANO (1475–1554)

Partly responsible for the classical revival in Europe

Italian architect and theorist. Serlio's great work was his *Treatise*, published in several parts during his lifetime and posthumously. It was essentially a practical handbook of the antique style of architectural detail and presented a number of models for copying. He was very influential in the classical revival that swept Europe during the Renaissance.

> I have bought [...] Serlio – his book of Architecture, edition of 1560 [...] This proved to be one of the best guides in my work.

Important architectural drawings

This entry of 1903 in *Index to the Story of my Days* indicates Craig's indebtedness to these books of architectural drawings. The most important and influential of these is reproduced on page 208. The classical themes provided him with ideas for a theatre of architectural forms as opposed to painted scenery.

Serlio, S.,   *The Five Books of Architecture*,   Dover, 1982. (Reprint of the edition of 1611)

NICHOLSON, WILLIAM AND PRYDE, JAMES: KNOWN AS 'THE BEGGARSTAFF BROTHERS'

Poster artists, book illustrators

In 1893, in the small country town of Uxbridge, Craig came to know the two men who practised as poster artists under the name of **The Beggarstaff Brothers.** When he met them they were about to achieve fame as the most original and outstanding artists of their day, on a par with Toulouse-Lautrec and Alphonse Mucha.

Bold shapes with vivid colours

They became renowned for their use of the woodblock as a means of printing a bold and often vividly coloured image; it was from these two men that Craig learnt the art of wood engraving:

> The idea of starting with the black background and slowly introducing light was what captured Ted's imagination. [Craig, E., 1968. p.85]

Wood engraving was like turning on a light on a dark stage

In other words, Craig was struck by the way a woodblock (black) might represent an unlit stage. Once a chisel had cut away the surface it produced a white space (light). The results had the potential for conveying clearly defined theatrical imagery: the dark invaded by light.

Craig published a magazine to promote his illustrations

Craig's early work under their tuition was often indistinguishable from his masters', but gradually he developed his own style. The first expression of that individuality was with the publication of a small magazine of the arts called *The Page*.

Scene: see section 3.1.3

At a later date (1907) Craig mastered the technique of etching as a means of expression, and this more subtle technique gave him the mastery to illustrate *Scene*. His evocative and challenging images were exhibited throughout his life, and combined with his writing were one of the main means by which he spread his theories.

Campbell, C.,   *The Beggarstaff Posters*,   Barrie & Jenkins, 1990

DUNCAN, ISADORA (1878–1927)

<table>
<tr><td>Introduced Craig to dance as pure movement</td><td>Not only was Isadora Duncan important herself as a great original creator of dance, she was also instrumental in introducing Craig to a wholly European perspective of theatre and performance and, through her innumerable contacts, to the most important individuals in that theatre.</td></tr>
</table>

From the moment they met and became lovers in late 1904, Craig rarely returned to the country of his birth, preferring a roving existence in the artistic worlds of Europe's capital cities.

<table>
<tr><td>Everyone was scandalised by her art</td><td>Duncan's extraordinary gifts as an interpretative dancer have to be seen alongside the generally accepted 'classical' training that a dancer of the time would undergo. A Europe that had been brought up on such principles had been astonished and scandalised by her example of free movement. American by birth and temperament, Isadora Duncan had no received notions of correctness and brought a refreshing challenge to the dominance of classical ballet.</td></tr>
</table>

> She threw away ballet skirts and ballet thoughts. She discarded shoes and stockings too [. . .] I shall never forget the first time I saw her come onto an empty platform to dance.
>
> [E.G.C., 1981. p.262]

Although their close relationship survived a mere two years, Gordon Craig was forever in her debt. Through her introductions he met the foremost theatre practitioners of Europe (most importantly Stanislavski in Moscow), all of whom wanted to work with him. Through her art Isadora made him aware of the nature and power of movement.

Steegmuller, F.,   *Your Isadora,*   Macmillan, 1974

SHAW, MARTIN (1875–1958)

<table>
<tr><td>Shaw introduced Craig to musical theatre</td><td>Shaw is an important figure in Craig's early life, since it was through him that Craig came to work on his first major productions.</td></tr>
<tr><td>Self-taught like Craig</td><td rowspan="2">He was born into a musical family, and said: 'I cannot remember a time when I could not play the piano and the organ' [Shaw, 1929. p.12]. He left music school without taking a degree, and was dissatisfied with the emphasis placed on the 'classical tradition'. He found that he was drawn to early English music: especially the operas of Handel and Purcell and the heritage of folksongs, which in the early 1900s were being rediscovered, written down and published.</td></tr>
<tr><td>Interested in early English opera and folk traditions</td></tr>
</table>

In 1900 he and Craig mounted a semi-staged version of Purcell's *Dido and Aeneas,* and the partnership flourished through all the productions that Craig accomplished before he left for Europe.

<table>
<tr><td>For a brief time acted as Duncan's musical director</td><td>Shaw joined Craig in Europe as Isadora Duncan's musical director, during the period when Craig was acting as both her lover and somewhat unsuccessfully as her business manager. His amusing account of the experience throws an interesting light on the wandering existence that Craig and Duncan led at that time.</td></tr>
</table>

Shaw also introduced Craig to Bach's *St. Matthew Passion*; it was designs and a model for this oratorio rather than a play that occupied Craig for many of the last years of his life.

He settled as an organist at a parish church in London and published a collection of folksongs. He also edited the *English Carol Book* (1913).

Shaw, M. F.,   *Up to Now*,   OUP, 1929

3.1.5 FOLLOWERS

YEATS, WILLIAM BUTLER (1865–1939)

A leader of the Irish Dramatic Movement

Yeats was an important influence on the formation of the Irish Dramatic Movement, which sought to return to that country a genuinely distinctive voice. He mastered the technique of playwriting and produced plays of poetic vibrancy, drawing strongly on Irish folklore for their themes.

In 1901 he was in the audience for the revival of *Dido and Aeneas* and he wrote congratulating Craig on the light, colour and feeling for space achieved by such simple scenic means: '... it was the most beautiful scenery our stage has seen.'

Friendship with Craig

A friendship developed, and Yeats realised that Craig's ideas were ideally suited to enrich the staging of his own poetic texts. It was not until 1909, however, that Yeats, on a trip to London, renewed his acquaintance with Craig, who then offered him a set of *Screens* for use at the Abbey Theatre.

Craig made designs for Yeats

After a series of textual revisions much influenced by the staging potential of the *Screens*, Yeats presented *The Hourglass* in 1911, with settings by Craig. More productions of other plays followed, for which Craig provided designs for sets and masks, and the *Screens* proved adaptable and useful for a number of years. It was ironic that in the same year as Craig was experiencing problems with *Hamlet* in Moscow, Yeats was enjoying the relative success of the *Screens* as a means of staging his plays.

O'Driscoll, R. & Reynolds, L.   *Yeats and the Theatre*,   Macmillan, 1975

SIMONSON, LEE (1888–1967)

Very critical of Craig and what he saw as impractical ideas

Lee Simonson was an American stage designer, who in 1932 published the most reasoned condemnation of Craig's work, entitled *Day Dreams: The Case of Gordon Craig*. Simonson supported his findings with conjectural three-dimensional reconstructions of Craig's designs, and made a strong case for their scale being unreasonable in relation to the then typical theatre space.

But Simonson failed to grasp just how visionary the original designs were meant to be, and it is more in sadness than in anger that he criticises their practical application.

A designer with a distinguished record

He had a very distinguished career of his own as a founder member of the Theatre Guild, an organisation not unlike the National Theatre in the UK, which sought to mount new plays with first-class production values.

A strong connection can be traced by examining his designs

Ironically, in view of his feelings about Craig's work, there are strong traces of an influence in his designs, particularly those that used a 'unit setting': permanent architectural frameworks that could be changed by the insertion of different scenic elements. Their simplicity and adaptability have strong echoes of Craig's *Screens*.

Simonson, L.,   *The Stage is Set*,   New York, 1932

BEL GEDDES , NORMAN (1893-1958)

He was interested in the architecture of theatres

Innovative ideas for new theatres

This designer and architect did much work on questioning the predominance of the proscenium arch. His exciting and innovative ideas, which he called *Theatre Number Six* (1922), are quite as valid now as they were then. His designs were based on the Greek model, with the audience linked to the stage by a shallow flight of steps. He placed the lighting control in the rear of the auditorium (now common practice) and his sets were raised to stage level by hydraulic lifts. This system is now in use for the Olivier stage (Royal National Theatre), where huge sets can appear and disappear at the touch of a button.

Worked on Broadway with Max Reinhardt

He had great success with his first designs for the German director Max Reinhardt in his New York production of *The Miracle*. For this epic, pageant-style play, set in the Middle Ages, Bel Geddes transformed the whole theatre into a cathedral, with soaring arches disguising the proscenium arch altogether.

Architectural shapes in strong chiaroscuro

In later projects he moved away from the representational towards the abstract, using steps, ramps and levels across and on which the action took place. Variations in mood were achieved with the most sophisticated lighting.

In his designs for plays such as *King Lear* and *Hamlet* there are strong 'Craigian' influences at work, with emphasis on the vertical and simple, rather monumental shapes.

After the 1930s he turned away from theatre and made his living as a successful commercial designer and architect.

Ridge, H.C.,   *Stage Lighting*,   Heffer, 1928

KOZINTSEV, GRIGORI (1905–73)

Hamlet on film

He tended to see *Hamlet* in elemental terms

Kozintsev was a Russian film director, whose version of *Hamlet* (1964) is indebted to Gordon Craig. He takes as his starting point elemental textures, such as earth, fire and water, rather than period stylisation. Like Craig, who had toyed with the idea of *Screens* made in wood and metal, Kozintsev deploys these elements to create moods which complement the episodes of the drama.

The beginning of the film is a perfect example of his treatment: the camera tracks Hamlet on horseback along the sea shore into the glowering castle, which closes its gates on the dwarfed figure of the protagonist, imprisoning him until the tragedy is played out.

Kozintsev treats Elsinore as a concept rather than a place, and says of Craig:

> [He] saw the visual imagery of Hamlet primarily as the interrelation of scale: the scale of huge walls, and that of the small figure of a man. It was a revelation of no small importance.
>
> [Kozintsev, 1967. p.237]

In the filmed version Kozintsev is able to do what Craig was unable to do even in his kinetic theatre. It is the camera that moves, rather than the *Screens*, and this mobile force is the one that takes us on the journey into the tormented mind of Hamlet. It is a striking and exciting version of the play, now available on video.

Kozintsev, G.,   *Shakespeare, Time and Conscience*,   London, 1967

SVOBODA, JOSEF (BORN 1920)

See Craig and architecture, pp.208–9

Trained as an architect in Czechoslovakia after the Second World War, he has risen to become one of the most sought-after designers in Europe. He has developed his striking scenographic (staging) techniques in a huge number of productions, from the domestic scale of Chekhov to the Wagnerian epic.

Technology harnessed for design

Projections, film and gobos create texture which can change and move

His use of technology of the most advanced kind gives his productions a certain recognisable quality. For example, he makes use of both abstract and figurative projections, not just on walls and floors but moving across mobile screens. Occasionally film is used to animate huge screens. Ramps, stairs and levels are changed by strong directional light and dark shadowed areas are contrasted with pools of colour through which the characters move.

A theatre of movement and changing moods

> I don't want a static picture, but something that evolves, that has movement, not necessarily physical movement of course, but a setting that is dynamic, capable of expressing changing relationships, feeling, moods, perhaps only by light during the course of the action.

Kinetic theatre enables quick changes of mood

Reference to his work quickly confirms his debt to Craig, as this quote underlines. His production of *Hamlet* (1959), which used stairs and screens, is a definite homage to Craig.

Anti-naturalism

Theatre of movement

It is not a theatre of naturalism; instead, he is concerned with a kinetic theatre, a theatre of changing shape and form, with expressive light playing a dominant role in changing the moods. As a designer he draws on all the available technologies of theatre; the result is often a quite abstract solution, providing a fluid and changing environment for the actors.

He is able to use this highly sophisticated technology in such a way as to enhance the figure of the actor, rather than diminish it, creating some of the most exciting and challenging designs that have been made this century.

Burian, J.M.,   *The Scenography of Josef Svoboda*,   WUP, 1971
Burian, J.M.,   *The Secret of Theatrical Space*,   Applause, 1993

3.1.6 SUMMARY: EDWARD GORDON CRAIG

This summary is written to draw together certain parts of the section on Edward Gordon Craig under particular headings. It should be considered with the student's own practical work in mind and/or the student's viewing of other productions. For example, Craig's 'Staging Form Adopted': as a student undertaking practical work you would wish to discuss how staging should be considered as architectural as opposed to painted and how this could be reflected in your own work. By isolating this convention/practice not only are you enhancing your own approach but you are able to make informed reference to his theories when viewing other productions.

THE SUBJECT MATTER
Poetic drama
Music/Pageant and processional drama
Shakespearian theatre
Dance

THE POLITICAL PURPOSE OR MESSAGE OR DRAMATIC INTENTION
A-political
Non-realist drama
Emphasis on the symbolic

THE ACTOR–AUDIENCE RELATIONSHIP
The actor as an embodiment of qualities/archetypes
The actor isolated in a spotlight
The actor as part of the total mise-en-scène
Strictly fourth wall/presentational.
The movement of the actor

THE STAGING FORM ADOPTED
Architectural (the Greek and Roman stage)
The stage as three-dimensional space
The stage floor as integral to the design
Abstract modernism. The use of steps to suggest mise-en-scène
Suggestive of time and place (anti-realism)
Kinetic

DIRECTORIAL INTERPRETATION /PRODUCTION STYLE
The director as overall co-ordinator
Emphasis placed on coherence
Unwillingness to compromise
Non-text based scenarios
Fast moving, colourful spectacle

DESIGN ELEMENTS
Design and planning led to an overall concept
Mood/atmosphere was created through synthesis
Exciting symbolic statements
Changes in scale
The actor dwarfed in his environment
Elemental

ROLE OF ACTORS AND PERFORMANCE STYLE	The actor as 'Ubermarionette' The actor as passionless interpreter. The masked actor The actor as dancer. The introduction of choreography Broad expressive movement Close attention to the speaking of the text The actor as pliable and responsive
TECHNICAL ELEMENTS	The proscenium arch as an adjustable frame Units that move during the action Theatre as a technological machine Fully controllable lighting which would mould form The abolition of the footlights
AUDIENCE RESPONSE	Kept at a distance to admire the changing spectacle

3.1.7 SUGGESTIONS FOR FURTHER STUDY

PLAYS

Craig produced designs for settings and masks for Yeats's plays (see section 3.1.5). Look at the four *Plays for Dancers* (1921), which were written out of interest in the Japanese Noh drama.

FILM

Hamlet (1948), directed by and starring Laurence Olivier

The designer Roger Furse produced an all-purpose setting in which the camera could move freely. There is a strong emphasis on stairs and moody lighting, and towering walls of stone.

Hamlet (1964), directed by Grigori Kozintsev

A version that takes enormous liberties with the text, but because this is spoken in Russian the spectator is free to concentrate on the stunning visual imagery, which the director uses to complement the narrative.

A THEATRE PRACTITIONER

Leopold Jessner was a German director who used the motif of a blood-red set of stairs in his production of Richard III (1920). In the finale of the play Richard was killed at the top and plunged to his death down several flights. Jessner's motif for this production was strongly reminiscent of the stairs in Craig's *Four Moods* (1905).

3.1.8 BIBLIOGRAPHY

Bablet, D.   *Edward Gordon Craig*   Heinemann, 1966   A most accessible and readable account

Craig, E.G.	*The Art of the Theatre*	London, 1905	
	On the Art of the Theatre	London, 1911 Heinemann, 1956	Contains essays on *The Art of the Theatre, First and Second Dialogues* and the key essay on *The Actor and the Ubermarionette*
	Towards a New Theatre	London, 1913	
	The Theatre Advancing	Boston, 1919	
	Scene	OUP, 1923	
	Index to the Story of My Days	CUP, 1981	
Craig, E.A.	*Edward Gordon Craig, The Story of his Life*	Gollancz, 1968	Quite critical of his father, and full of first-hand accounts of the life
Innes, C.	*Edward Gordon Craig*	CUP, 1983	An exhaustive account of theory and practice
Leeper, J.	*Designs for the Theatre*	Penguin, 1948	The designs are well produced, and Craig had a hand in compiling the bibliography
Walton, J.M.	*Craig on Theatre*	Methuen, 1983	Key essays, well illustrated
Senelick, L.	*Gordon Craig's Moscow Hamlet*	Greenwood, 1982	A very full and critical account of this event

Essays by Craig are not generally available, but there is a good summary of key texts in *Craig on Theatre*. It is also well illustrated.

3.1.9 QUESTION AND SUGGESTED FRAMEWORK FOR ANSWER ON EDWARD GORDON CRAIG

ACTIVITY   **Discuss those of Craig's theories and themes that in your opinion are still valid for the theatre of today.**

POINTS TO CONSIDER
- Start by looking at the **end** of the question. It asks you to consider the 'theatre of today'. So your starting point should be to choose a production or productions that you have seen or performed in to which you

can refer all your points. You will need to have a sound knowledge of current theatre practice.

- List the main theories and themes of Craig's working life. Then choose two or three to concentrate on which you really believe have a relevance for today's theatre.

- It is always advisable to support your answer with relevant quotations.

A DETAILED　*Introduction*
ANALYSIS　Briefly list your choices of theories and themes.

Main body

For each of the subsequent sections, take one of the theories or themes that you have selected. For each section explain:
- what it is
- where and how you have seen it used in a production
- how you feel it contributed to the production.

For example:

- The role of the actor: Craig looked for an actor who was part of the totality of the production, not a star performer. He believed in a theatre where the actor would be only one part of the whole. Productions by companies such as Théâtre de Complicité (see section 2.3) would provide a very clear example of how all elements of performance can be integrated. Discuss how the work of the actors contributed to the whole production.

- Production design: follow on by looking at Craig's views on how a production is designed, with every element being carefully considered, including the sets, costumes, props and lighting. (You would find it helpful to look at section 2.2 where we give a breakdown of the elements and how to analyse them.) Relate this to a production in which you have performed, or one you have seen, and discuss how a thoroughly considered approach was necessary for the success of the production.

- *Screens*: mention how important Craig considered these as providing a strong architectural and abstract setting for the actor. Discuss how light can affect the mood or create strong contrasts of light and dark. Reference to technical terms would be important here. Take the ideas of the *Screens* and explore how they changed the way people looked at stage space. Discuss one or two productions where something resembling *Screens* has been used. Describe these briefly and explain how they related to the overall production concept.

Conclusion

Point to the fact that Craig's theories are now part of current practice, making further reference to productions you have seen. Say why you find him interesting, for example for his visionary and provocative qualities. Name particular directors, designers or companies who have been influenced by Craig, if you can.

3.2 *Konstantin Sergeievich Alexeiev (Stanislavski) (1863–1938)*

Figure 3b Konstantin Stanislavski at the time of founding the Moscow Art Theatre

3.2.1 A CHRONOLOGY

Born into a very rich family

1863: Born 5 January into one of the richest families, if not *the* richest, in Russia.

1877: His father transforms a wing of their country house (dacha) into a theatre, for the entertainment of friends and guests.

Theatre was an early part of his life

1877, 5 September: First performances as an actor. From this first experience he begins the lifelong practice of making notes about his performance.

With a stage name, enrols for training

1884: Appears in operatic excerpts at the Conservatoire. Begins to use the stage name Stanislavski, acquired to keep his acting activities a secret from his family.

1885: Briefly enrols at the Moscow Theatre School, but leaves within three weeks, dissatisfied by the training.

1886: Invited to take over as chairman of the Russian Music Society and Conservatoire. His business plan for improving the Society's school is accepted.

Decides to take up acting as a profession

1887: A performance of the Russian premiere of *The Mikado* at his family's Moscow home is directed by Stanislavski. The event gains a professional review. Given permission by his father to continue a career as an actor, Stanislavski forms the Moscow Musical–Dramatic Amateur Circle.

Travels to see European theatre

1888: Founds the Society of Art and Literature with his colleagues Komisarjevski and Fedotov. This has a school attached. Travels abroad. Researches the rehearsal process at the Comédie Française and the teaching programme at the Conservatoire.

As an actor he begins to create more and more new roles. His work in the family business takes a back seat.

Is influenced by the Meiningen company

1890, April: Tour by the company of the Duke of Saxe-Meiningen. Stanislavski notes the radical production style, resulting in disciplined and artistically coherent productions.

Is now in control of a theatre company

1891: The affairs of the Society of Art and Literature are wound up, but the associated theatre company survives. Stanislavski takes absolute control. Tolstoi's *The Fruits of Enlightenment* is a great success, both as the new director's first production and for his acting role in it. Preparations had been made using the example of the Meiningen Company.

Acting with professionals he is out of his depth

1892: Acts with members of the Mali company (the leading professional company at this time) and, despite favourable opinions, finds himself out of his depth. Is urged to turn 'professional'.

1894–5: Produces *Acosta*, a now-forgotten drama, which he prepares with obsessive detail, in both the acting and the design. His performance is criticised for its anti-heroic, more natural elements.

Preparations include a search for detail	Begins to prepare for *Othello*, a part that had fascinated him for years. Extensive preparations involve a trip to Paris to buy books on costume and fabrics, and to Venice for research into the architecture and to buy props.
Shakespeare and psychological realism	**1896**: *Othello* opens to great critical acclaim. Stanislavski, though unhappy with his role, is deemed to have brought a deep psychological realism to the part.
Meets his partner Nemirovich for the first time	**1897**: Meets Anton Chekhov. They discuss the formation of a popular Russian theatre. Meets Nemirovich-Danchenko, who among his other duties is leader of the drama department at the Philharmonic School. Among his pupils are Olga Knipper (later to marry Chekhov) and Meyerhold.
The plan for a theatre takes shape	22 June: Stanislavski and Nemirovich agree to form an Art Theatre with a resident ensemble.
	1898, 9 April: Assumes the role of Principal Director of what is known as the Moscow Open Theatre. Begins to instil the disciplined working practices that he has planned for, heavily influenced by the Meiningen Company. Forms a lifelong friendship with Meyerhold.
The Seagull by Chekhov is a triumph	The first season includes *Tsar Fiodor, The Merchant of Venice, Antigone, Hannale* and Chekhov's *The Seagull*. The season opens to mixed critical notices and a number of outright failures. The opening of *The Seagull* is a triumph.
	The theatre is renamed the Moscow Art Theatre.
Uncle Vanya by Chekhov, another great success	**1899**: Directs première of *Uncle Vanya* and plays Astrov. A critical and artistic success. He is shouldering most of the administrative tasks as well as playing leading parts and directing.
	1900: Begins to rehearse Chekhov's new play, *Three Sisters*, while the author supplies continuous rewrites. Nemirovich contributes to the direction.
Three Sisters. His own role is considered his best yet	**1901**, 31 January: *Three Sisters* opens. He plays Vershinin at the last moment. It proves to be one of his greatest performances.
	1902: The company moves to a new permanent home. An existing theatre is gutted and rebuilt with the latest technical and lighting equipment. This forms the base for the Art Theatre for the next 70 years.
Realism/Naturalism: see pp.234–7 Gorki's *The Lower Depths* is a success	A new production of Tolstoi's *The Power of Darkness* highlights the conflict between 'realism' and 'naturalism'. Première of Gorki's *The Lower Depths;* despite rigid censorship, the play is a great success; Nemirovich takes over the direction at a crucial moment. The director and cast make extensive preparations in researching the characters from life.
Quarrels with his partner	Meyerhold leaves the company. Divisions begin to emerge between the directing styles of Stanislavski and Nemirovich, and although the breach is healed it is the beginning of the end of their close partnership.
Begins the habit of extensive pre-production Mise-en-scène: see Glossary	**1903,** October: Preparations for *The Cherry Orchard* begin. He prepares an extensive production plan, which details not only ideas for the mise-en-scène but also psychological motivations of the characters in some detail.
	1904: Chekhov's death at the end of June leaves him grief-stricken.

Symbolist dramas are seen as experiments	Begins to be influenced by the Symbolists, particularly the plays of Maeterlinck, a Belgian playwright (who much interested Chekhov towards the end of his life). Decides to direct three one-act texts by Maeterlinck. The plays are received badly as no one can make much sense of the style, not least the director.
Meyerhold in charge of the first Studio experiments

The first Russian Revolution | **1905**: Creates the Theatre Studio and gives the running of it to Meyerhold. It is intended for experimental work in new theatrical forms and texts. Meyerhold's experiments are a failure. Productions are shelved and the theatre is closed after the abortive revolution of 1905, which is brutally suppressed. He decides to take the company on its first foreign tour. |
International tour by the company	**1906**: Touring with, among other plays, *Uncle Vanya*, *Three Sisters* and *The Lower Depths*. They visit Berlin and towns throughout Germany and Austria. The tour is a triumph and succeeds in creating an international reputation for their work.
Draft of *A Manual on Dramatic Art*: the foundations of the System take shape	He begins to write a draft of *A Manual on Dramatic Art*. This is the first foundation of his 'System'. He returns to Moscow with the germ of an all-consuming objective.
A mission statement re-affirms experimentation	**1907**: He is isolated by the bad feeling in the company and the calls for his resignation. Writes an important letter restating his belief in the Art Theatre's mission of experimentation.
His role is redefined

He concentrates on the System | **1908**: Finally a solution is reached that satisfies. He is to mount one 'experimental' production each year and others by arrangement. His work as an actor in the company is to continue. Nemirovich becomes chairman of an administrative committee. Such an arrangement enables Stanislavski to concentrate his life on developing the 'System'. |
Isadora Duncan: see section 3.1.4	Meets Isadora Duncan. Is fired with enthusiasm for her dance and how it might relate to Maeterlinck's *The Bluebird*. Duncan writes enthusiastically to her ex-lover Gordon Craig about production possibilities.
His last spectacular production is a symbolist work	Begins to apply new methodologies (such as extended improvisations and discovering the 'objective') in the rehearsals of *The Bluebird*, much to the dismay of the company. The production is, however, a great success, much copied throughout Europe. It is the last of his spectacular productions.
First mention of Emotion Memory	Begins directing *The Government Inspector*. Mentions, for the first time, 'emotion memory'. Experiments with new rehearsal techniques, giving back to the actors responsibility for their work. The production is a critical success. Begins to leave behind his work as a director/actor, except as it advances the building blocks of the 'System'.
Craig: see section 3.1	Gordon Craig arrives in Moscow to discuss the possibility of directing/designing *Hamlet*. This is agreed.
	1909: Work begins on *Hamlet*, though it is not to be mounted for another year.
Collaboration with actors	Begins to direct Turgenev's *A Month in the Country*. Elaborate preparations are discarded; collaborative work with the actors is

paramount. The text is broken down into 'units'. The cast find rehearsals difficult; the 'System' is still in its infancy, but developing fast.

He contributes to Hamlet *rehearsals*

1910: Craig proves intractable and vague, so he takes control of *Hamlet* rehearsals. The actors are muddled between the new 'System' and the old methods of 'demonstration', to which he returns simply to achieve results. Craig is absent in Italy for much of the time.

Screens: see section 3.1.3

The production with Craig's screens is a partial success – at least Craig believes so, and continues to foster this view. Its notoriety transforms European stage practice for the next half century.

The Method: See section 3.2.5

1912: He establishes the (First) Studio, which is to recruit actors from both within and outside the company. Those that join include Richard Boleslavski, Vaktangov, Michael Chekhov (the playwright's nephew) and Maria Ouspenskaia. By **1914/15** the Studio is established as a centre for original and exciting experimentation.

Struggles continue to find ways through the System

1913: Rehearsals for various roles give opportunities for work on the System and its components. The outcome is not always successful. Outward transformations with make-up are not always matched with an inner truth.

The supreme actor of his time

1914: Great personal success in Goldoni's *La Locandiera*. Applying aspects of the System results in a superb performance, after sleepless nights of worrying and study. Acknowledged as 'the supreme actor of his time'.

Work on the subtext overwhelms the role Subtext: see Glossary

1915: The next role is a disaster. Playing Salieri in *Mozart and Salieri* he is savaged by the critics. Acknowledgement of the subtext overwhelms the part and leads to incomprehension.

Is so lost in the System that he is sacked

1916: Is sacked by Nemirovich from Dostoievski's *The Village of Stepanchikovo*, unable to reconcile his view with that of the director and obsessively self-critical. He is lost in the complexities of the System and its application to his own work.

Second Studio created.

Soviet state is created

1917: The Russian Revolution. The Moscow Art Theatre is anxious to be seen as sympathetic to the new ideas generated by the social and artistic upheaval.

1918–22: Continues to play major roles, teaches the System, directs or revives productions and creates an Opera Studio. Becomes active in the Professional Union of Moscow Actors.

Continues to teach

1919: All theatres are reorganised. The Art Theatre becomes a state 'Academic' theatre, with full independence and subsidy. The 'classics' are taken to new audiences in factories and the army.

Begins to lecture on the System

At the Art Theatre Stanislavski begins a series of lectures on theatre aesthetics, followed by a series on the System.

The Art Theatre is under attack

1920: The Art Theatre is under critical threat from all sides as an outdated and outmoded company. The most important work is being done in the 'Studios', leaving the main company to flounder with its outdated repertoire.

Working with the Habima Company	**1920–21**: Works with the Habima company, a group of Palestinian Jewish actors. Vaktangov is put in charge of a Third Studio, created especially for them. The culmination is an internationally famous production of *The Dybbuk*, by Solomon Anski.
Physical expression of the text	**1921:** Directs a revival of Gogol's *The Government Inspector*, with the leading actor Michael Chekhov. It is a huge success. The 'grotesque' and exaggerated physical style is perfectly in keeping with the current mode of production, though very different from the System.
Tours of Europe and America	**1922–3:** After months of discussion as to the way forward a foreign tour is agreed that will take in Berlin, Paris and for the first time the United States. A company is formed and a repertoire decided upon, which includes three plays by Chekhov, *The Lower Depths* and *Tsar Fiodor*.
Critical acclaim	The reputation of the company has preceded them and everywhere there is general critical acclaim.
Begins *My Life in Art*	While on tour Stanislavski signs an agreement with a publisher to write his autobiography. Now aged 60, he leads the company as teacher and actor. Begins to dictate the work that will become *My Life in Art*.
Meets his future 'editor' for the first time	**1924:** On returning to New York at the end of a gruelling tour, he meets the President. His interpreter is Elizabeth Reynolds Hapgood, who is later to become his editor and translator.
Meyerhold's theatre is now the most popular	**1925–6**: Returns to a changed Moscow. Meyerhold's anti-naturalistic theatre is in the ascendant and the Art Theatre repertoire is therefore considered politically unacceptable. Nevertheless, a new production of Ostrovski's *The Burning Heart* is a great success. He is acting as overall director, with younger assistants undertaking the day-to-day rehearsals;
Rewriting *My Life in Art*	he is then called in to supervise the last stages of production. He is working on the Russian version of *My Life in Art*.
A productive period of writing and directing	**1926:** With Nemirovich abroad on tour, he enters one of the most productive periods of his life, with new plays and a young company.
Uses a more physical approach to rehearsal techniques	**1927:** He is working with other directors on operas, where his main function, it is recognised, is to breathe new life into tired classics. Directs Beaumarchais's play *Le Mariage de Figaro*, which proves to be his last fully realised production. Is still breaking new ground, using
Technology of the Art Theatre	the technology of a revolve to keep the action in almost continual flow.
The year of his last performance	**1928:** Nemirovich returns and reassumes management. Offers of directing assignments pour in. The jubilee of the Art Theatre is celebrated. It is on this occasion that Stanislavski has a heart attack.
Seriously contemplates publication of the System Rethinking Emotion Memory	**1929–30:** Visits Berlin and meets the Hapgoods, who urge him to write a definitive version of the System. He is rethinking the use of Emotion Memory and beginning to propose the 'Method of Physical Action', which he develops in his teaching on his return.
Text of *An Actor Prepares* complete	By the end of his stay in Europe he has completed the text of *An Actor Prepares*, the intended first volume of two that will lay down the principles of the System.

He defends the theatre from
ideological attack

1931: The System is under attack by the Association of Proletarian Writers. The quality of productions at the Theatre is in danger of being compromised by the requirement to perform so often. He views this as short-sighted and says so; the Art Theatre has gained its reputation for quality with productions that are the outcome of long and detailed rehearsal periods. His protest has a positive result in the renaming of the company the Moscow Art Theatre of the USSR.

Prepares *Building a Character*

1933: He is 70. Travels abroad to recover his failing health. Continues work on the second half of what is known to him as *An Actor's Work on Himself*.

Stella Adler:
see section 3.2.5

1934: Meets Stella Adler and her then husband Harold Clurman in Paris. She is anxious for his help. Over a five-week period she takes classes with him, which are recorded verbatim. The outcome of this meeting is to have far-reaching influences on the development of the System in the USA.

An Actor Prepares is
published in America

1936: *An Actor Prepares* appears in the USA.

Dies on the eve of the
Russian publication of *An
Actor Prepares*

1937: He meets Meyerhold on a regular basis. He is anxious to leave a successor, and his colleague and friend seems the right choice. On the eve of the Russian publication of *An Actor Prepares,* he dies.

This chronology was compiled with the help of:

Benedetti, J.,   *Stanislavski, A Biography*,   Methuen, 1990

3.2.2 A BRIEF BIOGRAPHY

Important to understand the
context

Before we embark on a detailed examination of Stanislavski's theory and practice, it is important that we sketch in the circumstances and tradition of the Russian theatre that confronted him at the start of his career. It was just such a theatre that he dedicated his life to changing.

Russian theatre was a recent
development
Censorship was imposed

Since its infancy at the beginning of the 19th century, Russian theatre had been controlled by placing it under heavy censorship and the jurisdiction of the police. In the early years Moscow and St Petersburg were the only cities to sustain companies of any repute, while in the provinces theatre was little regarded or even known.

Gogol:
see chronology, 1908

By the middle of the century this had begun to change, more or less entirely due to the influence of a few dramatists, who delivered scathing attacks on authority disguised as social comedies. One such was Gogol (1809–52), who wrote plays such as *The Government Inspector* (1836), a portrait of corrupt small-town life which is still continuing to amuse and entertain over a century and a half later.

Gogol and Shchepkin:
see section 3.2.4

A discipline now in need of
renewal

Gogol is of special interest because of his friendship with the actor Shchepkin, which brought together two like-minded souls. They succeeded, temporarily, in imposing a disciplined and professional approach on a craft much in need of guidance in the early part of the 19th century. It was their combined and complementary attitudes to prevailing methods that made them of special interest to Stanislavski as he moved towards a soundly based practice.

Theatre standards were appalling	By the time Stanislavski came to work in the professional theatre, however, standards were as haphazard as they had ever been. His early years as a director were often taken up with mundane matters such as punctuality, drunkenness backstage and in some cases real squalor.
Haphazard staging methods	Rehearsals were often conducted in the most perfunctory manner. Experienced actors would simply inhabit the stage as they sought fit and deliver the lines of the text downstage centre and out front. There was no accepted convention that actors should address each other directly.
Traditions were outmoded and outdated	Settings were usually drawn from stock, doors and windows being placed conveniently, with no reference to reality. Costumes were often what the actor could provide, or were chosen simply because the theatre had them in store. Stanislavski's trips abroad to do research and buy props and fabrics for costume, as he did for *Othello* in 1894, were an unheard-of initiative. Stanislavski has left a vivid account of the theatre in which he gained his first experiences [Stanislavski 1993, Chapter VI].
His life was in the theatre from the beginning	It is important to remember that it was from the background of family amateur theatricals, indulged and supported by his father, that he emerged to become such an innovative director and actor. Not only was there an auditorium at the family home in Moscow, there was also one at their country home, where during the summer months the family could mount plays for their friends and relations.
The society that led to the formation of the Moscow Art Theatre	From this undoubtedly privileged background as an outsider he was in a particularly favourable position to view the work of the contemporary professional theatre. It was his influence and wealth that enabled him to create the first alternatives to such a theatre, with the founding of the Society of Art and Literature in 1888. So began an assault on what he observed as outdated and outmoded practice.
Worked on experimental texts	Throughout his life he insisted on experimentation, both for the actor and in the texts he chose to work on. His close relationship with Chekhov is crucial here, but he was also brave in his decision to work on such authors as Maeterlinck, and later Bulgakov. In the case of the former this was often in the face of incomprehension, in the latter fierce and dangerous official disapproval.
A quest for 'truth in art'	More than one biographer rightly lays stress on the fact that it was Stanislavski's quest for knowledge and his desire for perfection that led him from the closed world of semi-private companies into the national and eventually international world of the professional theatre. With little or no training, he embarked on a quest for truth in his art and devoted his life to that hard journey.
A systematic actor's training	His legacy was a **system** of approaching the inexact science of acting. He tried in a systematic way to lay down ground rules for approaching a character and for how an actor might employ his or her body, voice and mind in such a creation.
Influential as a teacher	He has been and remains enormously influential as a teacher and guide; he has also been much written about, argued about and interpreted by his disciples. But for his system to have any meaning it must be practised, and in the process it will be challenged and re-interpreted more than 50 years after his death.

3.2.3 THEORY AND PRACTICE

THE MOSCOW ART THEATRE

See section 3.2.8

The formation of this company is well documented, both by Stanislavski (*My Life in Art* [*MLIA*]) and Nemirovich-Danchenko (*My Life in the Russian Theatre*). By 1897, Stanislavski was becoming disenchanted with the life of an amateur part-time actor, and when he was approached by Vladimir Nemirovich-Danchenko, a teacher of acting at the Philarmonic School, he readily agreed to meet.

Meyerhold: see section 3.2.5

It so happened that in 1897 Nemirovich had an exceptionally talented group of actors, who would make the ideal basis for a new company. Among them were Olga Knipper (later to become Chekhov's wife) and Meyerhold, both of whom were destined to become founding members of the new theatre and Stanislavski's lifelong friends.

The meeting with Nemirovich lasted 18 hours, but by the end they had, in all but detail, laid the foundations for the policy of the theatre. They went as far as discussing individuals, and not for the last time, Stanislavski used the phrase when vetoing an actor: 'She is a good actress but not for us … *She does not love art, but herself in art.*' [*MLIA*, p.295. Our italics.]

Powers of veto and responsibilities

As Stanislavski records, he was to be predominantly responsible for artistic matters, such as devising the production plans and some directing, and would continue as an actor. Nemirovich would look after literary matters, such as choosing the repertoire, and would also direct.

Concerned for the proper function of theatre

Benedetti [1985. p.11] highlights five separate qualities that at this time concerned Stanislavski:
- Theatre was to be a moral instrument.
- Its function was to civilise.
- It was to increase sensitivity.
- It should heighten perception.
- It should ennoble the mind and uplift the spirit.

Shchepkin: see section 3.2.4

Fine sentiments, and built by Stanislavski on the foundations of the work and ethos of the great 19th-century actor Shchepkin, whom he quotes in *My Life in Art* [p.292]: 'Seek your examples in life.'

In other words, the actor had to go no further in his quest for truth than to base his art on his cumulative experience of the world around him, mediated and enhanced by the director's interpretation and the rehearsal process.

A permanent theatre is established

It took some time to acquire suitable premises and it wasn't until their fifth season that they moved into what became the Moscow Art Theatre. The stage was to be functional, the orchestra pit abolished, and the most up-to-date technical and lighting equipment installed (see Figure 3.10).

Unity and freshness to production values

Above all, the two men sought to bring a unity and freshness to all aspects of production and presentation. It was this vital philosophy that distinguished their work from the tired old ideals still so readily evident in the work of their rivals. It was to be a truly coherent company and it was to be based on the ethics and beliefs of the best of the past and present.

Figure 3.10   Fedor Shektel's design for the curtain and stage of the Moscow Art Theatre (1901). The seagull became the company's emblem.

To sum up they sought to:

- Choose plays from the classical repertoire, but also encourage new writing
- Treat actors with proper respect. They in turn would be expected to respond with total dedication to the new discipline
- Rehearse all plays for an agreed length of time and mount all productions with new designs and costumes.

REALISM AND NATURALISM

Realism was the guiding principle of his life

There is absolutely no doubt as to Stanislavski's position on Realism. He made the concepts embodied in it the guiding principles of his life and work and was totally opposed to what he saw as the meaningless experiments of the avant-garde. Though he was noted for groundbreaking productions in new styles, such as *The Bluebird* (1908), he totally failed to appreciate Gordon Craig's point of view when discussing their production of *Hamlet* (1910).

Realism in context

We need to be clear about the meaning of Realism, however, since there are as many definitions as there are contexts and the Moscow Art Theatre is no exception. Since Realism is often seen as synonymous with Naturalism, and since the term Realism is frequently used by Stanislavski, we must be convinced of the distinction.

Naturalism in context	Naturalism as a movement in literature and drama was associated with the work of the French novelist Emile Zola. His preface of 1868 to the second edition of his novel *Thérèse Raquin* explains clearly that he looked upon his task as a novelist much as a surgeon may look upon an examination of a human corpse:

> While I was writing *Thérèse Raquin* I was lost to the world, completely engrossed in my exact and meticulous copying of **real life, and my analysis of the human mechanism** . . .

> [Quoted in Rothwell, A. (trans), *Thérèse Raquin*, OUP, 1992. p.2]

Strindberg's Introduction to *Miss Julie*	This obsession with exposing a 'slice of life' was for a time very influential, and before the term was eventually subsumed into Realism there were some noted practitioners. For example, Strindberg applied the same principles to his characters in *Miss Julie* (1888) and, like Zola, wrote an introduction that explained his intentions.

> So I do not believe in 'theatrical characters'. And these summary judgements that authors pronounce upon people – 'He is stupid, he is brutal, he is jealous, he is mean,' etc. – ought to be challenged by naturalists, who know how richly complex a human soul is . . .

> [Quoted in Meyer, M. (trans), Strindberg, A., *Miss Julie*, Methuen, 1967. p.23]

An influential document	It was and remains an extremely influential document, calling into question the one-dimensional characters of 19th-century playwriting. It also questions the actors' insistence on facing the audience at all times.
The 'isms' can be interchangeable	However, one of the problems for us as readers is that Strindberg, even when writing this thesis, uses the terms Realism and Naturalism as interchangeable.
Obsessive themes of love and death	The term Naturalism applied to these two writers' work came to imply a concern with the suffering and degradation of the servant and working class and an obsession with love, death and moral decay.
Drama for a bourgeois audience	Realism grew out of Naturalism and superseded it. The desire for an indiscriminate reproduction of lower-class life, sometimes in all its squalor, ceased to fascinate. With few exceptions, the plays that Stanislavski mounted were peopled with characters who reflected the lives of their bourgeois audience, Gorki's *Lower Depths* being one exception to this rule.
Realism involved selection and distillation	Realism, then, could be recognised by its **selection** and **distillation** of the detailed observation of everyday life, not the life itself.
Naturalistic detail often swamped the text	We have touched on the distinctions between these two terms, but it has to be acknowledged that they are both used fairly indiscriminately by all practitioners, especially by Stanislavski. It might be argued that despite his desire to work towards the ideal of Realism, i.e. extracting the essence of a work, his practice was often otherwise, smothering the real in the detail of Naturalism (see Fig. 3.11).

Figure 3.11   A photograph of Stanislavski's production of Ibsen's *A Doll's House* at the Philharmonic School (later the Moscow Art Theatre), 1890. This is an example of the over-detailed naturalistic design that Chekhov found unacceptable.

Chekhov antagonistic to Stanislavski's approach	Meyerhold has left a record of Chekhov's antagonism to Stanislavski's over-detailed mise-en-scène for *The Seagull* (quoted in Braun 1978. p.30). Employing artists and designers whose style was highly naturalistic made it inevitable that the overall concept would be a faithful reproduction of
Over-representational	life, warts and all. While Stanislavski's instincts for the highest standards of representation for each new production were admirable, they often resulted in a stage picture that left little or nothing to the imagination.
Text and subtext	However, what above all distinguished Realism from other genres was its emphasis on the **subtext** of a play. Text was no longer a matter of surface meaning: characters could and did say things that had hidden agendas. It was on the way towards an understanding of this and how it could be communicated with feeling that many aspects of the System were devised.
Subtext: see section 1.1.3, pp.29–31	For a fuller discussion of subtext see section 1.1.3, but you may also find this summary useful.

Subtext, as the word suggests, is what can be identified under the text. It is the unspoken nuance that we as an audience recognise and which gives a character more depth or psychological realism.

Part of the pleasure we derive from watching or reading a scene is the fact that we can recognise the sense behind the words. This gives us insights into the characters' motivations often denied to those characters themselves. The subtext must, however, be acknowledged and understood by the actor.

Playwrights whose works we can identify as embodying these principles included Ibsen in Europe and, of course, Chekhov in Russia. It was through his work on Chekhov and then Gorki that Stanislavski was forced to tackle the issue of the subtext.

To sum up:

- Stanislavski was forced to acknowledge **subtext** as a way of deepening meaning.
- With Naturalism discredited he wished to **select** and **distil** detail and meaning on stage.
- A 'slice of life' had to be realised **selectively**, with truth and feeling.

THE SYSTEM: BEGINNINGS

In this section we examine the System, which Stanislavski developed over a period of 30 years. To understand fully **why** he thought it necessary to embark on such a journey, we have chosen **three** occasions which forced him to evaluate his work.

From the very beginning of his career Stanislavski kept a series of notebooks, annotating and evaluating all his performances and the processes that led to them. As we shall see, it was these records of his work that ultimately enabled him to formulate the theoretical objectives of his teaching.

SOCIETY OF ART AND LITERATURE (1888)
See chronology

First exposure to professional practice

Mannerisms were eliminated

Imitation rather than creation

There is a good account of the formation of this society in *My Life in Art* (Chapter XV), where Stanislavski records the long and painful process of rehearsing and performing in *The Miser Knight* by Pushkin, his first serious semi-professional role.

It was a daunting experience, but he was helped by a sympathetic director, Fedotov, who cut away his extraneous mannerisms. Although the work on his character was almost entirely a matter of imitation, and therefore little advanced on previous work, he considered it at least a qualified success.

An extravagant manner

He also described working on the second piece in the same season (*Georges Dandin* by Molière). He imported a kind of overblown extravagance of manner inappropriately based on his first-hand knowledge of Molière from visits to the Comédie Française the previous summer.

Imitation could be useful but it eliminated process

Again, Fedotov resorted to demonstration, which left Stanislavski baffled since it completely eliminated any *process*. However, he records how the 'accidental touch of the make-up brush' on his face suddenly animated what could have been a mere carbon copy.

To sum up:

- Professional directors sought to simplify his approach to the character.
- There was little or no process, imitation still being important.
- External details helped him to animate the part.

OTHELLO (1895)
A Shakespeare text as a test

Shakespeare's *Othello* had fascinated Stanislavski for years, and on the verge of the formation of the Art Theatre he decided to undertake both the direction and the leading role.

A trip to Venice to do research

As part of his plan of preparation he visited Venice in 1895, not only to research the locations but to buy fabrics, furniture and properties.

Meiningen:
see section 3.2.4

He prepared a detailed production plan, which fleshed out the meagre stage directions and gave life and vitality to the text. It was his intention from the first to reproduce as much of the reality of the play as possible, heavily influenced by the Meiningen tradition, and to his delight he also found his role model for the Moor:

A detailed character study, from direct observation

> In one of the summer restaurants of Paris I met a handsome Arab in his national costume [...] With the help of the waiter we made the designs of the costume. I learned several bodily poses which seemed to me to be characteristic.
>
> [*MLIA*. p.277]

Imitation again, but in a coherent framework

The production was a great success. Every aspect of the play was focused on the one objective: that of creating an overwhelming *psychological realism*.

The critic Marov, reviewing the performance, said: 'This is magnificent. What you see is not the way jealousy takes hold of his soul all at once but how passion, little by little, takes possession of his whole being.' [Quoted in Benedetti, 1990. p.53]

The actor Rossi, complimenting Stanislavski after his performance, also pointed a way forward:

Stanislavski urged to be self-critical

> God gave you everything for the stage [...] The matter is in your hands. All you need is art. It will come of course [...] I can recommend you only one teacher [...] You yourself.
>
> [*MLIA*. p.286]

To sum up:
- A detailed production plan with realist design was the basis.
- Imitation again supplied the method of preparation.
- The whole production was focused on an in-depth, realist approach, and his performance on a carefully considered psychological realism.
- He was encouraged by critics to be self-critical.

Figure 3.12   A photograph of Act 1 of *The Seagull* at the Moscow Art Theatre, 1898.

THE SEAGULL (1898)

See chronology

Mise-en-scène: see Glossary

By the time of the third and last example, Stanislavski was joint director of the Moscow Art Theatre. In 1898 a gamble was taken to revive Chekhov's *The Seagull* as part of the first season's repertoire.

For the task of constructing the mise-en-scène, Stanislavski adopted what by now was regular practice of heavily annotating the text with both visual elements:

What is mise-en-scène related to Chekhov?

> *The Seagull* notebook is full of stage designs, descriptions of settings, diagrams of movement and grouping, plus hundreds of notes on blocking, picturization, and visual rhythms . . .

and auditory elements:

> . . . notes about vocal rhythms, tempo, timbres, phrasings, sound effects, pauses . . .

> [Jones, D.R., *Great Directors at Work* UCP, 1986. p.19]

In practice it was too much detail

Despite his best intentions, Stanislavski produced imagery that almost threatened to swamp the text, and he was taken to task by Nemirovich for too much emphasis on the excesses of naturalism.

'Sound score' was much applauded

But this time the detail paid off and all critics agreed that the **'sound score'** (the balance of sounds on- and offstage) alone produced heart-wrenching moments of drama, as silence was juxtaposed with sudden bursts of half-heard sounds.

Subtext: see pp.29–31 and Glossary

The emotional motivation of the characters had been revealed through an acknowledgement and understanding of the **subtext,** and altogether the production confirmed a company working at the height of its potential.

To sum up:

- A detailed mise-en-scène was a successful way of unlocking the play's meaning.
- Chekhov's text demanded a deeply psychological approach.
- There was more to a play than surface meaning.
- Subtext had to be acknowledged and developed.

SUMMARY OF BEGINNINGS

We have focused on three distinct milestones in Stanislavski's early career as a director and actor and have identified in each case a particular learning process.

Time for reflection and consolidation

It was after the company's triumphant tour of Europe in 1906, and after an exhausting schedule of roles, that Stanislavski on his return took a much-needed holiday in Finland. There he began to reflect upon his life and work to date. After years of recording the agony of creation in his notebooks, he steadily began to sift his thinking and over the next two years he began to identify what finally became known as the System.

Begins to identify components of a System

Begins to use the company as guinea pigs for the System see pp.240–6

In his production of *A Month in the Country* (1909) these elements were confirmed through the rehearsal process, though the cast were baffled by aspects of the new language and rehearsals were fraught with personal anxieties. For the first time, exercises that later become identified as *Units and Objectives, Subtext,* the *Through-line of Action* and the *Super-objective* became defined. [Benedetti, 1985. p.41]

On the following pages we will discuss some of the most important elements that became the System, bearing in mind Stanislavski's dictum:

'The System as a whole way of life'

> ... the System is not a hand me down suit that you can put on and walk off in, or a cook book where all you need is to find the page and there is your recipe. No, it is a whole way of life ...
>
> [*Building a Character*, Chapter XVI. p.290]

THE SYSTEM IN DETAIL

The texts to look at

An Actor Prepares (*AAP*) is the key text from which we draw the main sub-headings for a discussion of the System. It is supplemented by *Building a Character* (*BAC*), which contains further thinking and modifications. References are made to *My Life in Art* (*MLIA*) but as an autobiographical record it is occasionally vague and imprecise.

ACTION

Action as the mainspring of drama

For Stanislavski this was one of the most important elements: he conceived **action** to be concerned with the meaningful, purposeful activity of an onstage actor.

Inner and outer action

From the start, Stanislavski makes the distinction between action for its own sake, as an outward and physical form, and action that can be seen as action because of a concentrated stillness on stage – which he calls 'inner intensity'.

Process of enactment

His objective is to demonstrate that there is never a point when the actor is not engaged in a process of *enactment*, but at the same time he suggests that it must always have purpose:

Acting with purpose

> Do not run for the sake of running, or suffer for the sake of suffering. Don't act 'in general', for the sake of action; **always act with a purpose**.
>
> [*AAP*, Chapter III. p.40]

and later:

> ... all action in the theatre must have an inner justification, be logical, coherent and real.
>
> [*Ibid*. p.46]

In other words, it must have a 'why'. Why am I coming through that door? With what purpose? What is behind the door? How might I approach the door?

ACTIVITY

Try some exercises based on ideas of entering and leaving a space. We do this a lot of times every day. Try it with different physical rhythms, with different intentions. You will need to justify the why of your action but it should be clear what **purpose** you want to communicate to an audience.

The 'why' of action | Stanislavski takes as an example the story of the insane man who lurks behind a door (a story that is returned to throughout these texts), and he uses the door and the dilemma of whether to open it or not as an indicator with which to focus the actor's purpose of action.

IF | Known as the '**magic if**', it opens up possibilities for the actor of 'creating a whole new life', of stimulating new emotions. What would happen if...?

The 'magic if' creates a whole new life | What would happen if all the canvas and paint were not just a representation but a real place? If the actor next to me were in fact a mother/brother/sister, etc?

What if...? | It remains for an actor to make believe: 'sincerely to believe in the possibility of what you are called upon to do on the stage', or what Stanislavski later calls the 'imaginative fiction of another person'. It is not just the person, but the circumstances in which that person can and will function.

ACTIVITY | Improvise: What would you do **if** the lights suddenly went out in the middle of a party? What would you do **if** the man who has escaped is behind the door? You receive a phone call to say your long-lost sister is arriving unexpectedly. What would you do?

But the '**magic if**' can only be sustained within the context of the next theme.

THE GIVEN CIRCUMSTANCE

What seems true in 'given circumstances'? | **Given circumstances** are the basis for an actor and his role, they are created by the playwright, the director and designer and form the context in which the the actor can ask: what **if**...?

Stanislavski's list | Stanislavski lists the circumstances:
- the story of the play
- its facts, events, epoch, time and place of action
- conditions of life
- the actor's and regisseur's (director's) interpretation
- the production, the sets, the costumes, the properties
- lighting and sound effects.

ACTIVITY | Decide on a set of given circumstances, taking the above points as a guide. It might be best to plan this round a story rather than a play. Develop a scenario and decide how best to communicate the circumstances. A family funeral? Packing to go on holiday? Create an environment and act out a moment from the scenario.

An actor's belief and the development of imagination | The actor must believe in the **given circumstances**; through this belief she or he will be able to function at a high level of involvement. The goal throughout is a quest for truth:

> ... it is necessary for the actor to develop to the highest degree his imagination, a childlike naivete and trustfulness, an artistic sensitivity to truth and to the truthful in his soul and body.

[*MLIA*. p.466]

THE IMAGINATION

Stanislavski then goes on to foreground this notion:

> . . . when you begin to study each role you should first gather all the materials that have a bearing on it, and supplement them with more and more imagination . . .
>
> [*AAP*. p.53]

Undergoing a visual journey

It is useful to note that Stanislavski's teaching here relies very much on visual stimulus for the development of this faculty. The chapter contains more than one exercise that demands that the actor undergo a **visualised** journey.

When, where, why and how

> If you speak any lines, or do anything, mechanically, without fully realising **who** you are, **where** you came from, **why**, **what** you want, **where** you are going, and **what** you will do **when** you get there, you will be acting without your imagination.
>
> [*AAP*. p.71]

ACTIVITIES

Develop an imaginative journey: there is a good starting point for one on page 61 of *An Actor Prepares*. After some preparation time question each other, so that gradually the whole group gets to know the story/journey you have developed. It can become quite complex as you have to answer the when, where, why and how questions.

Do some research: take a character from any of the major plays by Chekhov. By careful reading, find out what that character says about him/herself and most importantly what other characters say about that person. You will end up with a very rich study from which to develop further an imaginative life.

Find a photograph or a painting: construct a character study from the picture. Make a list of questions you would ask the person if you could meet them. Exchange your findings with each other. You need to provide an imaginary life, just as you can with a character from a play.

CIRCLES OF ATTENTION

A need to find ways of relaxing

During much of Stanislavski's early career he was concerned with his perceived inability to relax onstage and he therefore examined ways to help an actor relax and focus.

The actor as focus

Stanislavski uses a device that he calls Circles of Attention to illustrate his point. Its prime purpose is in giving the student a focus for his or her attention. Like ripples on a pond, these circles radiate from the centre of attention (the actor) and in ever increasing circumferences embrace the whole stage.

Ripples on a pond

In the smallest circle an actor can create what he calls **Solitude in Public**, a condition that focuses the actor within him/herself. By increasing the focus the actor can begin to take in further objects and gradually, by concentration, the whole of the stage/imagined world is brought into focus.

ACTIVITIES Sit in the middle of a large space. How can you make the audience want to watch you? By what you are doing? By what you are not doing? How can you extend the focus? By looking at another person in the space? Can we tell what you are thinking about them? How far can you extend the circle?

Find a hoop. Holding this at arm's length, walk in a controlled way round a space. Can you create **solitude in public**? Drop the hoop and stand within it. Now make your focus the whole space. Get rid of the hoop and do the exercise again. You should have a focus which is clear and concentrated.

UNITS AND OBJECTIVES

Units make the text 'manageable'

They have in-built objectives

A unit needs to be active

Like so many of the aspects of the System, these two are both distinct and inextricably entwined.

In essence, the idea of **Units** is common sense: a play can be broken down not just into acts or scenes by the author, but by the director or actor into **units of action.**

These units are dominated and controlled by the **objectives** within them; while it is useful to work on small and manageable chunks of text, each chunk will have its own in-built objective. A unit ends with the end of the objective.

Stanislavski warns against the creation of too many units: 'The part and the play must not remain in fragments.' Using a seagoing metaphor he likens the units to buoys in a channel, as guides for the actor in his voyage.

One of the most important features of the objectives contained within the units is that they are active, driving the text forward. For that reason Stanislavski insists on describing them with a verb rather than a noun. He uses the example of the noun 'power'. Simply by placing the words 'I wish to . . .' in front he begins the process whereby an actor can actively free the objective: 'I wish to obtain power over . . .'. Immediately, with a qualifying verb, 'power' becomes an active, less generalised, objective. As an example of an active objective we might examine what Stanislavski calls 'the right objective' and the example he gives (*AAP*, p.120). Here he suggests that the act of shaking hands with a person to whom you wish to apologise is not a simple act. It requires thought and the psychological exploration of many conflicting emotions. The active element is 'I wish to make an apology . . .', while the emotional subtext is dependent on the circumstances of the act within the action of the play.

ACTIVITY Look at the beginning of Act I of *The Seagull*. Where would you end the first **unit**? Just before the entrance of Sorin and Treplev? What is the **objective** for the actor playing Medvedenko? He is obviously in love with Masha, but she is uninterested. Is he seriously trying to make her love him? What verb would you give to the **objective**?

THE SUPER-OBJECTIVE AND THROUGH-LINE OF ACTION

Stanislavski emphasises firstly how important it is to identify an over-arching **objective** within a play. For example, *Hamlet* is about a man who wants to find a way through the muddle of his life so that he can make up his mind. Secondly, the **through-line** can be described as the main current 'that galvanises all the small units and objectives'. Useful diagrams (*AAP*, p.276) illustrate his points.

ACTIVITIES   Look at *The Seagull*. What is the **super-objective** of the play – the main theme? You might decide that it is how lives are lived in conflict with the creativity of acting and writing (two themes that were very close to the life of its author). However, there are other possibilities.

Now consider the character of Nina. She wants to be an actress. This is firmly fixed in the character's imagination, as well as evidenced in the text. This is her **super-objective**. Find how often she makes a statement about this conviction, but also see how her actions help to express the whole theme of the play and how in doing so she creates a **through-line** for herself.

EMOTION MEMORY

Just as your visual memory can reconstruct an inner image of some forgotten thing, place or person, your **emotion memory** can bring back feelings you have already experienced.

[*AAP.* p.168]

This aspect of the System was destined to become one of the most controversial, owing to its adoption by some practitioners of the American 'Method' in the late 1940s and 1950s. Stanislavski's almost complete disavowal of it in later life was because of both its limitations and the fact that it led to introspection and self-reflective performances that failed to communicate.

Affective memory

Recall of stimulus

His starting point was Ribot's *Problèmes de Psychologie Affective*, which dealt with the memory of feelings and emotions. It was Ribot's contention that the nervous system bore the marks of previous experiences, which could be recalled by a stimulus, such as a sound, smell or touch, in a similar way to the sensation of *déjà vu*.

Memory can be stimulated by experience

Memory as an aid to creativity

Stanislavski believed that it was an actor's duty to stimulate his or her 'emotion memory' by making a conscious effort to broaden his or her range of experience: to create, as it were, a reservoir of memory from which to draw and on which to build. This memory could then be tapped into when the actor was working towards the creation of a character. Equally, as Stanislavski found, it could be used to re-invent emotions that had been fixed in rehearsal and that needed reproduction in performance from night to night.

Always and for ever, when you are on stage, you must play yourself. But it will be in an infinite variety of combinations of **objectives,** and **given circumstances** which you have prepared for your part, and which have been smelted in the furnace of **your emotion memory**.

[*AAP.* p.177]

ACTIVITIES   Find a stimulus that will provoke a memory of some kind: a picture/ photograph; a piece of music; a smell. Construct the circumstances of that memory and devise a short improvisation to express your feelings from that time. Can you link this to a piece of text of your own choosing?

Make a direct observation of someone. Try to do this without them knowing. Record your impression and then try to recreate that person either by writing about them or by acting out a detail you remember.

**TEMPO–RHYTHM
IN MOVEMENT**

Dalcroze:
see section 3.2.4

Stanislavski's later preoccupation with this aspect of the System marks a significant move away from the internalised work of **Emotion Memory.** Through his study of yoga and the work of eurythmics advocated by Dalcroze, Stanislavski goes to great lengths to explain his ideas:

> Wherever there is life there is action; wherever action, movement; where movement, tempo; and where there is tempo there is rhythm.
>
> [*BAC.* p.198]

Rhythm connected with a musical beat

By setting a number of metronomes ticking at the same time but with different beats, Stanislavski shows how an actor must find his own rhythm (inner) while at the same time being surrounded by other actors, all of whom may have their own distinct rhythm (outer).

Inner and outer rhythms in conflict

Thus an actor who might be frantic with worry (inner rhythm) may be acting in a scene where everyone else is discussing something as mundane as the weather (outer rhythm). An inner turmoil could be identified through its outward manifestation, or concealed (in this case) by a show of calm. Two rhythms are created, the one contradicting the other, leading to interesting dramatic tensions within the performance.

Rhythms need to be rehearsed and agreed

It is important that rhythms are kept distinct. All too easily a group of actors can pick up each other's rhythms, creating a generalised beat, which all too often is the slowest. A well-rehearsed rhythm can drive the play forward, with an imaginary conductor keeping all the rhythms intact.

> You must get accustomed to disentangling and searching out your own rhythm from the general, organised chaos of speed and slowness going on around you on the stage.
>
> [*BAC.* p.187]

Stanislavski also tackles the way that different external, physical tempo-rhythms can affect the atmosphere of a particular text, for example a slow rhythm suggesting a ceremonial or a faster rhythm leading to a more chaotic scenario. He draws attention to the strength of stillness, which in itself is a tempo-rhythm, and how that can be contrasted with rapid movement by other characters in the same scene.

ACTIVITY

Look at *The Seagull* Act 4, when Nina arrives to confront Treplev after an absence of two years. He is disillusioned with his life as a writer, she with hers as an actress. Decide which actor is the still one and which the one who moves most. These contrasted rhythms can express each character's internal/external tempo and give us huge insights into the emotional state of these people.

**THE METHOD OF
PHYSICAL
ACTION**

Towards the end of his life, with *An Actor Prepares* all but published, Stanislavski increasingly placed emphasis on physical expression as a way of training.

Improvisation as physical action

Once objectives and lines of physical action had been identified, it was through the *physical*, 'the doing', that the actor might find 'solidity and depth'. What this boiled down to was more emphasis on **improvisation** as a way of unlocking aspects of both the text and the role.

Text was to be tried and tested in rehearsal

In the last stages of revision of his teaching he continued to refine and draw together the rehearsal process. There is a clear description of this in his biography [Benedetti, 1990. p.339]. Further detail on this later theoretical rethinking can be found in *Building a Character*.

FINALE

Stanislavski's System will be argued over and dissected as long as there are actors, directors, teachers and students to do so. Of all the practitioners discussed here, it was Stanislavski with his prescription for approaching the art of acting who dominated the 20th century.

Springing from the need for an absolute truth of thought, feeling and expresssion to be communicated by an actor to an audience, this System has ensured that the code of Naturalism and Realism has dominated theatre and, more especially, film for the last 50 years.

It was and is a difficult code to break, and interestingly all the other practitioners in this chapter made a concerted attempt to do just that, attempting to show that there were alternative ways of looking at the process towards the enactment of a text.

Stanislavski's legacy was a System that sought to present a methodical approach to the art of acting and directing. It was an enormous task, but it sprang from his own need to understand and wrestle with his own shortcomings.

As a series of documents, his books demand our attention for the personal and passionate way in which they seek to support and challenge an actor through his or her training, through rehearsal and the nightly task before an audience.

3.2.4 INFLUENCES

SHCHEPKIN, MIKHAIL SEMENOVICH (1788–1863)

Stanislavski enjoyed an unbroken connection to this great actor of the 19th century through his teacher and mentor Fedotov, from whom he took lessons in 1888. She had studied under the great actor and passed on to Stanislavski those qualities he in turn came so much to admire and live by.

Shchepkin had been born a serf and it wasn't until 1818, after a number of provincial successes as an actor, that he gained his freedom. He was noted for the fresh and simple way that he approached playtexts, predating the fashion for a more 'realistic' style. He was one of the first to recognise the virtues of ensemble playing and the need for company discipline. He also viewed the theatre as an almost sacred institution, in which plays by great writers could find their place. Stanislavski in *My Life in Art* quotes a letter from him:

Ensemble playing

The actor as self critic   Watch yourself sleeplessly, for although the public may be satisfied with you, you yourself must be your severest critic.

[p.85]

This was the ethos that inspired and guided Stanislavski throughout his life.

Worrall, N.,   *Gogol and Turgenev,*   Macmillan, 1982

GOGOL, NIKOLAI VASILIEVICH (1809–52)

Lifelong friend of Shchepkin   Gogol was a writer who lived a troubled life but who was to become a literary figure as much admired as Dickens in England, and who similarly created characters and stories that passed into the national consciousness. He found a like-minded friend in Shchepkin, with whom he shared a passion for theatre, having at one time contemplated acting as a profession.

Russian provincial life satirised   His most famous play, *The Government Inspector* (1836), takes up the theme of the absurdities of Russian provincial life. It came at a time when he was campaigning for a truly national drama, as opposed to imported classics from France and Germany:

> . . . for God's sake give us Russian characters, give us **our own selves**, our swindlers, our cranks! Onto the stage with them, for the people to laugh at.

[*Petersburg Notes of 1836*, quoted in Worrall, N. p.41]

In his *Advance Notice To Those Wishing To Act The Government Inspector Properly* he urges the actors to take the comedy seriously; then and only then will the trivial lives of his protagonists be revealed.

Theatre with a social purpose   His views on theatre as having a serious social purpose were handed down as part of Stanislavski's cultural heritage and were perfectly in tune with the ideas of the two men who founded the Moscow Art Theatre:

Theatre as a power for good   The theatre is by no means a trifle or a petty thing . . . It is a kind of pulpit from which much good can be spoken to the world.

[*On the theatre*, quoted in Worrall, N. p.43]

Worrall, N.,   *Gogol and Turgenev,*   Macmillan, 1982

THE MEININGEN COMPANY

Detailed realist productions   This theatre company, run by the Duke of Saxe-Meiningen, toured Europe extensively at the end of the 19th century. Through its advanced production techniques in the naturalist/realist style it was responsible for influencing a number of theatre companies, including Stanislavski and the Moscow Art Theatre.

Challenges to prevailing practice   Stanislavski first saw the company perform in 1890 and was immediately struck not so much by the acting, which was indifferent, but by the mise-en-scène, which sought to challenge prevailing stage practice using:
- settings placed on the diagonal, rather than parallel with the proscenium
- the choreographed movement of extras, which isolated the protagonists in dynamic stage pictures

- actors who could and did turn their backs on the audience if the production demanded it
- the placing of architectural or natural features across the stage floor, to reinforce the realistic settings.

The company was run with iron discipline by its autocratic director Ludwig Chronegk. Stanislavski remarked that despite himself he admired and wished to imitate the 'restraint and cold-bloodedness' of this man. Many of the values of this extraordinary company were adopted wholesale when it came to the setting up of the Art Theatre in 1898.

Braun, E.,   *The Director and the Stage*,   Methuen, 1982
Osborne, J.,   *The Nature of the Saxe-Meiningen*
                  Aesthetic,   *Theatre Quarterly*, May 1975. pp.40–54

CHEKHOV, ANTON (1860–1904)

A founder member of the Art Theatre

No study of this length can do proper justice to this man, who played such a crucial part in the fortunes of the Art Theatre. With Nemirovich-Danchenko and Stanislavski he was responsible for the values that the Theatre sought to embody and, after the success of *The Seagull* in 1898, productions of Chekhov's plays became the standard by which the ensemble work of the company was judged. All Chekhov's subsequent work was produced by the company, culminating in *The Cherry Orchard* in 1904, just before his death.

Integrated ensemble playing

Realism:
see section 3.2.3

Whilst he is often lumped together with other playwrights in the genre of Realism, what was it that distinguished him?

Let us be just as complex and as simple as life itself . . .

[Chekhov, quoted in Braun, 1982. p.62]

Figure 3.13   Anton Chekhov reading *The Seagull* to the actors of the Moscow Art Theatre.

Objectivity, observation and recording

He sought, by a process of selection and refinement combined with objectivity, to present his characters without moralising. As a one-time doctor he was attuned to the foibles of humanity and he used his gift as a writer to create compassionate statements about what many might consider as wasted lives.

A summary of Chekhov's qualities as a dramatist

One of his translators, Ronald Hingley, draws attention to the quality of the writing:

> . . . Chekhov's drama is essentially a study in moods: moods desultory, sporadically inter-acting, half-hearted, casual, yet somehow profoundly moving.
>
> [Introduction to *Five Plays*, 1985. p.xxviii]

Braun, E.,	*The Director and the Stage*,	Methuen, 1982
Chekhov, A.,	*Five Plays* (trans. Hingley, R.),	OUP, 1985

JACQUES-DALCROZE, EMILE (1865–1950)

Isadora Duncan: see section 3.1.4

Stanislavski met Isadora Duncan in 1908, when she was dancing in Moscow, and began discussions with her about her 'system' of movement. It soon became clear that she had no system that could be easily expressed, so Stanislavski turned to Dalcroze, whose work was becoming known throughout Europe.

A teacher of music who used movement

His career as a music teacher had led him to use movement as a way of instilling a sense of rhythm into his pupils. As that became successful he began to develop a system that sought to achieve '. . . harmony of body and spirit through a co-ordination of physical movement and sound movement, musical and spatial elements.' [Quoted in Volbach. p.87]

Co-ordination of physical movement

He called this system Eurythmics, and by 1910, with the help of his great friend Appia, he had opened a studio where some of the most famous theatre artists in Europe could see his experiments. The movement, like Duncan's, was free and expressive, making loosely choreographed patterns across open spaces, juxtaposed with massed groups on tiered steps.

Stanislavski reacted favourably to this work. As he devised such ideas as **Tempo–Rhythm in Movement**, he increasingly urged his pupils to include movement and dance in their training.

Volbach, W.,	*Adolphe Appia, Prophet of the Modern Theatre*,	WUP, 1968

3.2.5 FOLLOWERS

In this section we have been very selective. It is probably true to say that every actor in the Western world will at some time have been influenced by Stanislavski's teaching, so we have concentrated on key figures who were themselves very influential.

MEYERHOLD, VSEVOLOD (1874–1940)

A brilliant actor who was drawn to experimental texts

Meyerhold was one of Stanislavski's most original and brilliant pupils, and a founder member, with Olga Knipper, of the Moscow Art Theatre. However, from playing leading roles he gradually grew disenchanted with the rather conservative repertoire and left the company. He undertook several experimental theatre seasons in provincial capitals, which persuaded Stanislavski to make him the director of the Theatre Studio in 1905.

Symbolist dramas were unsuccessful

Poetic dramas

Here he embarked on a series of productions heavily influenced by Maeterlinck and Symbolism, but despite the best intentions they were a failure. Stanislavski commented: 'For the new art new actors were necessary, actors of a new sort with altogether new technique.' [*MLIA*. p.437] Dark, rather gloomy plays which expressed the poets' inner life were much concerned with dreams; they were in direct contradiction to the realism practised by the Art Theatre.

Sister of Komisarjevsky: see below

Anti-realist productions

Another significant venture was Meyerhold's work under the management of the actress Vera Komisarjevskaya in St Petersburg in 1906. His production of Ibsen's *Hedda Gabler*, again challenging realism, was the first in a number of vivid and daring experiments. Audiences and critics gave it a mixed reception.

Constructivism: see Glossary

By 1908 he had been dismissed by his employer, as the time was not yet ripe for these bold statements. It was not until his work in the **constructivist** style in the 1920s that he consolidated his reputation as one of the most innovative practitioners of the 20th century.

Stanislavski remained loyal to his friend all his life. As he lay dying he said, 'Look after Meyerhold, he is my sole heir, not in our own theatre but in general.' [Benedetti 1990. p.345]

But by then Meyerhold had fallen foul of authority. He was accused of not being able to toe the 'party line' and, with his benefactor safely dead, Stalin had him shot.

Braun, E.,	*Meyerhold on Theatre,*	Methuen, 1969
Leach, R.,	*Vsevolod Meyerhold,*	CUP, 1993

KOMISARJEVSKY, THEODORE (1874–1954)

A director from the Art Theatre who made the link with British theatre

He is important for having brought the influence of the Art Theatre to Britain. His sister, Vera (see Meyerhold), was considered to be one of the most talented actresses of her generation, and as part of her company he too worked with Meyerhold. Like his colleague he was active in 'experimental' theatre and by 1918 he was noted as a director with new and challenging ideas.

Chekhov with John Gielgud

Leaving Russia in 1919, he sought work in Europe and America, but it was not until 1925, when he was offered a season in a small theatre in Barnes, near London, that he made a dramatic mark on the contemporary audience. He decided to make Chekhov the focus of his work and was fortunate in being able to cast John Gielgud.

Chekhov discovered

Critics and public flocked to these 'new' plays, the British theatre having been generally ignorant of the playwright's work. A critic could say about a production of *The Three Sisters:*

It ... has brought to our actors a chance to cultivate under his direction new modes of dramatic expression.

[Quoted in *Theatre Notebook*, 1983. p.67]

The productions in this season confirmed Komisarjevsky's understanding of and sympathy with Chekhov and it would be fair to say that his influence in Britain as an innovative director was far-reaching and pervasive.

Gielgud, J.,   *An Actor and his Time*,   Penguin, 1981
Komisarjevsky, T.,   *Myself and the Theatre*,   London, 1929

THE METHOD

The influence of the Moscow Art Theatre

The Moscow Art Theatre toured America in 1923–24 and left behind two actors: Richard Boleslavski and Maria Ouspenskaya. Together they formed a school called the American Laboratory Theatre, where they began to teach, basing classes on their intimate knowledge and understanding of Stanislavski's System, up to the point that it had then been codified.

The formation of the Group Theatre

Among their students were two actors, Stella Adler and Lee Strasberg, who in 1931 became founder members of the Group Theatre. This based its work on a socialist/realist style and was noted for its fine ensemble playing, using Stanislavski's System as a basis for rehearsal.

The Actors' Studio used Emotion Memory, although discredited

Adler made it her business to meet and work with Stanislavski in 1934 and therefore renewed contact with the System. However, as leader of The Actors' Studio from the early 1950s onward, Strasberg continued to rely very heavily on Emotion Memory. Stanislavski had begun to discredit this in the mid-1930s as he moved towards publication of *An Actor Prepares*, appreciating its limitations and preferring a more outward and practical experimentation.

The Method actor might be characterised by heavy reliance on his or her own personality and a deeply emotional approach to performance. There is a good checklist of qualities associated with the Method in Vineberg, J., *Method Actors*, Schirmer Books, 1991 (pp.6–7). It has provided a sound and methodological training for actors in the American theatre and film industry, where value is placed on intense psychological realism in the construction of character.

The Method style still in evidence

The Actors' Studio nourished actors as diverse as Marlon Brando and Marilyn Monroe, and in the 1980s was still seen as an influence on such stars as Jane Fonda and Al Pacino, who were noted as intense and compelling film actors. This has resulted in some of the finest performances in the history of the cinema, in such films as *On the Waterfront* (1954) with Brando, and *Rebel Without A Cause* (1955) with James Dean. More recently the series of *Godfather* films, again starring Marlon Brando, as well as a new generation of actors like Al Pacino, has confirmed the 'Method's' training.

3.2.6 SUMMARY: KONSTANTIN STANISLAVSKI

This summary is written to draw together certain parts of the chapter on Stanislavski under particular headings. It should be considered with the student's own practical work in mind and/or the student's viewing of other productions. For example, Stanislavski's interest in the training of an actor: as a student undertaking practical work you would wish to discuss an aspect of this training that you have observed (such as the realisation of the super-objective) and how this could be reflected in your own work. By isolating this convention/practice not only are you enhancing your own approach but you are able to make informed reference to his theories when viewing other productions.

THE SUBJECT MATTER	Classic texts performed in realist settings Research as a method of realising the author's intention Plays about 'real life'
THE POLITICAL PURPOSE OR MESSAGE OR DRAMATIC INTENTION	Socially motivated texts The actor as an integral part of the mise-en-scène Texts that reflect the lives of the audience The use of subtext to reveal an emotional context
THE ACTOR– AUDIENCE RELATIONSHIP	Firmly established 'fourth wall' The audience as voyeur The actor removed from any contact with her/his audience The actor establishing an interior world. Character based An actor dedicated to his/her art
THE STAGING FORM ADOPTED	Heavily naturalistic/realistic The re-creation of reality in stage terms Detailed settings with many portable props
DIRECTORIAL INTERPRETATION /PRODUCTION STYLE	Detailed pre-planning Based on a 'system' Seeking the truth in the text by planned rehearsals Deeply psychological approach An ensemble approach to the text A methodical approach to the realisation of text
DESIGN ELEMENTS	Mood and atmosphere created through detailed realist settings Natural sound used to create a feeling of place/time The theatre of illusion. Confined within the stage picture Costumes to replicate those worn in real life
ROLE OF ACTORS AND PERFORMANCE STYLE	The use of improvisation in the creation of a character The actor part of a close-knit ensemble Realism/Naturalism. The desire to recreate real life
TECHNICAL ELEMENTS	The importance of the proscenium arch as a way of containing the picture 19th-century practice harnessed to new interpretations Machinery as a way of sustaining illusion
AUDIENCE RESPONSE	Onlooker through the 'fourth wall' A suspension of belief Seeking confirmation of their own bourgeois place in the world A desire to see great acting at work in the re-creation of character

3.2.7 SUGGESTIONS FOR FURTHER STUDY

PLAYS

The Seagull (1898), **Uncle Vanya** (1899), **Three Sisters** (1901), **The Cherry Orchard** (1904) Anton Chekhov

The Lower Depths (1902) Maxim Gorky

A Doll's House (1879), **Hedda Gabler** (1890) Henrik Ibsen

Miss Julie (1888), **The Father** (1887) August Strindberg
Strindberg experimented with many styles, but these two 'modern tragedies' are good examples of a detailed psychological realism.

Mrs Warren's Profession (1880) George Bernard Shaw

Shaw adapted much of his technique from Ibsen, and this early play is a good example of a social theme communicated by lively and well-rounded characters.

Playboy of the Western World (1907) John Millington Synge

A superb and entertaining 'slice of life' play, based on the life of a community in Ireland. A text of carefully researched realism.

All My Sons (1947) Arthur Miller

Sometimes labelled as 'new realism', Miller's writing was heavily influenced by Ibsen. Social themes in a well-crafted realist context.

Death of a Salesman (1949) Arthur Miller

This play combined strong scenes of realist dialogue with 'dream' sequences that owe something to an expressionist influence.

Live Like Pigs (1958) John Arden

This early play combines a social theme with inter-scene folk ballads. Its detailed setting and examination of 'real-life' characters make it part of the realist genre.

Look Back in Anger (1956) John Osborne

A highly influential play, which breaks new ground. It belongs firmly in the genre of realism.

Chicken Soup with Barley (1958), **Roots** (1959) Arnold Wesker

Part of a trilogy of plays. Aspects of the writing are realistic, but they were staged in a strongly 'Brechtian' style.

3.2.8 BIBLIOGRAPHY

PRIMARY SOURCES

Stanislavski, K. *My Life in Art*	Methuen, 1993	Despite the lack of dates, and chapters that are not arranged chronologically, it is a first-hand account.

	An Actor Prepares	Methuen, 1993	The primary text for a working through of the System.
	Building a Character	Methuen, 1993	The 'second' book of the System, published from notes after his death.
	Creating a Role	Methuen, 1993	The 'third' book in the trilogy. Useful for its perspective on later theory.
Benedetti, J.	*Stanislavski, A Biography*	Methuen, 1990	A comprehensive account of his life and work.
Benedetti, J.	*Stanislavski, An Introduction*	Methuen, 1985	An account of the System, its changes and growth.
Braun, E.	*The Director and the Stage*	Methuen, 1982	A useful companion to all the practitioners.
Cole, T. and Chinoy, H.	*Actors on Acting*	Crown, 1970	A reference book for accounts by actors of their craft.

FURTHER SOURCES

	Stanislavski and America 1	*Tulane Drama Review* Vol. 9, No. 1, Fall 1964	Original and very useful articles on and about the System and its American legacy.
Schmitt, N.C.	*Stanislavski: Creativity and the Unconscious*	*New Theatre Quarterly* No. 8, 1986	Concerns itself with readings of Ribot related to Emotion Memory.

3.2.9 QUESTION AND SUGGESTED FRAMEWORK FOR ANSWER ON STANISLAVSKI

ACTIVITY   Stanislavski said about his System: '. . . it is not a cook book where all you need is to find a page and there is your recipe. No, it is a whole way of life.'

Discuss this statement with reference to an actor's preparation for a role. Choose an appropriate play to illustrate your answer.

POINTS TO CONSIDER

- Choose a text that is suitable for this answer. This will be very important, and it would be quite appropriate if you had acted in it.

- Although it is a long question it is really quite simple: you are being asked to discuss an actor's preparation for a role.

- You should realise that the question is asking you to comment on 'a whole way of life' and that should be dominant in your mind.

- Relevant quotes could be useful.

A DETAILED ANALYSIS

Introduction

Name the play that you are going to use and the character in that text. Say why you have chosen the piece: for example, its relevance to Stanislavski's theories (realism and characterisation). Explain why the whole System would be useful if playing that character.

Main body

For each of the subsequent sections, take an important aspect of the character. For each section explain:
- what the aspect is and what evidence there is for it in the text
- which elements of Stanislavski's System would assist you, the actor, in creating the role
- *how* they could help you.

For example one aspect of the character might be his/her variety of moods. You should give examples of these from the text. You should then suggest elements of the System that might help you truthfully portray these: for example, Units and Objectives, Inner Tempo–Rhythm, Circles of Attention. Explain why each would be useful and how you would use it in rehearsal. It is important that you state that it is the *combination* of these elements that would be of particular use; one alone would not be sufficient to help you realise such a wide range of moods. You might also point out that the other elements of the System would be of additional use.

Another aspect of the character might be his/her relationship with another character. Again, give examples from the text. Name a number of elements that would help you: for example, If and the Given Circumstance, Emotion Memory. Continue as above. The format would then continue for other characteristics, if you have time.

Conclusion

Comment on the quote in the question. Do you agree with Stanislavski that you must use *all* the aspects of the System, or not? Justify your conclusions using examples from your earlier points and from your own practical experience in particular.

3.3 *Antonin Artaud (1896–1948)*

Figure 3c   Antonin Artaud

3.3.1 A CHRONOLOGY

1896: Born, 4 September, Marseilles.

1901: Contracts meningitis, which starts a lifelong history of nervous disorders; although he is cured it leaves him incapacitated.

Starts a literary review

1910: Starts a literary review while still at school and publishes his first poems, much influenced by the Gothic/Romantic poets Baudelaire (1821–67) and Edgar Allan Poe (1809–49).

First stay in a sanatorium

1915: Suffers from depression and destroys all these first works. His parents arrange for their son to go into a sanatorium. This first incarceration is a signal of a condition that is repeated throughout his life.

Addiction to drugs
Begins to draw and paint

1918: Under the care of one of his doctors he is prescribed opium (laudanum), which leads to a lifelong addiction to drugs of all kinds. While in care he draws and paints.

Contributes to a literary review

1920: Decides to go to Paris to undertake a career in film, theatre and and literature. His parents reluctantly agree and he is put in the care of a doctor who is studying the phenomenon of artistic genius. He contributes to a literary review edited by his doctor.

Works with Charles Dullin

1921: Makes his theatrical debut in a small part at the Théâtre de l'Oeuvre. Auditions for Firmin Gemier, who sends him to Charles Dullin (1885–1949). Dullin is running the outstanding experimental theatre in Paris, called the Théâtre de l'Atelier.

Artaud's personal relationships are made difficult because of his drug-taking habits.

Sees Far-Eastern dancers

1922: Active in theatre as an actor and designer. Publishes poems. For the first time sees oriental dancers from Cambodia, who are at the Colonial Exhibition in Marseilles, his home town. They make a deep and lasting impression.

Works with further experimental companies

1923: He is working for a number of directors who are interested in an international repertoire of plays, including Pirandello's *Six Characters in Search of an Author* and Strindberg's *Ghost Sonata*.

1924: Abel Gance offers him a role in the film *Napoleon*. He appears as the revolutionary Marat. Over the next years film work allows him a living.

Surrealism:
see section 3.3.4

At the invitation of André Breton he joins the Surrealist Movement.

Begins to write poetry

Correspondence is published

He submits poems to the editor of the literary magazine *La Nouvelle Revue Française*. Furious at being turned down for publication, he initiates a correspondence with the editor, Jacques Rivière. Ironically, it is these letters that are published, since they reveal a new writer in embryo.

Director of the Surrealist Research Centre

Writes manifestos

1925: Becomes the director of the Surrealist Research Centre. Is already making his mark on the philosophies of the group with his uncomfortable and highly emotional presence. Is responsible for the content of the third edition of *La Révolution Surréaliste*, the movement's newspaper, and continues to write further manifestos.

Writes poetry and plays	Publishes collections of poetry and a scenario for the 'surrealist play' *The Jet of Blood*.
Jarry: see section 3.3.4	**1926:** Begins to plan the Alfred Jarry Theatre, named after the playwright who in 1896 had written the scandalous *Ubu Roi*. He is joined in this venture by Roger Vitrac and Robert Aron and a manifesto is published.
Is expelled from the Surrealist Movement	Breton sees him as a threat and expels him from the Surrealist group. It is an acrimonious parting and 20 years later, in the last years of his life, it can still make him angry. The theatre project collapses.
Film: see section 3.3.3	**1927:** Begins a period of intense activity, not all of it successful. His scenario for the film *The Sea Shell and the Clergyman* is directed by Germaine Dulac, but much altered from the original. However, it paves the way for other surrealist films: *Un Chien Andalou* and *L'Age d'Or*, directed by Luis Buñuel with the participation of Salvador Dalí.
	Plays the part of a young monk in Dreyer's *The Passion of Joan of Arc*. His expressive performance is one of the surviving records of him as a performer.
Théâtre Alfred Jarry revived	A season at the revived Théâtre Alfred Jarry includes a wordless fragment by himself and contributions from his colleagues: *Gigone* by Max Robur (Aron) and *Les Mystères de l'Amour* by Roger Vitrac.
	He is penniless and practically starving. The season continues into 1928.
Acts of defiance in spite of censorship	**1928:** At the Théâtre Alfred Jarry there are two acts of defiance. The first is when the film version of Gorki's *The Mother* is shown, although it has been banned. Secondly, the author Paul Claudel has specifically refused permission for one of his plays to be performed and is outraged at the decision to present the final act. The Surrealists offer a temporary truce with Artaud, as they despise Claudel, but this is soon broken.
The Surrealists disrupt performances	Performances of Strindberg's *A Dream Play* are funded by a Swedish nobleman and consequently are disrupted by the Surrealists, who object to 'bourgeois' theatre. After a final performance in 1929 the Théâtre Alfred Jarry is dissolved amid much recrimination between Artaud and Vitrac.
See section 3.4.1	**1930:** Is in Berlin to film *The Threepenny Opera*, Pabst's version of the text by Bertolt Brecht. Sees Piscator's theatre.
Begins to plan a manifesto: *The Theatre of Cruelty*	**1931:** Continues to make films, but is in a state of acute poverty, living alternately with his mother and in cheap hotels. A growing reliance on drugs is taking its toll, sapping his strength and mind. Sees a performance of the Balinese dancers at the Colonial Exhibition in Paris. This initiates serious thought on his project entitled *The Theatre of Cruelty*.
Manifestos that become known as *The Theatre and Its Double* are published	**1932:** For the next years he is sustained by the patronage of the editor of *La Nouvelle Revue Française*, Jean Paulhan, who publishes several manifestos later to be collected under the title of *The Theatre and Its Double*.
	Meets the great novelist André Gide, who supports his theatre work over the next few years. He is so poor that he has to appeal to an emergency government fund for writers.
Continues to publish manifestos	**1933:** Continues to work on his collection of manifestos, including a lecture at the Sorbonne entitled *The Theatre and the Plague*. The audience leave the reading in disgust at his emotional rendering.

Scenario for *The Conquest of Mexico*	Writes the scenario for *The Conquest of Mexico*, which deals with the Spanish conquest of the Aztecs in 1519. Briefly works on a scenario for the composer Edgar Varese, entitled *There is No More Sky*, but it is unfinished.
	Takes a trip to the south of France in a desperate attempt at self-imposed detoxification.
Outline for *The Cenci*	**1934:** Continues to act in films, though this year sees the last of these roles. He is disenchanted with the cinema. He needs to take another treatment for his addiction, but again this is unsuccessful. Writes the outline for a treatment of *The Cenci*, a tragedy by the poet Shelley.
An end to theatre experiments	**1935:** *The Cenci* is presented for 17 performances, but does not attract an audience. This marks the end of experimentation and of *The Theatre of Cruelty* in action. Indeed, it is the end of any real practical involvement in theatre or cinema for the rest of his life.
Travels to find Indian rituals Is destitute	**1936:** Embarks on his ill-fated voyages of discovery, starting with a search for lost rituals among the Indians of Mexico. Obtains a government grant from the Ministry of Education, but by the time he reaches Mexico City he is penniless again. Commences a series of lectures for the intellectual elite, who are starved of European news.
Stays with Indian tribe Peyote dance	He arranges a trip to see the Tarahumaras Indians. It takes him on an arduous and dangerous journey and he stays with them for about a month, finally witnessing the peyote dance. He takes the drug peyote, during a ferocious and frightening ceremonial ritual. He is almost dead with withdrawal symptoms, having thrown away his supply of opium. Returns to France a broken man.
Unsuccessful cures for drug addiction	**1937:** Takes two cures for addiction but neither is successful; is spending more and more time in sanatoria trying to cure his drug habit. After giving a scandalous lecture in Brussels, he decides to visit Ireland.
Travels to Ireland	He acquires a walking stick which he believes to have belonged to Saint Patrick, and decides that it is his mission to return it to the Irish. Accordingly he sets out on what will prove to be his final journey. Increasingly, his fragile hold on reality evaporates, until he is finally arrested in Dublin after a series of street fights and deported to France.
Deported in a straitjacket	He arives back in a straitjacket and is immediately interned. The incarceration is to last the next eight years.
	1938: His essays and manifestos are collected together. Publication of a limited edition of *The Theatre and Its Double* (*T & ID*).
At the clinic in Rodez *Theatre and Its Double* published	**1943:** He is transferred to a clinic at Rodez, where he is cared for by Dr Ferdière. He remains there until his discharge in 1946. He resumes creative writing and drawing, and words pour out as in the days before his illness. Second edition of *The Theatre and Its Double* is published.
Drawing and writing continue	**1945:** Begins to re-live his experiences through drawing therapy, and these fractured images are accompanied by short texts in a language of his own devising.

He is returned to semi-freedom

1946: Arrangements are made for his release. He is to live in a small pavilion in the grounds of the asylum at Ivry, near Paris. He is returned to semi-freedom. Is well enough to sign a contract for his Collected Works.

A recording is made of his final text

1947: An abortive lecture at the Vieux-Colombier is a disaster. Plans are made to broadcast his text *Pour en Finir avec le Jugement de Dieu* (To have done with the judgement of God). Recordings continue into 1948.

Radio broadcast is banned

1948: His worst fears are confirmed – he is suffering from cancer in its advanced stage. The day before the broadcast the recording is banned. He is hurt and outraged, as are his friends.

Dies alone on 4 March, sitting at the end of his bed with a shoe still in his hand. He may have died of an overdose of chloral.

His friend Paule Thevenin is entrusted with the enormous task of editing his Complete Works.

This chronology was compiled with the help of:

Barber, S.,   *Antonin Artaud, Blows and Bombs*,   Faber, 1993

3.3.2 A BRIEF BIOGRAPHY

Offers radical scenarios

No other figure in the relatively recent history of the theatre has been so raided for his dreams for a new theatre and then so misunderstood as Artaud. Since his death, and since the publication of his key texts in the English language, however, Artaud has been acknowledged as offering radical scenarios for the development of theatre practice.

Labels which give us no definitions

Artaud has been labelled a prophet, a martyr, a cult figure, a madman and a drug addict. Since those who have written about him have labelled him thus, we must try to find our own way through to an objective consideration of his work.

This is no easy matter. His ideas and theories were bound up with his life and the style in which it was lived. Since that life could be likened to a journey through a 'darkness pierced occasionally by flashes of brilliant light', we need to hold on to those moments of clarity when we come to view his theory translated into practice.

A mass of written evidence

For a man of such chaotic tendencies he left an amazing amount of written evidence: correspondence, letters of protest, articles, scenarios, plays, adaptations of plays, poems, manifestos and the recollections of friends and enemies.

No clear progression

What makes this most confusing is that there is not even a hint of development to his theoretical outpourings. When we come to examine his life and therefore his work we are faced with an apparently chaotic choice of starting points. An examination of his followers (see section 3.3.5) will make clear that his objectives have been interpreted in a huge variety of ways.

Nine years lost	We should remember that for almost nine years of his life he was incarcerated in institutions, a voice silenced and unheard, and that throughout his life, for months on end, he was in voluntary exile undergoing detoxification. After the Second World War he emerged, a broken spirit, into a world that had all but forgotten him. It was only after his death that his thoughts, so painfully recorded, came to be recognised for what they were: an authentic rebellious voice in the chaotic days of post-war European theatre.
Recognition at the end of his life	

Nine years lost

Recognition at the end of his life

We should remember that for almost nine years of his life he was incarcerated in institutions, a voice silenced and unheard, and that throughout his life, for months on end, he was in voluntary exile undergoing detoxification. After the Second World War he emerged, a broken spirit, into a world that had all but forgotten him. It was only after his death that his thoughts, so painfully recorded, came to be recognised for what they were: an authentic rebellious voice in the chaotic days of post-war European theatre.

Unknown by his contemporaries in Europe as a practitioner

In his lifetime there was no one outside France who looked upon him as any kind of influence, not only because his writings remained untranslated, but also because he was simply never counted as a practising theatre innovator. By comparison with his contemporaries, Stanislavski, Craig and Brecht, Artaud lived the life of a hermit.

A lonely figure, who did not choose to collaborate

He did not choose to have fruitful collaborations with others; his ideas were too formless and individualistic for this to be a possibility. It is therefore in the context of his life as a lonely figure of revolt and rebellion that we must begin to consider him.

Man of vision

If we settle on a definition of him as a man of vision, what is it that distinguished him from his contemporaries?

Uncompromising ideas

Theatre of the senses

He was totally uncompromising, in that he advocated the complete abolition of the traditional boundaries between actor and audience. He combined this with an appeal for theatre to return primarily to an experience of the **senses**. The audience was to be unsettled and shocked to its very core by experiences of extreme power and beauty. Artaud was primarily responsible for the breaking down of audience–actor barriers, and the confrontational theatre of the post-war period (see section 3.3.5).

Ritual and ceremony

He believed the director should dominate the working through of scenarios which laid stress on **ritual** (see section 3.3.3). For Artaud, ritual involved a carefully worked out scenario with staging elements that by their visual and aural power would present a controlled sense of danger in their performance.

An actor with heightened gesture

Actors' bodies, gestures and voices were to be worked on and choreographed to create as much meaning as the spoken word. They could be accompanied by huge puppets, which had the effect of heightening the scale of the spectacle and creating a sense of **disorder** and **anarchy**.

Controlled chaos

Theatre as a weapon

If all this seemed to be working towards a sense of chaos, Artaud also made the point that it should be controlled and precise in order to achieve its objective. He saw theatre as a weapon to destroy present society and as such he realised that it could never be extreme enough to achieve this objective.

Peter Brook has commented:

> Artaud applied is Artaud betrayed: betrayed because it is always a portion of his thought that is exploited . . .
>
> [Brook, 1986. p.60]

Offering radical solutions

In retrospect, Artaud can be seen as the true man of vision, someone who appears to offer real and radical solutions to the theatre of conventionality. But the solutions are all too often based on contradictory statements, since Artaud never had the opportunity really to explore the implications of his ideas.

Theatre as a power to question society

Yet as a practitioner with an admittedly limited personal experience he left behind in his manifestos and writings enough ammunition to supply his inheritors with the weapons they needed for the re-invention of theatre.

3.3.3 THEORY AND PRACTICE

THE THEATRE AND ITS DOUBLE

Collection of manifestos

The title given by Artaud to the collection of essays and manifestos which were published in 1938 was encapsulated in a letter to his publisher:

An all-encompassing title

I think I have found a suitable title for my book.
It will be:
THE THEATRE AND ITS DOUBLE
for if theatre is the double of life, life is the double of true theatre ... This title will correspond to all the doubles of theatre which I thought I had found over so many years: **metaphysics**, **the plague**, **cruelty**.

[Quoted in Sellin, 1975. p.93]

Three definitions

This is a difficult definition to understand and like so many of Artaud's statements it has many readings.

The three doubles of theatre identified by Artaud come from three different essays in the collection:
- *Production and Metaphysics*
- *Theatre and the Plague*
- *Theatre of Cruelty, First and Second Manifestos.*

Thus the title carries with it some of the ideas that Artaud explores at some length and also hints at a fourth and less explicit idea: that of **the double**.

METAPHYSICS

Metaphysics is a difficult idea to deal with out of context, but generally it may be used to express anything that has no rational explanation. Hence Artaud's use of the word – for the logical and rational have very little place in his scenarios.

Metaphysics is further broken down

Artaud breaks **Metaphysics** down into a further three early influences, which he identifies as having contributed to a formulation of the Theatre of Cruelty. These are:
- Balinese dancers
- *Lot and His Daughters*, a painting by Lucas van Leyden
- The Marx Brothers.

Balinese dancers

Dance as the first expression

Artaud had seen a company of Cambodian dancers as early as 1922 in his home town of Marseilles, but it was his viewing of the **Balinese dancers** at the Colonial Exhibition in Paris in 1931 that proved such a hugely exciting experience and gave him one of the elements to formulate his Theatre of Cruelty.

Non-verbal signs for communication

What he admired and sought to translate, though not to copy, was the effect of gesture and facial expression on an audience's unconscious: how these signs could be seen to express and communicate far more than a mere substitute for words.

More than traditional mime

He maintained that in traditional mime, relying on the example of the Commedia dell'Arte, the skilled artist could communicate whole scenarios, but that these still relied on a fairly straightforward narrative explained in gesture.

Gesture with deep meaning

What Artaud was after was to attach deeper meanings to gesture: '...instead of standing for words or sentences [...] stand for **ideas, attitudes of mind**...in a tangible, potent way...' [*T& ID*, 1985. p.29].

A language of the senses

This language of 'signs' that so fascinated Artaud was one that would appeal to the senses and minds of his audience, giving them an 'intuition' that something more than words was being communicated. In addition, he wanted this process of communication to be a violent one – not so much in the physical sense, but in the way it might stimulate and conjure up 'mental poetry' in the mind.

True poetry is metaphysical

He explores this idea further by suggesting that 'true poetry is metaphysical', and it is in this statement that he really summarises his feelings about these dancers. If the audience is to be stimulated by the gestural dancers to formulate mental poetry, and if this poetry is to be

Explaining the unexplainable

metaphysical, then Artaud is reaching towards experiences for his audience that are beyond the logically explainable.

Gesture creates meaning

It is an exciting and radical concept, suggesting that gesture alone would have immense power to invent and discover a 'mystical meaning' in drama, beyond the overtly obvious.

Lot and His Daughters

Painting as influence

Artaud made many visits to the Louvre to see this painting and often took friends to see it as well, which gave him an opportunity to explain its importance.

The painting is described

He describes the painting in great detail, contrasting the apparent domestic calm of the father and daughters in the foreground with the cataclysmic destruction of Sodom in the background.

The foreground of the painting is suffused with the glow of the fireball that God has delivered to the wicked city, and Lot himself, far from being a paragon of virtue, is here depicted as no better than those left behind to die in the flame.

A dramatic spectacle

The painting summed up for Artaud a moment that had an inherently dramatic meaning. It explored space and disjointed perspective to

Simultaneous action

unsettle the eye of the spectator. It also appealed to his sense of simultaneous action, with people's lives threatened by catastrophe while they went about their day-to-day existence.

The Marx Brothers

Comedy is anarchy In the work of this extraordinarily anarchic team Artaud saw further evidence for his Theatre of Cruelty. As he describes in the manifesto *Production and Metaphysics*, what he found so appealing was the rapid juxtaposition of imagery. A woman who is about to be embraced becomes a cow, the transformation provoking a sudden release of laughter.

Figure 3.14   The Marx Brothers – Hollywood's alternative comedians.

Laughter as a liberator	He saw laughter as a great liberator, as powerful an emotion as that generated by a tragedy. The power of the cinema was to make possible
The power of cinema	these juxtapositions, moving an audience from tears to laughter by the power of editing. His theatre could do the same through such contrasts and he envisaged the use of puppets alongside the human actor to achieve this.

The Marx Brothers and Surrealism

He described the films *Animal Crackers* and *Monkey Business* as parallel to the works of Surrealism. Just as the Surrealists constantly made use of the invasion of the rational by the irrational, so the Marx Brothers created a world of their own which short-circuited a logical chain of events. In transcending what was physical and natural the action and imagery would be metaphysical.

THE PLAGUE

This was the second **double** that Artaud thought he had found.

Physical effects

This manifesto touches on a number of concerns, but above all it gives a frightening and vivid picture of the physical effects of the plague.

Allegorical concerns

Artaud uses the plague as an allegory for theatre, so that while he is discussing the former he is using it as a symbol for the latter. When he says, 'The plague takes dormant images, latent disorder and suddenly carries them to the point of the most extreme gestures. Theatre also

The collapse of society equated to theatre stripped of constraints

takes gestures and develops them to the same **limit**' [*T& ID*, 1985. p.18] he is using the inevitable collapse of society during a plague as an image to challenge our view of theatre. He is suggesting that theatre should be stripped of bourgeois constraints and all that these imply, just as a population in the grip of the disease would be.

There are no limits

Despite suggesting there is a limit, in reality of course Artaud is saying that there are **no real limits** to which theatre cannot aspire.

Definition of a 'real' play

A **real** stage play upsets our tranquillity, releases our repressed subconscious, drives us to a kind of potential rebellion.

[*T& ID*, 1985. p.19]

What theatre can do

Theatre is intended to challenge and disturb, to release in us a sense of free licence, to unlock our sense of decorum and to act as a catalyst for our dreams to become reality.

CRUELTY

The third **double** is cruelty.

Since we plan to discuss this central theme in more detail, it will be sufficient here to touch on what Artaud meant by cruelty:

A definition

. . . to go to the very end of all that the **director** can exert on the sensibility of the **actor** and **spectator**.

[Quoted in Barber, 1993. p.52]

The director, actor and spectator make theatre

Here Artaud is clearly indicating the combination of three presences involved in the process of making theatre. To paraphrase Artaud: **all** of them would be involved in a theatre that could become as much a part of us as our bloodstream, threading through our bodies like fire. The

A spectacular theatre of the mind

theatre that Artaud envisages is one that could awaken, organise and present the latent dream images of our mind, and would grip us with its power and amaze us with its spectacular presentation.

THE DOUBLE   The fourth **double** is the double itself:

> . . . for if theatre is the double of life, life is the double of true theatre.

Innes interestingly suggests that:

A definition
> Material existence is seen as an imperfect copy of what art – as a higher form of reality – symbolically expresses.
>
> [Innes, 1993. p.62]

The reverse of the usual definition   This is the reverse of the accepted relationship between art and life: Artaud is looking at theatre as an *enhanced* mirror image.

Surrealism: see section 3.3.4   What is also of interest to us here is the connection betweeen that 'higher form of reality' and Surrealism. In the *First Manifesto of Surrealism* (1924) the leader of the movement wrote:

Definition of Surrealism
> 'I believe in the future resolution of these two states – ouwardly so contradictory – which are dream and reality, into a sort of absolute reality, a surreality.'
>
> [Quoted in: Waldberg, P., *Surrealism*, OUP, 1978. p.66]

Art is dominant in life   So not only does Artaud's definition reverse the role of art and life but, like the Surrealists, of whom he was once a member, he suggests that life will take second place to an absolute and higher form of the real.

Edgar Allan Poe: See chronology, 1910   Artaud's choice of the double as a metaphor was no accident. With his early interest in the poetry of the Romantics and the poems and stories of Edgar Allan Poe, Artaud would have come across the concept of the **double** in 19th-century literature (see Fig. 3.15).

Figure 3.15   An illustration of a *doppelgänger* in Poe's tale, 'William Wilson'.

The concept of 'the double'   The primitive idea of a soul as having two parts, 'the person and the shadow', was developed by the Romantics into the concept of double or *doppelgänger*. In the case of Poe, as with other artists of this period, this was very much connected with mental instability, which blurred the distinctions between the real world and the dream world where the double belonged.

Mental instability

The *doppelgänger* only destroyed in death   Glimpsed in mirrors or in the darkness of shadowed rooms, the *doppelgänger* haunted the life of its originator and, as in the case of Jekyll and Hyde, it was only destroyed by the protagonist's murder. At the moment of death the protagonist was invaded by the double and so the dual soul was finally reunified.

We can see from this brief summary how pertinent this concept was to Artaud's own life and how the shadow of a double could give meaning to and haunt his theoretical writings.

SUMMARY OF THE THEATRE AND ITS DOUBLE

We have looked in some detail at Artaud's three components of the metaphysics of theatre:

- Dance and gesture could create meanings as valid as words.

- A painting could suggest scenarios and dramatic spectacle.

- Comedy and film editing could produce liberating laughter through anarchic images.

We have touched on the relationship between theatre and the plague:

- The plague became an allegory for theatre.

- Extreme emotions and actions arise out of a lack of controls.

- He re-defines what a play should be – a release for dreams and hidden emotions.

We have looked briefly at cruelty:

- There are no limits to what theatre can achieve in stimulating an emotional response.

- There are no limits to how this might be accomplished.

We have explored the notion of the double:

- Theatre is seen as an enhanced mirror image of life.

- Concepts of the double draw our attention to the inseparability of life and the theatre.

THE THEATRE OF CRUELTY

The Theatre of Cruelty is a name covering much of Artaud's work   This is the title of two manifestos within *The Theatre and Its Double* which give their name to a whole body of generalised shorthand when Artaud's writing is discussed.

A résumé of the manifestos   The *First Manifesto*, first published in 1932, concerns itself mainly with issues of spatial and physical presentation, and includes a short list of possible texts. The *Second Manifesto* extends the first, but concentrates

Plan showing the use of the deep stage

Plan showing the use of the proscenium stage

Plan showing the use of the centre stage

Figure 3.16 These drawings for Gropius's 'Total Theatre' make it clear that the proscenium arch relationship was to be challenged in favour of a space that could overwhelm an audience with auditory and sensory experience through the manipulation of technology and the relationship of actor to audience.

more on the form such a theatre might take, with an important discussion of language. It includes the scenario *The Conquest of Mexico*.

Not just blood and murder The title of the Theatre of Cruelty has generated much debate since it was proposed by Artaud, but it is important to remember that it is not just referring to blood, murder and chaotic acts of torture.

A definition . . . the spectator will be shaken and set on edge by the internal dynamism of the spectacle.

[Innes, 1993. p.65]

Theatre to challenge an emotional response This definition gets to the heart of the intention of the Theatre of Cruelty and sets up the relationship between stage and audience that Artaud envisaged. He intended the theatre to challenge and heighten the spectators' emotional response through the most carefully programmed set of circumstances. Through stimulation of the physical and emotional senses, the audience was to be maintained in a constant state of **Overwhelming catharsis** uncertainty, leading to overwhelming catharsis (emotional release).

These two documents have played a major role in the rethinking of staging conventions in the 20th century, and it is these conventions that we examine first.

STAGING THE THEATRE OF CRUELTY

AUDITORIUM AND AUDIENCE

The audience in the centre of the action

The auditorium will be enclosed within four walls, stripped of any ornament, with the audience seated below, in the middle, on swivelling chairs, allowing them to follow the show taking place around them.

[*T& ID*, 1985. p.75]

An audience trapped and powerless

No other practitioner in the 20th century sought such a radical solution to the actor–audience relationship. As an idea it continues to challenge us, since with its emphasis on 'enclosed' and 'below' it implies an audience both trapped and in a powerless position (see Fig. 3.17).

A sensory experience in a vortex

The issue of the audience in the centre is a vital one and, it has to be admitted, seldom achieved. What Artaud envisaged was the vortex, a circular and shifting shape into which the performance could erupt, drawing the audience (on its swivelling seats) into total sensory identification with the show.

The abolition of boundaries

Artaud goes further in suggesting that there will be '...a kind of single, undivided locale without partitions of any kind and this will become the very scene of the action' [*T&ID*, 1985. p.74]. In other words, the traditional separation of actor and audience will be abolished, enabling both to join in working out what he called 'The Show'.

A crucial development in 20th-century theatre

This invading of the audience by the actor was one of the most crucial practical developments from Artaud's theory and led to the creation of theatres where such boundaries were re-examined and, in some cases, abolished.

Figure 3.17 An artist's impression of Artaud's auditorium. With the audience on swivel chairs, the action could take place anywhere in the auditorium and the spectator could be overwhelmed by the spectacle.

Actors or audience could be in galleries

Further, Artaud suggested '...galleries right round the circumference of the room', extending the potential for actors to look down on their audience. This in fact led to quite the reverse, as theatres tended to place the audience in this position (the Cottesloe Theatre for example). However, actors could join and frequently did join the audience: a further breaking of traditional barriers.

Finally, Artaud envisaged theatres as '...some kind of barn or hangar rebuilt along lines culminating in the architecture of some churches, holy place...' [*T&ID*, 1985. p.74].

The development of 'alternative' theatre spaces

In short, Artaud pointed the way to the development of alternative performance spaces, with exciting and liberating results for audience and actor.

SOUND

Sound as a score for the text

In Artaud's vision of theatre there is always a great emphasis on sound. He realised its power to engage an audience's inner sense, and in his production of *The Cenci* (1935) he was able to demonstrate its potential with a carefully scored accompaniment to the text.

Recorded sound at full volume

Recorded church bells from the four corners of the theatre greeted the audience, performers' footsteps were recorded and played at full volume, and voices which shouted and whispered the name of Cenci rose in a crescendo that was then immediately silenced.

Musical instruments used as well

Music and musical instruments also played a part in the mise-en-scène; Artaud suggested that they might be part of the set and that through 'vibrations' the audience was to be charmed just like a snake with a pipe. Alternatively, almost as a form of torture, the captive audience should be subjected to '...a new scale in the octave [producing] an unbearably piercing sound or noise'.

Rock bands using sound as a sensory experience
The Doors and David Bowie

Since the 1970s rock artists have taken Artaudian themes and adapted them for their presentational effects. Groups such as The Doors, with Jim Morrison, and David Bowie in his incarnation as Ziggy Stardust, are good examples of performers who owe more than a little to Artaud for the carefully orchestrated excess of their art.

LIGHTING

Sophisticated lighting effects

By the time Artaud came to realise his ideas in *The Cenci*, lighting equipment was sufficiently sophisticated for him to flood the stage with blinding light or to pick out detail in a spotlight. However, he was interested in challenging the then current possibilities of this technology:

New forms

...we must discover oscillating light effects, new ways of diffusing lighting in waves, sheet lighting like a flight of fire-arrows.

[*T&ID*, 1985. p.74: *Theatre of Cruelty, First Manifesto*]

Lighting as an active force

Artaud saw lighting as a force, to be used in conjunction with other aspects of staging to become an almost physical part of the action. Nowadays, when we can use laser light across vast distances and strobes that distort our perceptions, we can match his aspirations.

Now commonplace in all forms of theatre

This technology, much of which was developed for rock concerts, can now be seen in all sorts of productions, from musicals to so called 'straight theatre'.

FILM

Not keen on the medium of film

Artaud was a noted film actor, so it is curious that he tended to be dismissive about film and the function it might have in theatre. The juxtaposition of live actor and film is an exciting combination, not least in the interplay of scale between the two. In the introduction to his scenario for the film *The Seashell and a Clergyman* (1927) he wrote:

Film as optic shock

> …we must look to films with purely visual situations whose drama comes from optic shock, the stuff of sight itself…
>
> [*Tulane Drama Review*, Film and Theatre, Vol. II No.I, 1966]

Film could move beyond the purely narrative

He hints at the possibilities for the medium of film to move beyond the purely narrative and how much it might contribute to '**optic shock**' in the right hands. However, the resulting film was a disappointment and it was this that may have made him disenchanted with the potential for the medium.

The lasting influence of Surrealist film-making

Two films by his contempories Salvador Dalí and Luis Buñuel, *Un Chien Andalou* (1929) and *L'Age d'Or* (1930), achieved more lasting notoriety. The former, with its opening sequence of an eyeball apparently being sliced by a razor, is still able to shock after all these years.

To sum up:

- Actor and audience will be joined in one shared space.
- Sound could provide an overwhelming sensory experience.
- Lighting we normally associate with rock concerts could be used in theatre.
- Film can shock by its juxtaposition of imagery.

THE ACTOR

All the other practitioners covered in this book have given a fuller account of their proposals for a 20th-century actor, Stanislavski and Brecht in particular foregrounding the actor in their theoretical writings. However, Artaud has some very pertinent points to make.

An actor's training must be like that of an athlete
Breath control is an important aspect

He envisages a rigorous, disciplined regime and takes as his example the training of an athlete. In particular, he makes extensive comment on the need for proper methods of breath control, and advocates the mystic, semi-ritualistic chants of Eastern religions as examples of how breath control might be achieved.

Tempo–Rhythm: see section 3.2.3

In an interesting parallel with Stanislavski's Tempo–Rhythm, he also notes how important 'a kind of musical tempo' is, and relates this back to breathing patterns. This 'athleticism' is seen as a necessary preparation for the physicality required of an actor.

He suggests the scream as a primal experience for freeing the actor:

The scream as an important emotional release

> In Europe no-one knows how to scream any more, particularly actors in a trance no longer know how to cry out, since they do nothing but talk, having forgotten they have a body on stage, they have also lost the use of their throats.
>
> [*T&ID*, 1985. p.95]

See chronology, 1947

He was only too well aware of how staid and unadventurous the bourgeois theatre of his day could be; this release would have seemed as shocking as he meant it to be. In his only radio broadcast the 'scream' is an important element, though to the uninitiated it is a dangerous way of obtaining release.

The actor working with puppets

Finally, we should not forget that he sought to include, alongside the actor, masks and puppets – 'objects of strange proportions' – to give his theatre that sense of 'magic beauty' that he sought in 'The Show'. As an actor himself he was able to appreciate what a challenging effect in terms of scale these gigantic figures would have when set beside the human actor (see Fig. 3.18).

Figure 3.18   These two larger-than-life-size figures clearly illustrate the relationship between actors and 'puppets' in the ritualised scenarios that Artaud had in mind.

To sum up:

- The actor's body should be highly trained.

- Breathing and the voice would be important.

- The actor would work with masks and puppets.

SCENARIOS

In his work there are many unrealised scenarios

Artaud's theoretical writings contain distinct kinds of texts that he found suitable to include. On the one hand there are accessible works, such as his early play *The Jet of Blood* (1925), which takes much of its imagery from Surrealism, and on the other hand scenarios like *The Conquest of Mexico*, which he intended as 'The first Theatre of Cruelty show', but which was not developed beyond an outline. Beyond that there are any number of unrealised ideas that are only hinted at in the manifestos of *The Theatre and Its Double*. For some reason Artaud chose not to work on his favourite play, John Ford's *'Tis Pity She's a Whore*, which he pronounced the ideal example of a Theatre of Cruelty text.

Evidence suggests that scenarios were carefully planned

His most fully realised theatre production was the short-lived *The Cenci* (1935). All the evidence from this production suggests that it was a most painstakingly detailed scenario, with text, image and sound carefully orchestrated to create the maximum visual and aural effect (see Fig. 3.19).

Extreme themes

In choosing to adapt Shelley's text Artaud was demonstrating his sympathy for dark, romantic imagery combined with extreme themes such as incest and rape.

The prompt copy is heavily annotated

The published mise-en-scène for *The Cenci* follows the pattern of a written text broken up by long and detailed stage directions. These in turn are supported on the opposite page by even more detailed choreographic notations, accompanied by small drawings of the actor's movements.

This extract from the prompt copy illustrates the point:

Extract from the prompt copy

Colonna comes back toward the guests, each one of whom is moving in a small circle that closes in a spiral. Colonna makes a larger circle around them. This takes about eight or ten seconds.
At the end of this whirlwind, the men find themselves outside of the circle, the women in a heap at the center. Each one is engaged in a struggle against a ghost. All men freeze for two seconds.

[Quoted in *Tulane Drama Review*, June 1972]

An intention to create an overwhelming sensory experience

Artaud was anxious to make every detail as powerful and as meaningful as possible. The choreographed acting, the amplified sound and the extremes of mood created by the lighting all contributed to the overall intention: drawing the audience into the action for an overwhelming sensory experience.

It is clear that in working on his scenarios Artaud was creating the maximum conditions of creative freedom for himself as director.

To sum up:

- There are many unrealised schemes for scenarios.
- Those that are accomplished are very detailed in terms of staging.
- These scenarios gave Artaud maximum flexibility as director.

Figure 3.19   Artaud (foreground, left) as Cenci in *The Cenci* (1935).

LANGUAGE

Language and the role of the actor

Artaud's ideas for a 'new language' are not clearly articulated, but can be culled from a number of his essays in *The Theatre and Its Double*. They are, however, very caught up with his views on the role of the actor. We have separated out discussion of these aspects of his theatre, but they should be seen as being inextricably linked together.

Dialogue is to take second place to signs

Artaud suggested that communication had to shed aspects of dialogue – what he called **'written poetry'** – and that actors should use a new **'bodily language'**, no longer based on words but on signs. These would emerge, rather inspecifically, through a maze of 'gestures, postures, and air-borne cries'. Proposals for this non-verbal language evolved in response to the performances of the Balinese Theatre that he saw at the Colonial Exhibition in Paris (1931).

In one of his clearest statements of intent he wrote:

Acknowledgement of the shortcomings of gesture

...I am well aware that a language of **gestures** and **postures**, **dance** and **music** is less able to define a character, to narrate man's thoughts, to explain conscious states clearly and exactly, than spoken language.

A break with psychological theatre

But whoever said theatre was made to define a character, to resolve conflicts of a human, emotional order, of a present-day psychological nature such as those which monopolise current theatre?

[*T&ID*, 1985. p.30]

A challenge to prevailing modes

So while admitting on the one hand that his theatre would be less able to deal with the subtleties of psychological representation, on the other he was challenging the prevailing monopoly that saw no alternative to such theatre. His theatre was to be anti-character and anti-psychological, as far away as possible from the Stanislavskian mode, and the emphasis was to be on languages of all sorts: physical, verbal and visual.

Language borrowed from the Surrealists

As a note to conclude this section it is worth looking at some aspects of verbal language that Artaud 'borrowed' from the Surrealists. Their interest in language, like so much of their work, stemmed from a consideration of the world of dreams. Artaud's play *The Jet of Blood* is a prime example of this tendency.

In terms of the Surrealists' interest in a completely new spoken language, Artaud's borrowings began to surface in his poetry after his release from Rodez. Here he was forming new images through repetition and pure sound. The following poem should be read aloud:

> **klaver striva**
> **cavour tavina**
> **scaver kavina**
> **akar triva**

[Reproduced in Barber, 1993. p.130]

This use of words as both poetry and incantation can be traced to the poets of Dada, a movement that preceded Surrealism.

In his *Phonetic Poem* (1917) Hugo Ball uses the technique of **onomato-poeia** to achieve this same effect:

KARAWANE

jolifanto bambla o falli bambla
grossiga m'pfa habla horem
egiga goramen
higo bloiko russula huju
hollaka hollala
anlogo bung
blago bung
blago bung
bosso fataka
u uu u
schampa wulla wussa olobo
hej tatta gorem
eschige zunbada
wulubu ssubudu uluw ssubudu
tumba ba - umf
kusagauma
ba - umf

[Quoted from Waldberg, P., *Surrealism*, Thames & Hudson, 1965]

Artaud used and adapted those elements of Surrealism that could elevate his theatre beyond the real.

To sum up:

- Language could be gestural and non-verbal.

- Theatre was to be anti-character.

- Dialogue would become just one of the means of communication.

- Pure sound patterns could replace traditional speech.

RITUAL

Influence of the Balinese dancers

Seeing the Balinese Theatre in 1931 started Artaud off on his journey in search of a Theatre of Cruelty. His manifesto on the subject had to find a Western parallel to describe the mesmerising context of the performance and, quite reasonably, Artaud lighted on holy **ritual.**

Artaud's theatre is ritual theatre

Primitivism and dark forces

In our response to Artaud's theatre this word has become a form of shorthand, since it seems to encapsulate all the elements he was aiming for. His theories on theatre seek to return to some notion of primitivism, aiming to release the mostly dark forces of our soul through a highly stylised form, in the 'church' (auditorium) of the 'faithful' (audience).

Rediscovery of ritual

Artaud was forced by his meeting with the Balinese dancers to re-invent and rediscover the root of this **ritual**. As he developed it he called upon all the discarded notions of what theatre had been and could be.

Influence of Nietzsche

He seems to have been heavily influenced by the writings of the philosopher Nietzsche, who in *The Birth of Tragedy* (1872) reminded scholars of the origins of tragedy in the Greek theatre. In contradiction to the 19th-century view that classical man was essentially pure and noble, Nietzsche drew attention to the real duality at the heart of the drama: the contest between the gods Dionysus and Apollo for the human soul.

Opposition between Apollo and Dionysus

The rational and irrational

For Nietzsche, the human race was composed of these two opposing elements: on the one hand the Apollonian man – rational and reasoning – and on the other the Dionysian man – irrational and passionate. He further maintained that it was important for a person to acknowledge this fact in order to find an inward balance.

Artaud favoured Dionysus

Artaud's theatre drew heavily on this concept, but favoured the path of Dionysus, the darker, more violent side of human nature. By doing so he hoped to show the world through his distorting mirror as essentially irrational and passionate, and by this example of theatre to unbalance an audience's view of itself.

A definition of ritual

This definition of ritual is helpful:

> A ritual generally takes the form of repeating a pattern of words and gestures which tend to excite us above a normal state of mind. Once this state of mind is induced we are receptive and suggestible and ready for the climax of the rite. At the climax the essential nature of something is changed.
>
> [Ann Jellicoe, quoted in Innes, 1993. p.219]

Gravity and danger of ritual

This quotation raises a number of questions, but it draws attention to the gravity of ritual, the danger at its heart and the nature of the Artaudian performance, which seeks to induce catharsis by a direct and compelling appeal to the senses.

To sum up:

- Artaudian theatre means ritual theatre.
- It is the theatre of Dionysus, i.e. of passion and irrationality.
- It appeals primarily to the senses.

FINALE

In *The Theatre and Its Double* Artaud wrote his contradictory and puzzling prescription for his theatre of the future. Critics have remarked how difficult it is to understand his concepts; just when one thinks one has, they tend to disappear into thin air.

But his work transformed 20th-century theatre practice in more subtle and lasting ways than we realise. If we accepted Peter Brook's contention that to apply Artaud is to betray him we would remain powerless in the face of such exciting and challenging prescriptions.

On the contrary, it would seem that if only a tiny part of his theory is realised through practice, his intention will be accomplished: to change the way we look at theatre, to do so with discipline and to shake an audience to their complacent foundations in the process.

Figure 3.20   A self-portrait drawn in 1946.

3.3.4 INFLUENCES

SURREALISM

Themes taken from Surrealism

Artaud was only briefly a member of this movement, but he generated so many potential themes from his association with its members that it is important that we discuss the term in appropriate detail.

Redefinition of reality

The first Surrealist **manifesto** was published in 1924, under the leadership of André Breton (1896–1966). It proclaimed its mission as that of 'revising the definition of reality' and to this end initially concerned itself with:

- drug-taking
- accounts of dreams
- automatic writing
- speeches made whilst in a trance.

Insights into the subconscious

What it sought was insights into the subconscious and a reliance on the non-rational. Its flirtation with the ideas of Freud (1856–1939) became notorious, since far from seeking a cure for the patient (society), Surrealism 'saw madness as a key to perception'.

Definitions of madness and non-madness	The well-known **lack of frontiers** between non-madness and madness does not induce me to accord a different value to the perceptions and ideas which are the result of one or the other. [André Breton]
Artaud expelled from the movement	This provocative statement was made to distance the movement from the prevailing safeness of bourgeois society in France at that time. Artaud, who was a candidate for the above definition if ever there was one, was ejected by Breton from the movement because as it became more politically aware he would not join the Communist Party. Artaud carried around with him the landscape of a gothic novel, torn by flashes of lightning. [André Breton]
Surrealism selected its membership	Conceived as an insult by Breton, this was probably truer than he realised. It says little for Surrealism that it was unable to contain the man whose work so closely reflected its own preoccupations with dreams, madness and the inversion of the normal.

Bigsby, C.W.E.,   *Dada and Surrealism*,   Methuen, 1972
Melzer, A.,   *Latest Rage the Big Drum: Dada and Surrealist Performance*,   UMI, 1980

JARRY, ALFRED (1873–1907)

Anarchy in theatre	Dead from alcohol poisoning at 34, Jarry was the epitome of anarchy in theatre, and it was no accident that in 1926 when Artaud decided to launch his theatre he should call it the Théâtre Alfred Jarry.
Ubu Roi: satirical and absurd drama	Jarry's main claim to fame was a satirical and absurdist piece called *Ubu Roi* (1896), which in short and rapidly moving scenes told of the killing of the King of Poland by two grotesque characters, Pa and Ma Ubu.
Influenced by puppets	Heavily influenced by the puppets of *guignol* (not unlike a French Punch and Judy), the plot unfolded in a number of locations indicated by placards in the Brechtian style.
Music-hall farce	The actors wore bizarre padded costumes and carried as props everyday objects such as a lavatory brush to represent a sceptre. Jarry conducted the proceedings in the manner of a master of ceremonies, which was entirely appropriate since the play was pure music-hall farce.
Use of language to shock	The audience divided into those who walked out on hearing the first word of the text – '*Merdre!*' (shit) – and those who stayed to applaud, among whom was the Irish poet W.B. Yeats.
Surrealists rediscovered the text	The play was immensely influential. It combined an attack on authority with a style of 'rough theatre' guaranteed to offend. Its author lived out his life like his hero Ubu. The Surrealists took it up after the First World War and it was through this connection that Artaud adopted Jarry's name and in his own style sought to shock a new generation.

Styan, J.L.,   *Modern Drama in Theory and Practice* Vol 2,   CUP, 1986

3.3.5 FOLLOWERS

As with any of the other practitioners in this chapter, it is certain that anyone who has played a role in world theatre will have heard or read about Artaud. To a greater or lesser extent their work will have been influenced by him, whether they acknowledge this fact or not. This short list gives an indication of Artaud's wide-ranging world influence.

Publishing history of The Theatre and Its Double

A note about the publishing history of *The Theatre and Its Double*: it was not available in an English translation until the 1950s, so although it had been published in 1938 it wasn't until 15 years later that Artaud's writings became known to an English-speaking audience. An explosion of theatre followed which fastened on to Artaud's radical ideas for its inspiration, some of which we can trace here.

BROOK, PETER (BORN 1925)

Experimental workshops

Peter Brook was one of the first to bring Artaud to the attention of an English-speaking audience. In 1963 he and Charles Marowitz set up an experimental workshop with actors from the RSC, and after weeks of rehearsal they

A challenge to realism

presented, among other items, Artaud's first play *The Jet of Blood*, scenes from Jean Genet's *The Screens* and a montage based on *Hamlet* by Marovitz. As performance it was only a partial success, but as an experiment it radically challenged the 'Stanislavskian ethic' of realistic theatre.

The Empty Space: influential essays

For Brook it also led to a complete rethinking of his style, which he recorded in the essay 'The Holy Theatre' (*The Empty Space*, p.47). Here he applauds Artaud's influence, but is cautious about its long-term ability to disturb:

> There is a joy in violent shocks. The only trouble with violent shocks is that they wear off.
>
> [*The Empty Space*, p.61]

Used the theories of Artaud in production

The work in this experimental season led directly to his production of Peter Weiss's *Marat/Sade* (1964) at the RSC. Here his debt to Artaud was seen at its most extreme, though in retrospect there were critics who recognised influences from Brecht just as clearly.

Actor and audience: see section 3.3.3

In his work at this time Brook encouraged an acknowledgement of the audience by the actor, notably in *U.S.* (1966), which was a collage of scenes based on the Vietnam War. Actors crossed the boundary of the 'fourth wall' and stumbled into the audience's territory. Whether this was an Artaudian gesture it is hard to say; it certainly united the faithful in the one shared space.

Brook's work since has in its turn been enormously influential, not least with his refusal to join the mainstream. His world view has taken theatre back to its roots in a search for an 'idealistic theatre in the rough texture of this real world' [Brook, 1993].

Brook, P.,   *The Empty Space*,   Penguin, 1986
Brook, P.,   *There are No Secrets*,   Methuen, 1993
Marovitz, C.,   *Artaud at Rodez* (play),   Boyars, 1977

GENET, JEAN (1910–86)

A writer whose plays have been influenced by association	It is debatable whether Genet owed anything to Artaud at all, but since first productions of his plays were directed by Peter Brook (*The Balcony*) and Roger Blin (who had worked with Artaud on *The Cenci*) the influences were emphatically there by association.
Genet interested in the dramatic possibilities of ritual	To a greater or lesser extent Genet's plays concern themselves with ritual acts: 'His plays are without comfort, and his ritual forms are built upon scorn and hate.' [Styan, 1986. p.146]
Ritual and ceremonial: see section 3.3.3	In *The Maids* (1947) Solange and Claire while away the time while awaiting the arrival of their hated mistress, 'Madame'. Dressing in her clothes, exchanging identities and willingly submitting themselves to the imposed tyrannies of her regime they ritualise their relationship with her by playing out a pre-determined ceremonial – with the bed and dressing table as the fetish objects of their dreams.
A dream world of unreality	In *The Balcony* (1956) the dream world of the brothel is the setting. Nothing is what it seems in this play. While the clients live out their fantasies in gigantic costumes like puppets, they are, it transpires, merely plumbers and businessmen. The whores, criminals and revolutionaries who pander to their needs make up the cast of this pretend world, where there is licence to dream.
Spectacular illusion	Styan has drawn attention to the fact that this play of illusions owes as much to the work of the playwright Pirandello as it does to Artaud. But whatever the source of his themes, the spectacular staging devices and the fact that 'the characters are ultimately actors' remind us that Genet's debt to Artaud is very explicit.

Innes, C.,	*Avant Garde Theatre,*	Routledge, 1993
White, E.,	*Genet,*	Picador, 1994
Styan, J.L.,	*Drama in Theory and Practice: Vol. 2 Symbolism, Surrealism and the Absurd,*	CUP, 1986

THE AMERICAN CONNECTION

Artaud used as a source	Artaud's work was translated into English in the early 1950s and was adopted very quickly as a source for much of the experimental theatre activity at that time. A number of companies and 'happenings' can be said to have used Artaud as a springboard for their work; if anything could be recognised as a common denominator in these, it would be a desire to free theatre from its traditional constraints.
Happenings Auditorium and audience: see section 3.3.3	This was accomplished through semi-spontaneous events (happenings), organised by artists, where the use of speech, dance, film, music and projections sought to involve the audience in the event as both spectator and performer. The main influence of Artaud came from his theories about the spatial relationships between actor and audience and the breaking of these boundaries.

See Brook: *The Empty Space*

The composer John Cage, who was heavily involved in the early 'happenings' said:

> . . . theatre takes place all the time wherever one is and art simply facilitates persuading us this is the case.
>
> [Quoted in Marovitz, 1970. p.266]

Mythic tales with puppets combined with actors

The Bread and Puppet Theatre (1961) combined huge puppets with actors, usually in street performances, with texts based on myths or folk tales. It took traditional myths as a source. Both the return to myths and the use of puppets to contrast with live actors were ideas suggested by Artaud in *The Theatre and Its Double* (pp.60 and 75).

Actors dressed as puppets

Another group to use puppets was the Open Theatre, New York, run by the director Joseph Chaikin. In this company's play *Motel* (1966) two actors dressed as dolls tear a motel room apart whilst a third comments on the action. Chaikin worked closely with playwrights, and Sam Shepard was an early contributor to the work of this company.

Grotowski: see below

Experiments with actor–audience relationships

The experimental director Richard Schechner, a one-time editor of the magazine *Tulane Drama Review*, which championed the work of Artaud, was very influenced by Artaud's theories. He was also influenced by Grotowski, and by 'happenings'; his theatre experiments worked towards a breaking down of actor–audience boundaries, sometimes with confrontational means, and towards the development of non-traditional spaces for performance. His later work has been in the area of performance analysis from a strongly theoretical perspective.

Actor–audience confrontations

The Living Theatre, run by Julian Beck and Judith Malina, became the most overtly political of all the companies. Their productions of *The Brig* by Kenneth Brown (1963) and *The Connection* by Jack Gelber, took the situations of these texts, respectively army life and drug addiction, and involved the audience in participation, blurring the distinction between the actor and his assumed role. The audience was encouraged to identify with the plight of the characters, and great emphasis was placed on a confrontational verbal language.

Spectacular and physical theatre

Their adaptation of *Frankenstein* (1965) was a spectacular welding of Artaudian theatre and storytelling, in which 20 actors made the body of the monster while Beck played the Doctor. Again, actors invaded the auditorium.

Actor and text: see section 3.3.3

By 1970 their experiments were all but over. They had used Artaud as their mentor, but although they 'embraced' their audience it is doubtful whether they simultaneously challenged them. It was in their work with the actor and his text that they most successfully developed Artaudian themes.

Marovitz, C. (ed),   *The Encore Reader*,   Methuen, 1970

GROTOWSKI, JERZY (BORN 1933)

Acknowledged Artaudian influences

Since the formation of this Polish director's Laboratory Theatre (1959) predates any knowledge of Artaud's writings, it is only on reflection that critics have linked their work, and Grotowski acknowledges that his theories have been supported by Artaud.

Spiritual theatre

The physicality of the actor

The main points of contact would be through their shared belief in theatre having a 'spiritual and religious role' and through the emphasis on the actor as a highly trained, athletic communicator. Grotowski's celebrated collection of essays, *Towards a Poor Theatre*, spells out his vision of a theatre stripped of its traditional trappings and, importantly, returning to its unique function in a world of film and television.

Returning theatre to its basic roots

> The acceptance of poverty in theatre, stripped of all that is not essential to it, revealed to us not only the backbone of the medium, but also the deep riches which lie in the very nature of the art-form.
>
> [Grotowski, 1994. p.21]

With the 'room' stripped bare it was inevitable that the actor would become the 'riches in the nature of the art-form' and the training that Grotowski initiated was extremely rigorous:

Interest in the actor and his physical and vocal equipment

> The actor makes a total gift of himself. This is the technique of the 'trance' and of the integration of all the actor's psychic and bodily powers which emerge from the most intimate layers of his being and his instinct...
>
> [Ibid. p.16]

Artaud's achievements

In his brilliant essay *He Wasn't Entirely Himself* (1967), Grotowski sums up Artaud's achievements as they reflect on his own practice and at the same time takes to task those who would seek to trivialise him.

Figure 3.21 Grotowski's staging for *The Constant Prince*. The spectator looks down into the pit where the action takes place, suggesting a bull-ring or an operating theatre – a place of ritual acts.

Artaudian visions and metaphors	The paradox of Artaud lies in the fact that it is impossible to carry out his proposals. Does this mean he was wrong? Certainly not ... He left visions, metaphors...
	[Ibid. p.86]

Grotowski, J.,   *Towards a Poor Theatre*,   Methuen, 1994

SHAFFER, PETER (BORN 1926)

Total theatre	Peter Shaffer has defiantly raided the storehouse of Artaudian themes, to create what we might call **Total Theatre**, 'involving not only words but rites, mimes, masks and magic' [Author's note to *Royal Hunt of the Sun*, 1964].
Artaudian influence	In this play, which bears a striking resemblance to Artaud's scenario *The Conquest of Mexico*, there are moments of visual and auditory splendour that far outstrip the narrative text in their power to move and excite an audience.
Theatre of power and beauty	Again, in *Equus* (1973), the basic theme, the blinding of horses by a young boy and the attempted 'cure' by his psychiatrist, is turned into theatre that has the potential for great power and beauty.
Sound used as a sensory experience	In this case both Brechtian and Artaudian influences can be traced, the spare Brechtian space being invaded by the Artaudian horses (played by actors in masks and raised boots). It is these figures that ritualise the blindings, in a physical orchestration of violence and terror. The accompanying sounds are part of the experience, numbing the audience with the sheer level of amplification.
Theatrical effects overwhelm the text	However, the somewhat banal conventional narrative fails to rise to the level of this spectacle, a common problem of marrying words to images, and the text is far outstripped by the displays of theatrical pyrotechnics.
Problems of synthesis	In Shaffer's work there remains the problem of how to marry the two apparently conflicting modes of expression: spectacular ritual theatre, which uses all the technology available to create a total experience, and more conventional means of storytelling, which involve character development at a realistic level.

Innes, C.,   *Avant Garde Theatre*,   Routledge, 1993

BERKOFF, STEVEN (BORN 1937)

Physical theatre	Berkoff is widely regarded as representing one extreme of a physical theatre tradition that is generally outside the mainstream of British theatre. His training as a mime artist at the Ecole Jacques Lecoq in Paris and an unhappy career in repertory theatre led him to create works for himself as actor and director.
A theatre of violence	After starting with the adaptation of such texts as *Metamorphosis* (1969) and *The Fall of the House of Usher* (1974), he began to write his own plays. The first of these drew on his experience of street life in the East

End of London: *East* (1975) was a savage evocation of the gangs of his birthplace, written in a parody of Jacobean blank verse. Its power to shock was soon recognised.

Berkoff followed this with *Decadence* (1981), an equally abrasive attack on the upper classes, which transferred to the West End and, ironically, attracted precisely the kind of audience it was satirising.

Expressionism: see Glossary

It would be true to say that all his work is heavily indebted to expressionist influences, from the language of the text to the setting and lighting. In this quotation he expresses his contempt for naturalist theatre:

> Naturalism is what you do when you don't know anything else. When you have little skill for anything else you automatically revert to the copying of everything around you . . .
>
> [Article in *The Guardian*, 16.7.92]

One of his fellow actors has likened a performance with him to 'going into a boxing ring'. It is his fierce and unrelenting exploitation of all the elements of theatre, especially with regard to the physicality of the actor in all its manifestations, that places him as a follower of Artaud.

3.3.6 SUMMARY: ANTONIN ARTAUD

This summary is written to draw together certain parts of the chapter on Antonin Artaud under particular headings. It should be considered with the student's own practical work in mind and/or the student's viewing of other productions. For example, Artaud's Theatre of Cruelty: as a student undertaking practical work you would wish to discuss what Artaud says about his theatre and how this could be reflected in your own work. By adopting this convention/practice not only are you enhancing your own approach but you are able to make use of the practice when viewing other productions.

THE SUBJECT MATTER
Surrealist dramas
Highly charged, immensely detailed scenarios
Renaissance Revenge tragedy

THE POLITICAL PURPOSE OR MESSAGE OR DRAMATIC INTENTION
To shock by the power of the spectacle
To subvert and challenge bourgeois theatre
Violence contained
A sensory experience

THE ACTOR– AUDIENCE RELATIONSHIP
Audience sitting in the middle of the action
The actor as a figure in ritual acts
The audience in the centre of a vortex

THE STAGING FORM ADOPTED
A space stripped bare
Total theatre
Anti-realist

DIRECTORIAL INTERPRETATION/ PRODUCTION STYLE	Gothic/Romantic sources Every aspect taken to extremes Concerned with the metaphysical
DESIGN ELEMENTS	Surrealist Actors representative of emotional states Fractured and unsettling
ROLE OF ACTORS AND PERFORMANCE STYLE	Anti character Sounds to replace accepted language Athletic bodies with well-trained voices Gestural
TECHNICAL ELEMENTS	Amplified sound to underscore the text Strongly directional lighting Changes in scale
AUDIENCE RESPONSE	To be moved and shocked by the show To have an intense sensory experience and be changed by this Catharsis encouraged

3.3.7 SUGGESTIONS FOR FURTHER STUDY

PLAYS

Ubu Roi (1896) Alfred Jarry

An amusing, highly satirical piece whose author gave his name to Artaud's theatre ventures in the 1920s (see section 3.3.4).

Murderer, Hope of Womankind (1907) Oscar Kokoschka

An early 'expressionist' text, discussed in detail by Innes in *Avant Garde Theatre*. It has been made into an opera with music by Hindemith (1895–1963).

Royal Hunt of the Sun (1964) Peter Shaffer

In its first production it caused a sensation, with its spectacular staging. A good example of 'total theatre'.

Equus (1973) Peter Shaffer

Another text that uses vivid visual imagery. The blinding of the horse is a potent and deeply disturbing theatrical moment.

Marat/Sade (1964) Peter Weiss

Best known by this its shorter title, this text has all the ingredients of an Artaudian experience. Peter Brook's production at the RSC (1964) was filmed.

Everyman (15th century)

A text that deals with an archetypal man's life journey and the qualities that he meets on the way to his inevitable death. It would adapt to a strong and relevant contemporary scenario.

POETRY

August Stramm (1874–1915)

An expressionist poet, known for his spare, one-word-per-line poems. Totally non-representational, they invite open interpretation. His play *Awakening* (1914) is a precursor for much modern writing.

Edgar Allen Poe (1809–49)

His short stories and poems are a good basis for adaptation into dramatic scenarios.

Charles Baudelaire (1821–67)

His collection of poems entitled *Les Fleurs du Mal* offers opportunities for dramatic adaptations.

Antonin Artaud (1896–1948)

His own poetry has not been acknowledged in this section, but it is important to note that it was as a poet that he began to write. Volume 1 of *The Collected Works* reproduces some of the texts.

OTHER THEATRE

DV8 Dance Company

Strange Fish (1992), which was adapted for television, is a good example of a company working in 'physical theatre' terms with movement-based scenarios.

V-Tol Dance Company

Their production of *32 feet per second per second* (1992) used film, back and front projection and 'physical theatre' techniques to create a dark and brutal scenario.

Théâtre de Complicité

A physical theatre company that primarily uses mime and movement to express its adaptations (see section 2.3).

Rock concerts

Videos are easily available and well worth a look: for example, Madonna, Michael Jackson and Prince. The extravagant style, the larger-than-life props, the lighting and the sound all stem from a concern with pushing back the limits of performance art.

Sutherland, L., *The Astonishing Art of Rock Concert Design*, Thames & Hudson, 1992

288 Antonin Artaud (1896–1948)

PAINTING

Paintings can be a strong stimulus for inventing scenarios (See *The Theatre and its Double*, p.255).

James Ensor (1860–1949)

A Belgian painter who used mysteriously masked figures in his pictures, bringing the nightmare of the dream world into the present.

Edvard Munch (1863–1944)

Dark and often immensely sad, his paintings suggest strong dramatic scenarios. Look at the *Dance of Life* series. It was no accident that the playwright Strindberg (*The Dream Play*) admired Munch's work so strongly for the passionate way he looked at the tragedy of life.

René Magritte (1898–1967)

One of the major representatives of Surrealist art. Strange juxtapositions lead to fantastic and mysterious pictures. (See also *After Magritte* by Tom Stoppard, 1970.)

MUSIC

Edgar Varese (1883–1965)

Despite a completed scenario by Artaud in the early 1930s, a collaboration came to nothing. Listen to *Ionisation* (1931) or *Arcana* (1927). This exciting modern music acts as a perfect example of the kind of sound contemplated in The Theatre of Cruelty.

FURTHER WORK

ACTIVITIES In groups work on frozen tableaux, expressing an emotional/physical state: anger, sadness, hunger. Emphasise largeness. Extend the body. Use hoops or sticks to make shapes outside the body.

Progress to using poems or sound patterns as a stimulus. Act out the sound. Don't just say the words. Hum/chant/spit the sound. Work in a circle. Pass sounds across the space. See *Soundtracking* in Neelands, J., *Structuring Drama Work*, CUP, 1991.

Work on *The Jet of Blood* (1925). The text lends itself to improvised movement. Work in a large group. Vocalise and physicalise the text. Take key lines and work towards a group version, repeating lines. Make sounds. Use simple percussion instruments.

Work on 'the plague'. Your body is infected. You begin to notice decay. Focus on a limb or a part of your body. It gets worse. Move for comfort to your neighbour. They are infected too. Move towards the centre of the circle. As a group react to each other. Freeze.

Choose a space and make it 'as unpleasant as possible to be in'. Introduce an audience (who don't know your intentions). How do they enter? Are there obstacles? Sounds? Can you disorientate them? Is it dark or light? Can they sit or do they crawl? Make something happen in ten seconds. Discuss.

Choose a text you'd like to work on. Start with Artaud's suggestions in *The Theatre and Its Double*. Adapt poems, stories, themes. Use music, masks, costume, puppets and/or lighting. Use video to record your work.

Create a tableau of grotesque and disorientating images. Use music and light to enhance the sense of terror. Invite an audience to view this 'museum' of the macabre.

Remember what Grotowski said: '. . . he left visions'.

3.3.8. BIBLIOGRAPHY

PRIMARY SOURCES

Artaud, A.	*Collected Works* Vol. 1 (trans: Corti, V.)	Calder, 1978	Useful for background reading, and for the texts of some poems.
	Collected Works Vol. 4 (trans. Corti, V.)	Calder, 1974	Contains *The Theatre and Its Double* and the text of *The Cenci*.
	The Theatre and Its Double	Calder, 1985	Indispensable reading. Barber has pointed out that in his opinion this is a poor translation, but it is the only one available.
Barber, S.	*Antonin Artaud, Blows and Bombs*	Faber, 1993	The most recent biography. Has a strong view about the importance of the last works.
Hayman, R.	*Artaud and After*	OUP, 1977	A useful chronology and well illustrated.
Innes, C.	*Avant Garde Theatre*	Routledge, 1993	A comprehensive view of Artaud in the context of 20th-century theatre
Styan, J.L.	*Modern Drama in Theory and Practice. Vol. 2: Symbolism, Surrealism and the Absurd*	CUP, 1986	Good bibliographies and time chart.

FURTHER SOURCES

	Various articles and interviews	*Tulane Drama Review* Vol. 7, No. 3, Spring 1963
	The Artaud edition	Vol. 8, No. 2, Winter 1963
	Translation of *To End God's Judgement*	Vol. 9, No. 3, Spring 1965
	Artaud on film and scenarios	Vol. 11, No. 1, Fall 1966
	The Cenci: diagrams from the prompt book and reviews of the production	Vol. 16, No. 2, June 1972
Luis Buñuel and Salvador Dalí	*Un Chien Andalou* CR 129 (film)	Connoisseur Video, 1994

3.3.9 QUESTION AND SUGGESTED FRAMEWORK FOR ANSWER ON ANTONIN ARTAUD

ACTIVITY   'The paradox of Artaud lies in the fact that it is impossible to carry out his proposals.' (Grotowski)

Discuss how far this statement is true in the light of what you know about his theories.

POINTS TO CONSIDER

- Look carefully at the quotation. What is it suggesting? What is a paradox? The statement challenges you to disagree: that is Grotowski's intention.

- Think about the theories. It is not a good idea to try to cover them all. Select a few that are relevant: for example, ones that you feel would be difficult to carry out. How will you connect them to the quote?

- You are asked to say how far you think the quote is true. This will be the main part of your answer.

A DETAILED ANALYSIS

Introduction

Discuss the quote. Begin to think how far it is true: is there a straightforward answer or a qualified one? Briefly mention Grotowski's position in relationship to Artaud. Explain that you are going to select a *few* of Artaud's theories.

Main body

In each of the subsequent sections discuss one of Artaud's theories. For each section explain:

- what the theory is and some information about why Artaud believed in it

- how this relates to practice in productions of the time that you have read about, or more recent productions that you have seen or in which you have performed
- how far the theory was impossible to carry out. Try to select a variety of circumstances to show that some theories can be realised, others not so easily.

For example, one theory might be Artaud's ideas on verbal and gestural language. Describe these and why they were of importance to Artaud. Give examples of productions you have seen or performed in that have used similar ideas. Describe the success or otherwise of the language and gesture.

Another of Artaud's ideas you could discuss might be ritual theatre. Describe what is meant by this term. Talk about the theatre of the senses and catharsis. Give examples by drawing on what you have experienced as part of an audience or as a performer. Describe whether you think it can be successful.

This format would continue for subsequent sections, suggesting different aspects of Artaud's work and discussing them with reference to relevant examples.

Conclusion
Sum up your conclusions by saying how far you agree with Grotowski, referring to your examples above. You might like to bring in references to other practitioners, for example Peter Brook, or to discuss specific examples from productions you have not mentioned so far.

3.4 *Bertolt Brecht (1898–1956)*

Figure 3d   Portrait of Bertolt Brecht by Rudolf Schlichter, 1926

3.4.1 A CHRONOLOGY

1898: Is born into a middle-class family in the small south German town of Augsburg.

Studies drama and theatre

1917: Theoretically a student of medicine, he actually studies drama and theatre history.

Begins to write his first plays

1918: Sickened by the effects of the First World War. Already active as a drama critic. Writes *Baal* and begins *Drums in the Night*.

Political cabaret

1919, Munich: Takes part in the political cabaret of Karl Valentin, in which he sings his songs accompanying himself on the guitar.

Wedekind:
see section 3.4.4

Frank Wedekind dies. Brecht is an admirer of this writer, who like him was a ballad singer, actor and playwright.

1921: He arrives in Berlin. Gets to know a large number of Berlin's leading actors and directors.

1922, Berlin: Directs *Parricide* by his great friend Arnolt Bronnen – his first production. This is less than successful as he quarrels with actors and another director is forced to take over – a pattern repeated all his life.

Première of first play:
see section 3.4.3

Munich: *Drums in the Night* is produced: a popular theme of a soldier returning from the war.

The Kleist prize

Berlin: Receives the prestigious Kleist prize, and is launched as a playwright of note.

Is known for his ability to charm an audience with his guitar playing. Sets his own songs and poems.

Neher:
see section 3.4.3

1923, Munich: Première of *In the Jungle of the Cities*, with sets by his childhood friend, Caspar Neher. It is presented like a boxing match. The play is considered scandalous. He is delighted.

Leipzig: World Première of *Baal*; he attends rehearsals. He has already achieved both fame and notoriety.

Epic theatre:
see section 3.4.3

1924, Munich: Première of the Brecht/Feuchtwanger adaptation of Christopher Marlowe's *Edward the Second*, with sets by Caspar Neher.

Two lifelong collaborators

Meets the actress Helene Weigel, whom he will later marry.

Meets the brilliant writer/translator Elisabeth Hauptmann, who will co-author a large number of works with Brecht.

1925, Berlin: Joins 'Group 1925', a group of younger dramatists who want to reform the German theatre.

Sergei Eisenstein:
see section 3.4.3

Sees the film *Battleship Potemkin*, directed by Sergei Eisenstein. This introduces him to the concept of 'montage'.

A theatre riot

1926, Berlin: Produces *Baal* (revised version) with his colleague, Elisabeth Hauptmann. Sets are by Neher. There is a riot in the auditorium. Publishes short stories with a major contribution from Elisabeth Hauptmann.

Darmstadt: World première of the play *A Man's a Man* (co-writer: E. Hauptmann), with sets by Neher. The play is set in a mythical India based on Rudyard Kipling. Fragmentary scenery with actors as soldiers on enormous stilts.

First lessons in Marxism

Begins to study Karl Marx's *Capital*, which gives him theoretical frameworks for his plays.

1927: Berlin radio broadcasts *A Man's a Man.*

Kurt Weill:
see section 3.4.3

Baden-Baden: First collaboration with the composer Kurt Weill in the world première of *Mahagonny*. Sets and background projections by Neher. It is set in a boxing ring (his interest in the sport dates from 1925), with huge overhead projections. Changes in lighting indicate songs. The orchestra is taken from the pit and placed on stage. Lotte Lenya (future wife of Weill) stars.

Piscator:
see section 3.4.4

Berlin: Works periodically with Erwin Piscator, noted theatre director, who begins to advertise his productions as 'epic'. Brecht is not really happy with the arrangement since this collective does not want to perform his work.

1928, Berlin: Première of the Piscator adaptation of *The Good Soldier Schweik*, from the novel by Hasek, with sets by the political cartoonist Georg Grosz. This dramatised version is the first from this source. Brecht adapts it as *Schweik in the Second World War* later in his career.

The Threepenny Opera:
first big success

Berlin: World première at the Am Schiffbauerdamm Theater (future home of the Berliner Ensemble) of Hauptmann, Brecht, Weill, Klammer's *The Threepenny Opera*, directed by Erich Engel with the active and not always welcome assistance of Brecht. Sets by Neher. A half curtain is used, which only partly conceals the scene changes. A huge box-office success.

1929: He marries Helene Weigel.

Berlin: Broadcast of Weill and Brecht's *Berlin Requiem*.

Lehrstuck:
see section 3.4.3

Baden-Baden: Brecht directs his first two didactic plays: *The Lindbergh Flight* and *The Baden Didactic Play*.

Failure of *Happy End*

Berlin: Première of Elisabeth Hauptmann's play (with music by Weill and some songs by Brecht), *Happy End*. The play is a massive failure. The outcome is partly a result of his indifference to the work.

1930, Leipzig: Première of *The Rise and Fall of the City of Mahagonny* (Hauptmann, Brecht, Weill, Neher), which is an extended scenario of the **1927** version. Sets and background projection by Neher. Performances are picketed by uniformed Nazis.

Meyerhold:
see section 3.2.5

He sees the Soviet director Meyerhold's theatre on tour.

Didactic plays:
see section 3.4.3

Berlin: The didactic play *The Yes Sayer* (Hauptmann/Brecht, with music by Kurt Weill) is produced at Berlin's Central Institute for Training and Teaching, using schoolboys and an amateur orchestra. The play's negative outlook is heavily criticised. He produces *The No Sayer* as an answer to his critics.

Première of the Hauptmann/Brecht didactic piece *The Measures Taken*, with huge Berlin workers' choirs.

1931, Berlin: He directs *A Man's a Man* and establishes himself as among the front rank of European directors. His work is favourably compared with Meyerhold's.

Threepenny Opera film — The film version of *The Threepenny Opera* opens in Berlin. He brings an unsuccessful lawsuit to counter changes that have been made, against his wishes, to the text.

The Rise and Fall of the City of Mahagonny opens successfully, after quarrels with all the collaborators. It marks the beginning of the parting of the ways for him and Weill.

Gorki: see section 3.2.4 — **1932:** Première of *The Mother* (a Brecht Collective adaptation based on the novel by Maxim Gorki). He and Weigel take it on tour to the working-class districts of Berlin on makeshift stages, illuminated by car headlights.

Radio broadcast of *St Joan of the Stockyards*, which like so much of his work at this time is set in a mythical America.

Film: *Kuhle Wampe* Agitprop: see 3.3.3 — The film *Kuhle Wampe* (written by Brecht in collaboration with the director Slatan Dudow) opens. It contains a sequence with a worker's agit(ation)prop(aganda) group. It is censored.

1933, Berlin: The Nazis come to power. He flees, leaving everything behind. Hauptmann rescues some of his library. The rest is confiscated and burnt by the Nazis.

Last collaboration with Weill — Paris: Première of *The Seven Deadly Sins* (Weill/Brecht). This is their last collaboration. Weill emigrates to the United States and is a hugely popular success. He dies at the tragically early age of 50 in 1950.

Brecht makes a home in Denmark with Helene Weigel and their two children.

1934: Publication of *Threepenny Novel* which makes enough money for him to live on. Also supported financially by Weigel's family.

Visit to Moscow — **1935:** Visits Moscow. Sees and much admires the work of the actor Mei Lan-fang. Uses the word *Verfremdungseffekt* for the first time, apparently a translation of the Russian term '*priem ostraneniye*' – a device for 'making strange'.

The political atmosphere in Russia is poisonous. Friends and colleagues 'disappear' during the next few years.

He is stateless — His citizenship is formally removed by the Nazis.

Visit to New York — New York: Is invited to see the 'Brecht Collective's' adaptation of Gorki's *Mother*. He is furious with their adaptation and has to be kept out of the theatre. The set is by Mordecai (Max) Gorelik, who becomes one of Brecht's strongest supporters in America.

1936, Copenhagen: Danish première at the Knight's Hall Theatre of *The Roundheads and the Pointed Heads.*

Dudow: see 1932

1937, Paris: The world première (in German) of *Mrs Carrar's Rifles,* directed by Slatan Dudow and with Helene Weigel in the title role.

The first 'model books'

Copenhagen: Danish première of *Mrs Carrar's Rifles,* directed by Ruth Berlau, another close collaborator, with her 'Worker's Theatre' ensemble. Brecht attends rehearsals. Berlau takes a large number of photographs of the production; these are seen as the first serious attempt at what would later be called 'model books' of his productions.

1938: Threatened by the Nazis, he moves to Stockholm.

Paris: World première in German of eight scenes from *The Fear and Misery of the Third Reich.* He is present for rehearsals.

Completes *The Life of Galileo.*

Is busy writing the last great plays

1939, Stockholm: After some preliminary work he begins on the actual writing of *Mother Courage and Her Children.* By early November the play is completed.

Moves to Finland

1940: As the Nazis march into Denmark and Norway he moves first to Helsinki in Finland and then, in July, to the country estate of the Finnish writer Hella Wuolijoki. While in Finland he virtually completes the play *The Good Person of Setzuan* and writes, with Wuolijoki, *Puntila and His Man Matti.*

1941: Works with Margarette Steffin (another collaborator) on *The Resistible Rise of Arturo Ui.*

Première in Zurich of *Mother Courage*

Zurich: The Schauspielhaus (one of the last free German-speaking stages in the world) gives the world première performance of *Mother Courage and Her Children.* The lead is played by Therese Giehse, who will join him after the war as one of his leading actors. Sets and costumes are by Teo Otto. He too will become a member of the Berliner Ensemble.

See 1949

Most of the blocking, sets and costumes are used again in Berlin in early **1949.** Mother Courage's wagon becomes a potent emblem of the success of the Ensemble: their work is always associated with this image and with Weigel as Mother Courage (see Fig. 3.22).

To America via Moscow

Brecht and his family and his two co-workers, Margarette Steffin and Ruth Berlau, leave for America via Leningrad, Moscow and Vladivostock. Steffin dies of TB in Moscow but the rest of the group reaches California on 21 July.

1941–7: Establishes himself in California. Tries to write film scripts, but concentrates much of his attention on attempting to get his works staged on Broadway.

Works on the plays *Schweik in the Second World War* and *The Caucasian Chalk Circle.*

Galileo with Charles Laughton

1947, Los Angeles: Première of *The Life of Galileo*. He prepares an English version with the famous film actor, Charles Laughton, who also plays the lead. He co-directs with Laughton, though the director on record is Joseph Losey.

Galileo is taken to Broadway.

Political persecution

Return to Europe

Brecht appears before the House of Representatives Un-American Activities Committee. (Following the war this committee is set up to root out Communism, but it also begins a witch-hunt against intellectuals.) Before the play opens he hastily returns to Europe. The California and New York productions of *Galileo* are extensively photographed by Ruth Berlau.

Switzerland: première of *Antigone*

1948, Chur, Switzerland: He directs the première of his adaptation of Holderlin's translation of Sophocles' *Antigone*. The performance is photographed by Ruth Berlau and a 'model book' of the production published in 1949.

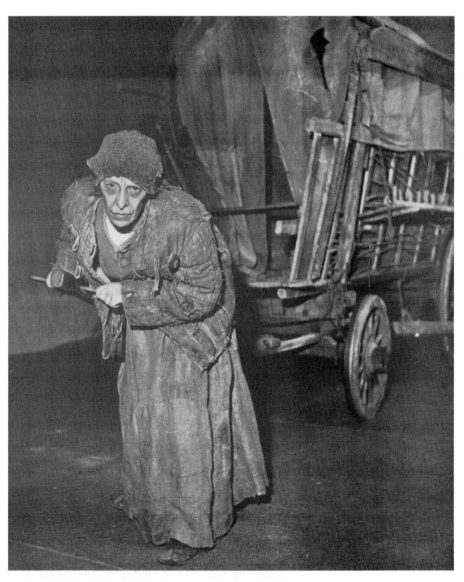

Figure 3.22   Helene Weigel as Mother Courage.

Zurich: Brecht and Hella Wuolijoki's play *Mr Puntila and his Man Matti* is produced at the Schauspielhaus. The set is by Teo Otto, who had designed the wagon and sets for the 1941 Zurich world première of *Mother Courage*. The music is by Paul Dessau.

1949, Berlin: Production of *Mother Courage and Her Children.*

Berliner Ensemble opens

He becomes artistic director

He goes on a recruiting tour to sign up actors for the proposed Berliner Ensemble. Helene Weigel is appointed administrative head of the Ensemble, while Brecht's position with the company is described rather vaguely as *Spielleiter* (this title roughly translates as *artistic* director).

Puntila opens the Berliner Ensemble.

Mother Courage in Munich

1950, Munich: A new production of *Mother Courage and Her Children.*

The Mother with scene projections

1951: Post-war Berlin première of *The Mother,* directed by Brecht. One of the very few post-war productions of Brecht that uses background scene projections.

Uprising in East Germany

1953: East German uprising. He sends a letter to the authorities, supporting their stand against the dissatisfied workers. He feels obliged to be seen as a loyal supporter of the new Communist regime, since it has helped establish his theatre.

Ensemble finds a new and permanent home

1954, Berlin: The company moves to a new home, the newly renovated Am Schiffbauerdamm Theater (see 1928).

Opening of *The Caucasian Chalk Circle,* directed by Brecht assisted by Manfred Wekwerth, with music by Paul Dessau and set and costumes by Karl von Appen.

Mother Courage on tour

The original Berlin production of *Mother Courage* is taken on tour to Paris, where it causes a sensation with international theatre audiences and establishes Brecht as *the* leading director in post-war Europe.

Tour to Paris
Tour to London

1955: *The Caucasian Chalk Circle* is taken on tour to Paris and to London in **1956,** where it causes a critical sensation. This production represents Brecht at the height of his powers as a director of a first-rate ensemble.

Dies of a heart attack
Helene Weigel is confirmed as his heir

1956: On his deathbed Brecht dictates a will containing the provision: 'I ask my wife, Helene Weigel, to continue to lead the Berliner Ensemble for as long as she believes the style of the theatre can be maintained.' Weigel directs the theatre up to her own death on 6 May, **1971.**

The preparation of this chronology owes a debt to:

Fuegi, J.,   *Bertolt Brecht: Chaos According to Plan,*   CUP, 1987

Other useful chronologies include:

Thompson, P. & Sacks, G. (ed),	*The Cambridge Companion To Brecht*,	CUP, 1994
Whittington, V.,	*Good Company Education: Study Pack: Bertolt Brecht,*	Brighton, 1991
Schneede, U.M.,	*George Grosz, His Life and Work* (pp.137–69),	Gordon Fraser, 1979

3.4.2 A BRIEF BIOGRAPHY

Born into a troubled period for Germany

Brecht was born into a world of conflict and contradictions. By the time he was 16 the First World War had broken out, which consumed Germany with its ferocity and accounted for the deaths of a number of those with whom he went to school. Financial, political and personal instability were a way of life and would remain so for Brecht until his death.

Figure 3.23   A cartoon of Bertolt Brecht.

Changes his name

Born **Berthold** Brecht, he changed his name to **Bertolt** (Bert for short), as he wanted to be identified with the heroes of American literature he so admired; throughout his life and after his death his wife, Helene Weigel, called him Brecht.

Experience of the First World War

During the war he managed to be posted as a medical orderly to his home town, so lived with his stable, middle-class family and escaped the real horrors of the trenches. His work, however, exposed him to the sight of terribly wounded soldiers and all his life he never forgot the smell of

Futility of war

death, brought about by the futility of war.

Escapes to Munich and Berlin

After this experience he felt ready to escape his provincial background, first with visits to Munich to find work in the theatre and soon after that to Berlin, where he settled on a more or less permanent basis.

He had the extraordinary knack of making friendships very easily: men and women were instantly attracted to him, despite his apparently unwashed state and the habit of having a lit cigar between his lips at all times. As a contemporary remarked, 'With his flapping leather jacket he looked like a cross between a lorry driver and a Jesuit seminarist.'

Working methods

His writing commenced at an early age, including poems, plays, stories, newspaper articles and theatre criticism. He made a habit of a punishing work regime, and simply to survive took on any and every chance to make himself known. Very quickly he assembled a devoted band of helpers who worked on his behalf. Thus began a lifelong habit

Collaboration: see section 3.4.3

of collaboration with others, not all of whom enjoyed the experience, though they would continue to serve him faithfully. He in turn thought nothing of passing their efforts off as his own. In financial matters he was astute and occasionally less than honest; he courted scandal and admiration in equal measure.

A short résumé of his early work

The 1920s was a period of intense activity. By the end of the decade he had divorced one wife and married a second and had written three plays – *Drums in the Night, In the Jungle of the Cities* and *Baal* – all of which had been directed by leading figures in the theatre and attracted, like their author, their fair share of scandal.

In the 1920s he also adapted Marlowe's *Edward the Second,* published a volume of short stories, directed his play *A Man's a Man* and undertook his first collaboration with the composer Kurt Weill in *Mahagonny,* followed closely by the sensationally popular *The Threepenny Opera,* which ran for 500 performances.

Didactic Theatre: see section 3.4.3

He also started to develop his didactic theatre pieces: *The Lindbergh Flight* and *The Baden Didactic Play.* The relative failure of *Happy End* in 1929 was the only real setback in an unbroken series of projects over eight years.

Three key periods in his life

Brecht's life has often been conveniently divided into three phases:
- Munich and Berlin: 1919–33
- The years of exile: 1933–48
- The Berliner Ensemble: 1949 until his death.

Major plays written during exile

Although this is a fair division, it takes no account of the work that went on wherever he was and with whom. The Brecht 'factory' was in production even at the most personally dangerous moments of his and his collaborators' lives. It is worth noting, for instance, that most of his major plays were completed before he reached the safety of America in 1941, but would remain unperformed for as long as seven years.

Theory evolved through practice

It is also important to remember that during these periods he changed his outlook on his work. His theoretical writings, for example, underwent enormous rethinking in the last years of his life. As with Stanislavski, the rigours of putting his theory into practice resulted in new ways of enquiring and reasoning.

Epic Theatre: see section 3.4.3

Brecht's passionate belief that theatre should not only reflect the world but, more importantly, change it, was the most important theme of his work. He used his theories of **Epic Theatre** to achieve this, in direct contradiction to the prevailing genre of naturalism.

To this end he drew on all the available resources: staging, collaborations with other directors, the help of designers and the catchy tunes of composers. Heavily influenced by the funfairs of his youth, street entertainments and political cabaret, he was able to draw all these together to make a totally new form of theatre.

Epic productions at the Ensemble

By the end of his life he was a world figure in theatre. The productions of the Ensemble had astonished Europe by their freshness, and the detail of their staging and acting, which was mesmerising in its apparent simplicity.

Peter Brook has said:

> . . . all theatre work today at some point starts or returns to his statements and achievement.
>
> [Brook, P., *The Empty Space*, Penguin, 1986. p.80]

Over 40 years since his death
What is relevant for theatre today

Today, over 40 years after his death, it is important that we find in Brecht's theory and practice lessons for evaluating and reflecting on theatre in our own time. In exploring his themes we shall demonstrate that theoretical perspectives need to be linked with practical realisations: theory alone is not enough. The vitality, excitement and strength of Brecht's plays can only be truly realised in the doing of them.

3.4.3 THEORY AND PRACTICE

THE FIRST PLAYS

These plays are:

- *Baal*: written in 1918, first produced in 1923 in Leipzig. Brecht took over key rehearsals.

- *Drums in the Night*: written in 1918, first produced in 1922 in Munich, and in Berlin at the end of the same year. Brecht attended many rehearsals. A critic of the first production remarked: 'Overnight the 24-year-old poet Bert Brecht has changed the literary face of Germany.'

- *In the Jungle [of the Cities]*: written in 1921; as *In the Jungle* the play acquired its fuller title in a revised version. The first production was in 1923 in Munich. Brecht contributed to every stage of rehearsals.

Experiments in playwriting These plays do not conform to the main thrust of Brecht's theory, since they were all completed before much of it was written down. But there are in all of them traces of methods and themes that were to recur later, in a modified and more considered form. He regarded them as 'experiments' and as such they are important in his development.

Baal

In some senses *Baal* is an anti-play, as it was written to express Brecht's dislike of Hanns Johst's *Der Einsame*. This had a similar theme and what Brecht considered to be the negative qualities of naturalistic writing and a sentimentalised conclusion.

Buchner: section 3.4.4 His text, by contrast, was heavily influenced by Buchner's *Woyzeck*, sharing with it a structure of episodic and subtitled scenes, which at the time was a novel and radical idea. Following Buchner's example, Brecht broke with the traditional three- or four-act structure and composed short scenes which could move around in time and place without any apparent continuity.

Epic Theatre: see pp.304–6 This first play, with its borrowed scene structure, is a precursor to how he would construct what he would later call **Epic Theatre.**

In his introduction to the complete plays of Buchner, Patterson [1987, p.159] makes a clear link:

Montage versus growth Buchner's technique anticipates Brecht's distinctions between the 'Aristotelian' (Dramatic) theatre [one scene leading to another: **growth**] and his own 'Epic Theatre' [each scene on its own: **montage**].

We shall be discussing the concepts of dramatic theatre and montage in more detail in the section on Epic Theatre, but it is important to note that from this earliest period Brecht was rejecting the style of contemporary theatre and borrowing ideas from the past to create his own form.

Baal: see chronology, 1923 *Baal* is certainly a text that could be taken as a partial self-portrait. Its anti-hero, Baal, is a poet and singer, who appears in cabaret and displays a contempt for social niceties, making it a relevant commentary on the young Brecht, who attracted and repelled his contemporaries in equal measure.

Drums in the Night

A popular theme of a soldier's return from the war His second play, *Drums in the Night*, took up a popular theme of the time: the return of a soldier from the war. By placing his protagonist in the centre of his post-war world, Brecht was again exploring the playing out of man's destiny in a hostile and revolutionary social environment. The year of its production (1922) was a particularly unsettled time in Germany.

Banners asking the audience not to stare romantically As part of the production, banners were placed in the auditorium which said, 'Stop that romantic staring', and 'Every man is best in his own skin'. Whether this was Brecht's decision is hard to tell, but we can see the first move to de-romanticise the act of watching, leading not to **empathy** with the characters but a distanced **objectivity.**

Anti-illusion in the stage
directions

In the last act the moon was a Chinese lantern that glowed red and in the final stage direction the soldier hurled his drum, '...which was a lantern, and drum and moon together fall into the river, which is without water'. Brecht was already demonstrating his dislike for any kind of **illusion** in the staging.

The Kleist prize

The critical reception of this play led to Brecht being awarded the prestigious Kleist prize, and immediately he became a much sought-after playwright.

In the Jungle of the Cities

Designed by Caspar Neher

Upton Sinclair's *The Jungle*

In his next play, *In the Jungle of the Cities*, Brecht enlisted the co-operation of his designer friend Caspar Neher. The play was presented like a boxing match and the action was set in an imaginary Chicago, inspired by the reading of Upton Sinclair's novel *The Jungle*.

Plays which use America as a
setting

This was not the last occasion on which Brecht placed his action in some imagined city. He repeated the Chicago setting for *St Joan of the Stockyards*, *Happy End* and *The Resistible Rise of Arturo Ui*. For Brecht, Chicago stood for all that he loved and hated in the 'American dream': fast cars, jazz, boxing fights, gambling and the dark world of gangsters, with death by machine-gun. Remember that he had changed his name to Bert to seem more 'American'.

Soho, London as a setting

In *The Threepenny Opera* he made Soho in London the setting, but it was not a city that anyone could recognise, while in *Mahagonny* it was Florida that stood for some North American dream world.

The boxing match as a
classless entertainment

The boxing ring metaphor of *In the Jungle of the Cities* would surface again in *Mahagonny*, where it became a tangible reality as a method of staging. The cast was literally raised on a platform within the ropes and lit with the harsh lights of a prize-fight. Brecht was fascinated and delighted by this sport, for in its staging it epitomised a democratic space in which all classes of persons could be together, eating, drinking, smoking and enjoying the entertainment.

This brief survey of the three plays has demonstrated that Brecht established aspects of form and content quite quickly and would develop them in his next phase of playwriting.

To sum up:

Epic Theatre:
see pp.304–6
Montage:
see p.307

- Aspects of **'Epic'** structure were in place in his first plays.

- The arrangement of scenes and their titles led to **montage**.

- Man within his social environment was a key theme.

Naturalism:
see section 3.1.3

- **Anti**-naturalistic presentation was an objective.

- By displacing the action into imagined worlds, the audience could be distanced from the human conflicts.

EPIC THEATRE

BEGINNINGS Epic Theatre created over a number of years Epic Theatre associated with the Berliner Ensemble	This title stands for a theatre of highly complex theoretical and practical ideas, which took Brecht some years to formulate. We have demonstrated that the early plays had traces of the 'Epic', but as we shall see it took a good ten years for all aspects to come together. It wasn't until the last great plays at the Berliner Ensemble in the 1940s and 1950s that Epic Theatre was finally firmly established.
	Throughout this section we will be making reference to the play *The Mother* (1932), which is a key text for an understanding of the Epic in practice.
Adaptation as a way of writing plays	It was after the scandalous success of *Baal* in 1923 that Brecht embarked on what could be recognised as his first 'Epic' production. This was his adaptation of Marlowe's *Edward the Second* (1924).
A text that had many aspects of the Epic within its structure	The choice of Marlowe allowed Brecht to develop the concept of the **Epic** within the Elizabethan context. Clearly, apart from the sensational subject matter, the elements that drew Brecht to the play were related to its structure and to its original mode of presentation in the Elizabethan playhouse:
Themes and mode of presentation	• an almost bare stage with the audience standing round it; • political and personal events unfolding in swiftly changing scenes • gripping stories of kings and their lives presented for a semi-literate audience • a performance that would have taken place in daylight.
Narrator as storyteller and titles	With designs by Neher he then 'distanced' his audience with soldiers in white faces to show they were 'frightened', a ballad singer and titles to introduce the scenes.
Brecht's theory influenced by popular entertainments	Fuegi [1987, p.6] suggests that Brecht's theory of theatre was well in place by his teens, and cites his fascination with travelling fairs to justify this theory. The entertainments at these fairs told tales of heroic deeds using a range of recognisable methods. These included: • a singer/narrator • stories with a moral purpose, underscored by pictorial illustrations • accompanying music on a barrel organ • a performance in daylight • the audience free to smoke and drink and to come and go as they pleased.
Components of popular theatre No illusions in a performance	This theory is a persuasive one, since it identifies quite complex theatrical means with components of popular theatre, and in particular leads to the realisation that all these storytelling techniques can be seen in Brecht's plays. The fairground showman had no reliance on the 'technology' of theatre to tell his tales, which made his methods very appealing to a playwright who desired to **demystify** the mechanics of a performance.

ACTIVITY   Look at the scene titles in *The Mother*. Make a list of them. How do they move the play from place to place? How is the time span constructed? What other information do they tell us? What is their message?

We can thus identify **two** sources for Brecht's theory:

- the Elizabethan theatre, with swiftly moving narratives concerning political and personal events
- popular entertainments, with a narrator who helped to explain the moral purpose, accompanied by musical interludes.

Notes on 'Epic' theatre

The first mention that Brecht makes of the term **Epic** is in 1926; however, it was in the notes that he wrote to the opera *The Rise and Fall of the City of Mahagonny* (1930) that he really began to clarify the issues. It is significant that by this time he had met and worked with the composer Kurt Weill.

Working with Kurt Weill

The function of the songs

Weill offered Brecht a much-needed way of enlivening and extending the work he was doing with texts. A musical score could include songs, which commented on the action and gave the actor/singer the opportunity to address the audience directly. They could also be sung by a chorus, which in plays like *The Mother* (1932) could address the characters with advice and warnings or take on the function of telling the audience the characters' unspoken thoughts.

ACTIVITY   Look at Scene 1 of *The Mother*. What is the function of the Chorus? Find the **three ways** in which Brecht makes it drive the play forward.

Unlike traditional opera, which Brecht regarded with suspicion because of its ability to overwhelm the spectator, this kind of musical contribution made a direct link between the actor/singer, his or her audience and the character in question.

Distinctions between Dramatic and Epic

Brecht needed to make clear the distinction between what he called **Dramatic** theatre and the **Epic**. He saw **Dramatic** theatre as representing all that he most hated, which was, of course, the prevailing form of theatre. It was a theatre of **illusion** - sucking the spectator into a dream world where all the problems were carefully resolved at the conclusion of the play, so that the spectator could leave those problems behind on leaving the theatre.

Dramatic theatre: the theatre of illusion

Epic theatre: the theatre of problems to be solved

Brecht defined his **Epic** theatre as challenging this dream world; he wanted a spectator who was awake and alert. His theatre would pose problems and, far from solving them, was designed to leave the spectator with a task to be accomplished in the real world.

A list of the distinctions

Brecht drew up a chart, placing elements of these two forms of theatre in opposition. This is reproduced below [Willett/BT, p.37]. We have slightly edited this list and added some comment.

Dramatic Theatre

- **plot:** has a beginning, middle and end and issues raised in the play are resolved

- **implicates the spectator in a stage situation:** suggests to the spectator that what she or he is watching is like real life

Epic Theatre

- **narrative:** begins anywhere, continues and stops. Issues are not resolved

- **turns the spectator into an observer,** but suggests that the spectator can question what she or he is seeing

Dramatic Theatre	Epic Theatre
• **wears down the spectator's capacity for action**	• **arouses the spectator's capacity for action**
• **provides the audience with sensations:** a theatre of illusion, with ideas reinforced	• **forces the audience to take decisions:** makes it clear that there are problems to be solved
• **the spectator is involved in something**	• **the spectator is made to face something**
• **suggestion**	• **argument**
• **instinctive feelings are preserved**	• **brought to the point of recognition**
• **the spectator is in the thick of it, shares the experience**	• **the spectator stands outside, studies**
• **the human being is taken for granted**	• **the human being is the object of the enquiry**
• **the human being is unalterable:** preconceptions are reinforced	• **the human being is alterable and able to alter:** change is possible, both in oneself and in the world
• **one scene makes another:** see plot	• **each scene for itself:** see narrative
• **growth:** events follow each other in a smooth progression	• **montage:** events are shown in self-contained scenes
• **linear development**	• **broken up**
• **a human being as a fixed point**	• **a human being as a process**
• **thought determines being**	• **social being determines thought**
• **feeling:** a theatre where the audience can allow itself to indulge in emotions	• **reason:** a theatre where the audience is made to question and think

To sum up:

- We have traced the beginnings of Epic Theatre.
- We have identified how it differed from 'Dramatic' theatre.
- We have discussed the role music was beginning to play in the structure of the plays.

We now need to consider other elements that Brecht assembled, from all sorts of sources, to help him realise his theatre. Some of these influential ideas were theoretical, others practical, but they all combined to create a distinctive alternative to the prevailing theatre of the 20th century.

MONTAGE
Theatre can be like film

Epic theatre proceeds by fits and starts, in the manner comparable to the images on a film strip.

[Benjamin, 1992. p.21]

Montage can shock

This short statement is part of our larger discussion of Epic Theatre, but it places in context Brecht's firm belief that **montage** could 'connect dissimilars in such a way as to "shock" people into new recognitions and understandings'. Brecht was interested in any device that could keep his audience alert and awake, and with montage he found a means to achieve this.

A technique of film editing

The term 'montage' came from the work of his friend, the Soviet film-maker Sergei Eisenstein. It was a technique of editing film by which seemingly unrelated images could take on new meaning by the way in which a film editor cut them together. The distinctiveness of montage was the way it could contract or extend real time by manipulating these images.

The silent cinema

For example, how we view a shot of an actor's expression of emotion is determined by the shots that come before or after it. Remember here that we are dealing with the silent cinema, so do not have the question of dialogue to think about. The visual elements are essentially the most important.

Because **montage** totally contradicted the realistic **growth** (plot and development) in dramatic theatre, it was useful to Brecht in a number of ways:

New shocks to keep the audience alert

- Short self-contained scenes could be juxtaposed with each other, creating new 'shocks'.

Absolute clarity of intention

- Because the emphasis was on the visual, Brecht took great pains to ensure that his arrangement of a scene was readable by a deaf person. There was to be not a single moment when such a person could not understand what was going on.

A storyboard

- Brecht organised rehearsals so that the designer (always an important figure) could help with drawings of possible stage arrangements. While he was working on *Galileo* in Hollywood, his director employed one of the foremost cartoonists of the day to 'plot' the production like the storyboard in a comic strip.

The epic actor

- In acting terms, the montage technique worked within the individual performance. The actor became aware of how he was recreating these pre-planned images.

A breaking down of action

Continuity broken

Thus we see that **montage** was a breaking down of action into minute details. Not a moment or gesture was to be wasted; clarity of intention was the goal at every moment. It was also a way in which continuity could be broken and fractured and through this the audience was to be kept in a constant state of alertness.

To sum up:

- Seemingly unrelated images juxtaposed together could shock.

- It drew attention to the content, because it proceeded in jumps not as a progressive growth.

- It was a way of structuring theatre that was totally opposed to the **dramatic**.

ACTIVITY   Look at the film *Strike*, directed by Eisenstein in 1924. The final sequence demonstrates how montage can be vivid and shocking, with its depiction of a worker's strike broken up by police. Eisenstein intercuts images of strikers being massacred with images of animals being slaughtered.

VERFREM-DUNGSEFFEKT

Chinese acting style

Brecht began to use this phrase after a visit to Moscow in 1935, where he had seen the Chinese actor Mei Lan-fang. He wrote a long article, entitled *Alienation Effects in Chinese Acting*, in which he explored the lack of illusion or empathy in the performance and commented upon the actor's ability to 'stand aside from his part'.

Making the familiar seem strange

In this article he also used the phrase 'to make the incidents represented appear **strange** to the public...' and here he was picking up the echo of another theme, as well.

While in Moscow he had heard the Russian phrase *'priem ostraneniye'* – the device or trick of making something **strange** – which originated with a group of philosophers known as the Formalists. This particular device as they saw it was a literary way of:

Renewing our interest in the familiar

> ...dislocating our habitual perceptions of the real world so as to make it the object of renewed **attentiveness.**
>
> [Bennett, T., *Formalism and Marxism*, Methuen, 1979. p.20]

We can see an example of this by looking at the phrase 'The sky is blue'. This tells us nothing about the sky we do not know already, but if we add: 'It was a sunny day and the sky was like a new sheet of blotting paper with the blue ink tipped into the middle of it' [Bennett, 1979. p.20], we are immediately struck by the vividness of the imagery and this increases our attentiveness to the nature of the sky.

Critics do not agree about the importance of this device to Brecht, but it certainly applied to his preoccupation with an actor's degree of identification with his part.

No identification with the characters

In other words Brecht's intention was that the actor could make himself the subject of 'renewed attentiveness' by not submerging himself in a character. By standing outside the character the actor forced the audience to look more closely at the mechanism of acting.

An Epic text: *The Mother*, 1932

Even before 1935 Brecht had already established the means for doing this, in the last play he directed before leaving Germany in 1933: *The Mother* (1932), which provides a very useful example of the working out of Epic Theatre in theory and practice. What Brecht found in **Verfremdungseffekt** was not so much a new idea, but a confirmation that his idea was a sound one.

ACTIVITIES

Reporting events to keep the audience at a distance

Look at Scene 5 of *The Mother* and see how Brecht recreates offstage events through the device of reporting them. The scene is no less tense and compelling for this **distanced** view, but the audience is kept at one remove from total involvement, since the actor is relating events rather than acting them out. The audience is not sucked into the living out of the story, but kept 'at arm's length'.

Try saying your lines in the third person, i.e., 'She/he said . . .', which turns direct speech into reported speech. This will 'distance' you from the role and at the same time you will find that the character is 'outside' yourself.

Problems of translation　There is some confusion over the translation of **Verfremdungseffekt,** and we would therefore suggest that instead of using the literal English translations – estrangement, alienation or disillusion, all of which are rather negative words – we adopt the word **distancing** as a more positive expression.

Distancing　Of all the other definitions we would warn against using 'alienation', as it suggests the making of a hostile relationship with an audience, which was not what Brecht wanted.

ACTIVITY　Work on *The Street Scene* (Section 29 in Willett/BT: p.121), sometimes called *The Street Accident*. In this proposed scenario Brecht uses the 'reported' nature of an accident to explain his theory of 'distancing'.

This final reference sums up Brecht's intention:

> We very readily cease to see the world we live in, and become **anaesthetized** to its distinctive features. The aim of poetry *[drama]* is to reverse that process, to **defamiliarize** that with which we are overly familiar . . . to indicate a new childlike, non-jaded vision in us. The poet *[dramatist]* aims to disrupt . . .' [*Our italics*]
>
> [Hawkes, T., *Structuralism and Semiotics*, Methuen, 1977. p.62]

Brecht's purpose was to **distance** his audience, to enable them to see more clearly the world in which they lived. Only then, he believed, would they be able to change it.

To sum up:

- **'Alienation'** doesn't really help us to identify this important idea; we are **distanced** not alienated.

- The 'effekt' is to keep the audience distanced from total involvement.

- There is no lessening of involvement, it is just more objective.

- Being distanced makes the audience see more clearly, rather than take things for granted.

GESTE　'*Gestus*', of which '*gestisch*' is the adjective, means both gist and gesture; an **attitude** or a single aspect of an **attitude**, expressible in words or actions. [**Our bold**].

[Willett/BT. p.42]

Geste means attitude

We have highlighted the word **attitude** in the above because it comes closest to explaining how we should view **geste** in translation, and how best to apply it to the text.

An actor's performance

It is not an easy concept, but it is very important because Brecht used it principally to describe the type of performance an actor should give in his Epic Theatre.

Charlie Chaplin

One reason that Brecht was such an admirer of the silent film star Charlie Chaplin was that he recognised in the actor's performance a control and concentrated attention to detail so great that were he to be behind a window we could still 'read' the performance. Chaplin's gestural cinema was for Brecht a summary of what he called 'making gestures quotable'.

ACTIVITY   In small groups, take an abstract word and create 'frozen' tableaux illustrating the word: for example, war, peace, terror, etc. Let one group guess what the others are showing.

Contrast to Stanislavski's work with actors

In interpretation, **geste** would exclude the psychological aspects of a character's development, and thus it can be placed in direct contrast to the sort of demands that Stanislavski was making on his actors. Feeling was to be externalised; the actor was to 'make himself observed standing between the spectator and the text'. [Willett, 1993. p.174]

ACTIVITY   Look at Scene 1 of *The Mother,* and read **aloud** the first monologue by Pelagea. Is she talking to herself or to the audience?

She gives us a lot of information about herself and her son. The direct address, the short sentences and the commentary on her dilemma all point to an actor *outside* the character. The writing demands a certain kind of delivery. Try to find the emotional attitude required by the text. How does she distance herself from herself and the situation? What do the final words of the scene tell us about the whole play?

Kurt Weill: see p.312

Kurt Weill, the first composer who worked with Brecht, also discussed **geste** and related it to the particular importance of music for the theatre:

> [music] can reproduce the *gestus* that illustrates the incident on the stage; . . . forcing the action into a particular **attitude** that excludes all doubt and misunderstanding about the incident in question. [**Our bold**]

> [Willett/BT. p.42]

Songs can comment on the action

Brecht used music in all his major plays

Weill expresses his feeling that music has the unique power to create a commentary on the action, to reinforce and exemplify the text's meaning. Brecht too recognised this. None of his major texts would be complete without their extensive musical component, acting as both a counterpoint to the text and as political and social commentary.

ACTIVITIES Look at Scene 2 in *The Mother* and the song Mascha sings to Vlasova. She uses the issue of the lack of soup as the subject of the poem, but then continues to urge Vlasova to see her dilemma in the context of social and political conditions.

Weill and Eisler: see p.312 Listen to recordings of songs from Brecht's plays. They are generally available, especially those from *The Threepenny Opera*, with music by Kurt Weill. Some of Brecht's poems set to music by Hanns Eisler are also available. The power of this music will help you understand why songs were so vital an element in a theatre of **geste**.

To sum up:

- **Geste** is an attitude towards performance which contrasts with naturalism.

- It means standing outside the character.

- In gestural terms it means that actions are in quotation marks, they are *shown*.

- In music it underlines and comments upon the message of the text.

COLLABORATION

All through his life, Brecht was a great collaborator with other writers, musicians, directors and designers and open to the most humble opinion during the rehearsal process.

His co-writer Elisabeth Hauptmann However, Brecht was apparently quick to claim work by others as exclusively his. Fuegi [1987] has suggested that much early work written with Elisabeth Hauptmann was more than 90 per cent hers and in later collaborations with the composer Kurt Weill it was Brecht's minimising of his colleague's invaluable input that led to the break-up of their partnership.

Parricide: see chronology, 1922 The fiasco of the production of *Parricide* in 1922, with its disastrous outcome, led Brecht to a lifelong practice. He found and cultivated trusted colleagues to carry out the function of director, while he interfered, usually unwelcomely, from the sidelines. Even in his later life, when the Ensemble was secure and he was able to initiate and see through any project, it was still in the collaborative mode.

MUSIC We have already touched on Brecht's fascination with the travelling fairs of his youth, with their musical element that he found so exciting and relevant in its appeal.

Epic Theatre: see p.304

Brecht as a singer of popular songs He was renowned for the singing of his own ballads, accompanying himself on guitar, and in the Munich of the 1920s he could be seen performing in the *Lachtkeller* (Laughing Cellar) with Karl Valentin, the brilliant stand-up comic and singer of satirical songs. However, he was not so accomplished that he could do without collaborators for the music in his plays.

Songs as a 'waker-up' Music for Brecht was a vital part of theatre, acting like the cabaret songs sung in a cellar, as a counterpoint to the text. It would function like other aspects of his Epic Theatre: separate, distinguishable from every other element and signalled by such staging devices as a change of lighting or a caption. It was to be a 'waker-up' of the audience, keeping them alert, and would be used to counter what Brecht firmly believed was the natural desire of an audience: to sit back and let theatre wash over them.

Opera like a heavy meal
Suspicious of Wagner

By contrast, Brecht labelled opera **culinary,** only good for eating; like a heavy meal it left one with indigestion. He was suspicious of such composers as Richard Wagner (1813–83), who sought to combine all aspects of theatre and subordinate them to his surging operatic music with its romantic librettos. Brecht saw this operatic form as leading to a suspension of an audience's critical faculties in favour of a wallow in emotion.

Nazis and their political rallies

He was proved right in his suspicions. The Nazis used 'Wagnerian'-type events to promote their distorted ideologies: huge crowds and orchestrated choirs, with banners waving and marching soldiers, to excite and impress the nation.

In Brecht's own anti-opera, ironically named *The Threepenny Opera* (1928), a strong statement was made as to its form. Not only was the orchestra pulled out of the pit to be put on stage, but the songs were signalled with their titles and a 'special change of lighting arranged'. The catchy and hummable music set feet tapping, further distancing the music from the unstoppable scores of opera.

Popular music forms

The music looked back to the fairground hurdy-gurdy, the beer-cellar and the hoarse and mesmeric singing of Brecht himself. It was to be truly popular, a far cry from the bourgeois world of the opera house.

Kurt Weill's popular musical forms

Chief among Brecht's musical collaborators was **Kurt Weill** (1900–50), who provided hugely popular scores to match the equally abrasive texts of such work as *Mahagonny* in both its versions (1927–30), *The Threepenny Opera* and *Happy End* (1929). He set poems by Brecht in *The Berlin Requiem* (1928) and some of the *Lehrstuck* texts. Their final collaboration was in Paris in 1933 with *The Seven Deadly Sins.*

Brecht acknowledged his debt to Weill as 'first providing what he had needed for the stage'.

Hanns Eisler shared political ideals

Hanns Eisler (1898–1962) matched Brecht's political commitment more closely. He composed scores both before the Second World War – *The Mother* (1932) – and after it – *Fear and Misery of the Third Reich* (1945), *Galileo* (1947) and *The Days of the Commune* (1950). He also composed numerous settings for Brecht's poems, and was in his own right a successful composer of film music.

Composed military marching tunes

We might characterise his music as more austere than Weill's, but he was capable of writing catchy military marching tunes for Communist youth groups that became popular all over Europe.

Epic productions for the Ensemble

Paul Dessau (1894–1979) was the last of Brecht's musical collaborators and is most associated with the big 'Epic' productions of the last years at the Berliner Ensemble.

To sum up:

- Brecht saw music as essential to his theatre.
- Because the music interrupted the text the songs were signalled in various ways.

- The music and songs were treated as separate elements.
- Songs could comment on a character's feelings as a third-person narrative, and thus were far from naturalistic.

DESIGN Brecht wrote of his friend, the designer Caspar Neher:

> Our friend begins in his sketches with people and with the things that happen to them and because of them. He does not do stage pictures, backgrounds and frameworks, but he **constructs** the landscape in which people experience life.

[*TDR*, 1968. p.136]

This admirable summing up of Neher's collaborative achievements draws attention to the importance that both Brecht and Neher placed on the job of a designer.

Neher is a stage builder not a picture-maker

They felt that he was a *Buhenbauer* – **a stage builder**, one who **constructs** – and infinitely preferred this term to *Buhenbildner* – **stage picture-maker** – which was the more commonly used term. Neher in particular hated this term, since it failed to acknowledge the necessary three-dimensional spatial qualities needed for the design.

The designer helps the director

Neher's special gift was not to subordinate his work to that of the playwright but to work in the closest possible collaborative contact. Brecht recognised that this contribution was as invaluable as any other. As late as 1950, while struggling to find the right spatial arrangement, Brecht gave up in despair and suspended rehearsals until Neher was available.

It was his colleague's delicate sketches (see Fig. 3.24) that had the power to create the right dynamic of relationships on stage and resolve the problem. The 'set' was to evolve as part of a creative partnership between actor, director and designer.

Figure 3.24   Neher's design for Scene 2 of *The Mother*.

Geste:
see pp.309–11

What Brecht enjoyed in Neher's work quite as much as in Weill's was his ability to adopt a political and intellectual attitude towards the events on stage. (We have discussed this vital element of 'geste' or attitude above.) Further, in referring to the staging of *The Threepenny Opera*, Brecht said:

Projections are separate

These projections of Neher are quite as much an independent component of the opera as are Weill's music and the text.

[Willett/BT. p.38]

Collaboration means every component being equally important

In other words, Brecht gave equal weight in the creative process to design, music and the text, but most importantly relished their separateness. It was to be a theatre of 'jumps', montages of different elements that would alert the spectators to the continuing dialectic (argument) taking place in front of them. It was these skilled practitioners, who were also collaborators, who could supply the right **attitude.**

At a time when the trend throughout the world of stage design was away from the **painted** world towards the **constructed** world, Neher and Brecht's other designers made visual statements which have become as much a part of Epic theatre as any of Brecht's theoretical writings:

The boxing-ring image

- the boxing ring for *Mahagonny* (1927), with placards, screen tiles and projections

Projections

- titles projected onto two screens on either side of the stage for *The Threepenny Opera* (1928), with the band onstage

- the lowering of the oil lamps during the songs

The half curtain

- perhaps most famous of all, the half curtain:

Figure 3.25   Staging for Epic Theatre, showing the half curtain.

Extract from the poem
The Curtains

...And please make
My curtain half-height, don't block the stage off.
Leaning back, let the spectator
Notice the busy preparations being so
Ingeniously made for him, ...

[Brecht (trans. Willett *et al*), 1979. p.245]

The mask

- the half mask, which in *The Good Person of Setzuan* (1940) was an integral part of the identity of the protagonist, reflecting Brecht's interest in Far-Eastern theatre. This was a device used again in *The Caucasian Chalk Circle* (1954)

The lighting

- not least, the lighting (about which he wrote another poem), which was to be as clear and sharp as the acting.

ACTIVITIES
Try working with half masks. Look at Part 1 of *The Caucasian Chalk Circle*. In the original production the Governor and his Wife were masked. Why do you think this decision was made? What can a mask do to you? How does it change you as an actor, in a scene with other unmasked characters?

Make some placards to accompany the telling of a story. Pick a newspaper story and dramatise it, by dividing it up into episodes and then titling these. How does this affect the way we receive the narrative?

Restricted colour schemes

In keeping with the drive towards simple and direct solutions, Neher's colour schemes were based on earth pigments and the fabrics for costumes were undyed, relying on their texture and quality to signal their function. The furniture was to have the look of having been used for a long time. Throughout any design scheme, only those bits of buildings which were needed to suggest a place and time were constructed.

Selective realism

The whole ethos of this collaboration was to work towards what Willett calls 'selective realism'; the audience, glimpsing these elements over the top of the half curtain during the scene changes, was never for a moment allowed to forget that it was sitting in a theatre.

To sum up:

- Brecht's designer was a stage builder, not a picture-maker.

- Selective realism provided the minimum to suggest time and place.

- The audience was to be kept alert by devices that reminded its members they were in a theatre.

THE *LEHRSTUCK* (LEARNING PLAYS)

See p.317

These plays, invariably set to music, were an important development in Brecht's work, since with the help of his collaborators he was able to challenge what he called 'culinary' art forms in bourgeois theatre.

The Communist Party

His desire in launching these plays was to explore an audience's active involvement in the medium of musical theatre. His move towards this kind of theatre marked his commitment to the KPD (German Communist Party).

Karl Marx:
see section 3.4.4

Since 1926 he had been reading the works of Karl Marx, where he found a philosophy that matched his plays. After absorbing the ideas, he was then able to write plays to match the philosophy. Although at no time did he feel that Marx had provided all the answers, the theories gave Brecht a pattern against which to measure his own thinking

Marx's *Capital* gave him insights

When I read Marx's *Capital* I understood my plays.

[Willett, 1978. p.23]

A committed political writer

Concern for change

By 1929 Brecht was a committed political writer; critics agree that his writing immediately gained in clarity and objectivity. To place his thinking in the simplest context, it would be true to say that henceforward he was concerned for **change.**

His desire was for a theatre that through its expression of particular opinions and attitudes could effect change in the material world. The change he sought was based on his belief that the oppressed working classes had to be empowered to alter their miserable lives through structured political action. This action was part of a continuing philosophical, historical and artistic process.

It is useful to quote the following list, which, it is suggested, best sums up his new-found philosophy:

A political system that demands answers
The individual as part of a collective system

Reform must be total

- Communism is simple, rational and depends on questioning and study.
- The party is immense, anonymous and indestructible; even if its policy is wrong it would be still more wrong for the individual to act on his or her own.
- Altering the world means dirtying your hands.
- Piecemeal reforms are inadequate.
- The rank and file of the oppressors are not all that different from the oppressed.
- An unfulfilled life is a fate worst than death.

[Willett, J., *Brecht in Context*, 1984. p.182]

Brecht's Marxism was a subject for criticism

It should be noted, however, that this summary does not represent a true Marxist model. Throughout his life Brecht was to find himself the target of much criticism from Communists for his unconventional views.

The Mother is a learning play

We can see many of his beliefs reflected in the text and songs for *The Mother* (1932), which was to come at the end of this phase of 'Learning Plays' and in many ways marked the conclusion of the working through of this theory in practice.

ACTIVITY   Look at Scene 10 in *The Mother*. It is a classic lesson in the need for and purpose of Communism, as explained by Vlasova in terms of a parable. Discuss the ways Brecht contrasts God with the realities of Vlasova's circumstances. There is no doubt as to her understanding of the need for change in an unjust world. How are we made to confront that need for change?

Figure 3.26 An artist's impression of the staging of a 'Learning Play', showing the choir and soloist, the orchestra and captions projected on a screen.

Lehrstuck: common form of presentation

Returning to our theme of 'Learning Plays', we need to examine the common threads in their presentation. Since they were mainly written for a music festival (Baden-Baden) and performed on a concert stage, there was no proscenium arch and Brecht and Neher were able to exploit this lack by involving the audience in the work.

Learning through dialogue

Active involvement by the audience

The main body of the texts was a dialogue between soloist and choir and at moments in the cantatas the audience was asked to join in by means of a text projected behind the orchestra. Through this active involvement Brecht hoped to draw his audience into the debates within the texts, which were based on moral and political dilemmas within the Communist arena.

The will of the individual against the collective

A number of the texts pit the individual against the idea of the 'collective', a Communist term meaning the community or group, to whom the individual was seen to be subordinate. The 'argument' was that the collective was all-powerful and that the individual should submit to it.

Audience could suggest rewrites

In some instances Brecht handed out questionnaires and asked the audience to involve themselves in a rethinking of the arguments. Rewrites were supposed to stem from their comments, as in the case of *The Yes Sayer* (see below).

THE PERFORMANCES
Boxing-ring stage

The first of these was *Mahagonny* (1927), in a collaboration with Weill. Neher designed a boxing-ring stage in which the singers stood. Lotte Lenya caused a sensation with her rendering of 'Alabama Song'.

Projected text so that the audience could join in

Lindbergh's Flight (1929), later retitled *The Flight Over the Ocean*, pitted its real-life 'hero' Lindbergh against a chorus which represented the hurdles he must overcome on his flight. The audience had copies of the score, the projected text urging them to 'sing along'. At a revival in 1994 actors were 'planted' in the audience, urging spectators to take part in the argument.

Man's inhumanity to man

In the same season, in *The Baden Didactic Play*, there was a sequence involving a huge dummy clown that was slowly dismembered by two other clowns in a demonstration of man's inhumanity to man. Combined with projections of dead bodies the spectacle horrified the audience, who left disgusted. The learning exercise was too negative and vivid an experience.

Outcomes could be changed by rewriting the text

Another didactic piece, produced in Berlin schools in 1930, was *The Yes Sayer*. Its unacceptably bleak conclusion, with a boy's death by the will of the collective, prompted Brecht to rewrite the scenario with a more positive ending. He called this *The No Sayer*, and the negative imperative became the reason for changing the custom rather than it leading to the boy's death. The two texts were then performed together.

The individual and the collective

Finally, in the same year, he presented *The Measures Taken*, a choral work with music by Hanns Eisler, which had China as its setting. Its theme was the individual's submission to the will of the collective, represented by the choir, while the individuals made a case for their complicity in the murder of an (offstage) comrade. Again, this somewhat bleak piece was staged on a concert platform, within the confines of a roped-off area and with a huge projection screen looming over the singers.

Instruction and learning

Through the rather abstract arguments deployed in the *Lehrstuck*, Brecht was able to initiate both instruction (the didactic) and learning. Mounting these texts in concert conditions, with largely amateur choral groups of workers, he seized the opportunity of turning theories into practice and bringing the results to the widest possible audience.

Political concepts in an Epic presentation

Looking back on the list of Brecht's convictions, we can see many of them reflected in these texts. But it was *The Mother* (1932), the last play he directed before leaving Germany, that captured the spirit of his new thinking – a play that promoted Communist ideals embedded in an **Epic** structure.

To sum up:

- Political commitment led to theory being tried out in practice.

- The influence of Marx was profound. Ideas were assimilated and altered.

- Change was sought through political action. The theatre could aid this process.

3.4.4 INFLUENCES

BUCHNER, GEORG (1813–37)

Influenced a number of playwrights in the 20th century	As a playwright, Buchner had an influence on a number of playwrights in the Germany of the early 20th century. When, after years of neglect, his texts became available, not only were they much performed but they also became a model for new constructions in writing.
Involvement in politics Wrote plays which remained unproduced	During his early years as a student he involved himself in radical politics, which nearly led to his arrest; when he fled Germany in 1835 it was to permanent exile. Here he wrote his major plays, totally unacknowledged, with only *Danton's Death* (1835) being published in his lifetime. Although the tone is pessimistic, one of the overriding themes in the plays is man's search for his destiny in a hostile world.
Expressionism: see p.323	Buchner is famous mainly for his influence on the Expressionists, which was due to the fact that, although his plays were written in the early 19th century, they were published only in the early 20th. What the Expressionists took from Buchner was his model of what they termed *Stationendrama* (literally: stations of drama), in which the protagonist would move through a sequence of 'dramatic incidents each having some psychological or symbolic importance in itself' [Styan, 1986, Vol. 3. p.13].
Drums in the Night: see section 3.4.3	While the Expressionists tended to depict the suffering of man on this journey as internal and overwrought, Brecht chose to model his heroes on a tougher, less romantic mould. In his first works, however, it is possible to trace strong Expressionist tendencies.
Baal: see section 3.3.3	For example, if we look at Buchner's play *Woyzeck* (first performed 1913, but written much earlier), we can see how it anticipates *Baal* (1923) with the tragedy of its low-life hero, and his inability to express himself:

Brecht influenced by *Woyzeck*

Woyzeck's powers of speech fall drastically short of the depth of his anguish . . . Woyzeck's agonized spirit hammers in vain at the doors of language.

[Steiner, G., *The Death of Tragedy*, Faber, 1982. p.275]

Buchner's influence on montage	This might well apply to Baal, who undergoes a similar journey, only to die like Woyzeck under the moon and stars. Brecht takes up the theme of this 'first real tragedy of low-life' and uses the same episodic scene construction that we can now recognise as an embryonic form of **montage**. Though *Woyzeck* has a sense of the tragically inevitable about it, in *Baal* Brecht is already alerting the audience to a distanced view of his hero as he blunders unwillingly to death.
Opera version of *Woyzeck*	The modernist composer Alban Berg created an operatic version, misnamed *Wozzeck*, in 1925, confirming the play's enormous influence, and critics since have continued to acclaim the play as a modern masterpiece.

Buchner, G. (ed. Patterson, M.),   *Complete Plays*,   Methuen, 1987
Steiner, G.,   *The Death of Tragedy*,   Faber, 1982

WEDEKIND, FRANK (1864–1918)

Statement by Brecht	Without actually seeing him buried I cannot conceive that he is dead. Like Tolstoy and Strindberg he was one of the great educators of modern Europe. [Willett/BT. p.4]

Wedekind as role model

See chronology, 1919

As we can see from this extract from an obituary written by the young Brecht, Wedekind was held in enormous regard by the struggling poet and critic. Wedekind, apart from his playwriting, was renowned as a cabaret artist, singing and accompanying his own songs on the guitar. Thus he acted as a close role model for 'Bert', who attracted his own share of scandal in the cabaret cellars of Munich and Berlin.

Structure of the plays influenced by Buchner

Wedekind's plays have a similar structure to those of Buchner: short scenes, seemingly unconnected, which by their relentless forward movement build to an often shattering physical climax. In *Spring Awakening* (1891) it is the death of a young boy driven to suicide by the oppression of those in authority, while in *Pandora's Box* (1903) we see the murder of its heroine Lulu at the hands of Jack the Ripper.

Contempt for bourgeois society

Like Brecht, Wedekind had a contempt for bourgeois society, and his plays tended to focus on the double standards of sexual morality in Germany, especially as they affected the young. His form and structure, particularly in what are known as the 'Lulu plays', use 'circus, clownish slapstick and heightened melodrama' to achieve a rawness and vitality later matched by Brecht, particularly in his early texts.

Boa, E.,   *The Sexual Circus, Wedekind's Theatre of Subversion*,   Blackwell, 1992

PISCATOR, ERWIN (1893–1966)

The careers of Brecht and Piscator were closely intertwined and it would be hard to ignore their parallel lives in Berlin in the 1920s.

Piscator, a socialist with a bourgeois lifestyle

Returning from the First World War, where he had experienced at first hand the horrors of the trenches, Piscator started his career as a maker of agitprop drama, then moved rapidly into the mainstream of Berlin theatre. If there was any critical distance between himself and Brecht it was that although Piscator espoused left-wing theatre he lived the life of a comfortable bourgeois artist in a flat designed by the Bauhaus: a contradiction that Brecht was not slow to note.

Agitprop theatre

Anti-establishment themes

However, Piscator's involvement with **agit**(ation)**prop**(aganda) theatre distinguishes him from Brecht. In the socialist movements that sprang up after the war, this kind of theatre was very popular. It was, as its name suggests, semi-revolutionary, taking anti-establishment themes and dramatising them into short sketches with songs, which were toured to workers' clubs and beer halls. These groups adopted evocative names such as The Red Review and The Red Megaphone. When in 1932 Brecht toured his production of *The Mother* to factories, he was following the same kind of impulse: the desire to entertain and re-educate the oppressed working class.

The Mother. see chronology, 1932

Brecht writing plays for Piscator

In the years 1927–8, when Brecht briefly joined Piscator's 'dramaturgical collective', they did undertake some fruitful collaborations. Brecht did some writing for the elaborate *Rasputin* (1927) and, more importantly, the next year he worked on the adaptation of *The Adventures of the Good Soldier Schweik*.

Film and slide projections

In both these productions Piscator used the most complex means of staging. In *Rasputin* he built a huge semi-transparent dome on a revolve, with panels that lifted out to reveal small interior scenes. Film was projected on to and above this enormous structure and as the whole unit moved round back-projected images changed the locale.

Mechanical staging

Schweik was similarly ambitious: two treadmills installed downstage allowed the Soldier Schweik to make a journey that could be fully realised. As he appeared to march forward, the treadmills could introduce new scenes, which were illustrated with film and animated cartoons. The satirical artist Georg Grosz (1893–1959) provided larger-than-life puppets so that the 'little man', as represented by Schweik, could appear to be threatened by these figures of authority.

Epic Theatre: a shared word but a different meaning

The most important concept that Brecht and Piscator shared was that of **Epic Theatre**. In fact, as early as 1924 a production of the play *Flags* at Piscator's theatre had been advertised as in the **'epic'** style. However, whilst Piscator tended to use extremely sophisticated and labour-intensive staging in his productions, Brecht resisted such extravagance and remained at a cool distance, selecting most carefully what elements to employ.

Differences in meaning

There is no doubt that Brecht was influenced by the physical elements of Piscator's staging, and to an extent they shared a political agenda, but Piscator's style was more grandiose and the moral and political outcome was often swamped by the technology.

At a later date Piscator recorded the differences he noted in meaning:

> B's starting point is episodic succession.
> P's is political fatality.
> B. demonstrates it in miniature.
> P. on the big scale. I wanted to comprehend fate as a whole, showing how it is made by men and then spreads beyond them. (Hence the machinery, film etc.).
>
> [Willett, J., *The Theatre of Erwin Piscator*, 1978. p.187]

Verfremdungseffekt: see section 3.4.3

Their paths crossed again in Moscow; it was Piscator who invited Brecht to the directors' conference in 1935, where Brecht was able to see the Chinese actor Mei Lan-fang. Piscator also looked after translations and publications of Brecht's plays in the USSR.

Brecht in Hollywood

They met again in exile in 1945. While Brecht had been languishing in California, Piscator had been enjoying a productive period in New York, running a theatre school and busily influencing a new generation of American actors and playwrights.

See section 3.4.3

While acknowledging their differences on the outcome of the epic, and despite his antipathy to Brecht's concept of **Verfremdungseffekt,** Piscator could say this in 1944:

> ...it is the business of the theatre to deliver a social message and this is as important as that it should be entertaining...Mere entertainment, 'art for art's sake', is not the reason for a theatre production.

[Quoted in Willett, 1978. p.167]

Willett, J.,   *The Theatre of Erwin Piscator*,   Methuen, 1978

MARX, KARL (1818–83)

Marx and Engels as a writing partnership

It would be true to say that in the last hundred years there has not been a socialist movement that has not traced its roots to this 19th-century philosopher. He lived in extreme poverty for most of his life, supported by his friend and fellow philosopher Frederick Engels (1820–95), with whom he wrote *The Communist Manifesto* (1848).

By the time of its publication Marx was living in London, where he also began *Capital*, the uncompleted volumes of which form the core of his life's work. London was his place of exile, and it was here that he died, barely recognised for his incalculable contribution to a doctrine of political thought. (His grave in Highgate Cemetery is still a place of pilgrimage.)

Marx provided the philosophy for the Revolution of 1917

It was not until 1917 that Marx's ideas found a natural outlet. His ideology was the guiding philosophy for the Russian Revolution of that year; many of his reforming ideas were incorporated into the new state.

See chronology, 1926
Brecht never joined the Party

It was in the disturbed and chaotic political days of post-First World War Germany that Brecht moved (unsuccessfully) to join the KPD (German Communist Party), which had been founded in 1917 as a radical anti-war party.

What must be remembered is that the context of Brecht's discovery of Marx is that of a pupil finding a relatively unknown master, and his gradual 'conversion' was all the more fresh and radical for that fact.

We have listed some of Brecht's convictions (see p.316) and it is clear that they relate directly to aspects of Marxist thought:

- A deep distrust of capitalism, which is unable to solve the problems of those who live in its system.
- The worker is 'alienated' by his labour for his master.
- Capitalism can only be defeated by alliances of workers.
- History is the life of people.
- Nothing is unchanging or fixed.

The *Lehrstuck*:
see section 3.4.3

This incomplete list highlights some of Brecht's concerns, as reflected in his plays, specifically the *Lehrstuck* and *The Mother*. In the former the dialectic (argument) was part of the dramatic process, while in *The Mother* he laid down a challenge to the view that history was only a series of big events. The character and development of '*The Mother*' specifically contradicted that view.

Marx interpreted in the 20th century

Like all ideologies, Marxism was subject to interpretation and the hostile and dogmatic model in Stalin's USSR was a particularly cruel one. It is well worth reading Marx's work, in particular the *Manifesto* (1848), to discover his still relevant arguments for the implementation of an ideal socialist world.

McLellan, D.,	*Marx,*	Fontana, 1975
del Rio, E.,	*Marx for Beginners,*	Pantheon Books, 1979
Schneede, U.M.,	*George Grosz, His Life and Work,*	Gordon Fraser, 1979

(This last book contains a very clear, well-illustrated account of the political situation in Germany from the end of the First World War to the rise of Hitler.)

EXPRESSIONISM

A movement including all the arts

Strictly speaking, this heading represents no one person, since the movement known as Expressionism was a catch-all title for a huge number of artists, architects, actors, directors of theatre and film, poets and playwrights, who worked in Germany from 1905 to about 1925.

Surrealism: see section 3.3.4

Dark worlds of the subconscious

Unlike Surrealism, which published regular manifestos, this loosely grouped movement can be identified only by its common thread of ideas and themes. These took the form of a preoccupation with the 'inner' person and the soul's journey, and a fascination for the irrational, madness and the dark world of the subconscious. Many of the most striking visual statements from this period represent a distorted and tortured view of the world, with angular and thrusting shapes that threaten to overpower the individual.

The movement of 'new objectivity'

Brecht's dislike of Expressionism

In theatre the movement was dominant before and just after the First World War, but by the time Brecht was writing his first plays this dominance was threatened by a 'new objectivity'. It is only in photographs of the first production of *Drums in the Night* (1922) that we have tangible evidence of an expressionist designer working on Brecht's work. Brecht disliked the production and Expressionism in general, since it placed so much emphasis on irrational dream worlds, and his writing soon lost any trace of expressionist influence.

Baal: see section 3.4.3

Source material

Baal, written in 1918 but not produced for some years, is the closest in form to an expressionist 'journey' play, with its emphasis on nature and the highly charged emotionalism of its hero. However, as we have noted earlier, the text was indebted to Buchner for its form and since Buchner also influenced the Expressionists Brecht inevitably shared some of their characteristics. But Brecht's distinctive voice was not to be tied to one movement; he took from the past what he needed and moved forward to create his own very personal style.

3.4.5 FOLLOWERS

Brecht is the key figure of our time, and all theatre work today at some point starts or returns to his statements and achievement.

[Brook, P., *The Empty Stage*, Penguin, 1986. p.80]

With this statement in mind, we have been very selective in choosing the practitioners in this section. Since it is acknowledged that Brecht's theory and practice have helped to change the direction of Western theatre in all its aspects, there is a long list of those we might discuss. Section 4.4.6 will suggest a number of areas for further research.

THE ENGLISH STAGE COMPANY

Based at the Royal Court Theatre

This was a company of directors, actors, designers and technical staff, created in 1956 by George Devine and Tony Richardson, which made its home at the Royal Court Theatre. One of the aims of the company was the encouragement of new writing, and with this initiative were linked new departures in design and a resident 'ensemble' of directors.

Visits to the Berliner Ensemble

Devine and others had visited the Berliner Ensemble in 1955 and there is no doubt that many of the decisions on company policy, particularly the design concepts, were confirmed by that visit.

The critic Ken Tynan promoted Brecht's theatre

In 1956 the Berliner Ensemble first visited Britain, where its season created a sensation. The influential critic Ken Tynan characterised the impression made, referring to the 'economy of staging, the lack of emotion, illusion and identification'. There was no talk of the politics, which was not surprising, since commentaries on Brecht's theory were not published for a further three years.

A production was 'imported' from the Ensemble

From the earliest days of the English Stage Company's history there was a desire to promote Brecht; he was not only a role model for the policy of the company but a 'new writer'. The company immediately mounted *The Good Person of Setzuan* (1956), with Peggy Ashcroft in the lead. The original designs were imported from Berlin and were adapted and recreated in London by Jocelyn Herbert.

It is worth noting that other equally radical new writing was emerging from the Royal Court during the same period, in the form of *Look Back in Anger* by John Osborne. This was typical of what could be termed 'new realism', with an examination of social class issues not hitherto seen on the English stage.

The work of the director William Gaskill and the designer Jocelyn Herbert

The issue of Brecht in English is best illustrated by an examination of two parallel careers in theatre, those of the director William Gaskill and the designer Jocelyn Herbert. Gaskill admits that Brecht 'changed my life'; he went on to work on a number of the plays, with Jocelyn Herbert as designer. They collaborated on *Baal* (1963) and in 1965 on *Mother Courage* at the National Theatre.

Influenced by Brecht

Looking at Herbert's designs it becomes clear how closely she and Gaskill followed the 'Brechtian' ethic: the plays are 'storyboarded' and in the case of *Mother Courage* Herbert admits that, '…despite myself, I got closer and closer to Brecht's production'. It seemed as if her own design instincts met with his text and the outcome became, in a sense, inevitable.

The following is worth quoting in full, since it admirably sums up how Gaskill saw the twin functions of Epic theatre and how this related to his designer who, in collaboration, provided the visual solutions.

> Brecht's Epic theatre is both aesthetic and didactic. Aesthetic because it makes beautiful pictures, didactic because the dramatist/director makes the audience focus on what will be instructive, moving his pointer round the stage like a school teacher on a blackboard … With Brecht no-one is so important that he may occupy the centre line. Often Brecht divides the stage in contrasting groups, which make a dialectic [debate] when seen together.

[Gaskill, 1988. p.19]

Other writers influenced by Brecht

Gaskill went on to help found the Joint Stock Theatre Group, where dramatists such as Howard Brenton and Caryl Churchill first workshopped their scripts. Both these writers, in turn, owe much to Brecht, and in the staging of the texts they both imply 'what will be instructive'.

Gaskill, W.,	*A Sense of Direction*,	Faber, 1988
Herbert, J.,	*A Theatre Workbook*,	Art Books International, 1993
Wardle, I.,	*The Theatres of George Devine*,	Methuen, 1978

LITTLEWOOD, JOAN (BORN 1914)

Ewan McColl, folk-singer

Joan Littlewood began what we might call a classical training at RADA but, disillusioned with theatre, cut it short and in 1934 made her life in Manchester. She very quickly became associated with socialist theatre groups, where she met Ewan McColl, writer, actor and folk-singer, who was to have a great influence on her life.

Agitprop:
see Piscator, p.320

It was an exciting period for agitprop theatre. Littlewood's group evolved a philosophy that had much in common with Brecht's theories, though at this time there would have been little, if anything, available in English. There was, however, a great deal of contact with other left-wing groups who shared similar ideas, and this prompted the following statement of aims:

A socialist manifesto

- an awareness of the social issues of the time, and in that sense, a political theatre;
- a theatrical language that working people could understand, but that was capable of reflecting, when necessary, ideas, either simple or involved, in a poetic form;
- an expressive and flexible form of movement, and a high standard of skill and technique in acting;
- a high level of technical expertise capable of integrating sound and light into the production.

[Quoted in Goorney, 1981. p.8]

Formation of the Theatre Workshop

It was in 1952, 20 years after the first Manchester productions, that the Theatre Workshop under Littlewood's direction, came to rest in London.

Ideals of European practitioners

Many of the ideals that Littlewood had worked towards in those years came to fruition at the permanent base in Stratford East. The theories of European practitioners were realised in production, directing, design and above all teaching. For Littlewood, like Brecht, theatre was a collaborative venture:

Collaboration

> I do not believe in the supremacy of the director, designer, actor or even the writer. It is through collaboration that this knockabout theatre survives and kicks . . .

[Marovitz, C., *The Encore Reader*, Methuen, 1970. p.230]

Brecht was a positive influence

Certainly Littlewood knew her Brecht. As early as 1938 she was working on a production of the Piscator/Brecht version of *The Good Soldier Schweik* and in 1955 she played the lead in *Mother Courage*. However, it is not so much for these isolated productions that she is included in this study; it is because, in a basically apolitical English theatre, she

Challenge to bourgeois ideals

represented a challenge to all its bourgeois ideals through the vitality of her work and those people she influenced.

Littlewood broke up the dominance of the commercial theatre

> Joan broke up the fabric of the English theatre, [. . .] We now look for our dramatic sustenance elsewhere . . . to the fringe, the Repertory companies and . . . the National and the RSC. I'm convinced this change would never have taken place without the erosion of the bourgeois theatre and its commercial organisation, by Joan.

[Harold Hobson, quoted in Goorney, 1981. p.183]

Goorney, H.,   *The Theatre Workshop Story*,   Methuen, 1981

3.4.6 SUMMARY: BERTOLT BRECHT

This summary is written to draw together certain parts of the chapter on Bertolt Brecht under particular headings. It should be considered with the student's own practical work in mind and/or the student's viewing of other productions. For example, Brecht's Epic Theatre: as a student undertaking practical work you would wish to discuss the theories of alienation/distancing by the actor as reflected in your own work. By adopting this convention/practice not only are you enhancing your own approach but you are able to make use of the practice when viewing other productions.

THE SUBJECT MATTER
Narratives are displaced in time and place
Political parables
Epic storytelling

THE POLITICAL PURPOSE OR MESSAGE OR DRAMATIC INTENTION
Heavily influenced by political ideals. Karl Marx
To arouse in the audience a need for change
To keep an audience thinking

THE ACTOR–AUDIENCE RELATIONSHIP
The role of the narrator/chorus. Direct address
The isolating of songs as a form of comment
The abolition of illusion
The audience encouraged to smoke and drink

THE STAGING FORM ADOPTED	The proscenium arch Epic as opposed to dramatic (Aristotelian) Swiftly changing scenes
DIRECTORIAL INTERPRETATION /PRODUCTION STYLE	The director as part of a team The use of music to comment on the action Very refined and specific detail Clear and carefully constructed stage pictures
DESIGN ELEMENTS	Realistic selective detail Very well-made props Costumes made to look well worn
ROLE OF ACTORS AND PERFORMANCE STYLE	The actor in a role not a character The actor as demonstrator The actor as the main source of distancing The use of gestus
TECHNICAL ELEMENTS	Hard white light from a visible source The half-curtain The revolve
AUDIENCE RESPONSE	The be alerted to the need for change To observe rather than empathise

3.4.7 SUGGESTIONS FOR FURTHER STUDY

PLAYS

Oh What a Lovely War (1963) Theatre Workshop Company

A musical drama based on events in the First World War, devised by Joan Littlewood's company. The cast performed in pierrot costumes recalling seaside shows of the period and added bits of uniform to suggest their characters. Popular songs were juxtaposed with subtitles showing numbers of casualties from the trenches. A classic piece that adapted 'Brechtian' theory into practice.

Vinegar Tom (1976) Caryl Churchill

The theme of the play is witchcraft in the 17th century, related to the lives of women in a small rural village, where jealousy and suspicion lead to a mass hanging. Short scenes are contrasted with songs that draw parallels with feminist issues from the 20th century.

Sergeant Musgrave's Dance (1960) John Arden

A group of recruiting soldiers visit a northern town in some unspecified past time and create havoc with their unwelcome pacifist attitudes to war and its outcomes. Prose, verse and songs mixed together give the play its anti-naturalist flavour.

MUSICAL THEATRE

Assassins (1991) Stephen Sondheim

A heavily satirical piece, detailing the lives and motives of some of those who have sought to assassinate American presidents. It is set in the imagined world of a fairground, and each character is given an episode in which to justify his action. A narrator is used as a linking device. Heavily influenced by Brechtian techniques such as distancing and the use of songs in the telling of the story.

EXPRESSIONISM

PAINTING Vassily Kandinsky, 1866–1944; Emil Nolde, 1867–1956; Franz Marc, 1880–1916.

THEATRE Oscar Kokoschka, *Murder Hope of Womankind* (1916); August Stramm, *Sancta Susanna* (1918); Georg Kaiser, *From Morn to Midnight* (1917); Walter Hasenclever, *The Son* (1916).

FILM *The Cabinet of Doctor Caligari* (1919); *Der Müde Tod* (1921); *Metropolis* (1926).

POETRY August Stramm (1874–1915).

3.4.8 BIBLIOGRAPHY

PRIMARY SOURCES

Bartram, G. and Waine, A.	*Brecht in Perspective*	Longman, 1982	Very useful chapters on all aspects of theory and practice, with a retrospective overview.
Benjamin, W.	*Understanding Brecht*	Verso, 1992	Written from first-hand knowledge of Brecht's theory.
Brecht, B. (trans. Willet, J.)	*The Messingkauf Dialogues*	Methuen, 1965	
Willet, J. (ed.) and Manheim, R.	*Poems 1913–1956*	Methuen, 1979	
Fuegi, J.	*Bertolt Brecht: Chaos, According to Plan*	CUP, 1987	The most recent biography.

Fuegi, J.	*The Life and Lies of Bertolt Brecht*	Harper Collins, 1994	In which he examines the real authorship of the plays.
Spiers, R.	*Brecht's Early Plays*	Macmillan, 1982	Very useful.
Styan, J.L.	*Modern Drama in Theory and Practice, Vol. 3: Expressionism and Epic Theatre*	CUP, 1986	One of a series of three. Very useful, well indexed and cross-referenced.
Thomson, P. and Sacks, G.	*Brecht: The Cambridge Companion*	CUP, 1994	This covers a lot of the theory in some detail.
Willett, J.	*Brecht in Context*	Methuen, 1984	
Willett, J. (ed.)	*Brecht on Theatre* (abbreviated to Willett/BT in the text)	Methuen, 1984	Willett has translated original statements and articles by Brecht.
Willett, J.	*Caspar Neher, Brecht's Designer*	Methuen, 1986	
Willett, J.	*The Theatre of Bertolt Brecht*	Methuen, 1993	
Wright, E.	*Postmodern Brecht*	Routledge, 1989	From a refreshingly new perspective.

FURTHER SOURCES

Brecht Edition	*Tulane Drama Review* Vol. 12, No. 1, Fall 1967
Article on Caspar Neher pp. 135–45	*Tulane Drama Review* Vol. 12, No. 2, Winter 1968
Brecht on Stage – videotape A319/16V (24 mins.)	Open University Educational Enterprises, 1992
Brecht Songs – audiotape A319 16Z	Open University Educational Enterprises, 1992

3.4.9 QUESTION AND SUGGESTED FRAMEWORK FOR ANSWER ON BERTOLT BRECHT

'The beauty of Brechtian settings is not the dazzling kind that begs for applause. It is the more durable beauty of use.' (Kenneth Tynan, quoted in *Brecht in Perspective*, p.212)

With reference to Brecht's theories and his productions, discuss the contribution set design and costume made to his Epic Theatre.

POINTS TO CONSIDER

- You will need to be able to summarise Epic Theatre.
- It would be advisable to have examples of Brecht's productions, not just the texts, in mind to which you can refer.
- You are concentrating on set and costume design, but these were only part of the collaborative process.
- Be aware of the relevance of the quotation.

A DETAILED ANALYSIS

Introduction

Give a summary of Epic Theatre, differentiating Dramatic and Epic. Mention the nature of collaboration in Brecht's work and the importance of set and costume design in that collaborative method of working.

Explain the quote. What does 'the dazzling kind that begs for applause' mean? What does Tynan mean when he refers to 'the more durable beauty of use'? Say that you intend to refer to certain of Brecht's productions to demonstrate Tynan's point.

Main body

Lay out Brecht's views on set and costume design. Use quotations where appropriate. Pay particular attention to collaboration. As you discuss the various points, mention appropriate productions: for example, *Mother Courage*. Discuss the symbolic wagon, which was so carefully constructed, the simple staging with the huge revolve that gave the impression of an epic journey and costumes that were broken down to look old and well worn. You may wish to mention the audience reception of these methods of staging.

Conclusion

Explain if you agree with Tynan. Then move on to discuss briefly the effect that Brecht's method of working had on dramatic writing and staging in the later 20th century.

3.5 *Jerzy Grotowski (1933–1999)*

Figure 3e   A sketch of Jerzy Grotowski

3.5.1 A CHRONOLOGY

Born in Eastern Europe

1933: Born in Rzeszow in Eastern Poland and remained there throughout the Second World War. The concentration camp Auschwitz is 60 miles away. He loses a year's schooling due to serious illness.

1945–6: Poland is occupied and administered by the Soviet Union.

1951: Applied for admission as a student to the State Theatre School in Cracow.

1953: Death of Stalin. Poland begins to experience a definite weakening of Soviet influence.

As actor, begins to explore world theatre

1955: Awarded an actor's diploma by the State Theatre School of Cracow. Attended a directing course at the State Institution of Theatre in Moscow. He studies the work of Stanislavski, Meyerhold and Vakhtangov.

1956: Travels to Central Asia. Becomes interested in Eastern philosophy. An active participant in the socialist youth movement, publishing dissident articles in support of de-Stalinisation.

1957: Visits France for the first time: International Youth Meeting, Avignon. Visits Paris.

Trains as director

1956–9: Director's training at the Stary Teatr in Cracow.

1959: Visits Paris. Meets the mime artist Marcel Marceau and is impressed.

FIRST PHASE 1959–69: THEATRE OF PERFORMANCE

Becomes director of a small susidised theatre

1959: Becomes director of the small provincial theatre – Teatr 13 Rzedow (Theatre of 13 Rows) – in Opole, Silesia, at the invitation of Ludwik Flaszen, critic. Flaszen is to remain as literary advisor and collaborator throughout the existence of what becomes known as the Laboratory Theatre. A very small subsidy sustains the work. Première of *Orpheus* by Jean Cocteau (1892–1963).

1960: Receives his professional Director's Diploma. A production of *Cain* by Byron. Poorly attended; the company's future in doubt. Final production of the first season is Mayakovsky's *Mystery-Bouffe* (first directed by Meyerhold in 1921).

Barba joins him

1961: *Dziady* (Forefather's Eve) by Adam Mickiewicz. Total integration of the spectators into the action. Eugenio Barba joins the company as assistant. Becomes recorder and popularises Grotowski's work in the West.

1962: *Kordian* by Julius Slowacki. Set in a mental hospital; the spectators become patients as well as audience. Followed by *Akropolis* by Stanislaw Wyspianski; the text is transposed to Auschwitz, where the spectators are forced to watch the most brutalising events at close quarters. His assistant is Eugenio Barba, who is to edit much of *Towards a Poor Theatre* (first published in English in 1969).

Travels to the West

This production tours extensively and introduces the work of the Laboratory Theatre to the West. Finland in 1962 and Warsaw in 1963.

1963: *Doctor Faustus* based on Christoper Marlowe's text. Restricted audience numbers are engulfed in the action.

1964: *The Hamlet Study.*

The Laboratory Theatre: Institute of Research into Acting Method

1965: The group move to Wroclaw, an academic centre in south-west Poland and change their name to Laboratory Theatre: Institute of Research into Acting Method. Systematic actor training now becomes the dominant work of the Institute. Many influences are in evidence including those of Meyerhold and his 'biomechanics', classical Chinese and Japanese theatre and the Kathakali dance drama of India.

1965: January: *Akropolis*.
April: *The Constant Prince*, based on Calderon's Spanish original. The elimination of plot and character. With Ryszard Cieslak, one of the original members of the company. (It is in the role of the Prince that Cieslak is a revelation to a Western audience, and becomes recognised as an extraordinary talent.)

Visits Brook in London at the RSC

1966: Is invited by Peter Brook (who knew of his work and writings) to conduct a workshop for his production of *U.S* with the RSC. The result is profoundly disturbing to actors trained in the English tradition.

1967: Gives workshops at New York University's School of the Arts. Meets Richard Schechner who has just formed The Performance Group, and Joseph Chaikin with his Open Theatre. He is immensely influential in the traditions they establish (see Followers, Section 3.5.5). Intense preparation for the next production combined with world tours.

Publication of *Towards a Poor Theatre*

1968: Publishes *Towards a Poor Theatre* in Denmark, edited by Eugenio Barba.

SECOND PHASE 1969–75 THEATRE OF PARTICIPATION

1969: *Apocalypsis cum Figuris*, a montage of 20th-century writing. The final production of The Laboratory Theatre. It was performed in various versions for the next ten years, and was regularly a curtain-raiser to workshops promoting the group's work.

Retires from production

1970: Experiences increasing disillusionment with the creative process. Announces his retirement from theatre. Journeys made alone to India and Kurdistan profoundly influence his work.

Works on 'paratheatre'

1970–5: Works with an enlarged group on what becomes known as **'paratheatre'**. Undertaken in a rural retreat it involves selected participants in what some critics termed release or encounter therapy. In June of 1975 the work is shared at a huge conference attended by Peter Brook, Jean-Louis Barrault, Joseph Chaikin, Eugenio Barba.

More interested in personal therapy

1975–7: The work is now directed by Jacek Zmyslowski, overseen by Grotowski. What becomes known as *The Mountain Project* takes its participants on a three-step journey spread over three days that is both physically and mentally exhausting. By now there is a definite move away from pure theatre towards a 'life experience' for all concerned.

1977: The work begins to fragment.

THIRD PHASE: THEATRE OF SOURCES 1976–82

1976–82: An intercultural group study yoga, voodoo, Sufi whirling, meditation, martial-arts training. Research continues. Leaves Poland during period of martial law.

1983: Becomes Professor at the School of Fine Arts at the University of California, Irvine. Requests political asylum.

1984: The Laboratory Theatre is dissolved.

1986: Forms the Workcentre of Jerzy Grotowski at the Centro per la Sperimentazione e la Ricerca Teatrale in Pontedera, Italy. Begins to realise the process of 'handing on' his teaching to Thomas Richards.

1990: Still actively involved in teaching and seminars at Irvine.

1992: Work ceases at Irvine.

1995: Thomas Richards publishes account of his latest work in *At Work with Grotowski on **Physical Actions***.

1999: Dies, aged 66.

3.5.2 A BRIEF BIOGRAPHY

When Jerzy Grotowski died in 1999, it was 30 years since the publication of his seminal book *Towards a Poor Theatre*. All his life he had relied on others to record his work, from Eugenio Barba on behalf of the Theatre of 13 Rows to that of his most recent disciple Thomas Richards, who in 1995 published an account of the work done in the last phase of his life, in Italy.

An intensely private individual, he gave his whole life to the exploration of the actor's relationship with his audience, and when he felt he had exhausted that challenge, he gave it all up and moved on to an even more intense period, which became known as 'paratheatre'. Here an invited public joined 'the work'. He never returned to the theatre as we know it, instead endlessly travelling and giving workshops and after a period as a professor of drama in the United States retired to relative seclusion in Italy.

The fact that Poland was an occupied country during Grotowski's most formative years is important; not only did the state provide him with the education he desired but when he set up the Laboratory Theatre in 1965 it gave him a small subsidy on which to survive, an enlightened act in a country so wary of freedom of speech. After a burst of political agitation while a student, once established at The Laboratory he forsook any political activity and over a relatively short time established what turned out to be one of the most influential theatre movements of this century.

When discussing Grotowski it is important to remember that of all the practitioners in this section he had the most thorough and extensive training as a director. Not only did he participate in a formal university course, but his subsequent subsidised travels, first to Russia and then to the Near and Far East, gave him unique insights into expressions of cultural diversity. It was this broad range of influences that he was able to harness in the work with his actors, in what he considered as 'scientific' study, drawing around him a small but trusted and totally committed group of writers, critics, actors and designers.

Much of the history of theatre can be analysed through movements that at any one time have sought to challenge stifling contemporary practice.

A radical practitioner
Sought to return to basic
roots of mythic and religious
symbolism

The last century is no exception and the radicalism of Grotowski is perhaps the finest example of a practitioner who sought to return theatre to its most basic roots of mythic and religious symbolism.

Grotowski's training had been dominated by the straitjacket of a Soviet-based culture and specifically 'realism', which was imposed on all the arts from the highest level. Grotowski's challenge was to question prevailing practice and to do so with a radical alternative, and he did this in a remarkably short time. From 1961, with his production of *Dziady*, to the final *Apocalypsis cum Figuris* in 1969 he had accomplished what he set out to do and had codified and published the experiments in *Towards a Poor Theatre*.

Experiments in Poor Theatre

In the harsh conditions of Western post-war commercial theatre it is hard to see how such a theatre could have survived in a world beyond what became known as 'the iron curtain'. Indeed, when a thaw in East–West relations allowed the Laboratory Theatre to travel in 1965, it was a revelation to those restricted audiences who saw the work, because to all intents and purposes it had been secret.

A revelation to a Western
audience

It would be wrong to suggest that Grotowski's theatre was exclusive or even elitist, though it must be admitted that few people saw the initial performances. Based on his belief that the audience needed to be shocked 'to get at those psychic layers behind the life-mask' [*Towards a Poor Theatre*, p.23] by the experience of total theatre, rather than by political arguments, the only solution was to confront the audience with 'close encounters' that demanded a spiritual re-examination on the part of the spectator.

Few people witnessed the
experiments

Confrontations led to spiritual
examination

With a number of international directors following his lead, the concept of 'laboratory theatre' began to be copied, but most of the experiments were considered by Grotowski as indulgent and undigested and indeed there were too many companies who, working in small, dark converted cellars, considered themselves faithful to the values of Poor Theatre.

Laboratory Theatre was much
copied

Grotowski's initiative in moving forward from performance was to take his loyal actors and begin the experiments that became known as 'paratheatre'. Community based and open to a selected public, these workshops had much to do with a desire to form new relationships with the natural world and developed into what one observer called: 'the confrontation of a man or a group of people with the open or prescribed space where their contact with others and with the phenomena of the perceptible world becomes the "work" itself.' [Quoted in Kumiega, 1987. p.166.]

New experiments in
paratheatre

Relationship with the natural
world

What transpired both in Poland and later in America was extended periods of time (which became known as 'special projects') when people living and working together created 'a natural human rhythm, freed from normal social constraints and determined by the bodies' own impulses' [Bradby and Williams, 1988. p.141].

Special projects

(These experiments can be compared to the rural retreats of Jacques Copeau (1879–1949) and his company in the wilds of Burgundy in 1925.)

Again Grotowski moved on and in 1975 was involved in what became known as the 'mountain project', another attempt at breaking down the final barriers between theatre and life. Throughout this period he had

Begins to lose control of
Laboratory Theatre

gradually relinquished control over the activities of the Laboratory Theatre and in 1984 at its final dissolution his name was absent from the list of signatories.

Martin Esslin in his obituary said:

A unique charisma

His total dedication, his saint-like integrity, and his quixotic striving for an unattainable ideal created a personality of unique charisma and lasting importance.

[*The Guardian*, 20.1.99]

Mystical relationship between
actor and audience

In retrospect *Towards a Poor Theatre* first and foremost placed the actor at the core of theatre practice at a time when the decorative/realist tradition was still dominant, and it refocused a whole generation on the essential and mystical relationship between an actor and his audience. As a document it will stand alongside *The Art of the Theatre* by Gordon Craig, *An Actor Prepares* by Stanislavski, *The Short Organum* by Brecht, *The Theatre and its Double* by Artaud and *The Empty Space* by Peter Brook, as a vital and challenging theatre document.

3.5.3 THEORY AND PRACTICE

INTRODUCTION

It is important to remember that Grotowski's overriding concern was to

. . . inaugurate a procedure of staging in which each production became an experiment per se in some aspect of the **actor/audience** spatial relationship . . .

[Kumiega, 1987. p.18].

Experiments had little effect
on contemporary theatre

What makes theatre unique?

Looking back now from the perspective of over 30 years it is possible to see that Grotowski's work, although much praised and copied by a number of practitioners at the time had little or no effect on a moribund commercial theatre. It is still questionable whether his policy for a 'poor theatre' has any relevance. In our high-tech, image-driven, short-attention-span world the idea of 'stripping away' to the essentials is a debatable aesthetic ideal. But Grotowski's point was: **what makes theatre unique?** and in asking that question he was driven to the conclusion that it is only the actor and the actor alone who can give us the spiritual and mythic experiences we seek, and which we so conspicuously lack in both our everyday lives and today's theatre.

Two distinct strands

This uniqueness was composed of two strands:

● the foregrounding of the actor as a holy and spiritual figure;

● the establishment of a unique and confrontational environment for each new production.

Synthesis

As we shall see from the close analysis of his productions that follows, these two strands became inextricably linked; it was the powerful result of this synthesis that so impressed and excited his privileged audience.

British Fringe

One of the most tangible signs of Grotowski's influence was the emergence in the 1960s in Britain of the so-called 'fringe' movement. Here the principle of small, intimate playing spaces with a limited number of audience led to visceral and emotionally charged experiences. However, it should be noted that, contrary to Grotowski's thinking, there was still a tendency for formal and fixed seating.

The actor in physical theatre

The actor took longer to emerge and when he did so, this could be recognised as being more in the mould of a generalised European tradition than in a specifically 'Grotowskian' form, which led in the 1980s to the movement we know as 'physical theatre'. This new theatre consciously drew from the continental tradition of the actor as 'comedian', a versatile and highly skilled actor whose intense **physical** presence was his overriding attribute. It was this theatre that could be recognised as having its roots in the experiments of the Laboratory Theatre.

The actor as the core of creation

Studying Grotowski we are reminded that in a theatre which has been dominated by the director and the mise-en-scène, we are in danger of losing touch with the actor as the core of creation.

Theoretical leads to the practical

A brief survey of the productions that led Grotowski 'Towards a Poor Theatre' will reveal theoretical perspectives as they developed alongside his unique practice. The first significant production in which tentative experiments led to new forms of staging was *Cain* in 1960.

CAIN 1960

Actors move into the auditorium

This production, although staged on the tiny platform at the end of the 'Theatre of 13 Rows', was the first consciously to move the actors into the auditorium. The actors addressed the audience directly and the audience themselves were given the roles of Cain's descendants. Despite the poverty of the theatre itself, quite elaborate stage techniques were used including loudspeakers through which the actor's text was broadcast, and in performance the actors displayed a high degree of physicality. This view by a contemporary critic gives a flavour of the work:

Styles of acting change

> In addition there is caricature, parody, satire, vaudeville, an operatic sketch, mime, a little ballet scene, and beside all that – an irreverent attitude towards the text. . . . There are continual changes in the acting . . . an actor among the audience, actors addressing the public, actors improvising during scene changes.
>
> [Quoted in Kumiega, 1987. p.24]

A wide range of sources

There is evidence of a very wide range of sources, all harnessed to the narrative, but the actors, despite their freedom to break out of the presentational mode, by all accounts remained mere puppets in the hands of a manipulative director.

DZIADY (FOREFATHER'S EVE) 1961

An intensely patriotic text that harked back to Poland's Romantic period, 'its loose form permitted a creative rather than representational response' [Kumiega, 1987. p.35], a hallmark of all future work; there was nothing sacrosanct about any text.

Scenic architect to design space

In this first most significant collaboration with his 'scenic architect', spectators were dotted at random around the space on little islands of chairs, the action taking place behind and around these groups. The audience's awareness of each other and their individual fragmented view of the production were both part of a performance style which sought to integrate the audience into what Grotowski called 'the relationship between ritual and play'. It was as if Grotowski was reinventing a treasured national myth in the terms of a child's playground, the actors encouraging a distanced participation in 'ceremony'.

Integration of audience into action

While Grotowski and the Laboratory Theatre were engaged in mounting a number of productions a rigorous and demanding training programme was being undertaken, and as that became more intensive the daily regime became separate from preparation for performance, work on 'self' became as important as the company's collaborations.

A training programme was started

To use scientific terminology, the productions were demonstrations of the **experiments** in **the Laboratory Theatre**, where work was **tested** by exposure to an audience. Grotowski always maintained a strict control over the number of people who at any one time shared in these experiments, a position that led to tensions and resentment when so many people wanted to share in his work. But in order for the vulnerable spectator to be brought face to face with the shock of seeing the actor

Productions are demonstrations of experiments

> ... divesting her or himself of the social, conditioned layers of the psyche, and revealing themselves at a level beneath the individual or personal.
>
> [Kumiega, 1987. p.132]

it was imperative that an intimate and intense relationship be created with him or her.

Vulnerable spectators in a confrontational theatre

TRAINING

Kumiega points out:

> ... There is very little in the way of technique that is in any sense unique to the Laboratory Theatre, an objective result of their research to be passed on.
>
> [1985. p.112]

This short statement summarises many of the dilemmas of studying Grotowski's training for the actor. A large section of *Towards a Poor Theatre* is devoted to just such a subject, but the danger as Grotowski saw it was that in writing down the many exercises he practised with the company, he was expected to endorse them as a path or 'method' for an actor's training. He very firmly resisted this idea:

The dilemma of recording technique

> In the final analysis there are no prescriptions. For every individual one must discover the cause which impedes him, hampers him, and then create the situation in which this cause can be eliminated and the process liberated.
>
> [Quoted in Kumiega, 1985. p.111].

Each individual makes his own discovery

In other words every actor had to find his own pathway. This attitude led to all sorts of confusions but it was the main reason that the company travelled so extensively during the late 1960s, performing and giving workshops, passing on at first hand what seemed so vital and extraordinary about their work.

The daily training for the actors of the Laboratory Theatre really took off while preparing the productions of *Doctor Faustus* (1963) and *The Constant Prince* (1965). Three categories of work developed:

Three categories of work
- exercises *plastiques*;
- exercises *corporels*;
- vocal and respiratory work.

These are well described in Actors Training (1959–62) in *Towards a Poor Theatre*, but briefly:

The *plastiques* the ***plastiques*** involved rotations of head, elbows, wrists, chest, hips and torso, the joints and limbs going in opposite or contradictory directions.

Body memory where impulses are released Grotowski related these exercises to what he called 'body memory', a belief that 'our entire body *is* memory, and it is by means of the "body memory" that the impulses are released' [Kumiega, 1985. p.120]. He went on to suggest that this 'memory' was only waiting to be released from a body which had stored certain experiences of life.

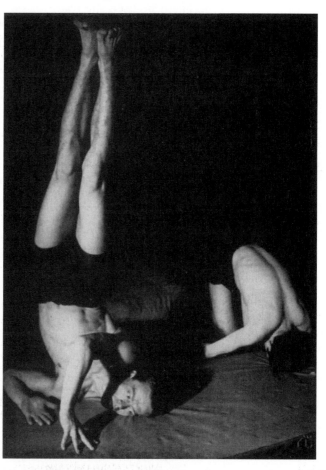

Figure 3.27 During training – which is part of the rehearsal process – each muscle is brought under the conscious control of the actor. Many of the exercises are drawn from yoga and the Chinese and Japanese classical theatres.

(The *'plastiques'* were to some extent based on the work of Jacques-Dalcroze, who had inspired Adolphe Appia (1862–1928) to develop his rhythmic spaces of 1910.)

The *corporels*

The *corporels* were based on the need for suppleness in the spine, the most well-known exercise being 'the cat'; a series of acrobatic jumps, somersaults, and stands all related to the freeing-up of the actor in space. Grotowski located the seat of this work in the base of the vertebral column and the lower pelvic area of the abdomen, both sites connected with yoga, for which these areas held a special meaning as concentrations of life's energy. By nature of their derivation they owed much to Grotowski's enthusiasm for Far-Eastern philosophies.

Exercises connected with yoga

Vocal and respiratory work

Vocal and respiratory work was considered to be a process of what Grotowski called 'unblocking', a physical as much as a psychological condition. Grotowski urged:

> Use the air. Don't economise. Take air when it's necessary, and afterwards don't economise on it. It is that that works, it's not only the vocal apparatus but the outbreath.

> [Quoted in Kumiega, 1987. p.124]

And again he used the traditions of yoga to illustrate his point:

> It is well known that the different schools of yoga – including Hatha Yoga – demand the daily practice of respiratory techniques in order to control and exploit the biological function of breathing which has become automatic.

> [Grotowski, 1981. p.116]

Five types of resonator

Grotowski goes on to discuss what he calls 'resonators', which he breaks down into:

- the upper or head resonator
- the chest resonator
- the nasal resonator
- the laryngeal resonator
- the occipital resonator.

Component parts are brought together

But he concludes his discussion with the statement that: 'the most fruitful possibility lies in the use of the *entire body* as a resonator' [ibid. p.123]. Like the breaking-down of gesture into component parts which are then brought together in performance as part of an actor's language, so too with the voice.

What should be emphasised is that while this intensive training was taking place, regular performances were testing the theoretical in practice, what might be called

> . . . the tuning of an instrument before a recital.

> [Bradby and Williams, 1988. p.123].

More interested in process than product

In fact, despite the extraordinary power of his productions, which stunned a receptive audience, Grotowski insisted time and again that he was interested more in process than product.

To sum up:

- Training was just as important as performance;
- It was intensely physical;
- It sought to isolate specific movements;
- The actor was to be a receptive and creative being.

KORDIAN 1962

The text, complex and disturbing, again from the Romantic period, details one man's search for personal salvation through self-sacrifice on behalf of his country. Judged insane, he is sent to an asylum where ultimately he is found not to be mad and consequently condemned to death.

The audience distributed through space

The spectators become part of the audience

The key to the production was the asylum, which it was decided would form the setting for the entire play (see Fig. 3.28). The tiered beds formed the basic acting areas with some of the spectators seated on the beds, on chairs distributed fairly randomly both on the floor and on raised areas (presumably to help with sightlines). Actors used the beds as performance platforms but the action in general was non-specific. Audience participation was encouraged in one scene with the singing of a song, a doctor in a white coat threatening anyone who did not do so. By virtue of their proximity to the actors the spectators became patients/inmates and as such became responsible for the fate of the protagonist, Kordian. At the moment that a doctor bled Kordian, representative of the hero giving blood for his motherland, Grotowski recalls that there were 'hysterical cries among the spectators' and noted with satisfaction that

very deep national values were attacked in order to revalue them.

[Schechner and Wolford, 1997. p.46].

Figure 3.28   A sketch of the setting for *Kordian*.

One of Grotowski's main aims had been accomplished, to reward the spectator who had

Confrontational situations

genuine spiritual needs, and who really wishes, through confrontation with the performance, to analyse himself.

[Grotowski, 1981. p.40].

AKROPOLIS 1962

Montage as a means of constructing a text

Akropolis was one of the first real international successes of the Laboratory Theatre, and marked Grotowski's first attempt at what he called 'montage'. This term derived from the Russian film-maker Sergei Eisenstein (1898–1948) and was an idea adopted by both Meyerhold and Brecht (see Brecht 3.4.2). Grotowski would have come across the concept during his Moscow training (see Chronology, section 3.5.1). In *Akropolis* he edited several texts together into the final version, allowing him to fragment the action in short highly motivated scenes.

Actors and audience separated

The audience were seated in a raised corridor formation and Grotowski, for the first time, deliberately kept actor and audience at a distance (see Fig. 3.29). In the middle of the room was another raised box onto which were piled the props and items to be used throughout the play, fulfilling Grotowski's insistence that nothing should be introduced into the space that wasn't there from the beginning.

They are two separate and mutually impenetrable worlds: those who have been initiated into ultimate experiences, and the outsiders who know only the everyday life; the dead and the living.

[Quoted in Kumiega, 1987. p.61]

The dead in this case were the resurrected survivors of Auschwitz concentration camp into which the setting had been transposed. Bearing in

Figure 3.29   Sketch of the arrangement of the audience at *Akropolis* (above) and the transformation of the theatre into crematoria for the end of the performance (below).

Figure 3.30   Jacob courts Rebecca in *Akropolis.*

Props were used to construct the setting

mind the relatively recent revelations about the camp (1945) and the fact that it had been on Polish soil, the decision was explosive. By the end of the play, the metallic scrap from the central area had been used to transform the theatre; hanging from the roof on ropes the pipes represented the re-creation of the crematoria into which the actors disappeared at the end. Sacking with holes revealed torn flesh, and clogs on their feet turned the actors into an anonymous group. In their search

Facial masks

for non-emotive expressions the actors had been working on 'facial masks' derived from studies of the Kathakali, with each individual face a reflection of the body's tensions and emotional temperature.

Parallels with Expressionism

It is worth mentioning that more than one critic has drawn parallels between much of this work and performances by the Expressionist actor (see Innes 1993, p.45). Specifically Innes discusses the role played by the 'ecstatic' style of acting so associated with the epic productions of Max Reinhardt, in which the actor sought through his excessive emotionalism to 'evoke the same emotional state in the spectators'. This is a very similar aim to that of Grotowski and the overriding reason why he insisted upon such small and intimate spaces in which to confront his audience.

To sum up:

- Montage was used as a method of assembling text;
- For the first time the audience was distanced;
- Nothing was used that wasn't in the space from the start;
- Emotional 'expressionist' performances shocked the spectator.

THE TRAGICAL HISTORY OF DOCTOR FAUSTUS 1963
Montage used again

In this production Grotowski again used 'montage' as a device for rearranging the text, the result of which is fully explored in 'Doctor Faustus: Textual Montage' in *Towards a Poor Theatre* [pp. 71–9]. As in *Akropolis* the decision was taken to transpose the action into one setting with the audience seated at two long tables, as at a feast, with a raised

An enclosed setting for actors and audience

third table at one end, the spectators becoming guests at Faustus's last supper, overhearing the history of his life, told mainly in flashbacks. The whole setting was enclosed in high walls cutting it off from any reference to the outside world. Faustus was cast as a saint/martyr whose desire for ultimate knowledge condemned him to seek salvation through his pact with the Devil.

Abandoning integration of actors and audience

From Faustus onwards Grotowski gradually began to abandon his attempts to integrate the spectator with the actor:

> We preferred to forget the spectator, forget his existence. We began to concentrate our complete attention and activity on, above all, the art of the actor.

[Quoted in Kumiega, 1987. p.54]

A religious feel to the production

The production had a deeply religious feel, the cast were dressed uniformly in monks' habits of different colours and to underline the church atmosphere, chanting at key moments could be heard from behind the enclosed box:

> ... wrapping us in the atmosphere in a way 'background music' in a proscenium rarely does.

[Quoted in Kumiega, 1985. p.68]

Figure 3.31   The set for *Doctor Faustus* at the Theatre Laboratory in Opole. Faustus awaits the arrival of his 'guests'.

Voice exercises and facial masks were used

The production revealed the extensive work that had been done on voice in the company's training sessions, with variations in level and pitch that amazed the critics. Similarly 'facial masks' were again used to create great mobility of expression, moving from calm acceptance to convulsive horror.

THE CONSTANT PRINCE 1965
Culmination of work in the Laboratory Theatre

This was the production that identified Ryszard Cieslak as one of the most outstanding actors of his generation, at the time acknowledged by some as the finest in the world, and it also marked the culmination of Grotowski's work with the Laboratory Theatre.

The text was an intense study of savagery and suffering in which the Prince, played by Cieslak, is tormented to death by his persecutors. In a review of the play one critic wrote:

> Cieslak's movements, facial expressions, tones do not express thoughts or external sensations but only emotional and volitional states of the spirit.

[Schechner and Wolford, 1997. p.125].

Transcendent performance

His performance was acknowledged as transcendent, the result of hours of individual work with Grotowski to whom he had committed his professional life. (At the end of his career he appeared in Peter Brook's *Mahabarata*, 1985.)

Spectators alienated from the action

The spectator as voyeur

This time the spectators were literally cut off from the action. As in a bullring or operating theatre they looked down on the actors, who functioned in an empty space except for a central raised dais that doubled as a bed, an operating table, the executioner's platform and a sacrificial altar. They were placed in the position of voyeurs, overseeing and hearing the terrible acts that took place below.

Figure 3.32 This exercise in developing the eye muscles is taken from the classical Kathakali theatre of India.

> The spectator, distanced in space, placed in a position of an observer who is not even accepted, who remains exclusively in the position of observer, is really in a position to co-participate emotively, in that he may eventually discover in himself the primitive vocation of the spectator.

[Quoted in Kumiega, 1987. p.69]

Simple costumes and few props

Costumes were organised to denote rank, mostly dark full cloaks for those in power, in contrast to the Prince who, representing the crucified Christ figure, wore white and a loin cloth to denote his vulnerability and nakedness. There were few if any props and the lighting, from pictorial evidence, was variable from open white to deeply shadowed directional sources for the Prince's death.

Parallels with Artaud

A shock to a receptive audience

It is worth noting here that parallels were noted between this production and Artaud's Theatre of Cruelty, although Grotowski always maintained that he had not read Artaud until 1964 when the Laboratory had already established its own style. The most recognisable similarity lay in his treatment of 'cruelty', by which he hoped to disturb and shock a receptive audience through the power of the 'show' to an emotional response.

To sum up:

- The actor is placed at the centre of the work;
- Spectators are cut off from the action, becoming voyeurs;
- Through observation the spectator experiences catharsis;
- Aspects of Artaudian theory are evident.

APOCALYPSIS CUM FIGURIS 1969–80

An introduction to company ethos

This was the final production by the Laboratory Theatre and the one that survived the longest since, when the main thrust of the company's work developed into teaching, it was often performed as part of a workshop by way of introduction to the company's ethos.

Self-exploration

Characters as archetypes

For the first time the text evolved out of exercises and improvisations which specifically sought to 'facilitate the actor's self exploration' [Innes, 1993. p.157]. In fact the result was one of the most inward-looking pieces that the Laboratory had devised; since it was more to do with self-development of the individual rather than a company piece, 'each actor was able to reach his or her own personal "Total Act"' [quoted in Kumiega, 1997. p.92]. Characters as such were built on archetypes, that is recognisable mythic and religious figures that an audience could identify with. The whole production was a vindication of the technique of 'montage' in the building of a compelling piece of theatre.

> We had material for twenty-four hours in the end. Out of that we had to construct something which would have its own energy like a stream. It was only then that we turned to speech.

Speech came last

[Quoted in Kumiega, 1997. p.90]

A wide range of texts

What written text there was derived from the Bible, the poetry of T. S. Eliot and Simone Weil and *The Brothers Karamasov.*

As a director, the work marked a radical departure for Grotowski; hitherto he had been quite dogmatic, shaping and orchestrating the final result. For *Apocalypsis* he was more of an observer, withdrawing to the sidelines and rarely interrupting. In retrospect this proved to be a turning point for the Laboratory; from now on the work would become more company centred and would move into the 'theatre as therapy' period, which became known as 'paratheatre'.

Grotowski as observer rather than director

Minimal technical resources

For this production the space was stripped bare to the vaulted brick walls. Properties were kept to a minimum. Two spotlights were supplemented by a number of candles, giving a distinctly claustrophobic air to the action. Audiences were seated on the floor and against the walls, and the actors, dressed in everyday clothes, were indistinguishable from the spectators.

A contemporary passion play

Critics likened the performance to that of a contemporary passion play:

> ... the action is set in a contemporary religious festival, among the touts and beggars camping out around the shrine, who play out the Second Coming as a brutal drunken game.

[Innes, 1993. p.155]

The text played with themes of blasphemy, parody, carnival, and ultimately salvation as a way of recreating Christian myth, which for Grotowski had lost its ability to awaken an audience to a sense of awe, now lost for ever in a cynical world.

A sense of awe

To sum up:

- Grotowski begins to withdraw from overall control;
- The text was a radical montage;
- The Poor Theatre was revealed at its most extreme.

From this brief survey of productions that effectively ended in 1969 (although *Apocalypsis cum Figuris* went on being performed for at least a further 12 years) the following general summary is possible:

Figure 3.33 Grotowski trains his actors to use their faces as masks. The results are closer to those of African and Oriental theatre than to the Western European tradition. Absolutely no make-up is used. Both faces above are from the production of *Akropolis*.

Summary

- the actor's training ran alongside regular public performances;
- the progressive actor training marked the emergence of 'the holy actor';
- classic texts drawn from Poland's Romantic past were adapted to meet the demands of the Laboratory's work;
- 'montage' was the means by which different sources were integrated;
- for each production there was created a unique actor/audience relationship;
- emotional 'expressionist' performances shocked the spectator;
- props were in evidence from the beginning of the work and nothing was introduced into the space that was not there at the start;
- costumes reflected the environment and had nothing to do with 'character';
- performance encouraged identification with the actor, by which means an audience would be moved to re-examine themselves
- the means was through a reconstructed mythic and religious text.

Section 3.5.3 is indebted to a reading of: *Kumiega, J., The Theatre of Grotowski* Methuen, 1987.

TOWARDS A POOR THEATRE
First published in Polish in 1965 and in English 1967

A summary of his achievements

By the time *Towards a Poor Theatre* was available in English, Grotowski's laboratory work was well advanced and in fact within three years would be almost over. The book therefore can be seen as a summary of work in progress which had been tested by the early productions and by the complementary practical work.

A comparison with Brook's The Empty Space

Its impact can be compared with that of Brook's *The Empty Space*, since it laid down a similar challenge to the rethinking of an actor's relationship with the space he worked in. But while Brook's essays were reflective on the state of theatre as he saw it, and were a résumé of current directorial purpose, Grotowski's book was more prescriptive, laying down quite specific conditions for the theatre advancing. The core of his arguments and proposition is contained in the first essay of the title:

The actor as core to the act of creation

- He maintained that 'the personal and scenic technique of the actor [is] the core of theatre art' [p.15], and further:

- '... everything is concentrated on the ripening of the actor ... a complete stripping down ... The actor makes a total gift of himself.' [p.16].

Inductive and deductive

- Grotowski goes on to suggest that, with the actor at the centre of creativity, rather than a training process that is **inductive** (a series of learnt skills), his actor's process was **deductive**, what he calls the **via negativa** or 'an eradication of blocks' [p.17].

Such an approach necessitates the stripping away of 'how to do', a mask of technique behind which the actor conceals himself, in search of the sincerity, truth and life of an exposed core of psycho-physical impulses.

[Bradby and Williams, 1988. p.124]

The actor as high priest The resulting work is based on the assumption that the actor as 'high-priest' gives totally of himself and in return the spectator is changed by this spiritual un-masking, acts which in their naked intensity with the '... integration of all the actor's psychic and bodily powers ... springing forth in a sort of "translumiation"' [p.16]. This concept is heavily

Catholic rituals reliant for its meaning on the intense rituals of the Catholic church.

- What is the theatre? What is unique about it? What can it do that film and television cannot?

Rather than a synthesis of creative disciplines, which makes what he calls **Rich Theatre**, Grotowski suggests that by the elimination of literature, sculpture, painting, architecture, lighting and acting one is left with the actor as pre-eminent. He wants to sweep away the attempts of theatre to ape the movies and television and with 'borrowed mechanisms' to compete in a losing battle. Rather he sees theatre as exploiting its intrinsic uniqueness:

Poor theatre [C]onsequently, I propose **poverty** in theatre'

[p.19].

The direct antithesis of Rich is **Poor**.

Different spatial relationships

Any number of spatial relationships

- He goes on to elaborate. For each new production he envisages a different space/relationship for actors and spectators. Actors can play among the audience, they can build structures among the spectators and 'thus include them in the architecture of the action' [p.20]. Or actors can play among the spectators but ignore them. The spectators can also be isolated from the actors by a physical barrier, for example looking down on the action from behind a fence (see *The Constant Prince*), observing the actors like animals in a ring or patients in an operating theatre. The entire space could become the location (see *Faustus*, where the whole hall became the setting for the 'baroque feast'). And finally:

The essential concern is finding the proper spectator–actor relationship for each type of performance and embodying the decision in physical arrangements.

[p.20]

Figure 3.34   The audience seated at two long tables for *Doctor Faustus*.

No artifice

- As far as the actor is concerned Grotowski is anxious to stress that Poor = the actor revealed. No false noses, no make-up, transformation was to be effected by using 'his own body and craft', the mask is to be achieved by the actor's own muscles not by a piece of painted papier mâché (see section 3.5.4, Influences, Kathakali). Transformation of objects is achieved by the way they are handled: the floor can become the sea, an upturned table a boat to sail on it. Such radical cutting away and denial of the tangible works towards the actor as a spiritual centre of all performance activity.

Transformation of space and objects

The re-enactment of myths

Grotowski maintained that with the death of religion the 'spiritual energy' of a community needed an outlet and it was the actor's duty to re-enact the **myths** for us (the spectator) and by doing so to awaken a sense of 'personal truth' and enable us to acknowledge that

> ... through fright and a sense of the sacred [we] come to catharsis.

[p.22]

Parallels with Greek tragedy

This is very like the intention of Greek tragedy, though in Grotowski's case the achievement was by the intimacy of shared suffering, rather than that of the Greeks which was society's way of keeping faith with its past. He concludes this most influential essay by expressing an almost tender regard for the actor:

- he must be attentive;
- confident and free;
- his growth is attended by observation;
- by astonishment;
- and desire to help;
- my growth is onto him
- or rather is found in him
- our common growth becomes a revelation.

> The actor is re-born – not only as an actor but as a man – and with him, I am reborn.

[p.25]

All quotations from *Towards a Poor Theatre* unless otherwise stated.

THE HOLY ACTOR

Much of the material for the definition of the Holy Actor is contained in the essay 'The Theatre's New Testament' [*Towards a Poor Theatre*, pp. 27–53]. In this interview-style essay with Eugenio Barba, Grotowski expands and elaborates ideas on the actor already briefly covered in the title essay.

The actor aspires to the spiritual

Grotowski begins by deploring the role of the actor in society, likening him/her to a prostitute who is paid to display his/her art. Rather he suggests that in offering his body publicly, the actor, through education (training), should be seen to move beyond the mere imitation of the everyday to a higher plane of spirituality where the outcome is evidence of his/her **holiness.**

Religious imagery

Interestingly despite his denial of belief ('I speak about **holiness** as an unbeliever' [p.34]), time and again Grotowski uses the religious imagery of death, profanation, sacrilege, burning, excess and self-penetration to illustrate his point. His Catholic upbringing obviously had a huge influence on his thinking.

He believes the actor's new '**secular holiness**' should be demonstrated in performances of such power and exposure of self that the spectator cannot fail to experience the same process for himself. By so doing the actor escapes the label of prostitute through his acts of self-revelation and what Grotowski calls his 'self-sacrifice'.

The actor's self-sacrifice

There are to be no tricks

For Grotowski the resulting '**holy actor**' is an actor who rids himself of 'tricks' and rather than accumulating a series of skills (**inductive** technique) he strips away inhibitions and lies to reveal the 'total act' (the **deductive** technique) [p.17]:

> . . . the body vanishes, burns and the spectator sees only a series of visible impulses.

> [Quoted in Bradby and Williams, 1988. p.125]

Stripping away reveals a spiritual force

He goes on: 'He must learn to use his role as if it were a surgeon's scalpel, to dissect himself' [p.37] – the act is to be both painful and totally revealing. He talks of stripping away the 'mask' of everyday, to reveal the 'innermost core' [p.37], which can be achieved only by 'mobilisation of all the physical and spiritual forces of the actor' [p.37]; Grotowski uses the word 'trance' to summarise the actor's state of mind and being.

The whole process is a conscious inward examination of what Grotowski terms 'our organism' [p.39], which for him is more than the body itself: it is also intuition, and those buried impulses that, through training, Grotowski seeks to reawaken.

Improvisation can be recalled

And finally the holy actor is one who self-composes the score of the production. With the guidance of the director, improvised moments are recorded and stored so as to be reconstituted in performance as self-remembered 'reflexes'. It is then the actor's job to reanimate these moments into a seamless 'score', 'retracing his personal route during the original creative process' [Bradby and Williams, 1988. p.132].

> Actors should be like martyrs burnt alive, still signalling to us from their stakes.

> [Antonin Artaud, quoted on p.93]

Parallels with Artaud

So ends Grotowski's essay in homage to Artaud (pp.85–93), of whom, despite their very many shared concerns, he is quite critical. The quotation sums up very well the potential for power and terror that both men held to be the prerogative of the actor. Artaud suggests in his *Theatre of Cruelty* (see 3.3.3) that the way forward is 'purification by violence and cruelty' [p.92], an extreme view of the actor's role. But Grotowski takes a step back from that position and insists that it is only through '**spiritual acts**' [p.33] that the actor is seen to transcend the everyday world.

The actor transcends the real world through spiritual acts

All quotations from *Towards a Poor Theatre* unless otherwise stated.

AFTER POOR THEATRE

Grotowski moves towards a more shared experience

Grotowski's disenchantment with theatre at the very height of the Laboratory's reputation led him away from the actor–spectator relationship towards a theatre of pure process, where members of the public under the direction of his immensely experienced company would work towards:

> … the possibility of authentic spontaneity, and the release of a creative flow of energy.
>
> [Kumiega, 1987. p.162].

Kumiega goes on to suggest that the proposed work was what might be recognised as 'de-conditioning', the sort of end-process that actors with the Laboratory had been striving for. The company worked on their own for a while, then in 1972 old farm buildings were acquired just outside Wroclaw and the first stage of the process began by moving from an urban base to that of a more ecologically focused relationship with the countryside.

Paratheatre. Through work to creation

In 1973 self-selected outside participants were invited to take part in the first **paratheatre** occasion, the basis of which was the channelling of 'innate impulses into dynamic physical action: work or play' [Bradby and Williams, 1988. p.141]. The hard work that was at the core of the activity involved simple everyday tasks, but in an environment divorced from the pressures of urban life. After initial events that took the participants on a series of individual journeys, the work quickly spread, particularly to America where in 1974 what became known as **Special Projects** were conducted in a rural locality. Running alongside this activity were performances of *Apocalypsis* and teaching workshops by members of the company.

The company become teachers

By the time this phase of the work was coming to an end, Grotowski was already embarking on the next, which came to be called the **Theatre of Sources**. This was more transculturally focused and began with an examination by a multicultural group of various rituals, including the voodoo of Haiti, and Sufic and yogic practices. In 1981 with the imposition of martial law in Poland, Grotowski sought asylum in America and never returned to his native land.

Leaves Poland for America

There were other projects: **Objective Drama** and **Art as Vehicle** were both based on interactive and exploratory group work. He never returned to theatre.

When he died in 1999, only the most well-informed theatre practitioners were able to recall work other than that under the title of *Poor Theatre* and if he has a legacy, it is for those early concepts and practice that he will be best remembered. There were critics who considered his later work as having more to do with personal therapeutic values than theatre, though at the time they attracted a huge following.

His legacy is 'Poor Theatre'

But if there is one aspect of his work that will endure, it is his insistence on a return to a theatre that could celebrate its **uniqueness** by placing the **holy actor** at the **core** of creation.

3.5.4 INFLUENCES

MEYERHOLD, VSEVOLOD (1874–1940)

(See also Stanislavski, section 3.2.5)

Grotowski, as part of his Director training, was in Moscow in 1955 and it was there that he first became acquainted with the theatre of Meyerhold. It is important to bear in mind that Meyerhold had become a forgotten figure, a victim of Stalin's purges, but in the late 1950s his reputation was slowly being rehabilitated. Indeed by the late 1960s, with the process complete, he was acknowledged as perhaps the greatest Soviet director of the 20th century. With his particular interest in the training of the actor Grotowski would have found Meyerhold's preoccupation with **biomechanics** both sympathetic and relevant.

An important figure rehabilitated

Biomechanics as a system of training

Biomechanics was related to an American system of time-and-motion study, known as Taylorism, named after its inventor. He had advocated the study of efficient movement-patterns related to the workplace but Meyerhold adopted and adapted the system to suit his own purpose. Thus:

> Straight line motions involving sudden and sharp changes in direction ... are preferred to smooth continuous, curved motions of the hands. ...

[Leach p.54]

As a minimum training the system taught the actor:

Awareness of three-dimensional space

- self-awareness in a three-dimensional space;
- the need for efficiency as well as expressiveness in movement;
- the essential rhythmic and dynamic qualities in stage movement.

Much of the work was based on the Constructivist values of man as worker (linked at the time to Stalin's push for industrialisation). These values foregrounded:

The body as machine

- the body as machine;
- the worker as machine operator;
- the actor must discover his own centre of gravity, his own equilibrium and stability;
- the actor must achieve co-ordination of bodily movements in relation to the stage platform, stage space and surrounding figures;
- a gesture is a motion of the entire body;
- body movement is the producer of external words.

But Meyerhold was interested in more than the mere 'mechanics' of acting. These ideas were combined with the super-theatricality of Commedia dell'Arte and the external techniques of Japanese and Chinese theatre.

Meyerhold used all the sources that were available

The parallels with Grotowski are evident. Though Grotowski worked towards an actor who relied less on the externals and more on the transcendent, Meyerhold, with his eclectic gathering of influences, would have appealed to a director when he was assembling his own international vocabulary.

Leach, R.,   *Vsevolod Meyerhold,*   CUP, 1993

NOH JAPANESE CLASSICAL THEATRE (1192–present)

An ancient dance drama

Noh evolved very slowly from fertility dances performed by the Japanese peasant population as part of their temple celebrations. From an early stage the dance performance was accompanied by flute/drum and harp and occasionally the dancers were masked. Influences from Korea and China in the 14th century led to a renaissance in the arts and Noh emerged as a secular art form along with the Zen garden and the tea ceremony as a triangle of deeply felt ceremonies. The language of Noh is that of medieval Japan so although the audience now may enjoy the spectacle they cannot understand a word, leading to the mistaken impression that it is an irrelevant form for the 21st century.

Stories were drawn from the tales and legends of the past, which were codified by the writer Zeami in the period 1363–1444 (around the time of England's Henry IV and Henry V).

Formal, robed and masked actors

In formalised staging of immense symbolic complexity, the robed and masked actor (Sh'te), assisted by one other, would relate the text, accompanied by the musicians. There were other assistants who were not masked and as such were considered invisible to the audience; they could place properties, remove discarded objects and change the costume of the protagonist. Training for the actor began as early as the age of 7, and by the time he reached 50 his career was considered as finished.

The actor as high priest

With movement, gesture and music Noh sought to present a highly formalised event to an audience who were complicit in the display of skills by the actor. 'Noh takes life and reduces it to ritual.' The actor as high priest enacts the same old stories, but it is how these are accomplished that gives the most pleasure to a discerning audience.

Rigorous training

Grotowski cites the Noh theatre as influential. What appealed to him most was the actor's rigorous training, the densely choreographed movement with inner and outer meaning and the skill of the actor as impersonator.

Teele, R.,   *No/Kyogen Masks and Performance*,   PCT, 1984

KATHAKALI – INDIAN DANCE (1650–present)

Dance theatre from Kerala, India

Kathakali is a marriage between a warrior class (the Nayers), who held the goddess Kali in great regard, and the more peace-loving Dravidians, who were driven out by the aggressor. Based in the south-western province of India known as Kerala, the dance theatre has evolved over a considerable time into one of the most vivid and compelling of Indian dances.

Evolved from training for war

The training for a Kathakali performer derived from the Nayers' highly organised preparations for war, in which, during a long and arduous apprenticeship, exercises and massage developed agility and strength. Traditionally, training also involved mime, gesture and acting, skills that were designed to give the warrior a psychological advantage over the aggressor. Martial dances and combat exercises honed skills in the handling of weapons, and the basic stance of the performer today derives from the body's position in hand-to-hand fighting; flexed knees held wide apart prepare the soldier/actor for a swift response and facilitate leaping and landing in this highly physicalised dance.

Highly physical training

Figure 3.35   Kathakali – King Lear

As the threat of war diminished companies developed under patronage and texts came to be derived from a number of sources, including the *Mahabarata* (see Peter Brook, section 3.6.3). Over time the performances became an immensely complex series of signs focused on the eyes, the face, the hands and the feet, with the eyes remaining the primary means of expression. But the hands, too, played a large part in the development of a hidden language, with more than 24 gestures all of which had infinite meanings depending on subtle changes. Building on this were the extremely elaborate make-up, costumes, jewellery and head-dresses which transformed the athletic performer into a complex hieratic image (make-up alone could take two to four hours).

Gesture and stylised movement

Complex stylised image

The attraction this art form had for Grotowski is clear:

- the intensive training of every aspect of the actor's body;
- limbs as independent means of expression;
- every aspect is developed separately and then brought together in one iconic whole;
- the face as a mask;
- physicality and energy.

This summary from the conclusion of a Kathakali performance could well apply to the aftermath of a Grotowski production:

> For some few hours the people have experienced the essence of primal passions in an unreal and unearthly atmosphere. With the rising of the sun they go home cleansed and uplifted, having walked with the gods.

[Massey and Massey, 1989. p.65]

Massey, R. and Massey, J.,   *The Dances of India*,   London, 1989

3.5.5 FOLLOWERS

BARBA, EUGENIO (Born 1936)

Assistant to Grotowski

Barba was an assistant to Grotowski during the Theatre Laboratory's most formative years and as such has been acknowledged as the only true 'disciple' of Grotowski's theatre. He broke away from Grotowski in 1964 and founded his own 'Odin Teatret' (its full title was Nordisk Theater-Laboratorium for Skuespillerkunst) in Oslo, later transferring to the small town of Holstebro in Denmark.

Formed his own theatre

It is worth noting that *Towards a Poor Theatre* (the collection of Grotowski's essays) was published under the auspices of the Odin Teatret in 1968, heavily edited by Barba. Barba is now best known for his work in what he termed 'Theatre Anthropology' – applying research into transcultural forms such as Noh, Kabuki, Kathakali and Balinese dance, he seeks to develop a Western form of physical stylisation. This is in conscious opposition to the preoccupation with the psychology of acting, which has dominated so much of an actor's training since Stanislavski published *An Actor Prepares*.

Theatre Anthropology

The values of the 'Third Theatre'

An encounter with the audience

Like Brook in *The Empty Space*, Barba has been preoccupied with the state of current theatre, identifying what he calls the First Theatre as that of the commercial and subsidised theatre, blooming but deadly; the Second Theatre as that of the avant-garde, which values the director above the actor; and the Third Theatre, where he places himself. This theatre is the theatre of confrontation, not in the accepted sense of an assault on the audience but a performance in which the actor confronts himself and offers the result of that encounter to an audience. It is a theatre of the actor as a member of a collective (see also Brook's company in Paris and The Performance Group in New York), in which the actor is his own creator rather than a servant of the dramatist.

Barba became fascinated by what he termed the pre-expressive:

> ... Why, when I see two actors doing the same thing, I get fascinated by one and not the other?

[Barba and Savarese, 1991. p.186]

Pre-expressive

In other words he is interested in what happens to an actor's body prior to expression, linking back to his early work in Eastern forms where performers were able to engage their energies in a way they did not in everyday life. In simplistic terms the pre-expressive might be translated as 'energy', a word in common usage in drama schools. Despite having his performances dubbed elitist for the very small audiences they attract, along with Brook, Schechner, The Living Theatre and others he has been one of the most inquisitive and persistent practitioners into the nature of the actor as performer.

Interested in the mystique of an actor's process

Barba, E. and Savarese, N.,   *The Secret Art of the Performer*,   Routledge, 1991

SCHECHNER, RICHARD (BORN 1934)

A follower of Grotowski

In 1968 Schechner published what he called Six Axioms for Environmental Theatre [*TDR* 39 Spring 1968], which laid out his understanding of the kind of performance style he was seeking. These are worth reproducing in full as they have much in common with Grotowski's own statements. At the time they were both teaching at the same university, and undoubtedly Schechner became aware of the concept of *A Poor Theatre* and the potential it had for his own work:

Six Axioms for Environmental Theatre

- It is necessary to accept a definition of theatre which is not based upon traditional distinctions between life and art;
- All the space is used for performance and all the space is used for audience;
- The theatrical event can take place either in a totally transformed space or in 'found space';
- Focus is flexible and variable. In environmental theatre the focus can be single, as in traditional theatre, or multi-focus, where the space is arranged so that the spectators cannot see everything without moving or refocusing, and more than one event is taking place at the same time, forcing the spectator to choose which to observe. Or there can be local focus where only a fraction of the audience can perceive the event;
- One element is not submerged for the sake of others. The performer is no more important than the other audible and visual elements. Sometimes performers may be treated as mass and volume, colour, texture and movement;
- The text need be neither the starting point of nor the goal of a production. There may be no text at all.

Theatre in alternative spaces

Schechner acquired an empty garage space furnished with several wooden towers. The audience sat on these as well as on the floor with the acting area in the middle; spectators could move into the central space if they wished but actors shared *all* the space. There was a total breakdown between performer and audience.

Favoured a shared participation

Work on *Dionysus in 69* (1968) confirmed Schechner's theatre as a theatre of participation, an anathema to Grotowski for while he often treated the audience as a congregation of equals, with the actors he kept the two within defined boundaries. Unlike in Schechner's theatre they never crossed the unspoken divide. The Performance Group had been using some of Grotowski's psycho-physical exercises as warm-ups and had even incorporated these into performance, but Grotowski distrusted group improvisations as he felt they removed responsibility from the actors by immersing them in what he termed 'the warm water of family relations' [Grotowski quoted in Shank, 1982. p.97]

Grotowski distrusted group improvisations

Schechner had an abiding interest in the actor as 'vulnerable', and nakedness played a large part in achieving this: the body exposed was no longer a secret container for character but a revealed performer where the social means of masking oneself had been removed.

Editor of influential journal

Schechner later went on to edit *Tulane Drama Review* (see Suggestions for Further Study) and was immensely influential in keeping Grotowski's work before a public.

Shank, T.,   *American Alternative Theatre*,   Macmillan, 1982

BROOK, PETER (BORN 1925)

(See also section 3.6)

Brook wrote in his Preface to *Towards a Poor Theatre*:

> In Grotowski's theatre as in all true *laboratories* the experiments are scientifically valid because the essential conditions are observed. In his theatre, there is absolute concentration by a small group, and unlimited time. So if you are interested you must go to Poland.

[*Towards a Poor Theatre* 1981, Preface by Peter Brook, p.11]

Friend and colleague

Brook has always acknowledged his debt to Grotowski. They were friends and colleagues and Brook had the foresight to invite him to participate in rehearsals for *U.S* (RSC in 1966) but it has always been clear that 'we share a same aim but our paths were different' [Brook, 1989. p.41]. Up to a point Brook was less a follower and more a fellow traveller.

A shared theatre

Brook maintained that Grotowski's methods led to an inward-looking theatre in which the audience played an increasingly minor role and in which the 'inner world' of the actor was paramount. By contrast he suggested that his theatre was one that was shared:

A theatre of celebration

> A strong presence of actors and a strong presence of spectators can produce a circle of unique intensity in which barriers can be broken and the invisible become real.

[Brook, 1989. p. 41]

Brook had no training as a director

In other words his was a theatre of community, one that reached across the divide between actor and audience uniting them in one shared act, a theatre of inclusion not exclusion. It is worth noting that Brook had virtually no specialist training as a director – it was his extended journey of discovery that became so important to him – while Grotowski had four years of extended study and travel in which to formulate his *Poor Theatre*.

Brook, P.,   *The Shifting Point*,   Methuen, 1989

CHAIKIN, JOSEPH AND THE OPEN THEATRE (1963–73)

Very influenced by Grotowski

Joseph Chaikin had been a member of The Living Theatre (see pp.397–400) in 1959 but a few years later broke away to found his own company, a company that proved to be one of the most influential in the 1960s. His theories derived from any number of sources but chiefly from Grotowski, from whom he took the intense psycho-physical exercises, the idea that theatre must be a radical alternative to cinema and television (see *The Poor Theatre*) and the notion that the emphasis must be on performer not character (Grotowski had visited the Open Theatre and given workshops with the company).

Concepts of 'outside' and 'inside'

One of Chaikin's key concepts was the 'outside' and 'inside' of a situation: outside was represented by the commercial theatre, the inside by abstract non-verbal improvisations with the actor as key participant. Performed texts tended to be collages of source material round which the company would improvise, the *mise-en-scène* also being created with props and simple units doubling as required. The use of hand-held percussion instruments interrupted and underlined aspects of the text. In the early stages the company went through a phase of direct bodily contact with the audience, what Chaikin called 'a celebration of presence', a means of getting the audience to confront themselves within the context of the work, but this experiment was abandoned (the Living Theatre continued to use this convention for many years, however).

Direct contact with the audience

Instead of exploration and change their very success required them to remain the same so the Open Theatre disbanded rather than face the inevitable commercial pressure. However, with their European tours and the consistently challenging nature of the work in their brief life, they were the most influential group to come out of America in the 1960s.

European tours

Note: The actor/playwright Sam Shepard (born 1943) began his writing career with the company and both he and Chaikin collaborated on a number of texts most notably *Tongues* (1978), in which there is percussion accompaniment, and *Savage Love* (1981).

Shank, T.,   *American Alternative Theatre*,   Macmillan, 1982
Chaikin, J.,   *The Presence of the Actor*,   London, 1994

3.5.6 SUMMARY: JERZY GROTOWSKI

This summary is written to draw together certain parts of the chapter on Jerzy Grotowski under particular headings. It should be considered with the student's own practical work in mind and/or the student's viewing of other productions. For example, Grotowski's writing on the training for an actor: as a student undertaking practical work, you would wish to discuss what aspects are relevant for an actor today and how these could be reflected in your own work. By adopting this convention/practice not only are you enhancing your own approach but you are able to make use of the practice when viewing other productions.

THE SUBJECT MATTER

Romantic texts from the past
Rethinking of classic texts
Improvisation combined with text
Montage of literary source material

THE POLITICAL PURPOSE OR MESSAGE OR DRAMATIC INTENTION	Drawing attention to past texts and their messages for the present The politics of self and roles in society
THE ACTOR– AUDIENCE RELATIONSHIP	Actors inhabiting the same space as the audience Proximity and distance The actor as holy, the actor as poor The audience as voyeur
THE STAGING FORM ADOPTED	Closed, claustrophobic space The audience as an active part of the setting The audience on levels A unique setting for each production
DIRECTORIAL INTERPRETATION /PRODUCTION STYLE	Director-led Actors encouraged to contribute Montage as a way of creating new texts
DESIGN ELEMENTS	Very stripped down Environments created for the whole play Costume to reflect types, not characters
ROLE OF ACTORS AND PERFORMANCE STYLE	The actor as maker of a text The importance of training Use of the body and voice to shock the audience Expressionist means
TECHNICAL ELEMENTS	Minimal lighting sources Intimate playing areas not separate from the audience No illusion, the actor as self
AUDIENCE RESPONSE	To be moved and changed by the visceral experience To recognise archetypes To achieve catharsis

3.5.7 SUGGESTIONS FOR FURTHER STUDY

OTHER SOURCES

Articles by and about Grotowski first found an English-speaking audience through the theatre magazine *Tulane Drama Review*. Copies can be found in good specialist drama libraries.

TDR 39	Spring 1968	'Six Axioms for Environmental Theatre'
TDR 41	Vol. 13 No. 1	'Interview with Grotowski' by Richard Schechner
TDR 46	Winter 1970	'*The Constant Prince*, a portfolio of critiques'
TDR 52	Vol. 15 No. 4	'Grotowski's *Apocalypse*'
TDR 63	September 1974	'Meyerhold's biomechanics and Meyerhold's centennial'
TDR 68	Vol. 19 No. 4	'Paratheatrical projects'
Theatre Quarterly	Vol. 3 No. 10 April/June 1973	' "Holiday", the meaning of meeting in everyday life'
New Theatre Quarterly	Vol. 1 No. 2 May 1985	'The four theatres of Jerzy Grotowski: an assessment'

FILM

My Dinner With Andre (dir. Louis Malle 1981 U.S 111 min.) with Wallace Shawn, Andre Gregory, Jean Lenauer, Roy Butler

A filmed discussion in which director Gregory recounts stories from his quest to 'find himself'. There is an extended section regarding his meeting with Grotowski and work on paratheatre.

3.5.8 BIBLIOGRAPHY

Barba, E. *et al.*	*The Secret Art of the Performer*	Routledge, 1995	A fascinating and well-illustrated account of performance styles.
Bradby, D. and Williams, D.	*Directors' Theatre*	Methuen, 1988	Chapter 5.
Braun, E.	*The Director and the Stage*	Methuen, 1986	Chapter 13, Grotowski's Laboratory Theatre, written by Jennifer Kumiega.
Grotowski, J.	*Towards a Poor Theatre*	Methuen, 1981	Edited by Eugenio Barba, his collaborator.

Innes, C.	*Avant-Garde Theatre*	Routledge, 1993	A comprehensive account of 20th-century alternative theatre.
Kumiega, J.	*The Theatre of Grotowski*	Methuen, 1987	The fullest account of work up until 1985. Sadly now out of print, but well worth tracking down.
Mitter, S.	*Systems of Rehearsal*	Routledge, 1992	Relating Brook's work to that of Grotowski.
Osinski, Z.	*Grotowski and his Laboratory*	London, 1986	
Richards, T.	*At Work with Grotowski on Physical Actions*	Routledge, 1995	Most recent first-hand account of his work with Grotowski.
Roose-Evans, J.	*Experimental Theatre*	Routledge, 1989	Chapters 15 and 16.
Schechner, R. and Wolford, L.	*Grotowski Source Book*	Routledge, 2000	To be published in paperback in late 2000.

3.6 Peter Brook (born 1925)

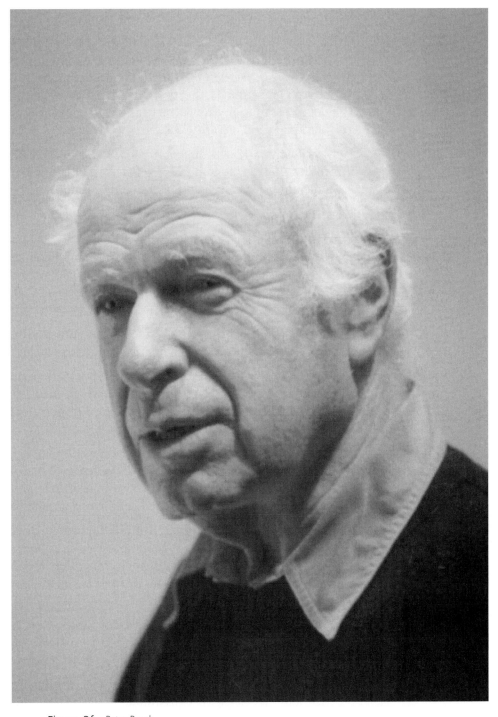

Figure 3f   Peter Brook

3.6.1 A CHRONOLOGY

FIRST PHASE 1942–63
Interested in film

1925: Born England. Son of Russian scientists. Interested from an early age in model theatres and an old film projector belonging to his father. 'The movies were my real windows on another world' [Brook, 1998. p.5]. Aged 15 spends two years in Switzerland to cure his TB.

1941: Takes a year off and works in a film studio. Learns the piano and becomes musically literate.

Directs his first production

1942: At the age of 17 goes to Magdalen College, Oxford. Directs an amateur production of Marlowe's *Doctor Faustus* at the Torch Theatre London.

Uses publicity to further his work

1944: Founds the Oxford University Film Society. Directs first (amateur) film, *A Sentimental Journey* by Laurence Sterne, using ex-service film stock. This film is the first in a lifetime of similar *causes célèbres*. He develops a facility for attracting adverse and notorious publicity for his work, a useful attribute for a life to be spent in theatre.

1945: Invitation to direct *Man and Superman* at Birmingham Repertory under Barry Jackson. His leading man is Paul Scofield. This first encounter leads to many later collaborations.

Also directs *King John* and Ibsen's *The Lady from the Sea*.

First production at Stratford-upon-Avon

1946: Barry Jackson, who has been asked to take over as director at The Royal Shakespeare Theatre, Stratford-upon-Avon, asks him to direct. He stages *Love's Labour's Lost*, designed after Watteau. Very well received. 'My obsession with film was helping me realise that a play is also a spool that unrolls; its truth comes to life shot by shot.' [Brook, 1998. p.37]

This marks the beginning of a long association with this theatre and later the Royal Shakespeare Company (RSC), first formed in 1961.

Sacked from Stratford

1947: *Romeo and Juliet* at Stratford. 'Hot violent and unromantic.' He is sacked for going over budget. Much wedded to the validity of the proscenium arch during this period: 'The so-called picture frame is an instrument of focus' [Brook, 1998. p.40].

He is drawn to the work of Jean-Paul Sartre

He stages two comparatively minor plays by Jean-Paul Sartre (1905–80): *Men Without Shadows* and *The Respectable Prostitute*. Both plays have a hint of the scandalous. They raise one of the questions that is already beginning to intrigue him: that of how to handle violence on stage.

Director of productions at Covent Garden

1948: Brook is made director of productions at Covent Garden, where he directs his first operas: *Boris Godonov* by Mussorgsky, designed by Frenchman Georges Wakhevitch, and *La Bohème* by Puccini. His eagerness to try all forms of theatre makes him seize this opportunity. He struggles for better rehearsal conditions.

Collaborates with Salvador Dalí

1949: Collaboration with Salvador Dalí at Covent Garden on a production of Strauss's *Salome*. He is looking to the Continent and specifically France for his texts and collaborators. He is again sacked.

1950: Directs *Ring Round the Moon* by Jean Anouilh (1910–87) with Paul Scofield. Works with Christopher Fry (b.1907) on the translation. The result is a much-admired production of an essentially empty text.

Measure for Measure with John Gielgud as Angelo. This production begins a long association with Gielgud.

Around this time reads *In Search of the Miraculous* by Peter Ouspensky (1878–1947) and subsequently begins to be influenced by the philosophies of the teacher and mystic Gurdjieff (1877–1949) (see Influences, 3.6.4.), who becomes a huge influence on his life and work.

1951: *A Penny for a Song* by John Whiting, *The Winter's Tale* by Shakespeare, and *Colombe* by Anouilh. Brook marries Natasha Parry, who like Brook is half Russian.

Engaged in a long succession
of popular 'West End'
productions

1953: *Venice Preserved* by Otway and *The Little Hut* by Rousin, the latter another example of a French boulevard comedy translated uneasily into English.

1954: *The Dark is Light Enough* by Fry with Edith Evans. Part of the shortlived revival of verse plays, popular at the time.

1955: Directs *The Lark* by Anouilh/Fry at the Lyric, Hammersmith. *Titus Andronicus* at Stratford with Laurence Olivier, when he rediscovers the play after a century of almost total neglect. Again deals with issues of extreme violence. He is also designer and composer for this production.

1956: *A View from the Bridge* by Arthur Miller (another production which courts controversy), staged in France but banned by the English authorities.

The year 1956 marks a dramatic change in the theatre climate in England. The arrival of such plays as *Look Back in Anger* by John Osborne, whose central character, Jimmy Porter, gives rise to the phrase 'angry young man', brings a new realism to bear on a distinctly moribund English theatre. Brook is untouched by these changes.

1957: *Eugene Onegin*, Tchaikovsky, Metropolitan, New York and *The Tempest*, Shakespeare, Stratford-upon-Avon.

1958: Directs *The Visit* by Friedrich Durrenmatt (b.1921). The production is unquestionably a political play, written after the model of Brecht's theatre, but Brook is untouched by this connection at this time and buries his version of the text in a realist narrative structure. Directs *Irma La Douce*, a lively and very popular musical, adapted from the French.

1960: Directs *Le Balcon*, by Jean Genet (1910–86) in Paris. Is now a regular commuter between London, Paris and New York.

1962: Brook's production of *King Lear* can be seen as a landmark in his career (see Theory and Practice 3.6.3). Brook himself designs an austere, spare set, lit by permanently bright light, and the actor Paul Scofield, as Lear, plays him with cold objective detachment (see Films and Videos 3. 6.7).

The production marks a major shift in Brook's thinking. Elaborate and decorative design is rejected in favour of stripping things down to bare essentials. Much influenced by the plays of Samuel Beckett, Japanese theatre and the Polish author Jan Kott (see Influences 3.6.4).

1963: A prolific year: his film *Lord of the Flies* appears (see Films and Videos 3.6.7). He produces *The Physicists* by Durrenmatt in London and his second version of *The Tempest* in Stratford-upon-Avon, with John Gielgud as Prospero.

He stages *Sergeant Musgrave's Dance* by John Arden in Paris.

He is given a sum of money by the RSC to work with a group of twelve actors on an experimental basis, taking the ideas of Artaud and his Theatre of Cruelty further.

SECOND PHASE 1964–70

Theatre of Cruelty workshop

1964: Brook collaborates with Charles Marowitz on the Theatre of Cruelty workshops inspired by Artaud.

After eight weeks an experimental programme of 'work in progress' is mounted at LAMDA under the title *Theatre of Cruelty*. This work leads directly to his sensational production of *Marat/Sade* in August at the RSC.

Grotowski works with Brook's company

1966: *Theatre of Cruelty* experiments continue with a production of *U.S* at the Aldwych, a play about the Vietnam War. He uses a multitude of contradictory techniques aimed at breaking down the boundary of the 'fourth wall' between actors and audience. Jerzy Grotowski (1933–99) is invited to work with the company.

1968: *Oedipus* at the Old Vic, London. Again with John Gielgud and Irene Worth.

The Empty Space is published

He publishes his collection of four essays, *The Empty Space*, setting out basic approaches to theatre. The first time he has published thoughts about his working process. An influential and well-regarded text.

Works in Paris

Invited by Jean Louis-Barrault to be a contributor to Théâtres des Nations, Paris.

He is becoming more involved with a group, led by Madame de Salzmann, who are exploring the life and work of Gurdjieff.

The student revolutionary unrest interrupts the Paris workshop and on his return to London with a small group stages a collage version of *The Tempest* at the Roundhouse.

THIRD PHASE 1970–PRESENT

1970: *A Midsummer Night's Dream* at Stratford. It is a triumph, and is probably the single most celebrated production the RSC has ever achieved.

Leaves London for Paris

In November finally leaves London for Paris where he sets up the International Centre for Theatre Research

1971: *Orghast at Persepolis*. Continues to test the possibilities of a non-narrative Western theatre, notably in an experiment at Persepolis in Persia (Iran).

1972–3: An adaptation of a 12th-century Persian text, *The Conference of the Birds*, is toured to West Africa to an audience unused to any kind of theatre experience.

International productions go on tour

1973–80: Following the *Conference of the Birds* produces *The Ik* – a true story of a displaced Ugandan tribe – and Jarry's *Ubu Roi* (see 3.3.4), the latter being performed virtually without masks or costumes and using a minimum of props. In a typical move he bypasses the big culture houses and plays Off-Off Broadway in La Mama's Studio. In 1980 all three productions are performed on consecutive evenings. The critics are ecstatic.

Settles in Paris   **1974:** Discovers a derelict theatre in the north of Paris which becomes the company's home

Returns briefly to the RSC   In between *The Ik*, *Ubu* and various productions of *The Birds*, Brook returns to Shakespeare with *Timon of Athens* (1974) and *Anthony and Cleopatra* (1978), a return to the RSC.

1979: Directs a film about the mystic Georgei Gurdjieff, *Meetings with Remarkable Men*.

Chekhov and Bizet   **1981:** Directs *The Cherry Orchard* at The Bouffes du Nord, Paris, and during the same year makes a triumphant return to opera with a radical production of Bizet's *Carmen*, pared away to its vital personal encounters.

Directs the ground-breaking   **1985:** *The Mahabarata* is presented in French at the Avignon Festival. A
Mahabarata   9-hour epic, it is performed over three evenings. It is the result of a 10-year collaboration with French writer Jean-Claude Carrière. The production tours the world (Glasgow, America, Japan) and is subsequently made into a film.

1990: *La Tempête* (*The Tempest*) in a version by Carrière, Bouffes du Nord, Paris. This is the third time Brook has tackled this text.

1993: Publishes *There Are No Secrets* containing further thoughts on acting and the nature of theatre. *L'Homme Qui* (*The Man Who*). Performed in English and French, it is based on the novel by neurologist Oliver Sacks, *The Man Who Mistook His Wife For a Hat*. It deals with the theme of madness, drawing Brook back to his early experiments with Artaud.

1996: He is 71. Directs a selection of scenes from *Hamlet*.

His memoir is published   **1998:** Publishes *Threads of Time*, a memoir.

Working in Paris and London   **2000:** Directs *Le Costume* at Bouffes du Nord, originally staged in London by the Market Theatre, Johannesburg. Revives *The Island*, by Athol Fugard, at the Royal National Theatre, London.

This chronology is indebted to:
Hunt, A. and Reeves, G.,   *Peter Brook*,   Methuen, 1995
(where a fuller play chronology can be found)
and
Brook, P.,   *Threads of Time, A Memoir*,   Methuen, 1998
(a very useful account of a life's work, although lacks specific dates).

3.6.2   A BRIEF BIOGRAPHY

A celebrated director at a   By the time Peter Brook was 22 he was firmly established as one of the
young age   most sought-after directors in the English-speaking theatre. Star actors were not only willing to work with him but actively sought him out to direct them, and he was a guarantee of a prestige production which more often than not attracted welcome notoriety. Luck seems to have played no small part in his meteoric rise: a meeting with Barry Jackson
Early success   at Birmingham Repertory Theatre when he was 20 led to seasons at Stratford-upon-Avon, where he made his mark with the little-regarded Shakespeare play *Love's Labour's Lost*.

Russian parents

Brook seems to have had a relatively untroubled childhood: his father and mother (both from Russia) escaped to England before the First World War, where they were quickly assimilated. They were part of the great diaspora thrown up by the Russian Revolution a fact worth remembering when we come to consider Brook's move to Paris in 1972. The dismay

Brook as part of a European sensibility

this generated was based on his supposed betrayal of his Englishness, but it should have been obvious that this first-generation Englishman was more a part of a European sensibility than anybody realised.

His schooldays were interrupted by illness. Two years spent in the Swiss Alps were what he called his 'merciful years of idleness' [p.18], and confirmed his abiding interest in film and toy theatre. 'The movies were my real window on another world' [p.6]. He spent a year as an

Apprentice in a film studio

apprentice in a film studio before university, which gave him the basic knowledge of production, and it was at Oxford that he formed the Film Society and directed his first film with fellow undergraduates.

Even at this early age he courted adverse criticism for his activities and it was the first in a lifetime of *causes célèbres*. All his life he has had a tendency to self-dramatisation and promotion, qualities it must be recognised are useful in the arts. But film was rapidly overtaken by ventures in theatre production and although he would make filmed

Theatre dominated his creative life

versions of his productions and direct a few original scenarios, for the rest of his life it was theatre that would dominate his creative process.

> 'My obsession with film was helping me realise that a play is also a spool that unrolls; its truth comes to life **shot by shot**.'

[p.37]

But he did not heed the logic of his own advice. Far from employing techniques associated with **montage** (see 3.4.3) and a political

A mainstream career in popular theatre

viewpoint, his subsequent mainstream career firmly maintained an allegiance to an escapist/realist/decorative narrative.

> . . . the theatre world to which I was now drawn was dominated by men with fastidiously draped muslin curtains at their windows . . .

[p.38].

He favoured what he called the 'romance' of the proscenium arch, which was epitomised by the impresario Binkie Beaumont who almost single-handedly dictated the style of West End theatre in the late 1940s and the 1950s.

When he later abandoned this theatre it was to move from the dominance of the proscenium arch to a shared space in which audience and actors were 'within the same field of life' [p.134]. At the age of 22

Failures at Covent Garden

he was director of productions at Covent Garden, a prestigious and important post, but this appointment was doomed to failure. What the Opera House wanted was a pliable and conservative administrator with qualities that were in direct opposition to Brook's practice. It is worth noting that while he was there he took the initiative of looking to Europe for his designers, signalling an early awareness of how European theatre, and specifically Paris, might play a part in his development.

Influenced by his travels

As a multi-lingual committed traveller he was already commuting to Paris on a regular basis and it is there that he came across the philosophical works that were to sustain and influence him for the rest of his life.

Studies the teaching of Gurdjieff

In his memoir he is vague about just what the influence of Gurdjieff (see Influences 3.6.4) was: phrases such as 'I learned to understand the oriental way' [p.69] do not reveal very much, though among Gurdjieff's followers, Brook is considered to be an important figure. Perhaps the most important aspect of Gurdjieff's teaching was his insistence on the oral tradition, that is, passing knowledge on by word of mouth. Brook's favoured method of working has always been through the practical before the theoretical.

Dismissive of Brechtian theatre

Despite a trip to Berlin to see the newly formed Berliner Ensemble in 1951, he remained unconvinced by Brechtian theatre and its associated theory (see 3.4). Though he was to use recognisable Brechtian techniques in *Marat/Sade*, this exposure was too early to have much effect as he was still mired in the theatre of illusion: 'For me the stage was still the world of illusion' [p.73], and indeed so it proved to be.

Popular theatre directed with immense skill and flair

With few exceptions, from *Ring round the Moon* in 1950 to *King Lear* in 1962 Brook continued to blaze a trail with dynamic and thrilling productions of second-rate works, many of these being translations of French texts. Hunt and Reeves suggest that Brook 'seems to have got his hands on the best available' [1995. p.25]. A few unqualified successes rose above the mundane: *Titus Andronicus*, with the Oliviers, toured to Europe in 1955 and brought Brook to the attention of Jan Kott (see Influences, 3.6.4). An emasculated version of *The Visit* by Durrenmatt played New York and London and was considered a daring and controversial choice and in 1957 his first attempt at *The Tempest*, with John Gielgud at Stratford, banished the over-decorative with his own designs and music concrete.

King Lear is a watershed in his career

King Lear (1962) (see 3.6.3) was a real watershed in his working life. He allowed himself to be influenced by the playwright Samuel Beckett (1906–89) and his play *Endgame* (1958) and Jan Kott, to whose book *Shakespeare our Contemporary* he had contributed an introduction. Both these men offered him an opportunity to rethink his approach to this text and specifically to 'remove facile sentimentality' and as a result deny his audience any 'spiritual reassurance'. This experiment, which ran so counter to his previous work, led two years later to the now

Theatre of Cruelty

celebrated workshop he called The Theatre of Cruelty.

Artaud's influence

Again this marked a radical shift in his thinking and although far from critically successful this exploration of Artaudian theory (see 3.3) gave him the opportunity to extend the improvisational techniques he had used in *Lear* and move towards a more fluid and rigorous process, where 'sound, gesture, rhythm, colour and music' were the primary means of expression. This workshop, funded by the RSC, led to further experimental work and directly to his sensational *Marat/Sade*.

'The fine muslin curtains over the windows in the beautifully decorated terrace houses' [p.138] had finally been pulled back and he was now embarked on the final productions of his years in England with a

Artaud becomes a huge
inspiration

Forms his own company

strengthened critical purpose. It was as if Artaud had opened the door, and was the much overdue inspiration that would sustain him for the rest of his working life. The move to Paris in 1970 marked another turning point in his work and with the foundation of the Centre International Recherches Théâtrales (CIRT), devoted as it was to exploration and unfettered by the demands of commercial production, Brook had found the ideal outlet for renewed creativity.

> 'We were there not to learn but to unlearn, discarding hard-earned skills so as to discover something from the most innocent of our members ...'

[p165].

An important practitioner

Here he embarked on a succession of productions which confirmed him as one of the most important and innovative practitioners of the late 20th century. Almost immediately (1971) he signalled his intentions (in collaboration with the poet Ted Hughes) with the *Orghast at Persepolis*:

> After years of involvement with wood, canvas and paint, spotlights and flood-lamps, here the sun, moon, earth, rock, and fire opened up a new world that would influence our work for years to come.

[p.176]

World travels

Further experiments took the company to Africa, Australia and the USA, always returning to their base at the Bouffes du Nord, a semi-derelict theatre in the north of Paris.

Figure 3.36   The derelict theatre stripped bare, Bouffes du Nord, Paris

International success

It was here in 1988 that the greatest test of his vision came to a reality in *The Mahabarata*, a retelling of the Indian epic. In three parts played over 8 hours, it stunned the imagination of its world audience with its vivid story-telling, visual magnificence and acting of refined athleticism.

He has denied that he is a 'guru', but there is no gainsaying his influence on the shape of theatre at the end of the 20th century. No other practitioner has had such a long and practically productive life; reinventing himself Brook has vindicated his work with this statement:

A statement of belief in theatre

> ... theatre is not just a place, not simply a profession, it is a metaphor. It helps to make the process of life more clear.

[p.225]

All page references are to Brook, P., *Threads of Time, A Memoir*, Methuen, 1999 unless otherwise stated.

3.6.3 THEORY AND PRACTICE

By examining a number of productions in some detail we are able to establish the progression of Brook's **practice**. It is important to remember that he saw theatre as a continuous act of discovery, in which process had equal weight with product and where theoretical concepts were always supportive of practice.

SEVEN KEY PRODUCTIONS

KING LEAR 1962   Pre-production

> This was a performance for our era; a harsh, brutally unsentimental *King Lear* set in a dismal and industrialised, abstract world.

[Helfer and Loney, 1998. p.111]

A complete rethinking of approach

From the start Brook's intention was to wrest this text from a century of patriarchal sentimentality and he did so through a close study of Jan Kott's seminal essay in *Shakespeare our Contemporary* (see 3.6.4). In preparation for a year, this was the first production that Brook admits to as representing a real shift in his thinking. Remember it comes at the end of a relatively populist period and just before the ground-breaking *Theatre of Cruelty* season.

Rehearsal

Working with trusted actors

'The communication between us was now so deep that it required few words' [Brook, 1999. p.34]. So Brook describes the ideal relationship that he had achieved with Paul Scofield over a period of 10 years.

Brook describes how Scofield seems to have worked from the outside in, starting with the picture of the man and 'by force of inner conviction' communicating his image of the man. There was no direct psychological examination of the character, Scofield maintaining that the 'text supplied all the necessary answers'.

Allowed experimentation

However, with the other actors Brook encouraged endless experimentation allowing them to move and speak until they themselves had 'found something', this being achieved through their response to exhausting rehearsals as much as by reason. Brook at times could be maddeningly vague but his constant elimination of all possibilities allowed the actor to arrive at the right solution, however late in the day that might be.

Rehearsal technique

Devices used to broaden the text were speeches prefaced by 'he said', which distanced the character from his text (a very Brechtian device) and the use of the mask to further differentiate character.

Scenography

Brook had taken responsibility for the designs of the previous Shakespeare productions of *Titus Andronicus* (1955) and *The Tempest* (1957):

The director as designer

I find that it is terribly important in Shakespeare in particular that I design myself ... If you are doing it yourself it means that over a long period of time your imagery and your staging evolve together.

[Brook, 1987. p. 91]

but *Lear* was the last time he cast himself as both director and designer. In the last week of pre-rehearsal he had abandoned his complex set realising that he had created a potential technical nightmare and as a result tore most of the model apart leaving the simplest of screens as a backing to the stage-bound action.

Simplifying the design

The set was open: two vast rectangular flats, the backcloth and stage all painted a subtle whitish, chalky grey – geometrical straight lines only broken by dangling squares and triangles of painted metal (for the palace) and three corroded metal thunder sheets (for the storm).

[Hunt and Reeves, 1995. p.48]

Influence of Edward Gordon Craig

The three huge thunder sheets, which had been extensively aged with paint, descended for the storm scenes and were animated by small motors to create a deafening roar. The set owed much to Edward Gordon Craig (see 3.1), with its strong vertical lines receding to a vast all-encompassing cyclorama, truly an '*Empty Space*'. Furniture was of natural hewn wood and all other props were of worn metal, suggesting the barbaric; a society that was past but had tangible objects to be sat upon and handled.

Clothes broken down

After the first preview all the clothes were considered too new-looking so a lot of work went into 'breaking them down' to make them look old and much used, as well as the furniture and props.

Open white light

The lighting was white, bright and unrelenting to match the tone of the production, taking inspiration from both Brecht and, as one critic recognised, 'Chinese theatre', a motif to be explored later in *A Midsummer Night's Dream* (1970).

Performance

Begins to question the
proscenium arch

In this production Brook had begun to question his concept of theatre as 'two rooms', the auditorium and stage separated by the proscenium arch:

> ... having the performers share one space intimately with the audience offers an experience infinitely richer than dividing the space into what one can call two rooms ...

[Brook, 1999. p.41]

House lights used to involve
the audience

There was little he could do in the vast unfriendly space of the Stratford theatre but what he did was to use the house-lights as a bridge between the two worlds; at specific moments the link was made explicit. On the blinding of Gloucester, at the point where he was allowed to drag himself off, the house-lights came up to underline the audience's complicity in the terror of the act.

Figure 3.37   A scene from *King Lear*, 1962

Summary

- A radical re-thinking of the text related to a theoretical perspective;
- Improvisation used as a way towards understanding and speaking text;
- Simplified design, influenced by Gordon Craig;
- The audience drawn into the action at specific points.

THEATRE OF CRUELTY

Artaud's influence

In 1964 Brook obtained funding from the RSC, where he was one of the co-directors, to initiate a workshop to explore the work and writings of Antonin Artaud (see 3.3). The workshop was christened ' The Theatre of Cruelty' in homage to the essay by Artaud in his *The Theatre and Its Double*.

> Both Marowitz and I admired the burning intensity of the positions Artaud took in relation to the safe theatre of his day.

[Brook, 1999. p.134]

Establishes a company   As Brook himself admitted, his intentions were pretty vague: primarily he looked on this period as a time to establish the beginnings of an ensemble, to experiment with voice and the body and, in what he termed 'research' conditions, to free the actor from the constraints of the proscenium arch.

> Our only public performances must indeed have seemed very strange, for they presented unearthly cries, long silences, splashes of red paint, Glenda Jackson stark naked, and lines of *Hamlet* shuffled out of all apparent order.

[Brook, 1999. p.137]

Much of the initial work stemmed from Brook, who was seeking to establish a new theatre language through the exploration of 'simple sounds', both man-made and mechanical, moving as far away as possible from the spoken word.

In performance to a select band of critics and colleagues, Brook reversed the actor–audience relationship by placing the audience on the floor and the actors on the raised rostra. Reactions were mixed. Ironically the most successful improvisations were the naked humiliation of Glenda Jackson related to the Christine Keeler case and the 20-minute collage *Hamlet* devised by Marowitz, both of which had little to do with Artaudian theory.

Mixed audience reactions

Led to further experiments   The subsequent record published by Marowitz in note form in *Tulane Drama Review* became the bible for improvisation classes at drama schools throughout the 1960s. The workshop had laid the basis for further experimentation with a permanent company who, at the conclusion of the workshop, embarked on a cut version of Jean Genet's (1910–86) *The Screens* followed closely by one of the most successful productions mounted by the RSC, *The Marat/Sade*.

Marowitz, C.,   *Notes on the Theatre of Cruelty*,   TDR, Vol. 1 No. 2 Winter 1966 pp.152–73 (re-published without the accompanying photographs in Williams, D., *Peter Brook*, *A Theatrical Casebook*, Methuen, 1988).

THE PERSECUTION AND ASSASSINATION OF MARAT AS PERFORMED BY THE INMATES OF THE ASYLUM OF CHARENTON UNDER THE DIRECTION OF THE MARQUIS DE SADE [Hereafter known as *The Marat/Sade*] 1964

Pre-production

> ... everything in this play is designed to crack the spectator on the jaw, then douse him with ice-cold water, then force him to assess intelligently what has happened to him, then give him a kick in the balls, then bring him back to his senses again ...

[Brook, 1988. p. 47]

Brook had seen a production of this play by Peter Weiss in Berlin in 1964 and recognised an opportunity to bring together all the work his company had done in the *Theatre of Cruelty* workshop, feeling that the text was as 'agile and penetrating as any Elizabethan equivalent'. The play purports to be a documentary-style performance by the inmates of Charenton reliving the assassination of Jean-Paul Marat by Charlotte Corday.

Supervising the proceedings is the Marquis de Sade, and the whole event is witnessed by the on-stage audience of the asylum's director and his family. Casting was from the *Cruelty* group and resident actors at the RSC. Brook also won an extended rehearsal period of 8 weeks to include a workshop on the text before beginning rehearsals proper. The intention was to blend aspects of Artaudian excess, as in the characters of the mad inmates, with the coolness of Brechtian distanciation in the play's most politicised moments. Although the play had a sort of muddled philosophical message – society's redemption through revolution versus personal salvation – in the end it was the remarkable visual images that Brook created which stayed in the imagination.

Experiments from workshops are used in production
Extended rehearsal schedule

Brechtian influence

Rehearsal
Workshop on madness

Brook began rehearsal with a workshop on madness:

> Brook was looking for kinetic images of insanity . . .
>
> [Hunt and Reeves, 1995. p.86]

This tested some of the cast to their limits, Glenda Jackson commenting that she thought they were all going 'looney'. Many of the rehearsal techniques were adapted from material used in the *Cruelty* workshop and in particular Brook stressed the need for the actors to confront their need for violence in themselves so they could in turn get the audience to do likewise.

Visual research stimulates imagination

Brook introduced a variety of images to the cast: pictures by Goya and Hogarth and articles on madness; they watched films of inmates in a French asylum in performance and a Nigerian documentary on savage ritual. 'Every rehearsal became a living process', Brook pushing and teasing ideas from his company, who when tired responded to the director's unflagging enthusiasm. Through his direction they achieved that rare state for an actor, 'being' rather than 'acting'.

> They were able to create a closed world which powerfully suggested that this was the world as it really is. Extremes of madness became the norm.
>
> [Hunt and Reeves, 1995. p.93]

Ensemble approach

When the play transferred to New York at least one critic remarked: 'It is the finest ensemble that this town has seen since the Moscow Art Theatre's visit' [Helfer and Loney, 1998. p.135].

Scenography
A visual triumph

What critics remarked upon most vividly was the total 'look' of the production.

This review from 1964 describes the set:

> A towering windowless silo walled with tiny bricks and booby-trapped with sunken pits. Among the inmates with their padded clothes and sunken faces, the devil-worshipping priests and burned-out whores, the lecherous ex-aristos and the lethargic ex-rebels, the childish voluptuaries and the aged virgins, move the black-eyed nuns and the muscle-bound warders.
>
> [Quoted in Williams, 1988. p.65]

Figure 3.38   A scene from *The Marat/Sade*, 1964

Props used and transformed

The set and costumes were bleached out into an overall grey/white tone, the only colours being the red and blue of the French flag. In a chilling moment in the guillotine sequence, paint of the same colours was poured from one bucket into another to represent the victim's demise. Props were created from what might have been found in such a bleak environment – scrubbing brushes, for example, being turned into puppets, old brooms into processional totems. The lighting was unremittingly stark, bright and unchanging throughout, as was the auditorium. Music for the songs was raucous and catchy, very much in the style of Kurt Weill's *Threepenny Opera* (1928), further underlining the Brechtian aspects of the production.

Performance

Lighting used to unite actor and audience

Brook's desire to link actor and audience went further this time, and he achieved this through several means. Principally it was through the stage lighting, which remained constant throughout, as did the lighting in the auditorium, bringing the audience into the action and making them complicit in the outcome.

> Throughout the play, Brook did not let the audience forget the line between them and the stage was very fine, the open stage and bath-house seeming like a single room.

[Helfer and Loney, 1998. p.133]

As the audience applauded the conclusion of the riot which finished the play, the wretched cast advanced to the front of the stage as if to assault the audience and ironically applauded them. To link the audience even further with the action, the asylum director and his family were seated on-stage and occasionally the former interrupted the proceedings when they threatened to get out of hand. So – Brook had inmates (actors) involved in a re-enactment of past events under the direction of the Marquis de Sade (Brook) watched by an exclusive audience of notables watched in turn by the theatre audience – a potent interweaving of theatrical conventions.

Complex actor–audience relationships

> More than a quarter of a century later, *The Marat/Sade* stands alongside Littlewood's *Oh, What a Lovely War* as one of the outstanding productions of post-war British Theatre.

An outstanding production

> [Hunt and Reeves, 1995. p.95]

Summary
- An opportunity to test Artaudian theories in production;
- Extensive text workshops prior to rehearsal;
- Very successful collaboration with a designer;
- The audience were drawn into the action.

OEDIPUS 1968

Pre-production
When Brook was asked to stage Seneca's *Oedipus* at the National Theatre, it seemed the perfect text upon which to further his research, begun in the Theatre of Cruelty workshop four years earlier. Seneca's Roman tragedies had preoccupied Artaud with their potential for performance:

Researches Artaud's interest in Seneca's tragedies

> I weep upon reading his [Seneca's] inspired drama, and in it behind the word I sense syllables crepitating in the most ghastly manner with the transparent boiling up of the forces of chaos.

> [Quoted in Sellin, E., *The Dramatic Concepts of Artaud*. p.32]

So Brook grasped the opportunity to further his researches into Artaud, at the same time coming closer to his ideals with a true ensemble production. He negotiated a new, unpunctuated, translation from the poet Ted Hughes (1930–99), which drew on barbaric animal imagery and which transformed what was essentially a text to be read into one that could be spoken.

Commissions new translation by a poet

> the plague began with the sheep   it began with the
> grass the grass was suddenly poison   the air was
> suddenly stench

Animal imagery

> the bull at the altar   massive animal   the priest had
> hoisted his axe steadied his aim   in that second

> before the axe fell   the bull was down   was it
> touched by the god   it was touched by the plague.

> [Quoted in Williams, 1988. p.118]

Ritual

The 'chaos' of Artaud was transformed into a carefully crafted ritual in which the modern poetry of Hughes sought to mirror the savagery of a primitive civilisation of pre-myth.

Remember that Brook was one of the first directors to rediscover the revenge tragedies of Shakespeare in his production of *Titus Andronicus* (1955). Shakespeare had drawn heavily on his knowledge of Seneca for his own work so in one sense Brook was returning to earlier preoccupations – the portrayal of violence on-stage and how it is resolved for actor and audience.

Violence on-stage

Rehearsal

Improvisation in rehearsal

Rehearsals proved to be most productive and challenging, reflecting Brook's growing confidence in using improvisation as a way into the exploration of a text. Since *Oedipus* had been written to be read not spoken the company were faced with a daunting task. How to animate a very static text?

While the principals rehearsed mainly with Brook the chorus occupied the deserted theatre, where they were able

> to find the precise point at which a living impulse could be truly passed around a group of people . . .

[Hunt and Reeves, 1995. p.123].

Problems of choral speaking

The aim was to unite a choral-speaking group who were scattered throughout the theatre.

The distinctive English text was full of vivid imagery but an unrehearsed reading could sound prosaic (a problem that Brook would re-encounter in *The Mahabarata*). The task was to transform and extend this blueprint into a recognisable text with the same power as the Greek original.

Sound pictures

When the chorus eventually met the principals they began the task of devising sound pictures to accompany their major speeches and to underline the emotional shifts inherent in the text. There were many physicalised improvisations, one of the most notable being that based on the plague, a theme for the first chorus in the play.

> Several of the actors became 'plague infested rats' and the rest had to get from one end of the room to the other blindfold without touching them.

[Hunt and Reeves, 1995. p.127]

Those who were touched caught the plague until the whole room was filled with victims; almost immediately the actors sat in a circle and tried to reproduce vocally the suffering they had just encountered.

Scenography

In a theatre which was essentially a Victorian playhouse the opportunities for experimentation were limited, but Brook was determined to further destroy the concept of 'two rooms', stage and auditorium, so he placed the chorus in the auditorium, lashed to the pillars, and actors came and went through the auditorium. This spreading of the chorus was a total

The chorus in the auditorium

reverse of the Greek idea that the chorus was essentially a massed body of like-minded individuals. But with Artaud in mind, Brook was once again exploring the idea of a vortex of sound in which the audience were caught up. It was also a chance to break through the proscenium arch, which had been a tentative move in *The Marat Sade* but which was now to be taken much further.

Another break with the proscenium arch

The set was a gigantic gold cube on a revolve, which opened to reveal a glittering interior, the four sides when lowered forming ramps. When not directly involved in the action the cast sat on the sidelines on benches.

Figure 3.39   A scene from *Oedipus*, 1968

'Timeless' costumes

Costumes went through several stages and eventually became as 'neutral' as possible, achieving a kind of timeless simplicity which had been so problematic in *King Lear*. Men wore roll-necked sweaters with trousers, the women were in very simple tunic-like dresses.

Performance

> . . . it had the feeling of being twentieth-century theatre and effectively banished those toga and fluted-pillar abominations for ever . . .

[Hunt and Reeves, 1995. p.131].

Fusions of text and man-made sound

The performance was notable for its complete fusion of text/sound. With the chorus scattered around the theatre not everyone heard every word, but at moments when sounds starting from the balcony spiralled to the chorus in the stalls, the whole theatre was transformed into a vibrant sound-scape.

Whole theatre becomes a performance space

Gielgud sums up the tone of the whole production: highly charged emotional moments diffused with ritualistic, almost catatonic movement. The 'coolness' of the acting reverberated against the unleashed terror, represented by the chorus.

> Antonin Artaud ... believed in the magical power of these primeval sounds ... Brook is the first to have used this storehouse of primitive emotion in a successful production in the theatre.

[Martin Esslin quoted in Williams, 1988. p.121]

Summary
- Research into Artaudian theatre continued;
- A new translation sought to create a mythic quality;
- Extensive chorus rehearsals created new sounds;
- The Empty Space was now both stage and auditorium.

THE EMPTY SPACE

Seminal text for generations of students

> I can take an empty space and call it a bare stage. A man walks across this empty space whilst someone else is watching him, and this is all that is needed for an act of theatre to be engaged.

[Brook, 1968. p.11]

With this often-quoted phrase Brook opens his volume of essays entitled *The Empty Space* (1968). Originally given as a series of lectures the collection represented much of Brook's theoretical thinking until that moment, and despite the fact that it is now over 30 years old it is still a passionate collective statement.

In four chapters, *The Deadly Theatre*, *The Holy Theatre*, *The Rough Theatre* and *The Immediate Theatre*, Brook explores his four themes.

The Deadly Theatre

The Deadly Theatre represents all that is bad about theatre, with such themes as commerce, the critics, deadly repetition, prices, an actor's training and the playwright, and concludes by asking the pertinent question of 'why theatre?'

The Holy Theatre

The Holy Theatre represents the theatre that Brook was pursuing at the time of writing. Here he looks at the theatre of ritual as expressed through Artaud, the rethinking of the actor/audience relationship, and how he has been influenced by other practitioners (see Influences 3.6.4).

The Rough Theatre (see Followers 3.6.5)

The Rough Theatre stands for what Brook sees as 'popular theatre', the theatre of laughter, of Joan Littlewood, of the breakdown in actor–audience relationships, of Brecht and the meaning of illusion versus alienation. This chapter demonstrates how wide ranging Brook was in his understanding of diverse forms, and in his belief that theatre was to be a theatre of 'truth' made evident.

The Immediate Theatre

The Immediate Theatre is a contemporary look at Brook's own best practice, examining such issues as design, the selection of actors for a company, the role of the director and rehearsals, acting, improvisation and the virtues of exploration.

Written in his distinctive didactic style the whole book remains a valuable primer for a would-be director.

Brook's Holy and Rough
= Theatre

The theatre Brook sought was a combination of *Holy* and *Rough* theatre, a theatre of shared concerns, an acknowledgement of the audience as part of the celebration, and with the actor, with all his powers, restored to the core of creation.

A MIDSUMMER NIGHT'S DREAM 1970

Anti-Romantic

Pre-planning
This was to be the most outstanding production seen at the RSC up until that date and some would argue till the present day. Early decisions included the desire to strip the play of all 19th-century Romanticism, to foreground the power of Shakespeare's text, to work with a white canvas on which to paint the action, and to treat the play as a 'celebration' in which the actors could reach out to their audience.

Rehearsal

Extended rehearsal

Again Brook fought for and obtained an extended 8-week period of rehearsal. Early rhythmic exercises with sticks being passed from hand to hand helped in learning basic dexterity both in movement and speaking the text. These extended to a rehearsal room that gradually acquired

'trapezes, ropes, plastic rods, spinning plates, tennis balls, hoops, paper, string, and a variety of musical instruments' . . .

[John Kane quoted in Williams, 1988. p.150]

Influence of Chinese circus

Sally Jacobs (the designer) and Brook had seen a Chinese circus in Paris and much was taken and adapted from these performers. The idea that spinning plates on the end of rods, with the addition of a humming sound, could stand for the magic flower, was indeed magical. There was an emphasis on increasing self-awareness, frustrated by Brook's inability or refusal to guide the actors at every turn.

Explore all possibilities

[He] asked them to look inside themselves to solve the 'mystery', to find their own individual rhythms, explore the limits of their own individual possibilities . . .

[Hunt and Reeves, 1995. p.153]

From chaos to selection

He talked a lot about the 'secret play', the hidden text which could only be revealed by the rehearsal process. One way this was achieved was through a rehearsal in which Brook allowed complete chaos to reign, the space literally reduced to a wreck but from which Brook was able, from his experience, to select and reject material for further work.

Scenography
This was to be the first Shakespearian production in which Brook collaborated with a designer and it was to be so successful that audiences were to remark on it and remember what it looked like long after the acting itself was forgotten.

A box of magical tricks

The desire to transform the RSC Stratford theatre from 'cruel' to 'kind' gave the impulse to the idea of a box, partly because it would improve the appalling acoustics, but mainly, like a box of tricks, it could become magical simply by the way it was to be used. Further it could be coloured white to act as a blank canvas on which to 'paint' the play, and with the idea of 'celebration' in mind the actors could be contained within the space by the expedient of having them watch the action simply by constructing a gallery above.

Figure 3.40   *A Midsummer Night's Dream.* The white box.

Into this 'squash court, gym, clinic and circus tent' the actors arrived with their simple loose-fitting multicoloured costumes in stark contrast to the traditional tight-fitting clothes worn by circus acrobats.

Open white light

The lighting remained as open-white for the whole play, as in *King Lear* eight years earlier; the lack of artifice was to be under intense scrutiny by an audience willing to suspend disbelief.

More like a gym than a set

Anti-naturalistic

Doors were cut into the four walls, and entrances right and left ran from the stage to the catwalk allowing access for Puck on his stilts. With a vertical ladder stage left and right access to the balcony was possible from stage level. As a result the play was totally contained within the parameters of this white space. There was absolutely no feeling of an off-stage world so usual in naturalistic drama, the world of the play began and ended within the white box. It was a total vindication of Brook's concept of 'the empty space'.

A form of nothingness

On a nothingness, moment by moment, something can be conjured up – and then made to disappear. The bare stage is a form of nothingness . . .

[Brook in Helfer and Loney, 1998. p.180]

Performance

Celebration

The concept of 'celebration' dominated the production, from the first entrance of the entire cast in their anonymous flowing white capes acknowledging applause, to the final moments when they stepped over the proscenium arch, acknowledging the audience with physical contact.

> Puck: Give me your hands if we be friends, And Robin shall restore amends.

> [Act 5 Sc 1]

The audience complicit in the action

During the course of the action speeches were frequently delivered into the auditorium making the audience complicit in the action, and with an entire lack of naturalistic detail a high level of imaginative response was demanded:

> The onlooker is a partner who must be forgotten and still kept in mind: a gesture is statement, expression, communication ... – it is always what Artaud calls a signal through the flames – yet it implies a sharing of experience once contact is made.

> [Brook, 1986. p.57].

and

Flowing over the footlights

> One really felt a desire on his part to make the play flow emotionally over the footlights, and to celebrate something shared with the audience ...

> [Kenneth Tynan in *New Theatre Quarterly*, No. 25 Spring 1977].

Highly physical

The lovers raced in and out of the doors, climbed the ladders, became stranded on the trapezes and, with Puck on stilts, raced in frustrated anger between his extended legs. Hermia was entangled in trees represented by huge coils of wire manipulated by the spirits/fairies, who were also responsible for the assorted musical effects played in full sight of the audience from the gallery. The trapezes became a central mechanism in the production – Titania took Bottom to her bed on one transformed with huge red ostrich feathers – and Oberon and Puck

Skilled in magic tricks

became so skilled in handling their spinning plates that they could pass one to the other while suspended several metres above the ground.

> It was poetry, ritual, ballet and circus all rolled into one ...

> [Ronald Bryden in *The Observer*. Quoted in Helfer and Loney, 1998. p.154]

Summary

- The production was anti-romantic;
- Rehearsals were highly physical;
- The all-white set was a box of tricks to be explored and played with;
- The production was a celebration, a reaching out to its audience.

Williams, 1988. pp.148–56

Selbourne, D.,   *The Making of a Midsummer Night's Dream*,   Methuen, 1982

THE MOVE TO PARIS
Establishing a company

By November 1970 Brook had finally achieved the reality of a fully funded company of actors and directors at the Mobilier National, Paris.

> How sad the setting seemed for a new beginning – yet it was this uninspiring bleakness that suddenly inspired its own solution ... Let's transform this **dreary room** and start with a **celebration**.
>
> [Brook, 1999. p.161]

From the start much of the work took its inspiration from outside Europe, Brook feeling that it should be

> ... outside the limiting framework and limited responses of the European theatre-goer ...
>
> [Williams, 1988. p.168]

A EUROPEAN SENSIBILITY

The composition of the company was such that cultural diversity could be seen as a reflection of the real world, and as Williams (1988) suggests, the result was much like a 17th-century troupe of the Commedia dell'Arte.

It was not until 1974 that the company found a permanent home at the forgotten Théâtre des Bouffes du Nord, in northern Paris and it was here that they were able to mount and present all future work before the inevitable international tours. The conscious decision to leave the fire-damaged theatre much as it was found was based on a number of concerns:

An old theatre is transformed

> ... that the old theatre may be a sacred place and that the ghosts of past productions are a reality and, if friendly, a benign presence. Slap on too much new paint and too much guilding and the ghosts will leave.
>
> [Mackintosh, 1995. p.84]

Returning from their travels where at best sand, sun and rock had been the company's environment, what better space could they reinhabit than that of a battered shell in which to recreate their experience?

Audience now part of the total space

The stage floor was levelled and extended into the auditorium, the proscenium being negated by this simple solution; cushions and simple benches created the equivalent of the stalls and the peeling stucco balconies were retained with new seating. The back wall was patched and left as it was, providing Brook with a stage 60 feet deep.

> An attempt to reunite the community, in all its diversity, within the same shared experience.
>
> [Williams, D., in *Theatre Quarterly*, February, 1985. p.41].

(Glimpses of the result can be seen in the opening sequences of the film *Diva* directed by Jean-Jacques Beineix, France 1981.)

ORGHAST AT PERSEPOLIS 1971

Pre-production

Now that Brook was established in Paris his changed circumstances allowed for a completely new approach to the creative process:

New approaches to creative process

- with funding in place, commercial concerns were no longer a priority;
- he was able to assemble a company and collaborators of his own choosing;
- he had a permanent base in which to conduct his research;
- he could begin to teach;
- he could organise his own international performances where theory could be tested.

A 'montage' of texts

Gradually text emerged from such writers as Aeschylus' whose play *Prometheus Bound* became the central image, plus text from the Spanish playwright Calderon, a chorus from an Armenian play, extracts from Seneca, and an exploration of Avesta, the ceremonial language of Iran. These combined with text by the poet Ted Hughes formed the core of *Orghast*. Innes [1993. p.137] draws attention to the similarities this experiment had to the word patterns of the French surrealists of the 1930s (see pp.275–6) and to Artaud.

Rehearsal

Before work began on the text itself, workshops concentrated on three themes:

Movement, voice and text become most important

Movement: Sticks, which had first been seen in *The Dream*, were used as a means of sharpening responses and as extensions to the body in group exercises. With Yoshi Oida, the Japanese actor, the company explored simple movements and sounds from the Japanese Noh theatre, and *t'ai chi*, an Eastern physical discipline which developed bodily awareness.

Voice and text: Early work resolved itself into a strange invented language that was used in improvisation, which was necessary because of the different nationalities of the actors at the Centre.

> The expressive qualities of tone, pitch and rhythm could be exploited, without the interference of conceptual meaning.
>
> [Innes, 1993. p.136]

Process is as important as product

There was now no division between process and product, the process was a continuous one that led naturally into performance and beyond. It is interesting to note how much longer the preparation had become at this stage: the balance had radically shifted from the 4-week rehearsal period of Brook's early career followed by a long run, to that of months of preparation followed by a quite limited and restricted performance schedule. (See also Grotowski, 3.5.)

Acquisition of ancient languages

When the company arrived in Iran, the task began of teaching the Iranian members of the cast how to tackle the demands of text and movement. The Iranians helped particularly with the ancient language of Avesta and working groups revolved around Brook and his assistants so that everyone could learn as fast as possible; much work was done on improvisation, which sought above all to integrate the two groups.

Scenography

This was the first of Brook's productions to rely on the elemental for its setting, the columns and tombs of forgotten kings being overpowering in scale and atmosphere. Other productions that recreated the natural environment were the African experience, with a carpet placed on a mud floor to give the performance definition, *Carmen* (1981), with sand on the floor of Les Bouffes, and finally the epic *The Mahabarata* (1987), with rock, sand and water imported to each new venue in which the production was recreated. Just as the Bouffes du Nord was a found object and left as it was, worn by fire and the elements, so these new settings would seek to find a solution using natural materials rather than any artificial construct.

Performance

The sheer scale of the setting encouraged the use of distance: actors as much as 200 yards away could begin their text while slowly advancing into the main arena. The whole experience was a vivid marrying of actor/music/text to one of the most awe-inspiring environments in the world. Lighting was minimal but since the performance began at dusk, flaming torches added greatly to the darkening atmosphere. Fire played a significant part in the performance, uniting the elements in the unfolding of the tragedy. Flaming torches, fires, the sun itself setting and rising – all contributed to an overwhelming sense of man in unity with nature.

> ... the association of the artificially constructed myth with archaic religion, gave *Orghast* a level of reality and intensity that could hardly otherwise have been achieved.

[Innes, 1993. p.141]

Summary

- The first experiment with a montage of texts;
- Extensive rehearsals worked on text and movement;
- Mythic theatre was recreated by returning to its roots in nature;
- The natural environment became the Empty Space.

TRAVELS IN AFRICA

On the return of the company from Iran, further experimental work was undertaken and in 1972 Brook set out for a 3-month journey in North and West Africa. Brook said:

> Behind this choice there were so many reasons: our already firmly established respect for the richness of African traditions, the feeling that there was something unique we could learn from the freedom of African performers, and above all the conviction that in Africa we would have no credit to draw on, no easy falling back on the shared references and topical jokes that never fail in a city. We would be out on a limb, and this danger was both stimulating and essential.

[Brook, 1998. p.179]

Improvisation becomes important

The resulting performances took the form of improvised scenarios supported by three distinct strands of research: the physical, the use of objects, the musical. The refining of the physicality of the actors was a constant preoccupation in Brook's improvisations, mainly based on simple themes such as hate, love or lust. The adoption of objects was an extension of this in which a prop such as a loaf of bread, a stick, a box, a shoe became central to the exposition of the drama. Finally there were musical forms, in which the group continued with work done in *Orghast* but also performed 'vocal exercises in non-naturalistic sound and collective choral work'.

The aim above all was to return to a kind of naiveté in performance, to develop a 'direct language of simplicity and precise economy'; for actors trained in a Western tradition these qualities were the hardest to acquire and then to sustain. This extended tour also marked the first appearance of the carpet as a way of defining theatrical space:

A carpet defines the space

> It became the very simple and direct expression of the difference between theatre and everyday life. Once on the carpet, a new intensity, a new concentration, a new freedom were acquired instantly.

> [Brook, 1998. p.181]

The carpet became both a theatrical expression of space and, in the dust of Africa, a definition between the earth of everyday life and the space for performance. Another Empty Space.

THE CONFERENCE OF THE BIRDS 1972–80

Pre-production
While Brook was travelling in Africa he was already thinking of his next project, which by the time it had resolved itself into a script in 1979 had been some six years in the making. When we compare this gestation period with the commercial work done with the RSC in the 1960s we can see how far the traditional barriers between rehearsal and performance had broken down. Now Brook was as deeply interested in the **process** as he was in the **product** and was in a situation where the latter was something of an afterthought to the all-important research.

Long period of planning

The text (adapted by Jean-Claude Carrière from the work of the Sufi poet Attar) was almost unknown at that time in the West, and was another example of Brook looking to the Middle East for inspiration, a search that would culminate in *The Mahabarata*.

Rehearsal
This term to describe process becomes, at this stage, inappropriate. If it can be taken to mean a fixed period in which a given text is explored, Brook was breaking all the rules in working on this partly improvised performance over such a very long period, and then presenting it in one long evening in a number of different versions.

Very long rehearsal period

A journey play

The poem describes a long and eventful journey by the birds to find a kind of salvation from their wars and quarrelling. Led by the Hoopoe bird they achieve their terrible journey but at the end find that it has all been an illusion. The peace they sought amongst themselves is achieved by the self-realisation they have acquired on the journey and finally by their meeting with the 'Simorgh'. In a highly abstract and spiritual conclusion the company of actors/birds, acknowledging the audience, are visibly changed by the highest form of enlightenment. The whole fable acted as a kind of metaphor for Brook's leadership of the company:

> In a sense the director is always an impostor, a guide at night who does not know the territory, and yet has no choice – he must guide, learning as he goes.

> [Brook, 1986. p.43]

Scenography

This aspect of the work only became important when the production was scheduled for the Avignon Festival in 1979. Brook turned to his long-time collaborator Sally Jacobs, whose task was to make concrete what had been heavily improvised. Three huge carpets were used to denote the acting area, two on the floor and the third hung on the back wall of Les Bouffes. Great emphasis was placed on the actor as storyteller, and *Simple means to illustrate the story* as this role was to be shared by the company, costume, masks and props had to be kept simple and interchangeable.

Brightly coloured costumes now took the place of the simple white robes which the cast had been wearing in Africa. Jacobs designed hand puppets to represent the birds with trailing fabric to show their plumage, and Brook *Use of masks* insisted on masks to distinguish types and help the audience identify characters in this sprawling story. Some were worn on the face, others hand-held a little way from the face and some were held in one hand and used like *Changes in scale* a puppet. While the birds were in flight, a human figure on the ground was represented by a tiny puppet, an actor taking its place as the birds landed.

Performance

Text into improvisation into performance In the first instance the raw text/poem was used as a basis for the group's improvisation skills; it then became the key text that over a number of years defined the evolving preoccupations of the company, the work always being tested against a huge variety of audiences and in any number of different spaces.

In Africa there was a carpet to play on, a simple device to mark out the area from the dust, where audiences who could not appreciate the subtleties of language gathered to watch a show that was mainly in song *Performance in the open air* and mime. It is important to remember that the company were playing in the open air.

In California they worked with a group who were dedicated to political action so the piece became a statement of agitprop; the company were able to marry the essentially spiritual with the political. Again they played in the open air to a multicultural audience.

Process as important as product We can see from this brief survey that **process** was now as important as **product** and, more importantly, that the piece was so flexible that the company were able to adapt their style of playing to particular audiences. In New York three different versions were played on the same night, from late evening to dawn, each one revealing a different aspect of the play's journey.

Various versions of the same
text

All were staged inside, but the approach varied according to the wishes of company members. In the first the carpet was again central and the text, accompanied by simple musical instruments, was played in a noisy exuberant style. In the second version, the space was transformed into a ritual environment, with 'the scent of cleansing incense' and delicate music played on small drums and a guitar. And finally the carpet was used again but in a hall lit with candles and Brook directed part of the performance in front of the audience.

When the final performances eventually took place in 1980, the audience found the result astonishing and spellbinding. It was the end of a long and complex phase.

To sum up:
- Process was now as important as product;
- Improvisation could be used to create a whole event;
- The designer used every means to further the storytelling;
- Work was presented to a multicultural audience;
- The Empty Space was defined by a carpet.

Heilpern, J.,   *Conference of the Birds: The Story of Peter Brook in Africa,*   Faber, 1979

THE MAHABARATA 1985

Pre-production

For his next project Brook again turned to a literary source and embarked on an adaptation that would prove to be the most challenging and complex of his entire career. He had come across the text as early as 1965, and his interest was later confirmed by a display of Kathakali (see 3.6.4) in which the dancer used a tiny part of the story as a basis for his work. The text was found to be so long (equivalent to fifteen times as long as the Bible) that it took Jean-Claude Carrière several years to untangle and adapt it. Several trips to India were made, and eventually the whole cast, the designers and the musicians went to soak up the atmosphere, this valuable exposure resulting in a production of stunning visual and aural images. Brook wrote this after a visit:

> 'The line between performance and ceremony is hard to draw, and we witnessed many events that took us close to Vedic times, or close to the energy that is uniquely Indian'.

[Quoted in O'Connor, 1989. p.56]

Rehearsal

Rehearsals lasted nine months, and marked the culmination of work done over the last two decades. They also brought together an international cast and synthesised all the influences that had become part of Brook's working practice. The starting point was improvisation though in this instance there was a firmly structured text (to be much adapted as rehearsal continued).

Brook's desire for an actor to 'find himself' could lead to endless experimentation as he stood back from the creative process, questioning only when he felt he needed to. Some actors found this approach both frightening and uncomfortable, until they realised that what he was seeking lay within the actor him or herself.

Margin notes: A complex challenge · Trips to India · Very long rehearsal period · Endless experiments

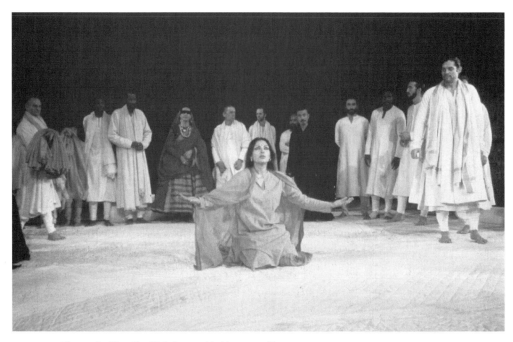

Figure 3.41   *The Mahabarata.* Mythic story-telling.

Very hard physical exercises

One of the actors has noted how hard the work was and how physical. For example, training lessons in archery gave the actors real skills but when it came to rehearsal they found they only had bamboo sticks. What interested Brook was that an actor could retain the gesture of shooting an arrow and reinvent this act from a physicalised memory.

The actor Vittiorio Mezzogiorno, confronted by the character of one of the protagonists, made this revealing statement:

> . . . I have to bring the character ever closer to me, bit by bit, as opposed to my trying to go towards something monumental. Such as I am, I cannot be a hero, but if I see the character as a human being, I can begin to work in a calmer way.

[Williams, 1988. p.376]

Scenography

In every account of the production, this aspect is the one that produced the most universal praise. The problem for Chloe Obolensky, the designer, was to give the appearance of an historical reality while elevating the characters to the status of mythic figures. To do this she studied the cut of historic clothes in museums and arrived at what she

Historical costume adapted

termed 'archetypal shapes', more sculptured than usual to help an essentially non-Asian cast.

The environment was more or less dictated by the exteriors in which the production played, so for the interior performances there was a conscious

Exteriors recreated

re-creation of the quarries of Avignon, bare earth floor, with a river and a pool. In the heat of battle handfuls of dry earth were tossed into the air to add to the feeling of heat and chaos. The background was the natural rock, which in the theatres became a complex painted wall. Fire was introduced at particular moments, flaring up around the pool and the

Elemental

cast held burning torches. The air was the space Brook created by playing out of doors and the sheer scale and sense of the infinite that so impressed the audiences. It was a truly elemental production.

Performance

Visual splendour

Most critics were agreed that in performance *The Mahabarata* was an overwhelming experience, but it is worth noting that it was for the visual spectacle rather than the text that it seems to have been remembered.

Infinite space

A viewing of the three-part film (available on video) gives a very good idea of performance styles, although the film does not convey the sense of the infinite space achieved in the environmental setting or the sense of what Brook calls 'completing the circle', that immediate relationship between the actor and his audience. Some splendid physical performances capture the essence of the epic, and there is an ease of playing that is impressive.

Elemental imagery

Carrière, who adapted the epic, had very carefully selected a language of imagery and was inclined to repeat it, until the overall effect reverberated throughout the text; life, blood, heart, fire, end. These very much echo the elemental design concepts.

To sum up:
- Detailed research revealed themes and established a cultural identity;
- A long rehearsal period was physically tough and vocally demanding;
- A strong, even overwhelming, visual statement;
- The four elements were a key concept;
- The environment played a central role, a truly Empty Space.

O'Connor, G.,   *The Mahabarata,*
                 Peter Brook's Epic in the Making,   Hodder, 1989
For a more critical view read:
Bharucca, R.,   *Theatre and the World,*
                 Peter Brook's Mahabarata,
                 A View from India   Routledge, 1993

THE EMPTY SPACE REVISITED – FINALE

Away from the proscenium arch

From this brief survey of key productions it is possible to trace a clear line of development in Brook's concept of The Empty Space. From the early days of his belief in illusion and the dominance of the proscenium arch Brook moved slowly towards the radicalism of *The Mahabarata*, where theatre was to all intents and purpose in the open air. The shift in his thinking seems to have occurred at the time of his African journey, when a carpet became the theatre of his itinerant group. It was at this time too, with a largely untutored audience, that the concepts of theatre as community and celebration were conceived and made important.

Towards celebration

Process of re-evaluation

Brook has never written a prescription for his theatre: there are pronouncements but they can be contradictory and vague if divorced from practice. Rather his unremitting energy and his search for the new has led to a continuous process of re-evaluation through practice, and his statements reflect this. He has established any number of spaces for theatre in his lifetime, not one of them the same as the other, and by so doing has redefined the validity of theatre as a shifting and evolving medium that reflects the mood of the time and the eternal truths it offers us.

3.6.4 INFLUENCES

The influence of others

I believe we are here to receive influences. We are constantly being influenced and in turn we influence other people. That is why, in my opinion, there can be nothing worse than giving oneself a trademark, acquiring a particular signature … We work in a field that must be one of free exchange.

[Brook, 1987. p.22]

CRAIG, EDWARD GORDON (1872–1966)

(See also 3.1)

By the time Brook met Gordon Craig in 1956, he was a well-established director, with 'ideas spun out of intuition' [*TQ* No. 25, 1977, p.22]; he was just beginning to search for theories of his own and saw in Craig someone who could offer him a perspective on over half a century.

The director in charge

He admired Craig's belief that the director was the person who really should be in charge, and that the writer was somehow an intrusion into the director's relationship with the actor. To someone who had directed a succession of immensely successful text-based productions, the idea that theatre could be more than an interpreted text must have come as a revelation. Brook's later work on improvisation as a way into text-based projects would be a vindication of Craig's influence.

The theatre of architecture

Brook also noted the key theme of Craig's work, that is, his desire to return theatre to a theatre of architecture rather than that of painted shadows. Again to someone who had pursued romantic realism as a solution Craig's suggestion that simplifying stage space into abstract symbolism must have been a real challenge.

The handing-on of theory and practice

But above all Brook recognised that Craig's ideas and influence had been passed verbally from generation to generation. This must have had great appeal to Brook who has relied on direct personal contact to inspire and motivate rather than write down definitive theories.

Brook, P.,   *The Shifting Point*,   Methuen, 1987, pp.23–5

GURDJIEFF, GEORGEI IVANOVITCH (1877–1949)

A philosophical model

Gurdjieff's influence on Peter Brook is self acknowledged, and, interestingly, what becomes very evident in any study of Brook is just how closely their lives mirror each other's. Gurdjieff was born in the Caucasus and spent most of his early life travelling in search of what he called 'esoteric' knowledge (Brook's film *Meetings with Remarkable Men* traces that journey). Esoteric is a difficult word to define because it suggests that which is hidden or only for the initiated, a fact that has kept the essential philosophies of Gurdjieff from attracting a wider audience.

International followers

By the time he settled in the West, in the 1920s, Gurdjieff had attracted a small number of followers, who in their turn split off into further groups, spreading his teaching mainly to Russia, America, France and England. And it was here that Brook became involved in the late 1950s, his teacher Jane Heap having been close to Gurdjieff and obviously as charismatic a figure as her mentor.

Briefly Gurdjieff sought to reawaken in urban man a realisation of self, which he felt had for too long been stifled by the concerns of the commercial world. Man, he suggested, was half asleep for most of his life and only a planned regime of rigorous study could develop what he termed his 'harmonious development'. For a brief while he founded an institute for his group and there he:

Rigorous self study

> ... tested and revised a system of study, self-observation, physical work and exercise aimed toward the reconciliation and union of the three basic human functions of thinking, feeling and physical activity ...

[Speeth, 1989. p.15]

Parallels with Brook's practice

From this statement it is possible to draw clear parallels with Brook's practice, particularly in respect of his later work in Paris. It is worth noting that Grotowski in his 'paratheatre 'period was also trying to accomplish many of these aims.

Themes in common

For further study the following themes would be worth investigating:
- Gurdjieff originated from a Near Eastern background from which Brook would draw inspiration. See *Orghast, Conference of Birds, The Mahabarata*;
- Gurdjieff's concept of a journey as a means of learning and discovery was taken up by Brook, particularly in his African travels;
- Gurdjieff believed in the oral tradition as a way of passing on knowledge. Brook has never written a book on training – his preferred method is by working with groups;
- Gurdjieff was a teacher and mystic. Although Brook denies his own guru status there is no doubt that he is regarded as such by some contemporary practitioners.

| Brook, P., | *Threads of Time,* | Methuen, 1998 pp. 66–9 |
| Speeth, K.R., | *The Gurdjieff Work,* | Penguin/Putnam, 1989 |

ARTAUD, ANTONIN (1896–1948)

(See also 3.3)

Artaud unlocked Brook's imagination

Brook has long acknowledged his huge debt to Artaud. As expressed elsewhere, it was really Artaud and his *Theatre Of Cruelty* that unlocked for Brook a long period of stagnation, and led to the radical production of *The Marat/Sade* in 1964.

For the first time in Brook's career he placed the emphasis on improvisation (with the help of Charles Marowitz), and through this technique he explored what pure movement, the making of sounds and intense physical activity could achieve. Artaud had made clear his opposition to character analysis:

Against character analysis

> ... whoever said the theatre was created to **analyse character**, to resolve the conflicts of a human emotional order, of a present-day psychological nature such as those which monopolise current theatre?

[Artaud, *The Theatre and Its Double* 1985. p.30]

By moving away from character and psychological analysis Brook was about to embark on a completely different route. It would take him some years to find his own style but by the time he reached *Orghast* (1971) and had completed his African journey (1972/3) free improvisation would play a crucial role in his creative process.

Free improvisation became dominant

CUNNINGHAM, MERCE (BORN 1919)

Influence of Martha Graham

One of America's foremost modern-dance exponents, Cunningham started life wanting to become an actor, but opted instead for dance. His studies of popular contemporary forms – folk, tap and exhibition ballroom dancing – gave him a grounding from which he moved towards modern dance and at a summer school he was asked by Martha Graham (1894–1991) to join her, in her company, as second male soloist. The most memorable role he created for her was the Revivalist in *Appalacian Spring* (1944). Between then and 1953, when he founded his own company, he had moved from dancer to choreographer and evolved his own distinctive style. He was helped towards this by his

Influence of John Cage

important lifelong collaborator, the composer John Cage (b.1912), and it was while he and Cage were in residence (1953) at the progressive Black Mountain College in North Carolina that they began to use the concept of 'chance structures' in their respective dance and music.

Freeing up dance

Briefly this meant that dance was to be freed from its tight narrative form, and was to be given the opportunity to be an activity governed by its own distinctive rules, in which after a series of carefully planned sequences of movement, time, sound and space the toss of a coin (literally) could determine the order and rules of the ensuing dance work.

Collaboration with artists

It was at this time that Cunningham's close friendship with the artist Robert Rauschenberg (b.1925), also in residence, led to a long and fruitful collaboration which in turn included such other leaders of the avant-garde art world as Jasper Johns, Frank Stella and Andy Warhol.

Cunningham consciously moved away from the lavish myth-telling of his teacher Martha Graham into a world in which pure dance had its own internal logic and meaning. The artist, the choreographer and the composer were all given equal right in the making of the dance and working independently, as they often did, the final result was often only made concrete on opening night.

> ... no implicit or explicit narrative but ... every spectator may see and hear the events in his own way.

[Percival, 1971. p.43]

Issues of gender

The gender of the dancers was no longer to be a stumbling block: women could lift women and men with comparative ease, and men could dance

<table>
<tr><td>Performance reaching out to the audience</td><td>with men without embarrassment. With his artist collaborators he shattered the confines of the proscenium arch and actively involved his audience. Famously in *Tread* (1970), giant industrial electric fans were spaced at regular intervals across the curtain line, blowing into the auditorium.</td></tr>
</table>

> Space … is important to him too, namely the space between movements, also the space between events. Just as Cage lets silence form part of his music, so Cunningham lets stillness form part of his ballets.

[Percival, 1971. p.44]

<table>
<tr><td>Improvised sound score</td><td>In 1964, during a world tour, Cunningham took the next step in the development of his aleatoric (depending on the throw of the dice) system. He devised a series of *Events*, evenings in which both old and new material was combined to the accompaniment of a totally improvised sound score. As a choreographer he was an innovator, making and experimenting rather than reviving old material. He was not interested in the dead hand of a repertory, endlessly repeated in debased and fossilised forms.</td></tr>
</table>

<table>
<tr><td>Improvisation based on learnt techniques</td><td>Cunningham was in Paris two years before Brook made his decisive move there, and given Brook's frequent visits it most probable that he saw the company. What he admired most was their ability to improvise, and to do so from a vast repertoire of acquired technique and feeling, just as he was beginning his long journey in the same direction.</td></tr>
</table>

> … to be more aware of the fine currents that flow within a movement as it unfolds for *the first time* … all is spontaneous and yet there is order.

[Brook, 1986. p.64]

<table>
<tr><td>An innovator</td><td>Brook saw Cunningham as a fellow traveller, a collaborator, one who was experimenting, moving forward, one who challenged the precepts of his art form and, more often than not, did so with a total disregard for the ensuing controversy.</td></tr>
</table>

> … and as he dances Merce Cunningham strives for a holy art …

[Brook, 1968. p.64]

Percival, J.,   *Experimental Dance*,   Studio Vista, 1971
Burt, R.,   *The Male Dancer*,   Routledge, 1995

GROTOWSKI, JERZY (1933–99)

(See also 3.5)

<table>
<tr><td>An investigation into the nature of acting</td><td>… No-one else in the world to my knowledge, no-one since Stanislavski, has investigated the nature of acting, its phenomenon, its meaning, the nature and science of its mental/physical/emotional processes as deeply and completely as Grotowski.</td></tr>
</table>

[Peter Brook in the Preface, *Towards a Poor Theatre*]

Travels in Asia and Russia

After a childhood blighted by illness, which reportedly changed his life, in 1951 Grotowski went to Moscow to train in the Stanislavski tradition and after an extended visit to Asia returned to his own country where he established a theatre first in Krakov and subsequently in Opole, where he became director of Teatr 13 Rzedow, committing himself to experimentation.

Physical theatre forms

Most important for my purposes are: ... Stanislavski's work on 'physical actions', Meyerhold's biomechanical training ... also particularly stimulating to me are the training techniques of oriental theatre – specifically the Peking Opera, Indian Kathakali, and Japanese Noh theatre.

[*TDR* Vol. 11, No. 3 p.60]

'Poor Theatre'

By 1965 his theatre, now called the Institute of Research into Acting, had been established in Wroclaw and a series of productions followed which were to make him into one of the most influential figures in world theatre. He coined the term 'Poor Theatre' to try to describe his theoretical impulses:

Performance simplified

By gradually eliminating whatever proved superfluous, we found that theatre can exist without make-up, without autonomic costume and scenography, without a separate performance area (stage), without lighting and sound effects ... It cannot exist without the actor–spectator relationship of perceptual, direct, 'live' communion.

[Grotowski, 1994. p.19]

This short statement sums up many of his intentions. By stripping the theatre of essentially realist concerns the focus shifted to the actor and in turn to his intimate and compelling relationship with his audience. The question 'what can it (theatre) do that film and television cannot?' was answered by a two-pronged attack. First he initiated probably one of the most rigorous actor-training systems ever devised and secondly performances were staged in the most intimate spaces, in which the audience were exposed to an assault on their intellect and their senses. [See 3.5.3]

An actor's training

Work with Brook and the RSC

Brook was well acquainted with Grotowski's work when in 1966 he invited him to the RSC who were preparing his production of *U.S.* The workshop that followed stretched the actors to the utmost of their capabilities. Brook summed it up:

The shock of the new

What did the work do? It gave each actor a series of shocks: the shock of confronting himself in the face of irrefutable challenges, the shock of catching sight of his own evasions, tricks and clichés; the shock of sensing something of his own vast and untapped resources; the shock of being forced to question why he is an actor at all.

[Hunt and Reeves, 1995. p.103]

Grotowski, J.,   *Towards a Poor Theatre*,   Methuen, 1994

KOTT, JAN (BORN 1914)

Drama critic and writer Kott is poet, critic and Professor of Literature at the University of Warsaw. In his youth he was associated with the Surrealist poets in Paris, and the progressive Catholic movement. During the Second World War he fought in the Polish army and the Underground Movement, since when he has concentrated on dramatic criticism and translations of classic texts.

A friend of Brook's Kott met Peter Brook in Warsaw in 1957, during the European tour of *Titus Andronicus*, which Kott much admired. Subsequently Brook read Kott's book *Shakespeare Our Contemporary* in French and when it was published in English contributed the Preface. Kott later acclaimed *His influence on Brook* Brook's *Lear* (see 3.6.3) as 'revelatory' and in his turn Brook acknowledged Kott's essay *King Lear or Endgame* as a huge influence on his production (1962).

In his review of that production the critic Kenneth Tynan (1927–80) compared *Lear* with Samuel Beckett's play *Endgame*.

> . . . Beckett and Shakespeare have more in common with each other than either has with the romantic, naturalistic theatre that historically separates them.
>
> [*The Observer*, November 1962]

He went on to suggest that for modern man without 'gods' the cathartic tragedy in *Lear* is no more than purely grotesque. 'The grotesque is more cruel than tragedy' [Kott, 1964. p.104].

Suggested rethinking of Shakespearian play This was born out by Brook's reading of the play in which his indebtedness to Beckett was made very clear, not only in the bleak, 'end of the world' *mise-en-scène* but also in the way catharsis was firmly resisted (see also the film version of 1971).

Kott, J., *Shakespeare Our Contemporary*, Methuen, 1964

BECK, JULIAN (1925–85) AND MALINA, JUDITH (BORN 1926) – THE LIVING THEATRE

Theatre in small spaces Performing first in New York in 1947, Beck and Malina staged their initial work in their own living room, to small invited audiences. They eventually transferred to a modified loft space and in 1952 were an immediate success with a repertory of one-act dramas. Their philosophies behind the creation of this 'alternative' theatre were:

> They would charge no admission, rehearse a play until they felt it was ready to open, and pay the talent by dividing up the contributions made at the door.
>
> [*TDR* Vol. 7, No. 2. p.196]

Texts based on controversial themes Two years later another suitable place was found and again a repertory was established including plays by Strindberg, Cocteau and Pirandello.

The theatre was closed by the authorities and in the summer of 1959 another new 'off-Broadway' theatre was established, opening with one of their most celebrated productions: Jack Gelber's (b.1925) *The Connection.*

This text sought to animate the theme of drug-taking and abuse interspersed with contributions from an on-stage jazz band, interruptions from the writer and director and two cameramen filming the show to give it the authenticity of a documentary. The authors' bleak assertion that all of us are 'hooked' in some way and that we all lead purposeless and self-annihilating lives was underscored by the late arrival of the dealer after which one junkie nearly died from an overdose. The proximity of the audience to the actors resulted in an overwhelming sense of involvement and shared pain, which was further enhanced by the actors, in role, joining the audience in the interval.

This was followed by the equally sensational *The Brig* by Kenneth H. Brown (b.1936) set in a military prison, where again the audience were, by their close proximity, complicit in the action. The recurring brutality and senseless routine combined to create an unremitting sensory assault on the both actors and audience.

Sensory assaults on the audience

The Living Theatre had begun by focusing on definably naturalistic productions laced with large doses of anarchy, but as their work progressed they became more interested in Artaudian principles and the possibilities of intense visual and aural experiences. These trends were exemplified in their adaptation of Mary Shelley's *Frankenstein* (1965), in which a multilayered scaffold became in turn the laboratory in which the monster is given life, the inside of the monster's head, and finally a prison representing the world itself where human prisoners die in an all-consuming fire. A company of 20 actors brought to life this vivid scenario in which victims of the system fled into the audience, from where they were dragged back 'to torture and imprisonment' on stage.

Followers of Artaud

By this time the division between actor and audience was becoming very blurred: not only were the actors encouraged to 'play themselves' with an increasing reliance on improvised moments, but as performers they crossed the boundaries (such as they were) into the audience, who were all too ready to be caught up in a mutually sensory experience. In the late 1960s The Living Theatre was synonymous with drug-taking (mostly the smoking of marijuana) and in performance encouraged the audience to strip off and 'free the theatre'.

Actor–audience divisions broken down

From 1964 to 1968 they toured Europe, and were notable by their actions in the student riots in Paris (May 1968); it was Malina and Beck who took over Barrault's Thèâtre de France and ousted the conservative director in favour of revolutionary action.

Politically active in Europe

Brook's admiration for the company is reflected in his writings:

> In the Living Theatre three needs become one: it exists for the sake of performing, it earns its living through performing and its performances contain the most intense and intimate moments of its collective life.

[Brook 1986. p.70]

A VIEW OF THE BRIG FROM ABOVE

Concrete wall
Heavy Chicken wire
White line

1. Large double doors
2. Storeroom door
3. Door to cell no. 1
4. Door to cell no. 2
5. Door to office
6. Door to inside compound
7. Door to outside compound
8. Freedom door
9. Head door
10. Large double gates

Figure 3.42 *The Brig.* With the audience in close proximity to the action, this production owed as much to Grotowski as it did to Brook's 'intense and intimate moments'.

A synthesis of sources

He goes on to suggest that without traditions of their own they are forced to borrow from other sources:

> . . . yoga, Zen, psychoanalysis, books, heresy, discovery, inspiration–a rich but dangerous eclecticism . . .

[Ibid. p.70]

But most of all Brook valued and maybe even envied their 'nomad' existence, which he copied as a means of creating a coherent group.

Tulane Drama Review,   Vol. 7 No. 2, Winter, 1962
Vol. 8 No. 3, Spring 1964
Vol. 13 No. 3

Styan, J. L.,	*Modern Drama in Theory and Practice*,	Vol. 2, CUP, 1986 (chapter 19)
Innes, C.,	*Avant-Garde Theatre*,	Routledge, 1993
Shank, T.,	*American Alternative Theatre*,	Macmillan, 1982

3.6.5 FOLLOWERS

In a recent article, the drama critic Michael Billington wrote:

Key practitioners

> Who is the key influence on modern British theatre? Paradoxically it is Peter Brook, who left these shores almost thirty years ago. A whole generation of directors – including Declan Donnellan, Simon McBurney, Deborah Warner, Katie Mitchell, Tim Supple and Mick Gordon – perpetuates the Brook principles: a belief in story-telling, in imaginative complicity between actor and audience, in the importance in found spaces.

[*The Guardian*, 15 January 2000]

Théâtre de Complicité

At the time of writing perhaps the most influential of these is **Simon McBurney**. As a founder member of Théâtre de Complicité he and the company have brought a whole new meaning to the term 'physical theatre', and almost single handedly have revitalised the art of improvisation into text.

Objectives

The most important objectives of the company are:
- complicity;
- collaboration;
- celebration.

Complicity refers to their belief that ideally there should be a strong bond between both the actors on stage and between the actors and their audience, leading to what Simon McBurney has called 'a sense of common understanding'.

Collaboration is a concept that drove Brecht to create his unique style. With complicity, the importance is in the way collaboration ensures a 'sense of shared understanding', particularly in the performers who, as a consequence, are given more creative control.

Celebration is a more abstract concept which accepts the audience as important in the sense that 'without them you're not going to make a whole'. This last objective has an important link with Brook, who all his life was searching for that Empty Space in which this celebration could take place.

It is important to remember that a number of Complicité's original company trained with the French mime teacher, Jacques Lecoq (b.1921) and the company has regularly drawn its members from Europe, integrating different skills and approaches, including languages, into a coherent physicalised theatre.

Théâtre de Complicité Education 020 7 700 0233

Deborah Warner is a freelance director who has demonstrated an ability to inhabit alternative theatre spaces with provoking and ground-breaking productions.

Katie Mitchell is a freelance director whose most recent work has been at the Royal National Theatre with a production of *The Oresteia* (2000).

Mick Gordon is artistic director of The Gate Theatre in Notting Hill, acknowledged as a fringe theatre with an international reputation.

Tim Supple is Artistic Director at the Young Vic, London, and his most recent work with the RSC, a production of Goldoni's *A Servant of Two Masters* and *Tales from Ovid*, both of which premiered at Stratford last year, will be in repertory during 2000.

Declan Donnellan founded Cheek by Jowl, with his long-time designer/ collaborator Nick Ormerod. His work has always been strongly ensemble based, and he is well regarded for his revivals of classic texts, often staged in new and exciting actor/audience spaces.His most recent work was at The Old Vic with a production of *Antigone* by Sophocles.

As a student of theatre it would be very worthwhile tracking these companies and directors and looking out for their work, but as Brook's influence has been so world-wide it should be possible to recognise his themes in many contemporary productions.

3.6.6 SUMMARY: PETER BROOK

This summary is written to draw together certain parts of the chapter on Peter Brook under particular headings. It should be considered with the student's own practical work in mind and/or the student's viewing of other productions. For example, Brook's The Empty Space: as a student undertaking practical work you would wish to discuss how Brook's concepts have developed over his working life and how these could be reflected in your own work. By adopting this convention/practice not only are you enhancing your own approach but you are able to make use of the practice when viewing other productions.

THE SUBJECT MATTER	Muticultural topics Adapted ancient legends and stories The Middle and Far Eastern cultures Re-examination of classic texts
THE POLITICAL PURPOSE OR MESSAGE OR DRAMATIC INTENTION	A-political The presentation of other cultures, safely Philosophical underpinning To include the audience
THE ACTOR–AUDIENCE RELATIONSHIP	Making the stage and auditorium one room Abolition of the proscenium arch Celebratory

THE STAGING FORM ADOPTED	Epic Productions in the open air Alternative theatre spaces Selective of content and form
DIRECTORIAL INTERPRETATION /PRODUCTION STYLE	The director as part of an ensemble Working through improvisation Searching for the truth Every aspect planned
DESIGN ELEMENTS	Elemental, a return to nature The use of natural materials, organic Heavily researched
ROLE OF ACTORS AND PERFORMANCE STYLE	Encouraged to search within themselves The actor in training for performance The actor equipped with skills
TECHNICAL ELEMENTS	White light, anti-illusion Maximum use of simple means Little or no technology
AUDIENCE RESPONSE	Invited to be part of the interaction Challenged to be imaginative

3.6.7 SUGGESTIONS FOR FURTHER STUDY

FILM AND VIDEO (unless otherwise stated all films are directed by Peter Brook)

A Sentimental Journey (1944 film GB b/w)
Amateur film made while Brook was at Oxford University.

The Beggar's Opera (1952 film GB colour) with Laurence Olivier, Dorothy Tutin, Stanley Holloway, George Devine

A failure at the box office, this was Brook's first feature film made within the confines of a studio. He quarelled with Olivier, who envisaged a quite different treatment and who threatened to take over as director. The film's most successful aspects were the big set pieces with the riotous inmates of Newgate prison, otherwise 'the over-all effect of the film is disturbingly jumbled' [Helfer and Loney, 1998. p.54]. Lack of continuity in the narrative makes it very difficult to follow.

Box for One (1953 television)

No record survives of the transmission.

King Lear (1953 USA/CBSTV b/w) with Orson Welles, Micheal Mac Liammoir, Alan Badel

A live transmission. Welles dominated the direction with his own version of the script.

The Birthday Present (1955 television GB b/w)

Report from Moscow (1955 television GB b/w)

Heaven and Earth (1957 television GB b/w)

Moderato Cantabile (1960 film Fr) with Jeanne Moreau, Jean-Paul Belmondo

A French entry at the 1960 Cannes Film Festival, it won for Jeanne Moreau the Best Actress award. Its style owed a lot to the New Wave and the films of Jean-Luc Godard, but critics found it slow and fragmented and the central relationship 'disastrously never felt'. Brook improvised around the script, and then filmed the result with a fairly static camera.

The Lord of The Flies (1963 film GB b/w) with James Aubrey, Tom Chapin, Hugh Edwards

Perhaps the best-known of Brook's films, as much for its Darwinian theme as for the brave performances of its amateur cast. Brook developed the script from the novel of the same name by William Golding, with much of the dialogue being improvised on location, and filmed by a largely inexperienced crew in quasi-documentary style. Much as one can admire the intention of the film the result is a curiously passionless statement, large parts of the middle section being formless and lacking in tension. It is only during the boys' final descent into total anarchy that the film begins to convince on all levels.

Despite the rather wasted opportunity the film does have interest as it signals Brook's obsession with violence and its aftermath, a theme that recurs in much of his subsequent work.

The Marat/Sade (film 1966 GB colour) with Ian Richardson, Patrick Magee, Glenda Jackson

The filmed version of Brook's sensationally popular production with the RSC cast. The film is the culmination of two years' work on this play and was made in just 15 days using traditional camera setups and a third roving hand-held camera. Brook comments that the shots obtained by this second unit were often the first choice in the editing process, the sudden wild abandon of the cast caught in vivid detail by the documentary style camera.

Critics praised the film for creating 'an uncomfortable proximity that makes us squirm a little more in our chairs than we ever did while watching the fascinating play onstage' [Helfer and Loney, 1998. p.141].

Tell Me Lies (film 1968 GB colour) with Mark Jones, Pauline Munro, Robert Lloyd

Filmed version of *U.S*, the anti-Vietnam war play which Brook, two years earlier, had devised with his cast at the RSC. It continued the themes of Artaud's confrontational theatre applied to a contemporary event. The production had been a much-discussed *cause célèbre* but the resulting film was described by critics as 'an extremely trivial enterprise'. The slapdash nature of the camera work and the variable quality of the performances all added up to what one critic described as 'abysmal and boring'. An instance where the filmed production failed to communicate the same excitement as the theatrical original.

King Lear (1971 GB b/w) with Paul Scofield, Irene Worth, Jack MacGowran, Alan Webb

(See also 3.6.3, Seven Key Productions)

A film version of Brook's ground-breaking RSC production of 1962, with a number of the same cast. Perhaps Brook's most truly original piece of cinema as opposed to a filmed production, it was shot on location in Denmark in most inhospitable conditions.

In the stage version more than one critic remarked on the bleakness of Brook's vision and his indebtedness to Jan Kott's famous essay *King Lear or Endgame* (see 3.6.4). Both the production and this film were compared to the apocalyptic world of Samuel Beckett's plays.

Huge close-ups dominate the narrative, and frequently Brook denies the viewer empathy with the characters by withholding the traditional reaction shots of classical realist editing. This alienates his audience, but at the same time focuses attention on the text, which is spoken, especially by Lear, in an almost unbroken husky monotone, unsupported by music.

Extremes of violence are again evident (see *Lord of the Flies*). The brutal deaths of the protagonists are handled in an almost ritualistic style, with an inevitability which is unremittingly savage. The viewer is appalled by the deaths but strangely unmoved, summed up by this comment: 'It is unthinkable that at some moment the destiny of Lear would not move one to tears. That moment never came in this film.' [Helfer and Loney, 1998. p157]

Meetings with Remarkable Men (film 1979) with Dragan Maxsimovic, Terence Stamp, Athol Fugard, Colin Blakely, Warren Mitchell, Natasha Parry

> Here is what I'll call a hero of our time, a man , a young man, with whom we can identify, because his primary situation is a hunger for understanding and a recognition that the answers that the world has given him in no way satisfy his demand.
>
> [Brook, 1987. p.212]

Based on the book of the same name by Gurdjieff (see 3.6.4), the film dramatises his early life in which he sought the secret sources of hidden knowledge. But it fails to make clear whether the so-called 'secrets' that he craved were revealed to him and damagingly the screenplay is at times both risible and portentous. The most interesting sequences are at the end when the protagonist reaches the secret monastery and witnesses the dances that Gurdjieff took and adapted for his work in the West.

Mesure pour Mesure (television 1979)

Carmen (television 1983)

A simplified and partly rewritten version of the Bizet opera, staged in very simple terms with a small orchestra and the minimum of settings.

Brook sought to get back to the basic story by Prosper Mérimée, and to examine in realist terms the central tragic relationships. Most critics found the result a triumph of clarity, though purist music critics were less enthusiastic. To take such a melodramatic piece and reclaim it for realism was a brave move, but Brook did not manage to stifle the melodramatic entirely and there was a worrying clash of genres in the tragic denouement.

Mahabarata (film and television 1989 Fr colour) with Urs Bihler, Ryszard Cieslak, Georges Corraface, Miriam Goldschmidt, Jeffery Kissoon

(See also 3.6.3, Seven Key Productions)

An epic in every sense of the word. A sprawling narrative adapted from its Indian source with roles for Brook's huge (cast of 42) international company. The three-part epic on stage lasted nearly 9 hours; it was then filmed for the cinema (3 hours) and then a longer TV version (5 hours) was produced. In the English video version the limitations of the translation are cruelly exposed.

Useful Addresses
Movie Mail
PO Box 220
Hereford HR1 2ZH
01432 262910

Film Vault Search Service
01865 361000

HMV Direct (mail order)
0990 334578

Relecting on the above very brief résumé of Brook's film career, there is an argument to be had about the purpose and nature of his filmed theatre. It has not been possible to validate all the films since many are virtually unobtainable, but an analysis of opinion and critical analysis would suggest that the films are a useful record of his work, the *Marat/Sade* being the most successful in purely cinematic terms. Ironically, since he set out to be a movie director, the original screenplays are the least satisfactory and on occasion it is difficult to reconcile these with his mainstream theatre career.

USEFUL REFERENCES   Colindale Newpaper Library
Colindale Avenue
London NW9 5H
020 7412 7353
Original press reviews and articles

Shakespeare Centre
Henley Street
Stratford-upon-Avon
01789 204016
Archive of RSC productions

The Theatre Museum
1E, Tavistock Street
London WC2E 7PA
0171 836 7891
Archive Library and Education

Offstage,
37 Chalk Farm Road
London NW1 8AJ
020 7485 4996
Theatre bookshop

3.6.8 BIBLIOGRAPHY

PRIMARY	Bradby, D. and Williams, D.	*Directors' Theatre*	Methuen, 1988	Chapter 6 is on Peter Brook.
	Brook, P.	*Threads of Time, A Memoir*	Methuen, 1999	A very personal review of his life's work. Very few dates make the chronology difficult to follow.
	Brook, P.	*The Empty Space*	Penguin, 1996	Very useful early essays that have not dated.
	Brook, P.	*There are no Secrets*	Methuen, 1993	
	Brook, P.	*The Shifting Point*	Methuen, 1989	Forty years of theatrical exploration 1946–87.
	Brook, P.	*The Book of U.S*	London, 1968	
	Helfer, R. and Loney, G.	*Peter Brook: Oxford to Orghast*	Harwood, 1998	A most useful resource with full credits for all major productions and critical analysis plus several useful interviews with collaborators.
	Hunt, A. and Reeves, G.	*Peter Brook, Directors in Perspective*	CUP, 1995	The most authoritative text, written by long-term collaborators. It is critical and analytical.

	Innes, C.	*Avant-Garde Theatre*	Routledge, 1993	As an overview of the 20th-century avant-garde this cannot be bettered.
	Williams, D.	*A Theatrical Casebook*	Methuen, 1988	(reprinting October 2000) An excellent collection of seminal essays.
SECONDARY	Davies, A.	*Filming Shakespeare's Plays*	CUP, 1991	For an extended analysis of Brook's *King Lear*.
	Grotowski, J.	*Towards a Poor Theatre*	Methuen, 1969	Very influential collection of essays.
	Heilpern, J.	*Conference of the Birds: The Story of Peter Brook in Africa*	Faber, 1979	An exhaustive account.
	Mackintosh, I.	*Architecture, Actor, Audience*	Routledge, 1995	A useful introduction to the evolution of theatrical space and with a section on Brook's Bouffes du Nord and the Winter Garden, New York.
	Mitter, S.	*Systems of Rehearsal*	Routledge, 1992	An analysis of Brook's work seen through the practice of Stanislavski, Brecht and Grotowski.
	Oida, Y.	*The Invisible Actor*	Methuen, 1997	Written by one of Brook's long-time colleagues.
	O'Connor, G.	The Mahabarata: *Peter Brook's Epic in the Making*★ (a Channel Four Book)	Hodder, 1989	Authoritative account of the genesis of this epic with particular reference to its filming. Splendid illustrations. ★Now out of print but libraries may have a copy.

	Roose-Evans, J.	*Experimental Theatre: From Stanislavski to Peter Brook*	Routledge, 1989	
	Smith A. C. H.	*Orghast at Persepolis*	Methuen, 1972	An account of the experiment in theatre.
VIDEO	Peter Brook interviewed by Melvyn Bragg	Thames Television, South Bank Show	Available from Thames Television.	Splendid resource with good extracts of all major productions.

Glossary

Antagonist
A character who acts in opposition to the **protagonist**. Generally, an adversary to the main character.

Anti-hero
A **protagonist**, but one who displays the less pleasant characteristics of human beings. One of the most famous anti-heroes in modern drama is Jimmy Porter in John Osborne's *Look Back in Anger* (1956).

Aside
Anything from a short phrase to a lengthy speech which is intended for the audience's hearing but not for those on stage. This may be spoken directly to the audience or simply out of the other characters' hearing. Certain *genres* of drama make more use of asides than others, e.g. melodrama, farce, Restoration comedy. However, asides also occur in more serious drama.

Blocking
This is the term that is used for the basic movements of the actors on the stage area. It is applied to the way that a director, in rehearsal, moves actors in the stage space. These moves are then recorded by the stage manager. Sometimes a director will prepare the blocking before the rehearsal process begins.

Chorus
A character or group of characters who comment on the action, providing a summary and a narrative link. In the original Greek theatre, the Chorus acted as the group who discussed events with the **protagonist**. The Chorus may be played by one actor or by a group, who do not have to speak in unison.

Constructivism
A method of production that influenced all the arts in post-revolutionary Russia. Associated in theatre with the director Meyerhold, it was typified by a use of materials that exposed the methods of construction. Totally non-realist, the forms resembled a giant children's playground, where abstract structures could take on many meanings.

Cue
This refers to the spoken line, movement, sound or any other form of stage action that is a marker for another spoken line, piece of action, sound effect, lighting change, and so on. For example, an actor moving from USR (see p.12) to DSL might be the cue for a change of lighting states. Alternatively, your fellow actor's line, 'Move along, please!' might be a cue for you to fall to the floor exclaiming, 'I never want to leave here'.

Diction
The rendition of words, particularly referring to clear or poor pronunciation.

Duologue

A scene in a play which consists of two actors holding a dialogue. This tends to be a clear-cut episode rather than a couple of speeches in the middle of a scene.

Epic

See p.304.

Epilogue

A final section of a play which often acts as a summary or 'coda' to the main play. It can encourage the audience to leave the theatre space considering some key theme or aspect of the play. For classic examples of epilogues, see Shakespeare, e.g. *A Midsummer Night's Dream* or *As You Like It*.

Fourth wall

This is a euphemism for the opening at the front of a stage, particularly on a proscenium arch stage (see p.5). The fourth wall is the imaginary wall or part of a wall through which the audience sees a room. This is traditionally associated with naturalistic drama, using indoor sets. We discuss the design of such a set on p.62. Note that the 'fourth wall' can actually be parts of two walls.

An appropriate use of the term might read:

> 'Ibsen's stage directions at the beginning of Act 1 of *A Doll's House* indicate that the setting would be naturalistic; there is even a fire in the stove. The audience would see the Helmers' home through the imaginary fourth wall, as this was the staging convention that was becoming popular at the time.'

Genre

A term originally taken from the French, meaning a 'species'. It refers to a dramatic form that has identifiable characteristics. The two most generalised and oldest genres are *comedy* and *tragedy*. However, these are subdivided and blended to such an extent that it has become impossible to identify all the different dramatic genres. Genre is easiest to detect in the film or television world. We are quite at ease with 'soap operas', 'detective series', 'Westerns' and recognise these as genres with similar features.

Examples of particular genres have been described within the text. For a description of the genre of Revenge Tragedy, see pp.119.

Lighting terms

See p.66.

Literary terms

See pp.74–81.

Mise-en-scène

A phrase that literally means 'put in the scene', i.e. the practice of stage direction in which things are arranged on the stage. This would include the setting, lighting, costumes and actors. When applied to film, it refers to whatever appears in the film frame, i.e. the way the director stages the event for the camera.

Monologue
A single lengthy speech, made when other people are present in the scene.

Performance spaces
See pp.3–11.

Prologue
The introductory section to a play, which acts as an entry into the piece for the audience. See its counterpart, **Epilogue**, above. Again see Shakespeare for many examples, e.g. *Romeo and Juliet*.

Protagonist
The principal character in a play. The protagonist is the person who initiates the action directly or indirectly. Some plays do not have protagonists, as no one character stands out.

Stage terms
See pp.11–14.

Style
Style relates to the language, tone and pace which comprise the *manner* of writing. It refers to the literary and dramatic composition, or form, rather than the content of a piece. However, the style will always be connected to the content, as the dramatist will find the most appropriate style in which to write in order to convey his or her ideas. The content and style are all part of the *meaning* of a playtext.

The style can refer to the manner of writing of one dramatist or of the writing of a group of dramatists of the same period. See p.7 for an example of the writing of Caryl Churchill and then compare it to the completely different style of writing of Oscar Wilde, p.36. The two playwrights use different types of language, tone and pace.

Style can also refer to the presentation or production of a text. An expressionistic production of Strindberg's *Miss Julie* will be performed in a completely different manner to a naturalistic one.

Subtext
The subtext is the information in the text about events and characters that is not directly made clear by the dramatist's written lines. It is the impressions we receive by 'reading between the lines'. See pp.30–1 for further details.

Symbolism
An international movement in all the arts, associated with Stanislavski and Meyerhold through the plays of Maeterlinck. The Symbolists refused 'to be satisfied merely to observe and portray the trivial, well-recognised truths, facts and realities of life'. Symbolist playwrights explored themes of death, madness and the dream world and looked to religious and mythical sources for their texts.

Index